STUDIES IN PHILOSOPHY

edited by
ROBERT NOZICK
PELLEGRINO UNIVERSITY PROFESSOR
AT HARVARD UNIVERSITY

A GARLAND SERIES

Risk, Ambiguity and Decision

Daniel Ellsberg

Routledge
Taylor & Francis Group

LONDON AND NEW YORK

First published 2001 by Routledge

2 Park Square, Milton Park, Abingdon, Oxon OX14 4RN
711 Third Avenue, New York, NY 10017, USA

First issued in paperback 2016

Routledge is an imprint of the Taylor & Francis Group, an informa business

Transferred to Digital Printing 2010

Library of Congress Cataloging-in-Publication Data
Ellsberg, Daniel.
    Risk, ambiguity and decision / Daniel Ellsberg.
    p. cm. — (Series name)
    ISBN-13: 978-0-8153-4022-5 (hbk)
    ISBN-13: 978-1-1389-8547-6 (pbk)

To My Father

Contents

Introduction
By Issac Levi*

DECISION MAKING WHEN PROBABILITIES ARE INDETERMINATE

IN HIS INSIGHTFUL and cogently argued doctoral dissertation, Daniel Ellsberg challenged the theory of rational decision that was then in the process of dominating the economics, statistics, social science, and philosophical literature on this subject. The publication of *Risk, Ambiguity and Decision* ought to confirm Ellsberg's position as an important pioneer in the study of patterns of choice behavior when decision-makers are reluctant to make quantitative or even comparative judgments of probability.

Risk Ambiguity and Decision was submitted to the Economics Department of Harvard University in April, 1962, within a year after Ellsberg had published "Risk, Ambiguity, and the Savage Axioms" in the *Quarterly Journal of Economics*. The article introduced into the literature on rational choice a type of problem that many are prone to solve in a manner that cannot be squared with the injunction to maximize expected utility.

Ellsberg noted that the cases of failure arise when the decision-maker is in an "information state" that "can be meaningfully identified as highly ambiguous."[1]

---

*Thanks are due to Daniel Ellsberg and Robert Nozick for helpful and interesting suggestions for improving the text.

[1]Ellsberg took for granted throughout both the paper and his dissertation that the consequences of an option are determined not only by the option being implemented but also by the "state of the world." The deliberating agent may be sure that a certain state is true. He may unsure but have information that he judges warrants assigning numerically determinate probabilities to conjectures as to which state is the true one. But Ellsberg is interested in situations where the information available to the decision-maker is "scanty, marked by gaps, obscure and

Ellsberg claimed (and considerable experimental research has confirmed his view) that the deviant behavior is deliberate and is often not readily reversed after careful review. He also claimed that the patterns of deviant behavior are not anarchistic but can be distinguished and described in terms of a decision rule. The decision rule is not the injunction to maximize expected utility but is a principle proposed by Ellsberg that is a novel variant of a proposal that had been advanced by Hodges and Lehmann (1952).

The published paper does not provide the elaborate argument that Ellsberg recognized as necessary to respond to the many followers of Ramsey, De Finetti and Savage who denied "ambiguity" in probability judgment. The dissertation supplies the lack in a detailed and philosophically sophisticated manner. And it proposes a different, more general criterion for rational choice, rather than the variant of the Hodges and Lehmann idea bruited in the paper.

All of this is done in the first seven of the eight chapters of the dissertation. The eighth chapter addresses, among other things, a problem posed by Allais that, like Ellsberg's problem, many respondents resolve in violation of expected utility theory. This problem presents a challenge to expected utility theory, as does Ellsberg's problem. It also creates puzzles for Ellsberg's proposed decision criteria; for the source of deviancy cannot be attributed to ambiguity in probability judgment. With characteristic honesty, Ellsberg acknowledged the point and made some heuristic suggestions as to how the Allais problem should be addressed, but left the issue unsettled.

Prior to the early 1970s, Ellsberg's discussion of decision-making when probabilities go indeterminate or "ambiguous" is the most comprehensive discussion of which I am aware.[2] Much of this discussion is instructive even in the contemporary climate. The attention directed to

---

vague" or is "plentiful and precise but highly contradictory"(p. 9). (Evidence, I conjecture, is contradictory for Ellsberg if part of it taken by itself would support one hypothesis and another, part would support another and there is no basis available to the decision-maker for resolving the issue, "all things considered.") It emerges subsequently that ambiguity is present when the decision-maker cannot rule out all but one probability distribution over the states of nature as representing the decision-maker's state of probability judgment. Ellsberg called such states of information "ambiguous" because of a precedent he found in the psychological literature (note 1, p. 1).

[2]There had been important discussions of indeterminate probability without special reference to decision-making in Koopman (1940), Kyburg (1961), and Good (1962). Discussions of indeterminate probability that do consider its impact on decision-making include, in particular, Good (1952), Hurwicz (1951), Hodges and Lehmann (1952), Smith (1961) and Wald (1942, 1947, and 1950).

Ellsberg's article in the *Quarterly Journal of Economics* focused on empirical studies of responses to Ellsberg-type predicaments or on damage control on the part of those who defend subjectivist expected utility theory and marvel at human foibles. Consequently, Ellsberg's positive discussions of probabilistic ignorance and partial ignorance, and of how to make choices in the face of such ignorance have not received a proper hearing. With the publication of Ellsberg's dissertation and the much more elaborate development of these positive proposals presented there, appreciation of the contribution of his work to the study of decision making when probability judgment is indeterminate or ambiguous ought to become more widespread.

THE BERNOULLI PROPOSITION

Ellsberg's paradox acquired the aura of paradox because reasonable and reflective individuals tend to respond to the type of decision problem he poses in ways that conflict with the precepts articulated in what Ellsberg called "the Bernoulli proposition":

> For a reasonable decision-maker, there exists a set of numbers ("von Neumann–Morgenstern utilities") corresponding to the uncertain outcomes of any given risky proposition or "gamble," and a set of numbers (numerical probabilities) corresponding to the events determining these outcomes, such that the ranking of mathematical expectations of utility computed for various gambles on the basis of these numbers will reflect his actual, deliberated preferences among these gambles. (p. 50, ch.2)

Consider any context where a "reasonable decision-maker" faces a choice between a set $A = \{a_1, a_2, \ldots a_n\}$ of options. (I shall assume the set of options is finite.) I shall suppose (as Ellsberg does) that from the decision-maker's point of view, the outcome o_{ij} of implementing a given option that is of interest to the decision-maker is uncertain. The outcome o_{ij} that will occur is determined (1) by the true state h_j of the world, and (2) by the option a_i chosen.

Figure 1 presents a familiar matrix representation of a decision problem so conceived.

Figure 1

Acts\States	h_1	$h_2, \ldots \ldots \ldots h_j, \ldots \ldots \ldots, h_m$		
a_1	o_{11}	o_{12}	o_{1j}	o_{1m}
a_2	o_{21}	o_{22}	o_{2j}	o_{2m}
a_i	o_{i1}	o_{i2}	o_{ij}	o_{jm}
a_n	o_{n1}	o_{n2}	o_{nj}	o_{nm}

According to the Bernoulli proposition, a "reasonable decision-maker" should assign real numbers to the outcomes o_{ij} determined by a von Neumann-Morgenstern utility function $u(o_{ij}) = u_{ij}$. Such a decision-maker should assign other numbers to the states according to a real valued probability function $P(h_j/a_I)$ defined over the h_j's conditional on the a_I chosen so that for each a_i and h_j, the following conditions hold:

(i) $P(h_j/a_i) = P(h_j)$

(ii) $P(h_j) \geq 0$.

(iii) $\Sigma_j P(h_j) = 1$.

Since a_I and h_j determine o_{ij},

(iv) $P(o_{ij}/a_i) = P(h_j)$.

The function u is a von Neumann–Morgenstern utility function in the sense that *if* there is a suitable probability P defined over the states, the value of each of the a_i's is equal to the expected utility $E(a_i) = \Sigma_j P(h_j) u(o_{ij})$.

The Bernoulli proposition asserts that reasonable decision-makers should evaluate outcomes of their options according to a von Neumann-Morgenstern utility function and assign numerically determinate probabilities to the states so that the value of the available options to the decision-maker should increase with increasing expected utility. The Bernoulli proposition as Ellsberg understood it *prescribes* that rational decision-makers *should* have the requisite probabilities and utilities, and *should* maximize expected utility according to those probabilities and utilities.

Ellsberg undertook to call into question some of the presuppositions of the Bernoulli proposition. Doing so was by no means a new activity. In the seventeenth century, Huyghens had taken for granted that utility is directly proportional to monetary price. Expected utility was therefore equal to expected monetary return. In the eighteenth century, Daniel Bernoulli modified this thesis in response to the St. Petersburg paradox by distinguishing the utility of money from monetary value. He was then able to say that decision-makers maximize expected utility without claiming that they maximize expected monetary value. Other authors had doubts concerning the availability of numerically determinate probabilities suitable for use in determing expected utility.

Such skepticism concerning the descriptive and normative status of the Bernoulli proposition had existed for some time. In the 1950s, however, thanks largely to the influence of the statistician L. J. Savage, a sophisticated "neo-Bernoullian" approach had begun to find broad support among decision theorists, economists, statisticians, and philosophers. Ellsberg's challenge was to this sophisticated neo-Bernoullian doctrine.

In order to appreciate the import of Ellsberg's ideas, therefore, a brief summary of the intellectual currents in the three decades prior to Ellsberg's work will be undertaken in the next three sections.

EARLY SKEPTICISM ABOUT THE BERNOULLI PROPOSITION: ORDINALISM

Statisticians, economists, and decision theorists prior to World War II were frequently prepared to concede that circumstances can arise where reasonable agents should have the appropriate numerical probability and utility judgments. There was, however, skepticism as to whether this was or should be so under all circumstances.

Many economists took the view that the decision problems facing participants in a market could be accommodated under the rubric of decision-making under certainty. Even when uncertainty and risk were acknowledged to play a role in deliberation, many authors doubted that there was a universally accepted method for taking risk and uncertainty into account that had any empirical import. They questioned, therefore, whether there could be an intelligible system of prescriptions regulating judgments of risk and uncertainty, conformity to which could be subject to public scrutiny.

Consider the behavior of consumers with fixed income deciding between rival commodity bundles while facing fixed prices. According to the theory of consumer demand, the consumer is endowed with a preference that weakly orders not only the commodity bundles actually available to him or her but those that would be available were the prices and consumer's income to change in a broad range of different ways.

These preferences over a domain of *potential* options (commodity bundles) were assumed not only to be weakly ordered but to be representable by indifference maps of the sort pioneered by Edgeworth, Pareto, Slutzky, Hicks, and Allen. The preferences represented by such an indifference map could in principle be elicited by interrogating the decision-maker as to how he or she would choose in various hypothetical decision problems where the set of available options is hypothesized to be a subset of the set of potential options. The preference ordering over a given subset is by itself hypothesized to be a restriction of the preference over the larger domain of potential options represented by the indifference map. Such choices would "reveal" the consumer's preferences in the sense that the consumer would choose a most preferred option from among those options available in the subset were members of that subset actually available to the consumer.

According to those who adopted this approach to characterizing decision-making, the only information of use for predictive, descriptive, or
prescriptive purposes concerns the preferences of decision-makers as
revealed by choice. And so-called revealed preference on this view is
completely characterized by ordinal conceptions of value. There is no
need to invoke a cardinal utility representation of the commodity bundles representing potential options in the example of consumer demand.

On this view, any uncertainty that a decision-maker might have concerning the consequences of the options available to him or her should be
integrated somehow into the decision-maker's comparative and ordinal
evaluation of the available alternatives. Only these comparative evaluations or preferences, as revealed in the choices the decision-maker would
have made in various hypothetical decision problems, are relevant to the
description and prescription of choice behavior. There is no need to consider the Bernoulli proposition.

VON NEUMANN–MORGENSTERN UTILITY

Skepticism regarding the need to invoke the Bernoulli proposition was
overcome for some contexts by the efforts of von Neumann and
Morgenstern (1944). They sought to show that when the set of potential
options over which the preferences that can be revealed by choice is constructed in a certain way, utilities appropriate for use in maximizing
expected utility are derivable. To the extent that they were successful,
they could argue that the "ordinalists," who restricted themselves to
comparative judgments of value among potential options, ought to be
committed to cardinal utilities for the consequences of potential options
and expected utilities for the options themselves.[3]

Von Neumann and Morgenstern considered preferences over a
domain of potential options that are "mixtures" or "roulette lotteries"
over some set of prizes.[4] A roulette lottery over the prizes $x_1, x_2, ..., x_n$ is
an option that yields prize x_i with objective or statistical probability p_i
where the probabilities of the n prizes sum up to 1. Included among the
potential options are "pure" options, where the decision-maker is
assured of receipt of prize x_i with probability 1. In addition, one can
choose compound lotteries where the payoffs are other roulette lotteries.
The set of options actually faced by the decision-maker X is a subset of
this domain of roulette lotteries. As in the case of consumer demand, the

---

[3]This observation is very much in keeping with a view expressed by Ellsberg
eight years before completing his dissertation. Ellsberg 1954, emphasized the
point that the measurable utilities obtained by the techniques of von Neumann
and Morgenstern satisfied the choice theoretic requirements on measurability
imposed by ordinalists.

[4]The distinction between roulette lotteries and horse lotteries I use here derives
from Anscombe and Aumann (1963).

preferences of the decision-maker X for the options X faces are by hypothesis embedded in the preference over the space of potential options.

Von Neumann and Morgenstern offered compelling axioms for preference over a domain of roulette lotteries that guarantee that the ordering of the mixed options could be represented by a von Neumann-Morgenstern utility function.[5] Choosing the best option from a finite subset of the mixture set should, then, maximize expected utility according to the von Neumann–Morgenstern utility and the objective probabilities specified for the mixed options. The terms of the Bernoulli proposition are shown to be satisfied—provided the consequences of the options available to the decision-maker could be guaranteed to be realized with known and definite objective probabilities conditional on the option being assessed.

The contribution of von Neumann–Morgenstern persuaded many to invoke the injunction to maximize expected utility when the options available to the decision-maker are roulette lotteries. Under these circumstances, advocates of the von Neumann–Morgenstern point of view could say to the revealed preference ordinalists that by enlarging the domain of potential options over which ordinal revealed preference is defined, and imposing compelling assumptions on such preference, a clear notion of cardinal utility can be constructed.

However, in the absence of an *objective* probability over states, many authors remained skeptical concerning the existence of a probability distribution suitable for determining expected utilities. Using the graphic terminology made familiar by Anscombe and Aumann, uncertain prospects for which such standardized subjective probabilities are not given shall be called "horse lotteries."

If the potential options to be evaluated are horse lotteries, where assignments of objective statistical probabilities to consequences are not available to the decision-maker, many authors were unprepared to endorse the Bernoulli proposition.

SUBJECTIVE PROBABILITY AND THE BERNOULLI PROPOSITION

Building on the pioneering efforts of Ramsey (1931) and De Finetti (1964), Savage (1954) offered a persuasive system of postulates for rational preference over potential options (Savage "acts") that need not be mixtures in the sense of roulette lotteries of pure options. Decision-makers, whose preferences agree with Savage's requirements, must evaluate these potential options (acts) *as if* the decision-maker endorsed a probability distribution over the states and the Bernoulli proposition is satisfied. These decision-makers maximize expected utility using "personal," "subjective" or "credal" probabilities representing their degrees of belief.

---

[5]See Luce and Raiffa (1957) for a useful discussion.

These degrees of belief need not be grounded in full belief in objective statistical probabilities.

Indeed, Savage, like de Finetti, was skeptical of the existence of objective probabilities. Both authors would have conceded that roulette lotteries can be reconstrued so that the probabilities are subjective or belief probabilities that most thoughtful agents would endorse under the circumstances specified for the problem. Thus, even though Savage's postulates do not entail that a given coin has an equal chance of yielding heads and of yielding tails on a toss, reasonable agents might agree in their probability judgments concerning the outcome of a specific toss of the coin. Objectivists might insist that such belief probabilities are grounded in information about objective, statistical probabilities. Savage would deny this but might, in some contexts, acknowledge that roulette lotteries are prospects where reasonable people assign subjective belief probabilities to hypotheses about outcomes in a determinate and standard manner. Whether such objective, statistical probabilities can be meaningfully posited or not, anyone whose preferences for acts conform to Savage's postulates is committed to endorsing a system of credal probability judgments. For the purposes of this discussion, we shall understand roulette lotteries in this fashion.

Savage's postulates were convincing to many students of rational choice as prescriptions constraining the way preferences among potential options ought to be structured in order to satisfy minimal requirements of rational consistency or "coherence." As Ellsberg observed, any pattern of choice contradicting the existence of appropriate von Neumann–Morgenstern utilities and of credal probabilities needed for computing the expected utilities of the options according to the Bernoulli proposition "must also violate certain proposed canons of reasonable behavior that are, undeniably, far more persuasive as normative criteria than is the 'Bernoulli proposition' itself."

INDETERMINACY IN PROBABILITY JUDGMENT

As Ellsberg rightly observed, the importance of Savage's contribution is to be found in his demonstration that someone who satisfies Savage's normative conditions on preferences over "acts" is constrained to endorse more than von Neumann–Morgenstern evaluations for consequences of his acts. The decision-maker should also act as if he endorsed numerically determinate probabilities for the "states" that, together with the act chosen, determine the consequence that will ensue.[6]

---

[6]Strictly speaking, the postulates for preferences over acts (formally functions from states to consequences) are representable by at least one probability-utility pair that determines an expected utility function for the acts that preserves the preference ordering. However, there is a continuum of many such probability-

Ellsberg insisted that reasonable agents often refuse to be committed to numerically determinate probability distributions over states or even to complete orderings of states with respect to probabilities. As a consequence, they could not, under all circumstances, be expected utility maximizers.

Ellsberg's critique of Savage's approach (for which he registered profound admiration) has three prongs.

The first prong points to work by authors such as Koopman (1940) and Good (1952, 1962) who proposed formal theories of probability that allow for interval-valued probability judgment based on the testimony of deliberating agents concerning their comparative judgments of probability in addition to their testimony concerning their choice behavior in actual and hypothetical contexts of choice. Ellsberg is aware that Savage is a program sought to rely exclusively on testimony of the second "behavioralist" type. But Ellsberg insisted on the "meaningfulness" of judgments of comparative probability of the nonbehavioralist "verbalistic" variety. He did not claim that such testimony was sufficient to establish the coherence of judgments of probability that are not determinate. He insisted only that they not be discounted as meaningless.

The second prong of Ellsberg's argument appeals to Smith's account of upper and lower probabilities (Smith 1961), which purports to invoke only data of the "behavioralist" variety to elicit such probabilities. We are entitled to entertain the suggestion that the interval-valued probabilities of Koopman and Good coincide with the interval values determined by Smith's upper and lower "pignic" probabilities.

If Savage's postulates are endorsed in their entirety as compelling conditions on rational agents, this "softening up" exercise will prove to be in vain. The third prong in Ellsberg's argument attempts to show that reasonable agents endorse choice behavior that violates the Savage postulates and that many such agents refuse to change their judgments when the fact of their violation is brought to their attention.

---

utility pairs. So it is misleading to claim that Savage's postulates determine a unique probability distribution over states, as Ellsberg suggests. What is true is that if one stipulates that the utility function must be state-independent (so that the utility of a given payoff is independent of the state as well as the act), there is exactly one probability that can serve in the representation. The postulation of state-independent utility cannot be formulated as a constraint on preferences over potential options of the sort that Savage calls "acts."

THE SURE THING PRINCIPLE

Ellsberg undertook to undermine the persuasiveness of one of Savage's postulates: P2. Ellsberg called this the "Sure Thing Principle."[7] I shall do the same. The content of P2 will be explained by considering the predicament of a decision-maker contemplating a (conceivably hypothetical) choice between options I and II in Figure 2, and also a choice between the options III and IV in Figure 3:

Figure 2

	H_1	H_2
Option I	a	c
Option II	b	c

Figure 3

	H_1	H_2
Option III	a	d
Option IV	b	d

The sole difference between the decision problem depicted in Figure 2 and the decision problem depicted in Figure 3 concerns the payoffs for H_2. In the Figure 2 predicament, prize c is obtained regardless of how the decision-maker chooses. In Figure 3 predicament, the prize is d instead of c. Prizes a and b are the same in both cases.

Savage's P2 stipulates that Option I should be preferred to Option II if and only if Option III is preferred to Option IV. Changing the utility values for the payoff to be received in case H_2 is true should make no difference to the preference for the pair of options. As formulated here, P2 applies to problems where there are two states. The principle can be generalized to apply to any system of states determining finitely many distinct payoffs.

The Bernoulli proposition presupposes satisfaction of P2 along with several other postulates including in particular the assumption P1. P1 is an assumption that Savage's neo Bernoullian theory shares with the ordinalist theorists of consumer demand and with von Neumann and Morgenstern. It asserts that preferences over potential options yield a weak ordering.[8]

---

[7]According to Savage (1954, p. 24), P2 captures a presupposition of "the first part" of the Sure Thing Principle. The second part is captured by P3. It has, however, become widespread practice to consider P2 to be the Sure Thing Principle.

[8]The relation "x is weakly preferred to y" (or "x is preferred at least as

To claim that preferences impose a complete ordering implies that no two potential options are noncomparable. Given any pair of potential options 1 and 2, then 1 is strictly preferred to 2, 2 is strictly preferred to 1, or 1 and 2 are equipreferred.

Ellsberg undertook to undermine the case for P2 while retaining P1. He attributed the failure of P2 to the circumstances that rational agents often cannot provide a complete ordering of probabilities of states of nature, even though they should as rational agents regard their options as comparable in value. Ellsberg claimed that common responses by deliberating agents to certain types of decision problems, including the examples instantiating the Ellsberg paradox, called P2 (the Sure Thing Principle) into question in a manner that showed that probabilities are not always completely orderable without casting doubt on the ordering of potential options.

UNCERTAIN PROSPECTS THAT ARE NOT RISKS

Consider the following scenario.

Urn_I contains 100 red and black balls in unknown proportion. That is to say, there are $r/100$ red and the remainder black where r ranges from 0 to 100. A single ball is selected at random from Urn_I. If a bet is offered where you (the decision-maker) receive $100 if a red is drawn, you are offered a bet on Red_I. Likewise you might be offered a bet on $Black_I$ (not-Red_I). Both of these bets are uncertain prospects that are not risks. The decision-maker does not know the objective probability of obtaining a red (or black) ball on a random selection from Urn_I.[9]

Let Urn_{II} contain 50 red balls and 50 black. A single ball is selected at random from Urn_{II}. If a bet is offered where you receive $100 if a red is drawn, you are offered a bet on Red_{II}. Likewise you might be offered a bet on $Black_{II}$ (not-Red_{II}). Such bets are uncertain prospects that are risks.

Consider a choice between sampling from Urn_I and betting on Red_I or sampling from Urn_{II} and betting on Red_{II}.

---

much as y") weakly orders the potential options if and only if the following conditions hold: (1) weak preference is transitive; (2) weak preference is complete (for every pair of potential options x and y, x is weakly preferred to y or y to x). As a consequence, weak preference is reflexive (for every potential option x, x is weakly preferred to itself).

[9]De Finetti and Savage alike questioned the very intelligibility of notions of objective or statistical probability. Hence, characterizing decision-making under uncertainty, as I have done in the text, would seem question-begging to them and their supporters. But instead of speaking of unknown objective probabilities, say in uncertain prospects that are not risks, probabilities are not given in the model.

Consider the corresponding choice between betting on Black$_{jI}$ and betting on Black$_{II}$.

Ellsberg pointed out that registering indifference between betting on Red$_I$ and Black$_I$, and between betting on Red$_{II}$ and Black$_{II}$ mandates indifference between betting on Red$_I$ and Red$_{II}$, and also between betting on Black$_I$ and Black$_{II}$ if Savage's P1 and P2 are to be obeyed.

But many who are indifferent in confronting the first two decisions favor Red$_{II}$ over Red$_I$ and Black$_{II}$ over Black$_I$. This suggests a partiality for uncertain prospects that are risks over uncertain prospects that are not.

Moreover, this partiality obtains regardless of whether the choice is between bets on Red$_I$ and on Red$_{II}$ or between bets on Black$_I$ and on Black$_{II}$. This implies that the probability judgments for Red$_1$ and Black$_I$ not only are not numerically determinate but also cannot be weakly ordered. Partiality for risk over uncertainty might seem to suggest that the probability of Red$_{II}$ (which equals 0.5) should be greater than Red$_I$. But then the probability of Black$_I$ (that equals the probability of not-Red$_I$) should be greater than 0.5 and, hence, should be greater than the probability of Black$_{II}$. This should require a preference for the gamble on Black$_I$ over the gamble on Black$_{II}$. This is not the preference that prevails among those partial to risk over uncertainty! (Ellsberg cites some experimental work by John Chipman [1960] in support of his empirical claims.)

THE THREE-COLOR URN PROBLEM

The partiality for risky rather than uncertain prospects exhibited in the decision problems just described undermines the contention advanced by Savage that, even in the absence of objective probabilities, rational agents should have subjective probabilities that insure satisfaction of the Bernoulli proposition. And this calls into question whether, in the absence of objective probabilities, both Savage's P1 and P2 are satisfied. But Ellsberg did not claim that, on the basis of the reactions displayed, one could argue that P2 is violated. To argue for this conclusion, Ellsberg appealed to the responses of experimental subjects to the three-color urn problem—also known as Ellsberg's paradox.

Consider an urn containing 90 balls, 30 of which are known to be red. The remaining balls are black and yellow balls in some unknown proportion. Figures 3 and 4 describe a pair of decision problems each involving a choice between two options. A ball is to be selected "at random" from the urn and the subject is to be paid $100 or nothing, depending on the color of the ball drawn and the option chosen according to the schedules given in figures 3 and 4.

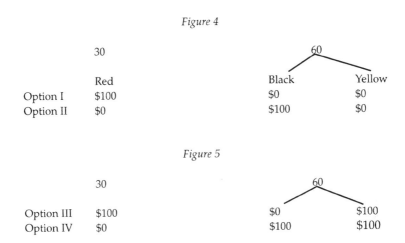

Figure 4

Figure 5

In Chapter 5 of his dissertation, Ellsberg invited the reader to consider carefully how he or she would choose in each one of these predicaments. He claimed that if "you" (the reader) favor I over II and IV over III, you are normal. Ellsberg reported on students' responses in Howard Raiffa's classes in the Harvard Business School, and since that time this type of response has been confirmed as typical over and over again.[10] He took this pattern of choice behavior to reveal a readiness to violate P2, or the Sure Thing Principle.

Many respondents who initially respond to the three-color urn problem in the manner described by Ellsberg change their minds upon reflection. Recognizing that they must be violating the Bernoulli proposition or one of Savage's postulates, they acknowledge the normative force of Savage's postulates for them and adjust their judgments to conform. But Ellsberg pointed out that many intelligent individuals refuse to adjust upon full consideration of the matter. The normative force of Savage's postulates does not appear to be universally applicable to all reasonable-seeming agents. Ellsberg (who counted himself among those who resist the sovereignty of Savage's postulates) argued that this circumstance suggested that modification of the expected utility model and of Savage's postulates should be sought. The modified approach should provide a more comprehensive decision criterion acknowledging the expected utility theory as a special case of a more general approach.

In Chapter 6, Ellsberg embarked on this exploration.

---

[10]MacCrimmon and Larsson (1979, section 6) report on studies that check on responses to Ellsberg type violations of the Sure Thing Principle.

PROBABILITY AND IGNORANCE

Ellsberg began Chapter 6 by noting that in the three-color urn problem, the Bernoulli proposition fails due to the absence of information about the constitution of the urn relevant to determining probabilities. The decision-maker can determine an expected utility for each option on the assumption that some specific characterization of the percentages of red, yellow, and black balls in the urn is known. But the decision-maker lacks an unconditional probability distribution over the several hypotheses concerning the percentages of balls of the several colors in the urn. And in the absence of such information, the decision-maker cannot derive an expected utility for each of the options. In the terminology adopted by Luce and Raiffa (1958), such a predicament approximates a case of "decision-making under uncertainty."

Ellsberg pointed out that the three-color urn problem is not precisely a case of decision-making under uncertainty. The decision-maker knows that one third of the balls in the urn are red. Hence the objective probability of obtaining a red ball is 1/3. The ignorance of probability required in decision-making under uncertainty is not total. But the predicament is not a case of decision- making under risk where the probabilities as well as the utilities are given, nor where they are derivable from what is given.

Ellsberg considered four rules for decision making under uncertainty discussed in the classic work by Luce and Raiffa (1958), and wondered whether they can be extended to apply to the three-color urn problem (p. 216). The four rules are the Laplace rule; minimax loss, proposed by A. Wald; maximizing an optimism-pessimism index, proposed by Hurwicz (1951); and minimax regret, proposed by Savage (1954). Ellsberg noted that such rules are intended for use under "complete ignorance" of the states of nature. In the discussions of Luce and Raiffa, complete ignorance is characterized by two constraints: (1) preference among options is independent of the labeling of states of nature; and (2) adding a new column (state) to the payoff matrix identical with one of the old ones does not influence the ordering of options.

If in the three-color urn problem we take the states to be obtaining a red ball, obtaining a yellow ball, and obtaining a black ball, the application of each of the four rules may be characterized as follows.

The so-called "Laplace rule" computes expected utility based on uniform probability over the states. Consequently, obtaining a red, obtaining a yellow, and obtaining a black are assigned equal probability of 1/3. The expected utilities of I and II are both equal to 1/3. The expected utilities of III and IV are both equal to 2/3. Hence the Laplace rule recommends indifference between I and II and between III and IV, and is no more successful in accommodating deviations from expected utility maximization exhibited in the three-color urn problem than is Savage's theory. In any case, it fails to satisfy the second condition on complete ignorance.

Minimax loss urges decision-makers to choose the option with the highest security level, where the security is the lowest payoff in utility yielded for any state. The security levels for options I and II are both 0, so are the security levels of acts III and IV. The deviant choice behavior frequently found in the three-color urn problem is not allowed.

Let the "regret" yielded by a given option a in state S be the difference in utility between outcome in S yielded by the option a^* and the outcome in S yielded by a. Minimax regret recommends maximizing security with respect to regret. According to this approach, I and II are treated the same as III and IV.

The Hurwicz optimism-pessimism rule urges maximizing for a fixed value of $\alpha (0 \leq \alpha \leq)$ a weighted average $\alpha u^* + (1-\alpha)u_*$ of the best utility payoff u^* and the worst utility payoff u_* yielded by an available option.[11] Again, there is no basis for discrimination. These recommendations do not accommodate the choice of I over II or IV over III that is the most frequent response to the three-color urn problem.

Ellsberg claimed that "it is not too surprising" (p. 216) that typical decision-makers do not conform to the Laplace rule, the Wald minimax loss, the Hurwicz optimism-pessimism rule, or Savage's minimax regret rule in confronting the three-color urn problem. This is because all four rules require that the decision-maker be totally ignorant of the objective probability of the state of nature. We are not totally ignorant in the case of the three-color urn. We know that one third of the balls in the urn are red. So we are given an objective probability of 1/3 for obtaining a red ball on a draw. If objective probabilities are dismissed as metaphysical moonshine, we can replace them in this example by a physical condition (the presence of red balls in the urn in the proportion of 1/3). This condition provides an objective basis for assigning a subjective probability of 1/3 to obtaining a red on a draw from the urn.

Ellsberg pointed out that the rules just mentioned can be reintroduced as applying relative to states of nature spelling out each of the 61 possible frequencies with which yellow balls may exist in the urn. Shifting from the three states of nature to 61 in this manner allows us to think of the decision-maker as totally ignorant of the 61 states of nature. However, the payoffs for the acts, given the state of nature, are now, in the cases

---

[11]Ellsberg pointed out that Shackle's (1949, 1961) account of decision-making (which was regrettably ignored by Luce and Raiffa) is a generalization of the Hurwicz optimism-pessimism rule (p. 218). To my knowledge, Ellsberg is the first commentator in print to provide an accurate characterization of Shackle's principle of choice. Arrow and Hurwicz (1972) endorse a similar view. Levi (1980b section 10) discusses the relation between Shackle's view and Hurwicz.

under consideration, expected payoffs conditional on choosing the acts in the the given state of nature.[12] Ellsberg did not claim that the new states are properly considered to be states of nature. He suggested that subjects act "as if" they are. (p. 228).

Ellsberg's ambivalence about the status of statistical states as states of nature is understandable. If a state of nature together with an option is supposed to completely determine a payoff, statistical states do not qualify. They provide only probability distributions over payoffs. If these probabilities are objective statistical probabilities, the option cum statistical state yield a roulette lottery as outcome. For objectivists, this may be enough to qualify statistical states as proper states of nature. But Ellsberg apparently did not wish to beg questions against those who, like Savage and De Finetti, thought objective probability is meaningless. This suggested that no assumptions involving objective probability should be irreplaceable in any model of a decision problem being examined.

Ellsberg saw an equivalence between, on the one hand, a state of complete ignorance about a set of statistical hypotheses specifying objective probabilities for outcomes of experiment that together with the option implemented, determine that the payoff is true, and on the other, a model that makes no appeal to objective probabilities. Multiply each of the statistical probability distributions corresponding to a simple statistical hypothesis by its subjective probability according to some probability distribution over the simple statistical hypotheses. The result is a subjective or personal probability over the outcomes. If the decision-maker endorsed such a personal probability, he or she could compute an expected value for each option and preferences for options assessed in a manner conforming to the Sure Thing principle.

---

[12]In point of fact, Wald understood states of nature and minimax loss in precisely this manner (Wald 1942, 1947, 1950). Ellsberg recognized that minimaxing could be applied to expected losses but only for "mixed" options. The application of minimax to expected losses for pure acts when states are statistical is not considered. By way of contrast, for Wald, each potential option is a function from states to n-tuples of payoffs where for each state, a probability distribution over the payoffs is given. Thus, for each state and option, an expected value is given. The minimum loss (maximum) incurred by exercising an option is the least *expected* loss conditional on a state of nature. Savage's own account of the objectivist position concurs with this (Savage 1954, 9.3, 9.4, 9.8). Savage's attempt to rationalize minimax theory as an account of group decision-making in a manner consistent with his personalism replaces Wald's minimax (expected) loss with minimax (expected) regret (Savage 1954, ch.10). Savage stated that he originally thought that Wald intended his decision rule to be the same as the Savage rule. And it is true that Wald restricts his discussion to cases where minimax loss and minimax regret are equivalent. The three-color urn problem is not such a case. In this context, the minimax loss rule does recommend choosing I over II and IV

Each of the 61 possibly true statistical hypotheses corresponds to a definite distribution over the outcome of sampling (to wit, when probability 1 is assigned to a given statistical state. But there are continuumly many other distributions over the statistical states each of which yields a probability distribution over the outcomes of sampling. L. Hurwicz (1951) had already suggested that complete ignorance with respect to a given space Ω of states or possibilities could be characterized by the set Y of all probability distributions over the Ω allowed by the calculus of probabilities. Partial ignorance with respect to Ω could be characterized by a subset Y^0 of Y. This, in turn, can be treated as complete ignorance with respect to Y^0. If Ω is taken to be a set of states that determine payoffs given the choice of an option, we can dispense with talk of statistical states and rely on the set Y^0 to represent the decision-maker's state of information about Ω. This state of information Y^0 is a state of subjective probability judgment of a special kind not countenanced by neo-Bernoullians ("strict Bayesians" as I have called them). It is a state of "ambiguity" or a state of indeterminate probability judgement where more than one distribution is "possible" as Hurwicz would say or is "permissible" as I would prefer to say.[13]

Hurwicz proposed adopting his optimism-pessimism criterion using Y^0 as if it were the set of states and the payoffs for options are their expectations conditional on the elements of Y^0. Ellsberg called this the restricted Hurwicz Criterion.

Ellsberg noticed that when this criterion is applied to the three-color urn problem, for $\alpha < 0.5$, I is chosen over II and IV over III. When $\alpha > 0.5$, II is chosen over I while III is chosen over IV. When $\alpha = 0.5$, I and II are both allowed choices, as are III and IV. Only in this last case is P2 satisfied, according to Ellsberg. In the first case, P2 is violated in the manner exhibited in the manner that a substantial plurality of respondents indicate. It is also violated in the second case.

Thus, what Ellsberg called "the Restricted Hurwicz Criterion" can accommodate those who violate P2 in both possible ways and the "Restricted Minimax Criterion" accommodates the most common of these ways. Ellsberg regarded the Restricted Hurwicz Criterion superior to the Restricted Minimax Criterion precisely because it was capable of recognizing a wider variety of choice behaviors exhibited by reasonable agents than the Restricted Minimax can.

---

over III. Indeed, the minimax loss rule corresponds to the rule Ellsberg called "restricted minimax" in his dissertation. He saw it as a special case of the "restricted Hurwicz" principle he recommended.

[13]To call such probability distributions "possible" is to suggest that they carry truth-values. Subjectivists have tended to think that probability distributions lack truth-values. I prefer to use "permissible" because such distributions are permissible to use in evaluating the expected utilities of options up for choice. (Levi,

THE RESTRICTED BAYES/HURWICZ CRITERION

Ellsberg was not satisfied with resting at this point. The Hurwicz construction allows us to regard the decision-maker as completely ignorant with respect to the set Y^0 of distributions over Ω. Consider, then, X, who confronts the three-color urn problem. Offer X a gamble, where X receives 1 utile if there are 0 yellow balls in the urn and nothing otherwise and ask him how much he is prepared to pay. Do the same putting the stake of 1 utile on the proposition that there are more than 0 balls in the urn. According to Smith's requirements for coherence, the highest amount X should pay for the first bet plus the highest amount he should pay for the second should not be less than 1. Ellsberg claimed that decision-makers might, however, be prepared to take such gambles. He wished to accommodate such behavior as reasonable. He suggested that a decision-maker who has failed to rule out any one of a set Y^0 of distributions as unacceptable might, nonetheless, regard one as distinguished from the rest by its reliability. Call this "best guess" distribution v^0. Compute the expected utilities of the options under consideration using v^0. Multiply the expectation of a given option by a nonnegative factor ρ less than 1. Multiply the Hurwicz optimism-pessimism value of this option by $1 - \rho$.

The most general criterion of choice recommended by Ellsberg is that X should maximize the value of this index. This criterion is called the "Restricted Bayes/Hurwicz Criterion." (pp.193–194). If $\rho = 1$, the decision-maker regards the best guess distribution as his personal probability and behaves like an expected utility maximizer. If $\rho = 0$, the decision-maker is in complete ignorance as to which of the elements of Y^0 to use. The decision-maker follows the Restricted Hurwicz Criterion. Intermediate values of ρ reflect a compromise between these extremes.

In the 1961 paper, Ellsberg had recommended a weighted average of the expectation according to v^0 and the security level of an option. This suggestion is, as Ellsberg acknowledged, a variant of a proposal for a "restricted Bayes solution" by Hodges and Lehmann (1952). Ellsberg called it "Restricted Bayes/minimax" in his dissertation. One of the significant differences between the dissertation and the earlier paper is Ellsberg's argument for Restricted Bayes/Hurwicz over Restricted Bayes/minimax. According to that argument, Restricted Bayes/Hurwicz accommodated a still wider variety of patterns of behavior which reasonable agents could endorse.

1974, 1980a). How the set of expected utilities is then used in assessing the available options in order to identify "best" options is a controversial matter. But the permissibility of the probability distributions does not imply that they carry truth-values.

At the beginning of Chapter 8 (the last chapter of his dissertation), Ellsberg summarizes his case for the Restricted Bayes/Hurwicz Criterion as follows:

> In the last two chapters the following testable propositions have been advanced: (1) certain information states can be meaningfully identified as ambiguous; (2) in these states, many otherwise reasonable people tend to violate the Savage axioms with respect to certain choices; (3) their behavior is deliberate and not readily reversed upon reflection; (4) certain patterns of "violating" behavior can be distinguished and described in terms of a specified decision rule; (5) this decision rule is one which has, in the past, been recommended or suggested as appropriate by reputable theorists; (6) many of the people concerned recognize the rule as reflecting the sort of considerations that influence their behavior and the rough character of actual mental processes by which they arrive at their decisions.

The discussion in chapters 6 and 7 that culminates in the proposal and elaboration of the Bayes/Hurwicz Criterion is a sustained effort to support these claims. By invoking a wide variety of problems and delivering verdicts that reasonable agents *might* deliver, Ellsberg argued for his Restricted Bayes/Hurwicz Criterion as the one that manages to accommodate the varieties of choice behavior that should be recognized as "reasonable" or "rational."[14]

As Ellsberg acknowledged, however, his critique of the personalist or "neo-Bernoullian" point of view, given exquisite expression in the axiomatic theory of Savage, might itself yield recommendations that "otherwise reasonable" people tend to violate. In Chapter 8, Ellsberg took up some challenges to the Bayes/Hurwicz Criterion and sought to respond to them.

INDETERMINACY IN PROBABILITY AND THE VON NEUMANN–MORGENSTERN AXIOMS.

A main theme of Ellsberg's dissertation is that failures of the Sure Thing Principle (or Savage's P2) arise in contexts where indeterminacy is present in subjective probability judgment. The famous three-color urn problem, often called "Ellsberg's paradox," is adduced in support of this idea. And Ellsberg's argument for the Bayes/Hurwicz Criterion is based on this problem and many other kinds of problems where indeterminacy or "ambiguity" arises in probability judgment.

---

[14]In his doctoral dissertation published one year after Ellsberg's, Nozick discussed Ellsberg's Restricted Bayes/minimax rule suggested in his 1961 paper. After registering some interesting doubts about this rule, Nozick suggested, in effect, that the Restricted Bayes/Hurwicz Criterion would be an improvement. Nozick remained skeptical at the end of this discussion as to the merits of this

suggestion (Nozick 1963, 214–223).

But the Sure Thing Principle, or variants of it, surfaces as postulates in Von Neumann–Morgenstern theory. In this theory, the potential options are roulette lotteries. The Independence Postulate asserts that if one such lottery L_1 is preferred to another L_2, then a compound lottery $<L_1, p, L_3>$ where L_1 is received with probability p and L_3 is received with probability 1-p, should be preferred to compound lottery $<L_2, p, L_3>$.

Ellsberg argued that there is nothing wrong with endorsing the Independence Postulate and rejecting the Sure Thing Principle. The Independence Postulate corresponds to the Sure Thing Principle restricted to bets where determinate probabilities are given for the payoffs. Endorsing it does not imply the full sweep of the Sure Thing Principle which covers horse lotteries as well as roulette lotteries.

Ellsberg's effort to seal off hermetically the Independence Postulate from the alleged excesses of the Sure Thing Principle was publicly challenged by Raiffa (1961). Ellsberg also mentioned similar challenges by Pratt in private correspondence. In the first part of Chapter 8, Ellsberg offered an extensive discussion of these challenges.

The flavor of the challenges and Ellsberg's responses may be gathered from a consideration of the following objection by Raiffa to choosing I over II and IV over III in the three-color urn problem.

Suppose one were offered two lotteries. Lottery A offers a 50–50 bet on the toss of a fair coin, paying with option I if heads and option IV if tails. Lottery B offers a bet paying option II if heads and III if tails. If I is preferred to II and IV to III, lottery A dominates lottery B. So A should be preferred to B. But lottery A pays $100 with a probability of 0.5, and 0 otherwise. So does B. So they should be equipreferred, and we have an inconsistency.

Ellsberg agreed that A and B are to be equipreferred. But there is no inconsistency. The appeal to dominance to sustain preference for A over B is unwarranted. Raiffa's dominance argument assumed that the states are the outcomes of the toss of the coin. But the payoffs from such states are not roulette lotteries. The probabilities of payoffs from lotteries A and B are indeterminate. The payoffs from tossing the coin are lotteries A and B and these are horse lotteries. In such cases, appeal to dominance arguments presuppose the Sure Thing Principle in its full generality and not its specialization as the Independence Postulate, which is restricted to roulette lotteries or prospects where the probabilities are determinate. Dominance arguments that used as states specifications of the outcome of tossing the coin and the color of the ball drawn would have been cogent had they been applicable. But in the case under consideration, neither option dominates the other relative to such states.

THE ALLAIS PROBLEM

Up to this point, Ellsberg had diagnosed the source of the breakdown of the Savage postulates as due to indeterminacy in probability. However, some alleged counterinstances due to Allais (1952, 1953) seem immune to this diagnosis. Ellsberg frankly concedes the point:

> Before studying carefully certain hypothetical examples proposed by Allais, I would have conjectured that the Savage postulates would prove acceptable to me as normative criteria in any situation providing a clear basis for "definite" probabilities: e.g., urns with known proportions of balls.... Now I am not so sure. (p. 256)

Suppose a ball is to be selected at random from an urn containing 10 red balls, 1 white ball, and 89 blue balls.

Figure 6 presents two decision problems, the outcomes of whose options are determined by the result of the selection.

Figure 6

	10 Red	1 White	89 Blue
Case 1:			
Option 1	$500,000	$500,000	$500,000
Option 2	$2,500,000	$0	$500,000
Case 2:			
Option 3	$500,000	$500,000	$0
Option 4	$2,500,000	$0	$0

In this pair of decision problems, the probabilities are determinate. Yet a large number of those who are invited to decide between them choose 1 over 2 in Case 1 and 4 over 3 in Case 2. Savage's postulates are violated. Ellsberg, like Allais, saw the violation as a deviation from P2—the so called "Sure Thing Principle." Here not only do agents disobey the recommendation to maximize expected utility; they also disobey the Bayes/Hurwicz criterion that Ellsberg advocated in Chapter 7.

In spite of this, Ellsberg criticizes Savage's reasoning in seeking to explain away his own attraction to the choices of 1 and 4. His own response is encapsulated in the following remarks:

> The "recognizability" of behavior-patterns such as those Allais describes, which involve violations of the Sure-Thing Principle even when personal probabilities are "definite," suggests that the following notion may have considerable heuristic value: *Certainty is to Risk, as Risk is to Ambiguity.* This expression suggests a relationship between the sorts of violations of Savage's postulate 2 discussed by Allais and those I have described. In the Allais examples, a change in the payoffs for which two actions "agree" (e.g., the payoffs in a "constant column") converts *one* of two alternative actions from a risky proposition to a "sure thing." Correspondingly, in the

"three-color urn" example, a shift in the rewards on which the two actions "agree" (the payoff under Black) can produce a "definite" probability distribution over payoffs for *one* of the actions, where both actions before had been associated with an "ambiguous" set of mathematical expectations of utility corresponding to different, reasonably acceptable; probability distributions over payoffs. In either case, there may be many people for whom this change makes a significant difference (not necessarily always in a direction favoring the action no-longer-risky or no-longer-ambiguous. (p. 263)

Ellsberg's remarks here do not constitute the presentation of a comprehensive decision criterion that accommodates both the Allais examples and his own three-color urn problem. Nor has he made out the case for at a least a "heuristic" analogy between the Allais examples and the three-color urn problem. The sensitivity to determinate or "unambiguous" probabilities that he claimed is manifested in the three-color urn problem is itself a consequence of the Bayes/Hurwicz Criterion. Ellsberg did not show that the sensitivity to certainty manifested in typical responses to Allais puzzles is a consequence of some general decision criterion covering cases where indeterminacy in probability is not an issue. In particular, it is unclear how far-reaching a retrenchment Ellsberg would have to make from his commitment to the expected utility theory when probabilities are determinate. In all fairness, Ellsberg did not claim to have given a full response to the question of how to square his proposals with the Allais proposal. Ellsberg left the issue of the Allais problem hanging in the air.

Ellsberg finished the dissertation with a further discussion of the extent to which one may wish to impose restrictions on the use of von Neumann–Morgenstern utility axioms and a review of some earlier unpublished suggestions he had made concerning Russian roulette.

COMMENTS

Ellsberg's distinctive contribution to decision theory is his correct observation that indeterminacy in probability judgment can lead intelligent and reasonable agents to reverse their choices in binary, constant column choices where utilities of payoffs are determinate but probabilities are indeterminate. He combined this insight with the laudable ambition to devise a general criterion for choice that would accommodate all those patterns of choice behavior to which reasonable agents might conform in their practice. The result is a powerful argument for abandoning the "neo-Bernoullian" or strict Bayesian view that probability judgment should be numerically determinate.

Ellsberg diagnosed the deviation from neo Bernoullian standards of rationality to be due to refusal to submit to P2, or the Sure Thing Principle. That is because he interpreted reversal of choice to be reversal of preference. He refused to countenance the possibility that P1 rather than P2 ought to be rejected. In this respect, his approach shares much in common with many of those who take indeterminacy in probability judgment seriously.

However, Ellsberg himself acknowledged that when a decision-maker lacks a determinate probability distribution over states but fails to rule out any distribution in a set Y^0, to any available option "there will correspond, in general, a *set* of expected utility values, among which he cannot discriminate in terms of 'definite' probabilities" (p. 346). It is but one very short step from this observation to the conclusion that, when evaluating all of the available options with respect to expected utility, the decision-maker cannot weakly order them. If preference is to agree with expected utility, as a "neo-Bernoullian" would require, P1 will be violated. This must be true in Ellsberg's three-color urn problem.

If that is so, it is no longer clear that those who choose I over II and IV over III are violating P2, the Sure Thing Principle. That principle is a constraint on *preference* for potential options or acts. Such preference could be interpreted as preference with respect to expected utility.

When all expected utility functions that are "permissible" because they are derived using permissible probabilities in Y^0 agree in ranking option x over option y, then option x is strictly preferred to option y with respect to expected utility. If all permissible expected utility functions rate x as good as y, x is weakly preferred to y with respect to expected utility. If all permissible expected utility functions rank x and y as equal, x is equipreferred to y. When none of these conditions obtain, x and y are noncomparable with respect to expected utility.

Thus in the three-color urn problem, it is false that I is strictly preferred to II or IV to III with respect to expected utility. In point of fact I and II (III and IV) are noncomparable with respect to expected utility. So there cannot be a violation of P2 as long as preference is understood as preference with respect to expected utility.

Preference, however, is often understood differently. Define binary revealed weak preference so that x weakly prefers (as revealed in binary choice) option 1 to option 2 if and only if in a choice between 1 and 2, x is prepared to choose 1. x strictly prefers 1 over 2 if and only if x weakly prefers 1 to 2 and does not weakly prefer 2 to 1. In that case, when confronted with a choice between 1 and 2, x is prepared to choose 1 but not 2. If weak preference holds in both directions, x equiprefers 1 and 2 (x is indifferent between 1 and 2).

According to this criterion, weak preference is complete by definition as long as we suppose that x is always "prepared" to choose at least one of the options in binary choice. It is logically possible that a rational decision-maker who finds options I and II to be noncomparable with respect to expected utility could find I strictly preferred to II in the sense of binary revealed preference. Similarly III and IV could be noncomparable with respect to expected utility but IV strictly preferred to III with respect to binary revealed preference.[15]

Thus the behavior that Ellsberg reported as illustrating deviation from the Sure Thing Principle does violate P2 according to binary revealed preference but does not violate P2 according to preference with respect to expected utility. The same result obtains if we use Ellsberg's own Restricted Bayes/Hurwicz Criterion of choice to derive recommendations for choice. That criterion implies violation of P2 according to binary revealed preference for suitable choices of the parameters α and ρ. But Ellsberg's own characterization of the sets of "reasonably acceptable" expected utilities of options implies that P2 is not violated if preference is taken to be preference with respect to expected utility.

All of this is predicated on the assumption that it is reasonable for decision-makers to make decisions under partial ignorance where the decision-maker's personal judgment as to which probability distributions are acceptable cannot restrict the set of permissible distributions to a unit set but allows Y^0 to have more than one member.

One of the central ambitions of Ellsberg's project is, however, to cover all reasonable patterns of choice behavior. Consider then the following scenario:

> An urn contains 100 balls, at least 40 of which are red and 40 yellow. X is offered a choice between three options:

Figure 7

	Red	Yellow
Option 1	55	-44
Option 2	0	0
Option 3	-45	55

Here Y^0 consists of all probability assignments to Red from 0.4 to 0.6 inclusive. Let the "best guess" distribution v^0 assign equal probability to both colors. And let the value of α (the weight attached to the best utility according to the Hurwicz optimism-pessimism index) be close to 0. It should then be clear that Option 2 is recommended as long as the reliability ρ of v^0 is not very high.

To me (among others), however, recommending Option 2 is not allowable in the three-way choice under any circumstances. That is because it fails to be optimal according to any probability distribution in Y^0. (In this particular example, the same holds even if Y^0 = Y.) Choosing 2 is not, in

---

[15]There is a rather substantial literature on revealed preference. Sen gaves a clear account and survey enriched by his own contributions (1982, ch. 1 and ch. 8). Another helpful and important contribution is Herzberger (1973). For a contrast between revealed preference and "categorical" preference, see Levi (1986, ch. 6). Preference with respect to expected utility as construed in the text is categorical preference when categorical preference is guided by expected utility.

this sense, a "Bayes Solution."[16]

Those who insist on restricting choices to Bayes solutions, or E-admissible options, as I call them (Levi, 1974, 1980a), are free to supplement this requirement with further principles.[17] One might in particular, use the Doubly Restricted Bayes/Hurwicz Criterion, which differs from Ellsberg's requirement only in that it restricts choices to Bayes solutions before applying the Bayes/Hurwicz Criterion. This would recommend Option 1 when ρ is near to or equal to 0 — the conditions under which Ellsberg's proposal recommends choosing 2.

Consider now the binary revealed preferences among these options. Option 2 is chosen over 1 and hence revealed to be preferred to 1. Option 1 is chosen over Option 3. And Option 2 is chosen over Option 3. It would appear that, according to revealed preference, Option 2 is best. But Option 1 is chosen. So the decision-maker cannot be maximizing preference as construed according to revealed preference.

It is also true that the decision-maker is not maximizing preference with respect to expectation. That is because there is no maximum. However, choice is made according to a principled procedure that allows for recommending options as optimal if and only if they are most preferred according to expectation.

Thus, if one recommends restricting choice to Bayes solutions, preference in the sense that guides choice is given by specifying the permissible set of expectation functions. This means that the Sure Thing Principle is not violated *in the relevant sense* in the three-color urn problem. However, Savage's P1 is.

As a bonus, this approach allows for addressing the Allais paradox by taking the utility of money as indeterminate. Indeterminacy of utility and indeterminacy of probability would be responsible in that case for indeterminacy of expected utility. This provides a unitary way of addressing the two alleged failures of the Sure Thing Principle in a unitary way. In both cases, the failure of the Sure Thing Principle proves illusory. In

---

[16]Wald (1950) showed that minimax always yields Bayes solutions when the set of options is in effect the set of mixtures (roulette lotteries) of some finite set of pure options. But if mixtures of options were also options, there should be no talk of preference revealed by binary choice; for there could then be no binary choice. In any case, the idea that the mixture of a pair of options is always an available option is a sheer fantasy. Tossing an unbiased coin to decide between 1 and 2 need to not be feasible.

[17]Many authors who take sets of probability seriously in studying decision-making do so in the context of offering an account of decision-making for groups seeking a consensus on the basis of which to reach a collective decision. Savage (1954) devoted considerable attention to this problem. On pp. 122–124, he modeled a decision problem with two states that resembles very closely the predicament of Figure 6 and endorsed, in effect, the requirement of E-admissibility. But

both cases, weak ordering of options fails instead.[18]

The line of argument just deployed appeals to contexts of choice where Ellsberg's approach to principled decision-making by reasonable agents comes into conflict with a rival approach that, unlike the strict Bayesian or neo-Bernoullian approach, acknowledges that to be in a state of indeterminate probability judgment is no sin against rationality. Both this approach and Ellsberg's share an ambition to be as permissive as feasible of patterns of choice behavior adopted by reasonable agents. They both acknowledge that indeterminacy in probability judgment is too important a phenomenon to be dismissed as the product of confusion or imprecision in a decision-maker's judgments about his views. Both approaches are indistinguishable when considering recommendations for binary choice.

When it comes, however, to choices between three or more options, Ellsberg's proposal comes into conflict with the approach that insists that recommended options be E-admissible. Ellsberg's approach allows for choices that the requirement of E-admissibility prohibits; but it seems far from obvious that reasonable decision-makers who have thought carefully about problems like that presented in Figure 6 would condone tolerance of deviation from Bayesian requirements to the extent that Ellsberg defends.[19]

Many contemporary authors who have written on decision-making when probabilities go indeterminate take Ellsberg's side in the dispute. In recent years, Gärdenfors and Sahlin (1982) have defended reducing a set Y of probability distributions over states in Ω by weeding out "unreliable" ones to form a set Y^0. Decisions are based on maximizing minimum expectations. These authors guarantee that the available options are weakly ordered by binary revealed preference. They reject the

---

unlike me, his attention in this setting is group decision-making. I have taken the view that normative group and individual decision making ought to be governed by the same principles in those cases where groups are subjected to principles of rationality (Levi 1982). Savage's approach is explored by Kadane, Schervish, and Seidenfeld (1999). Their approach endorses the E-admissibility requirement for group choice. They direct insightful critical responses to my approach (ch. 1.1.) I have sought to reply in Levi 1990. A further response to this and other objections is found in Levi 1999.

[18]This approach to the Ellsberg and Allais problems was floated in Levi 1986a, 7.7 and 7.8, and in Levi 1986b.

[19]Seidenfeld (1988) has presented a powerful and, to my mind, decisive argument against those who, like Ellsberg, think that problems like the three-color-urn problem and the Allais paradox should constitute violations of Savage's P2 rather than P1. McClennen's commentary and Rabinowicz (1995) seek to defuse Seidenfeld's objection. Hammond's commentary on Seidenfeld's paper is a sophisticated defense of both P1 and P2.

requirement of E-admissibility. Walley (1991) has proposed that, given a set Y^0 of distributions, one should choose an option x that is "maximal" in the sense that there is no option y that carries greater expected value than x relative to every distribution in Y^0. Walley's view does not insist on obedience to P1, but it does not rule out non-Bayes solutions to decision problems.

These authors and the advocates of E-admissibility agree that the probability judgments of rational agents are often indeterminate. And unlike many other advocates of indeterminacy in probability judgment, they take seriously the need to supply a suitable decision theory to go with the account of indeterminate probability they favor.

In this respect, they are all following in the footsteps of Daniel Ellsberg. Ellsberg's contributions to an account of decision-making when probabilities go indeterminate are philosophically and technically first-rate. The publication of his dissertation will make this apparent to a wider audience than hithertofore.

REFERENCES

In recent years the literature related in one way or another to the question of indeterminate probability has grown substantially. A substantial and growing bibliography now appears on the Web at http://ippserv.rug.ac.be/biblio/biblio.html. This bibliography was compiled by Gert de Cooman and Peter Walley for the First International Symposium on Imprecise Probabilities and their Applications, held at Ghent in 1999. The proceedings may be found at http://decsai.ugr.es/~smc/isipta99/proc/proceedings.html. A second such symposium is planned for 2001 at Cornell. The following list consists exclusively of references for this Introduction.

Allais, M. (1952) "The Foundations of a Positive Theory of Choice Involving Risk and a Criticism of the Postulates and Axioms of the American School." Translation of "Fondement d'une théorie positive des choix comportant un risque et critique des postulats et axiomes de l'école américaine," in *Expected Utility Hypotheses and the Allais Paradox*, by M. Allais and O. Hagen, Dordrecht: Reidel, 1979, 27–145.

Allais, M. (1953) "Le comportement de l'homme rationnel devant le risque: Critique des postulats et axiomes de l'école americaine," *Econometrica* 21, 503–46.

Anscombe, F. J., and Aumann, R. (1963) "A Definition of Subjective Probability," *Annals of Mathematical Statistics*, 34, 199–205.

Arrow, K., and Hurwicz, L. (1972) "Decision Making under Ignorance," in *Uncertainty and Expectation in Economics: Essays in Honour of G. L. S. Shackle*, Oxford: Blackwell.

Chipman, J. (1960) "Stochastic Choice and Subjective Probability," in *Decisions, Values and Groups*, ed. D. Willner. New York: Pergamon, 70–95.

De Finetti, B. (1937 [1964]) "Foresight: Its Logical Laws, Its Subjective Sources," translated from the French by H. E. Kyburg and H. E. Smokler, in *Studies in Subjective Probability*, New York: Wiley, 95–158.

De Finetti, B. (1972) *Probability, Induction and Statistics*, New York: Wiley.

Ellsberg, D. (1954) "Classic and Current Notions of 'Measurable Utility,' " *Economic Journal* 64, 528–56.

Ellsberg, D. 1961, "Risk, Ambiguity, and the Savage Axioms," *Quarterly Journal of Economics* 75, 643–669.

Gärdenfors, P., and Sahlin, N.-E. (1982) "Unreliable Probabilities, Risk-Taking and Decision Making," *Synthese* 53, 361–86.

Good, I. J. (1952) "Rational Decisions," *Journal of the Royal Statistical Society*, Ser. B 14, 107–14.

Good, I. J. (1962) "Subjective Probability as a Measure of a Nonmeasurable Set," in *Logic, Methodology and Philosophy of Science, Proceedings of the 1960 International Congress*, ed. by Nagel, P. Suppes and A. Tarski, Stanford University Press, 319–29.

Herzberger, H. (1973) "Ordinal Preferences and Rational Choice," *Econometrica* 41, 187–237.

Hodges, J. L., and Lehmann, E. L. (1952) "The Uses of Previous Experience in Reaching Statistical Decisions," *Annals of Mathematical Statistics* 23, 396–407.

Hurwicz, L. (1951) *Optimality Criteria for Decision Making under Ignorance*, Cowles Commission Discussion Paper, Statistics, No. 370 (mimeographed).

Kadane, J. B., Schervish, M. J., and Seidenfeld, T. (1999), *Rethinking the Foundations of Statistics*, Cambridge: Cambridge University Press.

Koopman, B. O. (1940) "The Bases of Probability," *Bulletin of the American Mathematical Society* 46, 763–74.

Kyburg, H. E. (1961) *Probability and the Logic of Rational Belief*, Middletown, CT: Wesleyan University Press.

Levi, I. (1974) "On Indeterminate Probabilities," *Journal of Philosophy* 71, 391–418.

Levi, I. (1980a) *The Enterprise of Knowledge*, Cambridge, MA: MIT Press.

Levi, I. (1980b) "Potential Surprise: Its Role in Inference and Decision Making," in *Applications of Inductive Logic*, ed. L. J. Cohen and M. Hesse, Oxford: Clarendon Press, 1–27. Reprinted as the first part of chapter 14 of I. Levi, *Decisions and Revisions*, Cambridge: Cambridge University Press, 1984.

Levi, I. (1982) "Conflict and Social Agency," *Journal of Philosophy* 79, 231–47. Reprinted in *Decisions and Revisions*, Cambridge: Cambridge University Press, ch. 16, 1984.

Levi, I. (1986a) *Hard Choices*, Cambridge: Cambridge University Press.

Levi, I. (1986b) "The Paradoxes of Allais and Ellsberg," *Economics and Philosophy* 2, 23–53. Reprinted in I. Levi, *The Covenant of Reason*, Cambridge: Cambridge University Press,1997, ch. 10.

Levi, I. (1990) "Pareto Unanimity and Consensus," *Journal of Philosophy*, 87, 481–92.

Levi, I. (1999) "Value Commitments, Value Conflict and the Separability of Belief and Value." *Philosophy of Science*, 66.

Luce, R. D., and Raiffa, H. (1957) *Games and Decisions*, New York: Wiley.

Nozick, R. (1963) "The Normative Theory of Rational" *Choice*, Doctoral dissertation, Princeton University.

MacCrimmon, K. R., and Larsson, S. (1979) "Utility Theory: Axioms versus Paradoxes," in Allais and Hagen, *Expected Utility Hypotheses and the Allais Paradox*, Dordrecht: Reidel.

Rabinowicz, W. (1995) "To Have One's Cake and Eat It Too: Sequential Choice and Expected-Utility Violations," *Journal of Philosophy*, 92, 586–619.

Ramsey, F. (1950) "Truth and Probability," in R. B. Braithwaite, ed., *Foundations of Mathematics*, New York: Humanities Press, 156–203.

Savage, L. J. (1954) *The Foundations of Statistics*, New York: Wiley.

Seidenfeld, T., (1988) "Decision Theory without 'Independence' or without 'Ordering': What Is the Difference?" *Economics and Philosophy* 4, 267–90; Commentary by P. J. Hammond and E. F. McClennen, 292, and a rejoinder, 309–15.

Sen, A. K., (1982) *Choice, Welfare and Measurement*, Cambridge, MA: MIT Press.

Shackle, G. L. S. (1949) *Expectations in Economics*, Cambridge: Cambridge University Press, 2nd ed. 1952.

Shackle, G. L. S. (1961) *Decision, Order and Time in Human Affairs*, Cambridge: Cambridge University Press, 2nd ed. 1969.

Smith, C. A. B. (1961) "Consistency in Statistical Inference," (with discussion), *Journal of the Royal Statistical Society*, Ser. B 23, 1–25.

Von Neumann, J., and Morgenstern, O. (1944) *Theory of Games and Economic Behavior*, Princeton: Princeton University Press.

Wald, A. (1942) *On the Principles of Statistical Inference*, Notre Dame, IN: University of Notre Dame.

Wald, A. (1947) *Sequential Analysis*, New York: Wiley.

Wald, A. (1950) *Statistical Decision Functions*, New York: Wiley.

Walley, P. (1991) *Statistical Reasoning with Imprecise Probabilities*, London: Chapman and Hall.

Further Readings on Choice Under Uncertainty, Beliefs and the Ellsberg Paradox

Compiled by Mark J. Machina

The appearance of Ellsberg's classic 1961 article posed such a challenge to accepted theories of decision making that, after an some initial rounds of discussion,[1] the issues he raised remained well-known but largely unaddressed, simply because researchers at the time were helpless to address them. It took more than a quarter of a century, and the successful resolution of separate issues raised by Allais (1953), before decision scientists were in a position to take on the deeper issues raised by the Ellsberg Paradox. The last decade or so has seen an explosion in the amount of research attempting to measure, represent, understand and explain the seemingly anomalous yet ubiquitous aspects of beliefs and behavior that Ellsberg first brought to light. The following is a selected bibliography of both early and current work in this area. Section 1 consists of literature reviews of the challenges to classical decision theory posed by Ellsberg, Allais and others. Section 2 consists of books of readings on decision theory, which contain many of the important contributions to the field. Section 3 is a list of research papers and books on uncertain beliefs and the issues inspired by the Ellsberg Paradox—this list is necessarily selective, both because of the current extent [2] and continuing nature of work in the field.

---

1. Ellsberg (1961,1963), Fellner (1961,1963), Raiffa (1961), Brewer (1963), Roberts (1963), Becker and Brownson (1964) and Brewer and Fellner (1965).

2. A recent check of the Science Citation Index, Social Sciences Citation Index, and Arts and Humanities Citation Index reveals more than 450 scholarly articles that reference Ellsberg (1961).

1. LITERATURE REVIEWS

Camerer, C. and M. Weber (1992). "Recent Developments in Modeling Preferences: Uncertainty and Ambiguity," Journal of Risk and Uncertainty 5, 325–370.

Epstein, L. (1992). "Behavior Under Risk: Recent Developments in Theory and Applications," in J.-J. Laffont, ed., Advances in Economic Theory, Vol. II. Cambridge: Cambridge University Press.

Fishburn, P. (1981). "Subjective Expected Utility: A Review of Normative Theories," Theory and Decision 13, 139–199.

Karni, E. and D. Schmeidler (1991). "Utility Theory with Uncertainty," in W. Hildenbrand and H. Sonnenschein (eds.) Handbook of Mathematical Economics, Vol. 4. Amsterdam: North-Holland Publishing Co.

Kelsey, D. and J. Quiggin (1992). "Theories of Choice Under Ignorance and Uncertainty," Journal of Economic Surveys 6, 133–153.

Machina, M. (1987). "Choice Under Uncertainty: Problems Solved and Unsolved," Journal of Economic Perspectives 1, 121–154. Reprinted in Hamouda and Rowley (1997b).

Munier, B. (1989). "New Models of Decision Under Uncertainty: An Interpretive Essay," European Journal of Operations Research 38, 307–317.

Starmer, C. (2000). "Developments in Non-Expected Utility Theory: The Hunt for a Descriptive Theory of Choice Under Risk," Journal of Economic Literature 38, 332–382.

Sugden, R. (1986). "New Developments in the Theory of Choice Under Uncertainty," Bulletin of Economic Research 38, 1–24. Reprinted in Hey and Lambert (1987).

Sugden, R. (1991). "Rational Choice: A Survey of Contributions from Economics and Philosophy," Economic Journal 101, 751–785.

Weber, M. and C. Camerer (1987). "Recent Developments in Modeling Preferences under Risk," OR Spektrum 9, 129–151.

2. BOOKS OF READINGS

Allais, M. and O. Hagen (eds.) (1989). Expected Utility Hypotheses and the Allais Paradox. Dordrecht: D. Reidel Publishing Co.

Arkes, H. and K. Hammond (eds.) (1986). Judgment and Decision Making: An Interdisciplinary Reader. Cambridge: Cambridge University Press.

Bacharach, M. and Hurley, S. (eds.) (1991). Foundations of Decision Theory. Oxford: Basil Blackwell Ltd.

Edwards, W. (1992). Utility Theories: Measurements and Applications. Dordrecht: Kluwer Academic Publishers.

Gärdenfors, P. and N.-E. Sahlin (eds.) (1988). Decision, Probability, and Utility: Selected Readings. Cambridge: Cambridge University Press.

Geweke. J. (ed.), (1992). Decision Making Under Risk and Uncertainty: New Models and Empirical Findings. Dordrecht: Kluwer Academic Publishers.

Hamouda, O. and J.C.R. Rowley (eds.) (1997a). Expected Utility, Fair Gambles and Rational Choice (Vol. 1 of Foundations of Probability, Econometrics and Economic Games). Cheltenham, U.K.: Edward Elgar Publishing Ltd.

Hamouda, O. and J.C.R. Rowley (eds.) (1997b). Paradoxes, Ambiguity and Rationality (Vol. 2 of Foundations of Probability, Econometrics and Economic Games). Cheltenham, U.K.: Edward Elgar Publishing Ltd.

Hey, J. and P. Lambert (eds.) (1987). Surveys in the Economics of Uncertainty. Oxford: Basil Blackwell Ltd.

Kyburg, H. and H. Smokler (eds.) (1980). Studies in Subjective Probability, 2nd Ed. Huntington, New York: Robert E. Krieger Publishing Co.

Moser, P. (1990). Rationality in Action: Contemporary Approaches. Cambridge: Cambridge University Press.

3. RESEARCH ARTICLES

Allais, M. (1953). "Le Comportement de l'Homme Rationnel devant le Risque, Critique des Postulats et Axiomes de l'Ecole Américaine," Econometrica 21, 503–546.

Allais, M. (1979). "The Foundations of a Positive Theory of Choice Involving Risk and a Criticism of the Postulates and Axioms of the American School," in Allais and Hagen (1979). English translation of Allais (1953). Reprinted in part in Moser (1990).

Anscombe F. and R. Aumann (1963). "A Definition of Subjective Probability," Annals of Mathematical Statistics 34, 199–205.

Barberá, S. and M. Jackson (1988). "Maximin, Leximin, and the Protective Criterion: Characterizations and Comparisons," Journal of Economic Theory 46, 34–44.

Baron, J. and D. Frisch (1994). "Ambiguous Probabilities and the Paradoxes Of Expected Utility," in G. Wright and P. Ayton (eds.), Subjective Probability. Chichester, U.K.: Wiley, 273–294.

Becker, S. and F. Brownson (1964). "What Price Ambiguity? Or the Role of Ambiguity in Decision-Making," Journal of Political Economy 72, 63–73.

Bernasconi M. and G. Loomes (1992). "Failures of the Reduction Principle in An Ellsberg-Type Problem, Theory and Decision 32, 77–100.

Blume, L., A. Brandenberger and E. Dekel (1991). "Lexicographic Probabilities and Choice Under Uncertainty," Econometrica 59, 61–79.

Brady, M. (1997). "Decision Making under Uncertainty in the ," History of Economics Review 26, 136–42.

Brady M. and H. Lee (1989). "Is There an Ellsberg-Fellner Paradox - A Note On Its Resolution," Psychological Reports 64, 1087–1090.

Brewer, K. (1963). "Decisions Under Uncertainty: Comment," Quarterly Journal of Economics 77, 159–161.

Brewer, K. and W. Fellner (1965). "The Slanting of Subjective Probabilities: Agreement on Some Essentials," Quarterly Journal of Economics 79, 657–663.

Chateauneuf, A. (1985). "On the Existence of a Probability Measure Compatible with a Total Preorder on a Boolean Algebra," Journal of Mathematical Economics 14, 43–52.

Cohen, M. and J. Jaffray (1980). "Rational Behavior Under Complete Ignorance," Econometrica 48, 1281–1299.

Cohen, M. and J. Jaffray (1983). "Approximations of Rational Criteria Under Complete Ignorance and the Independence Axiom," Theory and Decision 15, 121–150.

Cohen, M. and J. Jaffray (1985). "Decision Making in the Case of Mixed Uncertainty: A Normative Model," Journal of Mathematical Psychology 29, 428–442.

Cohen, M., J. Jaffray and T. Said (1985). "Individual Behavior Under Risk and Under Uncertainty: An Experimental Study," Theory and Decision 18, 203–228.

Curley, S. and F. Yates (1985). "The Center and Range of the Probability Interval as Factors Affecting Ambiguity Preferences," Organizational Behavior and Human Decision Processes 36, 273–287.

Curley, S. and F. Yates (1989). "An Empirical Evaluation of Descriptive Models of Ambiguity Reactions in Choice Situations," Journal of Mathematical Psychology 33, 397–427.

Curley, S., F. Yates and R. Abrams (1986). "Psychological Sources of Ambiguity Avoidance," Organizational Behavior and Human Decision Processes 38, 230–256.

Davidson, P. (1991). "Is Probability Theory Relevant for Uncertainty? A Post Keynesian Perspective," Journal of Economic Perspectives 5, 129–143.

Eichberger, J. and D. Kelsey (1999). "E-Capacities and the Ellsberg Paradox," Theory and Decision 46, 107–140

Einhorn, H. and R. Hogarth (1985). "Ambiguity and Uncertainty in Probabilistic Inference," Psychological Review 92, 433–461.

Einhorn, H. and R. Hogarth (1986). "Decision Making Under Ambiguity," Journal of Business 59, S225–S250. Reprinted in Hamouda and Rowley (1997b).

Ellsberg, D. (1954). "Classic and Current Notions of 'Measurable Utility'," Economic Journal 62, 528–556. Reprinted in Hamouda and Rowley (1997a).

Ellsberg, D. (1961). "Risk, Ambiguity, and the Savage Axioms," Quarterly Journal of Economics 75, 643–669. Reprinted in Gärdenfors and Sahlin (1988), in Moser (1990), and in Hamouda and Rowley (1997b).

Ellsberg, D. (1963). "Risk, Ambiguity, and the Savage Axioms: Reply," Quarterly Journal of Economics 77, 336–342.

Epstein, L. (1999). "A Definition of Uncertainty Aversion," Review of Economic Studies 66, 579–608.

Epstein, L. (2000). "Are Probabilities Used in Markets?" Journal of Economic Theory 91, 86–90.

Epstein, L. and M. Le Breton (1993). "Dynamically Consistent Beliefs Must be Bayesian," Journal of Economic Theory 61, 1–22.

Epstein, L. and T. Wang (1996). " 'Beliefs about Beliefs' without Probabilities," Econometrica 64, 1343–1373.

Fellner, W. (1961). "Distortion of Subjective Probabilities as a Reaction to Uncertainty," Quarterly Journal of Economics 75, 670–689.

Fellner, W. (1963). "Slanted Subjective Probabilities and Randomization: Reply to Howard Raiffa and K. R. W. Brewer," Quarterly Journal of Economics 77, 676–690.

Fellner, W. (1965). Probability and Profit. Homewood, Illinois: Richard D. Irwin.

Ferreira, P. (1972). "On Subjective Probability and Expected Utilities," Annals of Mathematical Statistics 43, 928–933.

Fishburn, P. (1983). "Ellsberg Revisited: A New Look at Comparative Probability," Annals of Statistics 11, 1047–1059.

Fishburn, P. (1986). "The Axioms of Subjective Probability," Statistical Science 1, 335–345. Reprinted in Hamouda and Rowley (1997b).

Fishburn, P. (1991). "On the Theory of Ambiguity," International Journal of Information and Management Science 2, 1–16.

Fishburn, P. (1993). "The Axioms and Algebra of Ambiguity," Theory and Decision 34, 119–137. Reprinted in Hamouda and Rowley (1997b).

Fishburn, P. and I. LaValle (1987). "A Nonlinear, Nontransitive and Additive-Probability Model for Decisions Under Uncertainty," Annals of Statistics 15, 830–844.

Ford J. and S. Ghose (1998). "Ellsberg's Urns, Ambiguity, Measures of Uncertainty and Non-Additivity: Some Experimental Evidence," Applied Economics Letters 5, 147–151.

Franke, G. (1978). "Expected Utility with Ambiguous Probabilities and 'Irrational Parameters,'" Theory and Decision 9, 267–283.

Frisch, D. and J. Baron (1988). "Ambiguity and Rationality," Journal of Behavioral Decision Making 1, 149–157.

Gärdenfors, P. and N. Sahlin (1982). "Unreliable Probabilities, Risk Taking, and Decision Making," Synthese 53, 361–386. Reprinted in Gärdenfors and Sahlin (1988).

Gärdenfors, P. and N. Sahlin (1983). "Decision Making with Unreliable Probabilities," British Journal of Mathematical and Statistical Psychology 36, 240–251.

Ghirardato, P., P. Klibanoff and M. Marinacci (1998). "Additivity with Multiple Priors," Journal of Mathematical Economics 30, 405–420.

Gilboa, I. (1987). "Expected Utility with Purely Subjective Non-Additive Probabilities," Journal of Mathematical Economics 16, 65–88.

Gilboa, I. and D. Schmeidler (1989). "Maximin Expected Utility With a Non-Unique Prior," Journal of Mathematical Economics 18, 141–153.

Gilboa, I. and D. Schmeidler (1994). "Additive Representations of Non-Additive

Measures and the Choquet Integral," Annals of Operations Research 52, 43–65.

Grant, S. (1995). "Subjective Probability Without Monotonicity: Or How Machina's Mom May Also Be Probabilistically Sophisticated," Econometrica 63, 159–189.

Grether, D. (1980). "Bayes Rule as a Descriptive Model: The Representativeness Heuristic," Quarterly Journal of Economics 95, 537–557.

Hacking, I. (1967). "Slightly More Realistic Personal Probability," Philosophy of Science 34, 311–325. Reprinted in Gärdenfors and Sahlin (1988).

Hazen, G. (1989). "Ambiguity Aversion and Ambiguity Context in Decision Making Under Uncertainty," Annals of Operations Research 19, 415–434.

Hazen, G. (1992). "Decision versus Policy: An Expected Utility Resolution of the Ellsberg Paradox," in Geweke (1992).

Heath, C. and A. Tversky (1991). "Preferences and Belief: Ambiguity and Competence in Choice Under Uncertainty," Journal of Risk and Uncertainty 4, 5–28.

Hirshleifer, J. and J. Riley (1992). The Analytics of Uncertainty and Information. Cambridge: Cambridge University Press.

Hogarth, R. (1989). "Ambiguity in Competitive Decision Making: Some Implications and Tests," Annals of Operations Research 19, 31–50.

Hogarth, R. and H. Kunreuther (1985). "Ambiguity and Insurance Decisions," American Economic Review 75, 386–390.

Hogarth, R. and H. Kunreuther (1989). "Risk, Ambiguity and Insurance," Journal of Risk and Uncertainty 2, 5–35.

Kadane, J. (1992). "Healthy Skepticism as an Expected-Utility Explanation of the Phenomena of Allais and Ellsberg," Theory and Decision 32, 57–64. Reprinted in Geweke (1992).

Kadane, J. and R. Winkler (1988). "Separating Probability Elicitation from Utilities," Journal of the American Statistical Association 83, 357–363.

Kahn, B. and Sarin, R. (1988). "Modeling Ambiguity in Decisions Under Uncertainty," Journal of Consumer Research 15, 265–272.

Karni, E. (1996). "Probabilities and Beliefs," Journal of Risk and Uncertainty 13, 249–262.

Karni, E. (1999). "Elicitation of Subjective Probabilities when Preferences are State-Dependent," International Economic Review 40, 479–486.

Karni, E. and P. Mongin (2000). "On The Determination of Subjective Probability by Choice," Management Science 46 233–248.

Karni, E. and Z. Safra (1995). "The Impossibility of Experimental Elicitation of Subjective Probabilities," Theory and Decision 38, 313–320.

Karni, E., D. Schmeidler, and K. Vind (1983). "On State Dependent Preferences and Subjective Probabilities," Econometrica 51, 1021–1032.

Keller, R. (1985). "The Effects of Problem Representation on the Sure-Thing and Substitution Principles," Management Science 31, 73 8–751.

Keynes, J. (1921). A Treatise on Probability. London: Macmillan and Co.

Knight, F. (1921). Risk, Uncertainty and Profit. Boston: Houghton Mifflin.

Koopman, B. (1940). "The Axioms and Algebra of Intuitive Probability," Annals of Mathematics 41, 269–292.

Kraft, C., J. Pratt and A. Seidenberg (1959). "Intuitive Probability on Finite Sets," Annals of Mathematical Statistics 30, 408–419.

Kreps, D. (1988). Notes on the Theory of Choice. Boulder, Col.: Westview Press.

Kuhn, K. M. and D. V. Budescu (1996). "The Relative Importance of Probabilities, Outcomes, and Vagueness In Hazard Risk Decisions," Organizational Behavior and Human Decision Processes 68, 301–317.

Kunreuther, H. and R. Hogarth (1989). "Risk, Ambiguity, and Insurance," Journal of Risk and Uncertainty 2, 5–35.

Lawson, T. (1985). "Uncertainty and Economic Analysis," Economic Journal 95, 909–927.

LeRoy, S. and L. Singell (1987). "Knight on Risk and Uncertainty," Journal of Political Economy 95, 394–406.

Levi, I. (1974). "On Indeterminate Probabilities," Journal of Philosophy 71, 391–418. Reprinted in Gärdenfors and Sahlin (1988).

Levi, I. (1980a). The Enterprise of Knowledge. Cambridge, Mass.: MIT Press.

Levi, I. (1980b). "Potential Surprise: Its Role in Inference and Decision Making," in L. Cohen and M. Hesse (eds.) Applications of Inductive Logic. Oxford: Clarendon Press.

Levi, I. (1986a). Hard Choices. Cambridge: Cambridge University Press.

Levi, I. (1986b). "The Paradoxes of Allais and Ellsberg," Economics and Philosophy 2, 23–53. Reprinted in Hamouda and Rowley (1997b) and in I. Levi, The Covenant of Reason, Cambridge: Cambridge University Press, 1997.

Luce, R. (1991). "Rank- and Sign-Dependent Linear Utility Models for Binary Gambles," Journal of Economic Theory 53, 75–100.

MacCrimmon, K. (1968). "Descriptive and Normative Implications of the Decision-Theory Postulates," in K. Borch and J. Mossin (eds.), Risk and Uncertainty. London: Macmillan.

MacCrimmon, K. and S. Larsson (1979). "Utility Theory: Axioms Versus `Paradoxes,'" in Allais and Hagen (1989).

Machina, M. and D. Schmeidler (1992). "A More Robust Definition of Subjective Probability," Econometrica 60, 745–780.

Machina, M. and D. Schmeidler (1995). "Bayes without Bernoulli: Simple Conditions for Probabilistically Sophisticated Choice" Journal of Economic Theory 67, 106–128.

Maher P. and Y. Kashima (1997). "Preference Reversal in Ellsberg Problems," Philosophical Studies 88, 187–207.

Malmnäs, P.-E. (1981). From Qualitative to Quantitative Probability. Stockholm: Almqvist & Wiksell International.

Marschak, J. (1975). "Do Personal Probabilities of Probabilities Have an Operational Meaning?" Theory and Decision 6, 127–132.

Marschak, T. (1986). "Independence versus Dominance in Personal Probability Axioms," in W. Heller, R. Starr and D. Starrett, eds., Uncertainty, Information and Communication: Essays in Honor of Kenneth J. Arrow, Vol. III. Cambridge: Cambridge University Press.

Maskin, E. (1979). "Decision Making Under Ignorance with Implications for Social Choice," Theory and Decision 11, 319–337.

McClennen, E. (1983). "Sure-Thing Doubts," in B. Stigum and F. Wenstøp (eds.), Foundations of Utility and Risk Theory with Applications. Dordrecht: D. Reidel Publishing Co. Reprinted in Gärdenfors and Sahlin (1988).

McClennen, E. (1990). Rationality and Dynamic Choice: Foundational Explorations. Cambridge: Cambridge University Press.

Montesano, A. (1994). "Non-Additive Probabilities and the Measure of Uncertainty and Risk Aversion: A Proposal", in B. Munier and M. Machina (eds.), Models and Experiments in Risk and Rationality. Dordrecht: Kluwer Academic Publishers.

Montesano, A. (1994). "On Some Conditions for the Ellsberg Phenomenon", in S. Rios (ed.), Decision Theory and Decision Analysis: Trends and Challenges. Dordrecht: Kluwer Academic Publishers.

Montesano, A. and F. Giovannoni (1996). "Uncertainty Aversion and Aversion to Increasing Uncertainty," Theory and Decision 41, 133–148.

Myerson, R. (1979). "An Axiomatic Derivation of Subjective Probability, Utility, and Evaluation Functions," Theory and Decision 11, 339–352.

Nakamura, Y. (1990). "Subjective Expected Utility with Non-Additive Probabilities on Finite State Spaces," Journal of Economic Theory 51, 346–366.

Nau, R. (1991). "Indeterminate Probabilities on Finite Sets," Annals of Statistics 20, 1737–1767.

Pratt, J., H. Raiffa and R. Schlaifer (1964). "The Foundations of Decision Under Uncertainty: An Elementary Exposition," Journal of the American Statistical Association 59, 353–375.

Raiffa, H. (1961). "Risk, Ambiguity, and the Savage Axioms: Comment," Quarterly Journal of Economics 75, 690–694.

Raiffa, H. (1968). Decision Analysis: Introductory Lectures on Choices Under Uncertainty. Reading, Mass.: Addison-Wesley.

Ramsey, F. (1931). "Truth and Probability," in Foundations of Mathematics and other Logical Essays. London: K. Paul, Trench, Trubner & Co. Reprinted in Ramsey (1978) Foundations: Essays in Philosophy, Logic, Mathematics and Economics. Atlantic Highlands, New Jersey: Humanities Press; in Kyburg and Smokler (1980); and in Gärdenfors and Sahlin (1988).

Roberts, H. (1963). "Risk, Ambiguity, and the Savage Axioms: Comment," Quarterly Journal of Economics 77, 327–336.

Sarin, R. and M. Weber (1993). "The Effect of Ambiguity in a Market Setting," Management Science 39, 602–615.

Sarin, R. and P. Wakker (1998). "Revealed Likelihood and Knightian Uncertainty,"

Journal of Risk and Uncertainty 16, 223–250.

Savage, L. (1951). "The Theory of Statistical Decision," Journal of the American Statistical Association 46, 55–67.

Savage, L. (1954). The Foundations of Statistics. New York: John Wiley and Sons. Revised and Enlarged Edition, New York: Dover Publications, 1972.

Savage, L. (1961). "The Foundations of Statistics Reconsidered," in Proceedings of the Fourth Berkeley Symposium on Mathematics and Probability. Berkeley: University of California Press.

Savage, L. (1967). "Difficulties in the Theory of Personal Probability," Philosophy of Science 34, 305–310.

Savage, L. (1971). "The Elicitation of Personal Probabilities and Expectations," Journal of the American Statistical Association 66, 783–801. Reprinted in Kyburg and Smokler (1980).

Schmeidler, D. (1989). "Subjective Probability and Expected Utility without Additivity," Econometrica 57, 571–587.

Segal, U. (1987). "The Ellsberg Paradox and Risk Aversion: An Anticipated Utility Approach," International Economic Review 28, 175–202.

Seidenfeld T. (1988), "Decision Theory without 'Independence' or without 'Ordering': What is the

Difference?" Economics and Philosophy 4, 267–290, with discussions by P.J. Hammond (292–

297) and E.F. McClennen (298–307) and a rejoinder by Seidenfeld (309–315).

Seidenfeld, T. and M. Schervish (1983). "A Conflict Between Finite Additivity and Avoiding Dutch Book," Philosophy of Science 50, 398–412.

Shackle, G. (1949). "A Non-Additive Measure of Uncertainty," Review of Economic Studies 17, 70–74.

Shafer, G. (1978). "Non-Additive Probabilities in the Work of Bernoulli and Lambert," Archive for History of the Exact Sciences 19, 309–370.

Sherman, R. (1974). "The Psychological Difference Between Ambiguity and Risk," Quarterly Journal of Economics 88, 166–169.

Shimony, A. (1967). "Amplifying Personal Probability Theory: Comments on L. J. Savage's 'Difficulties in the Theory of Personal Probability,'" Philosophy of Science 34, 326–332.

Sinn, H.-W. (1980). "A Rehabilitation of the Principle of Insufficient Reason," Quarterly Journal of Economics 94, 493–506.

Siniscalchi, M. (1997). "Conditional Preferences, Ellsberg Paradoxes and the Sure Thing Principle," in P. Battigalli, A. Montesano and F. Panunzi (eds.), Decisions, Games, and Markets, Dordrecht: Kluwer Academic Publishers, 1997.

Slovic, P. and A. Tversky (1974). "Who Accepts Savage's Axiom?" Behavioral Science 19, 368–373.

Smith, V. (1969). "Measuring Nonmonetary Utilities in Uncertain Choices: The Ellsberg Urn," Quarterly Journal of Economics 83, 324–329.

Smithson, M. (1989). Ignorance and Uncertainty: Emerging Paradigms. New York:

Springer Verlag.

Smithson, M. (1999). "Conflict Aversion: Preferences for Ambiguity vs. Conflict in Sources and Evidence," Organizational Behavior and Human Decision Processes 79, 179–198.

Suppes, P. (1956). "The Role of Subjective Probability and Utility in Decision Making" Proceedings of the Third Berkeley Symposium on Mathematical Statistics and Probability, 1954–1955, 5, 61–73.

Toulet, C. (1986). "Complete Ignorance and the Independence Axiom: Optimism, Pessimism, Indecisiveness," Mathematical Social Sciences 11, 33–51.

Tversky, A. and C. Fox (1995). "Weighing Risk and Uncertainty," Psychological Review 102, 269–283.

Tversky, A. and D. Koehler (1994). "Support Theory: A Nonextensional Representation of Subjective Probability," Psychological Review 101, 547–567.

von Neumann, J. and O. Morgenstern (1944). Theory of Games and Economic Behavior. Princeton: Princeton University Press. 2nd Edition, 1947. 3rd Edition, 1953.

Wakker, P. (1989). "Continuous Subjective Expected Utility With Non-Additive Probabilities," Journal of Mathematical Economics 18, 1–27.

Weber, M. (1987). "Decision Making Under Incomplete Information," European Journal of Operations Research 28, 44–57.

Whalley, P. (1991). Statistical Reasoning with Imprecise Probabilities. London: Chapman and Hall.

Winkler, R. (1991). "Ambiguity, Probability, Preference and Decision Analysis," Journal of Risk and Uncertainty 4, 285–297.

Yates, F. and L. Zukowski (1976). "Characterization of Ambiguity in Decision Making," Behavioral Science 21, 19–25.

Zadeh, L. (1978). "Fuzzy Sets as a Basis for a Theory of Probability," Fuzzy Sets and Systems 1, 3–28.

Acknowledgments

NEARLY EVERY PAGE of this study testifies to my intellectual debt to L. J. Savage, whose developments in "Bayesian" statistical decision theory provide the starting-point and main focus for the present work. Savage's *Foundations of Statistics* (New York, 1954) constituted my introduction to these problems and remains the single most important influence upon my thinking in this area. If my comments upon that work in this study are mainly critical, and by some standards heretical with respect to "Bayesian" principles, it is because I am concentrating here upon certain aspects in which it seems to me that current doctrines need and can find improvement in terms of goals which, I believe, I share with Savage and his colleagues.

I am grateful to Savage personally for encouraging me to believe that the arguments and counterexamples presented here deserved serious consideration: once at the very outset of my interest (February, 1958, when I proposed to him the counterexamples discussed here in Chapter Five, just then developed) and again in March, 1962, when he gave time generously to a discussion of the main ideas advanced in this study.

Both I. J. Good—with whose position on these matters I am in the closest accord—and L. J. Savage did me the favor of furnishing pre-publication copies of their recent papers, which were of considerable aid in my exposition of their views. Correspondence with Maurice Allais, I. J. Good, John Pratt, Howard Raiffa and Thomas Schelling was also extremely helpful to me.

I have benefited greatly from many discussions, and/or arguments, with Kenneth Arrow, Norman Dalkey, Jacob Marschak, Andrew Marshall, Howard Raiffa, Thomas Schelling, Martin Shubik, Lloyd Shapley, Sidney Winter and Albert Wohlstetter; also with innumerable colleagues in seminars at Harvard, Chicago, Yale and Northwestern Universities and at The RAND Corporation. I hardly know to which I am more grateful: to those who gave me the right answers to my hypothetical questions, who said they thought I was on the right track and generally cheered me on; or to those who disagreed (and disagree) wholeheartedly, but who have taken the time and trouble to tell me why.

I owe particular thanks to Armen Alchian, Allen Ferguson, Egon Neuberger and Russell Nichols for last-minute editorial comments and criticism under extreme time pressure; and to my secretary, Susan Simek who labored under extreme time pressure from first minute to last, yet remained tolerant of ambiguity, and of me.

The fundamental ideas advanced in this study were developed while I was a member of the Society of Fellows, Harvard University (1957–1959). They were first published in "Risk, Ambiguity, and the Savage Axioms," *Quarterly Journal of Economics,* Vol. LXXV, 1961, pp. 643–669. I have drawn heavily upon that paper here, without citation, but these areas of direct overlap account for less than ten per cent of the present study, which concentrates upon materials and aspects of the analysis considered subsequently to its acceptance for publication. This latter research was undertaken as part of a continuing research project supported by Project RAND, a program of research conducted by The RAND Corporation for the United States Air Force.

Whereas the present study is limited to the analysis of terminal decisions (no further information is presumed available prior to choice), with no explicit reference to uncertainties relating to a rational opponent, further aspects of this continuing research on decision-making under conditions of extreme uncertainty include application (partially completed, but not reported here) of the basic concepts and decision criteria presented here to: (a) conceptual problems of measuring the value of information, flexibility and insurance under circumstances when more information can be obtained, at a cost, by observation or experimentation; (b) conceptual problems of conflict and bargaining (i.e., the analysis of "games" as special cases of decision-making under—occasionally extreme—uncertainty); (c) specific problems of political/military decision-making.

I wish particularly to express my appreciation for the support and encouragement of Joseph Kershaw, who gambled on an extremely ambiguous prospectus in backing this work and subsequently resisted all temptations to hedge his bet, protecting me from all other demands during the process of writing. His investment in this research is second only to that of my wife, who may have had a clearer picture than Kershaw, or I, of just how long the writing might take and how much support and encouragement would be called for: yet who gave both generously.

Note to Reader

TWO TERMS THAT recur frequently in the course of this study deserve special comment: "you" and "I."

We shall be concerned with theories that lead to measurements and expressions of personal opinions, that assert rules of consistency among uncertain beliefs, and that propose decision-making criteria relating deliberate choices to the opinions and values of a given person in a given state of mind. As various hypothetical decision problems are discussed in terms of these theories, it is productive for the reader to try to put himself mentally in the place of the hypothetical decision-maker in question. As L. J. Savage informed a lecture audience: "It will be the right approach for each of you to think that you are the person under discussion." To encourage and assist this effort, in his path-breaking *Probability and the Weighing of Evidence* (1950) I. J. Good introduced the usage of *"you"* as a *technical term* for "the person who is doing the believing (inferring, deciding, preferring, acting)." "Subjectivist" expositions have relied upon this technical device ever since, as I shall do throughout this study.

The second term, "I," occurs sometimes in discussion of the calculations, reflections and responses of one particular subject with respect to the hypothetical examples considered, observed over a long period of conscientious deliberation; these "results" are intended to illustrate the sort of relevant data each reader can and should provide, if he accepts the challenge above to test the adequacy *for his own decision-making* of every normative theory proposed. More often the term occurs in a wholly, unashamedly non-technical usage. As Savage testified in his preface to *The Foundations of Statistics:*

> A book about so controversial a subject as the foundations of statistics may have some value in the classroom, as I hope this one will; but it cannot be a textbook, or manual of instruction, stating the accepted facts

about its subject, for there scarcely are any. Openly, or coyly screened behind the polite conventions of what we call a disinterested approach, it must, even more than other books, be an airing of its author's current opinions.

A reader unfamiliar with recent literature related to the present subject may find most of the opinions I express quite ordinary: and so they seem to me. They would hardly be worth mentioning—certainly, they would not deserve the lengthy exposition, illustration, the repetition and emphasis they receive here—were they not contradictory to sophisticated, elaborately developed views being advocated, with increasingly wider success, by some of the very ablest and most respected decision theorists today. Once more, Savage has aptly expressed my own feelings in this position; assessing the relation of his views to those of earlier, "objectivist" statisticians he has commented (in "Bayesian Statistics"; see bibliography):

> Sometimes people hearing that there is a new movement in the foundations, or theory, of statistics leap to the conclusion that such a movement must concern only specialists and have no immediate practical implications. After all, it would seem reasonable to suppose that a generation of bright people working in the subject would not overlook major opportunities to exploit common sense, but the unreasonable seems to have happened.

I would be quite willing to accept the dusty mantle of "common sense" for my own notions in this area, but I would have to fight the "Bayesians" for it. In such circumstances, it is unproductive to waste much time arguing which of two mutually exclusive, strongly defended intellectual positions is really more "intuitively self-evident." The reader is simply warned that "obviousness" is not a reliable index, in either direction, of truth or importance in these disputed matters. Any comparison of normative theories of judgment and decision must appeal directly and fundamentally to introspection: but not to casual introspection.

For which of "you" is this study primarily intended? On the one hand, I have assumed very little prior knowledge of decision theory or of foundational work on "personal probability"; I have included considerable introductory exposition and avoided, in general, abstract symbolism, though at the cost of increasing the length and of telling almost any given reader more than he cares to know about certain of the subjects covered. Yet if the discussion were truly intended entirely for the uninitiated, it could almost surely make its points effectively with far less repetition, citation of authority, emphasis, or close analysis of texts. Readers who were unfamiliar with sophisticated counterarguments, or who had already resisted indoctrination on other lines, would undoubtedly find many of the arguments quickly acceptable (whether wisely or not) without such reinforcing.

For all its introductory tone, it is really to the currently convinced—of opposing view—that this study is most directly addressed. The readers whose anticipated responses have most influenced the inclusion of otherwise redundant material are those I have characterized in the text as the "neo-Bernoullians." Very simply: I wish to change their minds. I hope to convince them of the importance of certain questions and problems, of the need and possibility for including in their formal theories certain considerations now explicitly ignored; and to persuade them there are more ways of being reasonable under uncertainty than they currently imagine.

1

TO ACT REASONABLY one must judge actions by their consequences. But what if their consequences are uncertain? One must still, no doubt, act reasonably; the problem is to decide what this may mean.

I wish to consider the problem of reasonable choice among given alternative actions on the basis of *highly incomplete information*. Let us begin by defining these special circumstances of information; the nature of a theory of reasonable choice; and the uses of such a theory.

AMBIGUITY AND RISK

The consequences of an action depend upon facts, not all of which may be known with certainty to the actor. Alternatively, we will say that the uncertain consequences depend upon the "state of the world" that "obtains", or upon the occurrence of certain events (which may be regarded as subsets or classes of states of the world), or upon the truth or falsity of certain propositions.

We shall be concerned primarily with circumstances *of decision-making* in which information bearing upon these relevant facts, (or states, events, propositions) is scanty, marked by gaps, obscure and vague, or on the contrary plentiful and precise but highly contradictory. These two distinguishable information-states are classed together in some psychological literature as "ambiguous."[1] Among the relevant facts on which information is ambiguous may be the parameters of certain empirical frequency distributions.

---

[1]See, for example, E. Frenkel-Brunswik, "Intolerance of ambiguity as an emotional and perceptual personality variable," *Journal of Personality*, Vol. 18, 1949, pp. 108–43. A more recent article, by V. Hamilton, "Perceptual and Personality Dynamics in Reactions to Ambiguity," *British Journal of Psychology*, Vol. 48, 1957, pp. 200–15, has a fairly complete bibliography of psychological literature on this subject. This experimental work has not, of course, focussed upon criteria of reasonable choice, but upon individual differences in response to ambiguity, and related personality structures: e.g., correlates of willingness to *recognize*, and report, ambiguity.

Daniel Ellsberg

Decision-making under uncertainty, even in Frank Knight's sense which distinguishes "uncertainty" from "risk," may be considered a broader problem, which includes decision-making under "ambiguity" as a special, extreme case. As Knight describes the more general situation:

> It is a world of change in which we live, and a world of uncertainty. We live only by knowing *something* about the future; while the problems of life, or of conduct at least, arise from the fact that we know so little. This is as true of business as of other spheres of activity. The essence of the situation is action according to *opinion,* of greater or less foundation and value, neither entire ignorance nor complete and perfect information, but partial knowledge.[1]

Of the bread class of circumstances in which opinion, degree of belief, partial knowledge or partial ignorance influence choice, the authors of a recent formal analysis of decision-making under uncertainty assert:

> In most applied decision problems, both the preferences of a responsible decision maker and his judgments about the weights to be attached to the various possible states of nature are based on very substantial objective evidence; and quantification of his preferences and judgments enables him to arrive at a decision which is consistent with this objective evidence.[2]

We shall consider at some length the means and uses of thus quantifying preferences and judgments in such situations; but with the aim eventually of focussing upon quite different circumstances, in which "objective evidence" is, on the contrary, extremely insubstantial, of dubious relevance or conflicting import. It is a principal point at issue whether or not this may indeed be a "difference that makes a difference" to a hypothetical, decision-maker who, as these authors put it,

> wishes to choose among [alternative actions] in a way which will be logically consistent with (a) his basic preferences concerning consequences, and (b) his basic judgments concerning the true state of the world.[3]

In particular, we shall consider whether the quantification (i.e., measurement and representation) of judgments or opinions in terms of definite numerical probabilities is equally feasible and useful when the evidence underlying partial belief is vague and confusing as when it is less

---

[1]Frank H. Knight, Risk, *Uncertainty and Profit,* Boston, 1921, p. 199.
[2]Howard Raiffa and Robert Schlairer, *Applied Statistical Decision Theory,* Boston, 1961, p. vii.
[3]*Ibid.,* p. 3.

"ambiguous." If not: then how are "vague" opinions to be expressed, and how may consistent action usefully be founded upon them?

An extreme position on this question has been taken by G.L.S. Shackle, who rejects numerical probabilities for representing uncertainty not only when information is peculiarly ambiguous but in *any* decision whose outcome, dependent upon a single choice of action, may be of crucial importance to the decision-maker. For such decisions, he insists that even "substantial objective evidence" in the form of precise, reliable, statistical information on frequencies within a large class of repetitive events is strictly irrelevant to choice.

> It is because I belive most occasions of choosing are, and are felt to be, crucial that I attach so much more importance to the unique or isolated experiment than to the kind typified by drawing balls from an urn or tossing a coin (except when the latter is for choice of stations in the Boat Race or of innings in a Test Match).[1]

On the other hand, Shackle's expressed intuitions on the uncertainties (presumably, relatively unambiguous) normally associated with cointossing, even in Test Matches, suggest that this total rejection of numerical expression may be premature, or undiscriminating. Shackle maintains that in situations where all the potential outcomes seem "perfectly possible" in the sense that they would not violate accepted physical laws and thus cause "surprise," it is impossible to distinguish meaningfully, either in behavioral or introspective terms, between the relative strengths of a person's (or one's own) expectations or degrees of belief in the various outcomes. In throwing a die, for example, it would not "surprise" us in this sense if an ace came up on a single trial, nor if, on the other hand, some other number came up. So Shackle concludes:

> The fact that out of 600 throws a die has shown an ace 100 times tells us that out of 6000 throws it will show an ace about 1000 times. But what does it tell us about the *next* throw, the 601st? Suppose the captains in a Test Match have agreed that instead of tossing a coin for choice of innings they will decide the matter by this next throw of the die, and that if it shows an ace Australia shall bat first, if any other member, then England shall bat first. Can we now give any meaningful answer whatever to the question "Who shall bat first?" except "We do not know"?[2]

---

[1]G.L.S. Shackle, *Uncertainty in Economics,* Cambridge, 1955, p. 63.

[2]*Ibid,* p. 8. The discussion of this example is drawn from my earlier article, "Risk, Ambiguity, and the Savage Axioms," *Quarterly Journal of Economics,* Vol. LXXV, No. 4, November, 1961, pp. 644–661.

Most of us might think we could give better answers than that. We could say, "England will bat first," or more cautiously: "I think England will probably bat first". And if Shackle should challenge us as to the *meaning* of "probably" in that statement, it would be natural to reply: "We'll *bet* on England; and we'll give odds."

In this case, it happens that statistical information (on the behavior or dice and coins) is readily available and does seem relevant even to a "single shot" decision, our bet; it will affect the odds we offer. Moreover, it is hard to believe that it would seem any less relevant to the captains of Australia and England, no matter now "crucial" their decision.

Yet in other situations our opinions may be just as definite, our uncertainties as unambiguous, the betting odds we find acceptable or unacceptable as well-defined; though evidence on the relevant events may be quite nonstatistical. In 1926 Frank Ramsey suggested that, in general, "The degree of a belief is . . . the extent to which we are prepared to act upon it," and pointed toward a certain class of actions—choices among *bets* on given events at varying odds—as leading directly to a quantitative *measurement* of partial belief.[1] Ramsey postulated *constraints on a pattern of bets which, if obeyed, would ensure that numerical, subjective probabilities over all events could meaningfully be inferred from such choices.* This approach has been enthusiastically developed in recent years by theorists who argue, cogently, that such constraints effectively *define* reasonable behavior under *all* conditions of uncertainty: i.e., that the problems specified above have satisfactorily been *solved,* in even more general form,[2] and with the special consequence that for a reasonable man all "uncertainties," in Knightian terms, may be expressed numerically as "risks".

The boldness of this claim,[3] and persuasiveness of the supporting arguments have in the last dozen years infused the analysis of "reasonable"

---

[1] F. P. Ramsey, "Truth and Probability" (1926 in *The Foundations of Mathematics and Other Logical Essays,* ed. R. B. Braithwaite (New York, 1931). L. L. Savage has recently drawn attention to an earlier paper by E. Borel, cited below in Chapter Four, presenting similar proposals.

[2] This seems a fair description of the point of view developed most fully by L. J. Savage, in *The Foundations of Statistics,* New York, 1954, and other papers cited below; it underlies the approach of Raiffa and Schlaifer, *op. cit.*

[3] "In our more enthusiastic moments, we even feel that only a completely Bayesian attitude towards statistical thinking is coherent and practical." (D. V. Lindley, "The Use of Prior Probability Distributions in Statistical Inference and Decisions," *Proceedings of the Fourth Berkeley Symposium on Mathematical Statistics and Probability,* Berkeley, 1961, Vol. 1, p. 453.)

Many assertions even more exuberant might be quoted (this is not said in criticism).

behavior with unwonted energy and intellectual interest. In my opinion, the efforts of this "neo-Bayesian"[3] school of statistical decision theorists have attained a very considerable measure of success. They even come within sight of the achievement they claim: close enough that one can discern rather clearly the tests that a better theory, or a more general one, must pass. Chief among these, as identified even in current "Bayesian" literature, is a more satisfactory treatment of problems associated with "vagueness" of opinion, "ambiguity" of information, and differences in the intensity of these qualities.

The spectrum of uncertainties such a theory must encompass range from the unequivocal "risks" of familiar production decisions or well-known random processes (coin-flipping or roulette, certain chemical/ physical phenomena) to the amorphous anticipations of the results of long-range Research and Development, the performance of a new President, the consequences of major departmental reorganization, the tactics of an unfamiliar opponent, or the secrets concealed by an efficient security system.

In terms of Shackle's cricket example: Imagine an American observer who had never heard of cricket, knew none of the rules or the method of scoring, and had no clue as to the past record or present prospects of England or Australia. If he were confronted with a set of side bets, even with large, potentially "crucial" stakes, on the proposition that England would *bat first*—this to depend on the toss of a coin or a die—it is hard to believe, with Shackle, that his general bemusement would prevent him from obeying pretty closely in his choice of gambles the plausible constraints

---

[1] So-called because they assign subjective probabilities to statistical hypotheses and use Bayes' Theorem to infer the effect of experimental results or observed samples upon their "degrees of belief"; Savage has recently summarized the development of the "Bayesian outlook" in, "The Foundations of Statistics Reconsidered," *Proceedings of the Fourth Berkeley Symposium on Mathematical Statistics and Probability*, (Berkeley, 1961), Vol. I, pp. 575–587. As discussed below, there would be some point in describing the strict approach rather as "neo-Bernoullian" after Daniel Bernoulli. There is also a question of how broadly the term is to be applied. Various definitions given by I. J. Good, who terms himself a "neo-Bayesian" along with Savage, would definitely include the present work as "neo-Bayesian" both in outlook and detail; and indeed, the hypotheses and decision rules I shall propose are closely related, in some cases identical, to some advanced by Good himself, though contrary to positions held, to the present (March, 1962) by such other Bayesians as Savage, Raiffa or Schlaifer. (See, for example, Good's definition of the "neo-Bayes/Laplace philosophy", discussed later, in "Significance Tests in Parallel and in Series," *Journal of the American Statistical Association*, Vol. 53, No. 284, December, 1958, p. 803).

postulated by the "neo-Bayesians": certainly to the point of discriminating between the probabilities of various outcomes of the toss and perhaps to an extent permitting precise measurement of his felt "risks." Yet it is easy to imagine a different state of mind (to which Shackle's speculations may be much more pertinent)—and, conceivably quite different betting behavior—if he were forced to gamble heavily on the proposition that England would *win the match*.

As early as *The Foundations of Statistics*, in a section headed "Shortcomings of the personalistic view" Savage noted as a "difficulty":

> the vagueness associated with judgments of the magnitude of personal probability. The postulates of personal probability imply that I can determine, to any degree of accuracy whatsoever, the probability (for me) that the next president will be a Democrat. Now, it is manifest that I cannot really determine that number with great accuracy, but only roughly.[1]

In more recent writings, Savage has continued to emphasize this as a problem, frankly though somewhat fatalistically:

> There is, however, an important respect in which the personal theory of probability and utility does seem inadequate. It is not really true that any of us knows his own mind, so-to-speak. If 'you' had a consistent and complete body of opinion, then every event would have a well-defined probability for you and every consequence a well-defined utility. Actually, vagueness, or indecision, intervenes at several stages to prevent this. . . . It has been suggested that some formal modification of theories of choice, like the theory of utility or that of personal probability, might give a realistic account of vagueness and indecision. I don't think that any such attempts have yet been very successful.[2]

VAGUENESS, CONFIDENCE AND THE WEIGHT OF ARGUMENTS

The phenomena of vagueness, imprecision or relative lack of confidence in certain of one's subjective judgments are given central importance in the work of I. J. Good, who, in contrast to Savage, approaches the theory of personal probability as a theory of consistent judgment rather than consistent

---

[1]Savage, *The Foundations of Statistics*, p. 59.

[2]Savage, "The Subjective Basis of Statistical Practice," University of Michigan, July, 1961, hectographed, p.2.14. I shall criticize, subsequently, Savage's implicit assumption, here and elsewhere, that "vagueness" is inevitably linked with "indecision."

action. Like B. O. Koopman, Good bases his theory upon intuitive judgments of relative degree of belief, and admits as evidence verbal statements of introspective probability comparisons. Though we shall concen-
trate in this study upon the Ramsey/Savage approach, which bases all
inferences upon non-verbal behavior such as choices among gambles or
upon verbal statements of *preferences* among actions, the language of the
Koopman/Good theories has one marked advantage for my particular
purposes; it is much easier in their approach to talk formally and precisely
about vagueness. Moreover, when statements of belief are admitted
directly as evidence, one can hardly postpone for long recognition of the
ubiquity of vagueness.

> Statisticians live with vagueness, yet most of their published work is pre-
> cise. There are some problems, however, where vague questions may
> require fairly vague answers . . .

> As I understand it, statistics is not primarily for making objective state-
> ments, but rather for introducing as much objectivity as possible into our
> subjective judgments. It is only in limited circumstances that fully objec-
> tive statements can be made, although the literature of theoretical statis-
> tics is mainly concerned with such circumstances. The notion that it must
> all be precise is harmful enough to be worth naming. I shall call it the "pre-
> cision fallacy."[1] If we refuse to discuss problems in which vagueness is
> unavoidable then we shall exclude a large proportion of real-life problems
> from consideration. In fact every judgment involves vagueness, because
> when it becomes precise it is no longer called a judgment.[2] Vagueness will
> not disappear if we bury our heads in the sand and whistle.[3]

Of the particular assumption that all degrees of belief may be represented by definite, uniquely-defined *numbers*, B. O. Koopman speaks also

---

[1]On the last page of his "Last Papers" (1929) Frank Ramsey supplied another
name, in addressing his own profession: "The chief danger to our philosophy, apart
from laziness and woolliness, is *scholasticism*, the essence of which is treating what
is vague as if it were precise and trying to fit it into an exact logical category."
("Philosophy," in *The Foundations of Mathematics*, p. 269.)

[2]Compare the remark attributed to Admiral Arthur Radford (Time Magazine,
February 25, 1957, p. 27; cited in Barry Ransom, *Central Intelligence and National
Security*, Cambridge, 1958, p. 6): "A decision is the action an executive must take
when he has information so incomplete that the answer does not suggest itself."

[3]I. J. Good, "Significance Tests in Parallel and in Series," *Journal of the American
Statistical Association*, Vol. 53, 1958, p. 799.

for J. M. Keynes and Good in complaining that it "commits one to too great precision, leading either to absurdities, or else to the undue restriction of the field of applicability of the idea of probability." The latter restriction arises from inability to apply such a theory to "events of such elaborate and individual nature as to defy numerical evaluation of probability, yet which can often be definitely compared as to their likelihood of occurrence."[1]

Like Koopman and Keynes, Good defines the theory of probability as "the logic (rather than the psychology) of degrees of belief": "a fixed method which, when combined with ordinary logic, enables one to draw deductions from a set of comparisons between beliefs and thereby to form new comparisons."[2] He defines a "body of beliefs" as "a set of comparisons between degrees of belief of the form that one belief is held more firmly than another one, or if you like a set of judgments that one probability is greater than (or equal to) another one."[3] But, again like Koopman, "Degrees of belief are assumed (following Keynes) to be partially ordered only, i.e., *some pairs of beliefs may not be comparable.*"[4]

Where a theory of *decision* can, if so desired, interpret every choice as indicating definite preference and even indecision as revealing definite "indifference," a theory of *judgment* based upon verbal (or introspective) comparisons must allow for the statements: "*I don't know*" or "*I'm not sure*" (as in, "I'm not sure which proposition (I think) is more probable").

[1] B. O. Koopman, "The Axioms and Algebra of Intuitive Probability," *Annals of Mathematics,* Ser. 2, Vol. 41, 1940, p. 270. See also: "Intuitive Probabilities and Sequences," *Annals of Mathematics,* Ser. 2, Vol. 42, 1941, pp. 169–187; and "The Bases of Probability," *Bulletin of the American Mathematical Society,* Vo. 46, 1940, pp. 763–774. For further discussion of Koopman's approach to the measurement of "intuitive probabilities," which represents an alternative to the Ramsey/Savage approach upon which this study mainly focusses, see Chapter Four.

[2] Good, *Probability and the Weighing of Evidence,* (London, 1950), pp. v, 3.

[3] Good, "Rational Decisions," p. 109.

[4] *Ibid.,* p. 108; my italics. A "partially ordered system is defined as one whose elements are related by a relationship ≤· which is: (a) reflexive: for all X, X ≤{ X; (b) anti-symmetric: if X ≤{ Y ≤{ X, then X = Y; and (c) transitive: if X ≤{ Y and Y ≤{ Z, then X ≤{ Z. (See Garrett Birkhoff and Saunders MacLane, *A Survey of Modern Algebra,* New York, 1950, pp. 312–331). It is not assumed, under this definition, that for every pair of elements X, Y in a partially ordered set, either X ≤· Y or Y ≤{ X; a partially ordered set in which the latter property holds for every pair of elements is said to be *connected* and is termed a "simply ordered set" or "chain."

Thus, where Ramsey and Savage assume the system of personal probabilities to be "simply ordered," Keynes, Koopman and Good assume a partial ordering only.

Thus, Keynes, in *A Treatise on Probability* (1921), introduced formally the notion of *non-comparability* of beliefs.

> Is our expectation of rain, when we start out for a walk, always *more* likely than not, or *less* likely than not, or *as* likely as not? I am prepared to argue that on some occasions *none* of these alternatives hold . . . If the barometer is high but the clouds are black, it is not always rational that one should prevail over the other in our minds, or even that we should balance them.[1]

However, as Keynes later points out, while it may be impossible for a given person on a given occasion to compare definitely the probability of "rain" to that of "not-rain," it may be possible to compare each of these to the probabilities of certain *other* propositions, to which it may even be possible to assign numerical values (by processes we have not yet considered); it may then be possible to make meaningful statements of the form, "the probability of 'rain' for me is greater than that of proposition X, which has probability = .3, and less than of proposition Y, which has probability = .7." Unless the resulting inequalities confine the probability of 'rain' "within narrow numerical limits," Keynes tends to say that a probability "does not exist,"[2] rather than that it is "unknown," but I. J. Good objects to both phrases, preferring the point of view that:

> The initial probabilities may always be assumed to exist within the abstract theory, but in some cases you may be able to judge only that they lie in rather wide intervals. This does not prevent the application of Bayes' theorem: it merely makes it less effective than if the intervals are narrow.

> It is hardly satisfactory to say that the probabilities do not exist when the intervals are wide, while admitting that they do exist when the intervals are narrow.[3]

To suppose that initial probabilities, in problems of inference, can always be judged precisely is an example of the precision fallacy, Good asserts. He emphasizes that most judgments of relative probability are in the form of *inequalities*, A "more probable than" B, rather than precise equalities; a body of judgments of this form can be described numerically, but the description is generally in terms of *intervals* of probability numbers, circumscribed by inequalities (the process by which Koopman and Good

---

[1] John Maynard Keynes, *A Treatise on Probability* (London, 1952), p. 30.
[2] Keynes, *op. cit.*, p. 31.
[3] Good, *Probability and the Weighing of Evidence*, p. 40.

propose to give operational meaning to such numerical, descriptive statements is discussed briefly in Chapter Four).

Thus, in summarizing his own views, Good lists the tenet: "Subjective probabilities are not usually precise but are circumscribed by inequalities ("taking inequalities seriously" or "living with vagueness").["] Though this view is in considerable contrast to such "neo-Bayesians" as Savage, Raiffa and Schlaifer, whose proposed postulates of rational behavior imply that all reasonable opinions may be represented by perfectly precise probabilities (Good has commented that, "The main difference between my theory and that advocated in Savage's book is that his 'subject' or 'person' does not take inequalities seriously"[2]), Good describes it as "neo-Bayesian": "since its opponents are primarily frequentists, and since Bayes' theorem is restored to a primary position from which it had been deposed by the orthodox statisticians of the second quarter of the 20th century, especially by R. A. Fisher."[3]

> By a neo-Bayesian or neo/Bayes-Laplace philosophy we mean one that makes use of inverse probabilities, with or without utilities, but without necessarily using Bayes's postulate of equiprobable or uniform initial distributions, and with explicit emphasis on the use of probability judgments in the form of inequalities.[4]

At this stage in our discussion, the operational meaning of such statements has not been made explicit (it is not taken as self-evident that they are meaningful at all); I have introduced them here only to suggest the flavor of a theoretical approach that admits vagueness as an explicit factor without apology and provides a formal vocabulary for discussing it. It so happens that all the patterns of behavior I shall examine in this study and all decision criteria I shall espouse are compatible (even when they violate various of the Ramsey/Savage postulates) with all axioms proposed by Good for consistency of beliefs, and with conjectures advanced by him specifying rules for reasonable action based upon consistent beliefs. By his definition, then, my own approach is thoroughly "neo-Bayesian" in spirit. (For reasons that will become apparent in Chapters Two and Three, I shall distinguish those "Bayesians" who insist upon the precise measurability of probabilities and utilities for "reasonable" subjects as "neo-Bernoullian").

---

[1]Good, "Kinds of Probability," *Science,* Vol. 129, 1959, p. 446.

[2]Good, "Discussion on Dr. Smith's Paper (C. A. B. Smith, "Consistency in Statistical Inference and Decision"), *Journal of the Royal Statistical Society,* Series B, Vol, 23, 1961, p. 28.

[3]Good, "Kinds of Probability," p. 446.

[4]Good, "Significance Tests in Parallel and in Series," p. 803.

The feeling (a) that it is sometimes difficult or impossible to *compare* the strength of one's degree of belief in two given propositions (facts, events) is often closely linked to feelings: (b) that one's information concerning one or both of these propositions is inadequate or conflicting, "ambiguous"; and (c) that one lacks "confidence" in any one stated probability comparison or definite probability distribution.

Keynes, in particular, introduces a notion of "the *weight* of arguments" (as opposed to their relative probability) which seems closely related to our notion of "ambiguity":

> The magnitude of the probability of an argument . . . depends upon a balance between what may be termed the favourable and the unfavourable evidence; a new piece of evidence which leaves this balance unchanged, also leaves the probability of the argument unchanged. But it seems that there may be another respect in which some kind of quantitative comparison between arguments is possible. This comparison turns upon a balance, not between the favourable and unfavourable evidence, but between the *absolute* amounts of relevant knowledge and of relevant ignorance respectively.

> As the relevant evidence at our disposal increases, the magnitude of the probability of the argument may either decrease or increase, according as the new knowledge strengthens the unfavourable or the favourable evidence; but *something* seems to have increased in either case,—we have a more substantial basis upon which to rest our conclusion. I express this by saying that an accession of new evidence increases the *weight* of an argument. New evidence will sometimes decrease the probability of an argument, but it will always increase its 'weight.'[1]

Earlier he had related the possible difficulty of comparing the probabilities of "rain" versus "no rain" to the sort of *conflict of evidence* we have included in the notion of "ambiguity": "If the barometer is high, but the clouds are black, it is not always rational that one should prevail over the other in our minds, or even that we should balance them."[2] But low "weight" he relates primarily to scantiness of evidence of any sort.

Keynes gives detailed and convincing arguments why the notion of "weight" cannot satisfactorily be expressed in terms of probabilities, "probable error," or the shape of a probability distribution. Summing up, he asserts:

---

[1] Keynes, *op. cit.*, Chap. VI, "The Weight of Arguments," p. 71.
[2] *Ibid.*, p. 30.

An argument of high weight is not 'more likely to be right' than one of low weight . . . Nor is an argument of high weight one in which the probable error is small; for a small probable error only means that magnitudes in the neighborhood of the most probable magnitude have a relatively high probability, and an increase of evidence does not necessarily involve an increase in these probabilities.[1]

Speaking metaphorically, Keynes suggests that the weight measures the *sum* of the favourable and unfavourable evidence, the probability measures the *difference*.

Finally, differences in relative "weight" seem related to differences in the "confidence" with which we hold different opinions, a notion to which Savage alludes though his approach permits no formal expression of it:

. . . there seem to be some probability relations about which we feel relatively "sure" as compared with others. When our opinions, as reflected in real or envisaged action, are inconsistent, we sacrifice the unsure opinions to the sure ones. The notion of "sure" and "unsure" introduced here is vague, and my complaint is precisely that neither the theory of personal probability, as it is developed in this book, nor any other device known to me renders the notion less vague.[2]

Actually, the theories of Koopman and the more recent analyses of I. J Good seem to me to go far toward rendering the concepts of relative "sureness" and "vagueness" less vague in themselves. I hope in the present study to add to that development; and beyond that, to develop meaningful and useful hypotheses on appropriate decision criteria for basing action, reasonably and systematically, upon "vague" and "unsure" opinions.

That such factors are, to some degree, measurable and must, somehow, be relevant to decision-making was stressed by Frank Knight:

The 'degree' of certainty or of confidence felt in the conclusion after it is reached cannot be ignored, for it is of the greatest practical significance. The action which follows upon an opinion depends as much upon the

---

[1] *Ibid.*, pp. 74–78. See footnote reference below, this section, to the similar discussion by Raiffa and Schlaifer of the impossibility of representing "vague" opinions, *in general*, by a given probability distribution of whatever shape; though they and Keynes both point out that "vague" opinions, or as Keynes says, opinions based on arguments of low "weight," may *often* be associated with "diffuse" probability distributions over certain arguments, or estimates with high "probable error."

[2] Savage, *Foundations of Statistics*, pp. 57–58.

amount of confidence in that opinion as it does upon the favorableness of the opinion itself.[1]

But *how* does it depend? *How* may the web of action systematically reflect the varying degrees of "vagueness" of "ambiguity/weight," of "confidence" in our judgment? On that question, which is of central interest in this study, Knight is virtually silent, as are Savage and Keynes (Good makes several conjectures, identical to some examined in Chapters Six and Seven). It is a puzzle, they agree.[2] Knight offers the comment: "The ultimate logic, or psychology, of these deliberations is obscure, a part of the scientifically unfathomable mystery of life and mind."[3] But where the recent "neo-Bernoullians" tend to shrug their shoulders at the difficulties of expressing these factors and measuring their influence, effectively ignoring them in their formal theorizing, Keynes, like Knight, emphasizes that these matters do seem relevant to decision-making, though admitting frankly his own vagueness and lack of confidence on this particular question:

> In deciding on a course of action, it seems plausible to suppose that we ought to take account of the weight as well as the probability of different expectations. But it is difficult to think of any clear example of this, and I do not feel sure that the theory of 'evidential weight' has much practical significance.[4]

> If two probabilities are equal in degree, ought we, in choosing our course of action, to prefer that one which is based on a greater body of knowledge?

> The question appears to me to be highly perplexing, and it is difficult to say much that is useful about it. But the degree of completeness of the information upon which a probability is based does seem to be relevant, as well as the actual magnitude of the probability, in making practical decisions . . . If, for one alternative, the available information is necessarily small,

---

[1]Knight, *op. cit.*, pp. 226–227.

[2]"So we ask, but we seldom receive an answer: the [probability theorists] have turned away, and like antique heroes we only know that we have been talking with the immortals from the fact that they are no longer there." (H. R. Trevor-Roper, "The Mind of Adolf Hitler," introduction to *Hitler's Secret Conversations*, New York, 1953, p. vii) [paraphrased].

[3]*Ibid.*, p. 227.

[4]*Op. cit.*, p. 76. Keynes is equally apologetic in introducing his chapter on "The Weight of Arguments": "The question to be raised in this chapter is somewhat novel; after much consideration I remain uncertain as to how much importance to attach to it." (*Ibid.*, p. 71.)

that does not seem to be a consideration which ought to be left out of account altogether.[1]

When John Maynard Keynes expresses himself with so much diffidence on a subject, it is, perhaps, excusable when later theorists shy from committing themselves upon it and make some effort to build theories on other foundations; but it seems incautious of them to try to ignore that subject entirely. In Chapter Five I shall argue, and propose some evidence, that theories that do so are for that reason inadequate. In Chapters Six and Seven I shall examine a number of decision criteria, and support several, that give formal roles to factors that may plausibly be identified with the concepts of "vagueness," "ambiguity" and "confidence" discussed above and that imply systematic influence by these variables upon decision-making: influence of a sort that is ignored (indeed, ruled out as "unreasonable"—a judgment I shall challenge) by the "neo-Bernoullian" decision theorists.

Thus, I regard as premature the resignation expressed by L. J. Savage:

> Some people see the vagueness phenomenon as an objection; I see it as a truth, sometimes unpleasant but not curable by a new theory.[2]

Though inspired by my own sense of the current inadequacies of the neo-Bayesian approach, the present work may be interpreted as a direct response to the challenge implicit in the last quotation above. I accept fully the point of view of personal probability as being "nothing else than the expression of beliefs about unknown facts";[3] but I am impressed by the fact that any single, definite probability distribution seems a profoundly *bad* expression of vague, semi-formed beliefs in situations of extreme ambiguity.[4]

---

[1] *Ibid.*, p. 313.

[2] Savage, "Bayesian Statistics," lecture at the Third Symposium on Decision and Information Processes, April, 1961, to be published in *Decision and Information Processes*, Macmillan.

[3] Bruno de Finetti, "The Bayesian Approach to the Rejection of Outliers," Proceedings of the Fourth Berkeley Symposium on Mathematical Statistics and Probability, Berkeley, 1961, Vol. I, p. 199.

[4] For an excellent critique of the plausible, but mistaken, view that a single distribution of appropriate shape (e.g., "broad," high variance) can capture meaningfully, in general, the notion of vague initial opinions or "low initial quantity of information", see Raiffa and Schlaifer, *op. cit.*, pp. 62–66; "*The notion that a broad distribution is an expression of vague opinions is simply untenable . . .* We cannot distinguish meaningfully between 'vague' and 'definite' prior distributions." (p. 66, italics in original). The authors do point to some related distinctions that *can* be made, though these do not seem relevant in the present context; they will be discussed later.

It is a form of expression, that is to say, which seems much more appropriate some times than others, and its worst shortcoming is that it totally obscures *differences* in clarity of underlying information and opinion: differences that seem to me important to discriminate, measure and express, whether my purpose is to communicate my uncertainties or to act upon them and in spite of them. This seems to me a defect that might well be curable by a new theory: one built upon and around the current structure and reproducing its propositions for those important, special circumstances (now, purported to be general) when they are most appropriate. In any case, that is what I propose to try.

Recent developments in the field of statistical decision theory, notably the work of L. J. Savage, thus provide stimulus, points of departure, and major influences upon the present study. But it is worth recalling that the concepts and point of view of that new discipline have their roots in economics; indeed, it is described by Savage as "the economic analysis of statistical problems"[1]: the conception of statistics as "an economic science, that of wise decision under uncertainty."[2] Any study which focuses upon the question "What is it reasonable to do . . .?" has its most direct application, of course, to the process of making and recommending decisions, rather than predicting or describing them; yet still that question serves as divining rod to springs of economic theory.

While the progress of economics as positive science has far outrun the formal development of "political economy," economic analysis of choice (as represented by theories of the firm, consumer behavior, welfare economics, bargaining theory) remains relevant to both. Economic theory can contribute not only to the formulation of economic policy in business and government, but to an understanding of the process of "economizing" in its widest application. Expertise in this broad area has come to be increasingly valued. As technological revolutions succeed one another with increasing rapidity and political/diplomatic/military challenges ramify, the complexity and unfamiliarity of required choices in many fields have magnified the role of calculation and analysis in the decision-making process, relative to that of direct intuition and experience.

The new art of "systems analysis" has evolved, unsystematically, to meet these needs, and the conceptual tools of the economist have been invaluable in shaping its methodology.[3] They remain perhaps the best

---

[1] Savage, "The Foundations of Statistics Reconsidered," p. 576.

[2] Savage, "Bayesian Statistics," p. 1.

[3] See C. J. Hitch and R. N. McKean, *The Economics of Defense in the Nuclear Age,* Cambridge, 1960. Also see C. J. Hitch, *The Uses of Economics,* RAND Corporation Paper P-2179-BC, for an incisive discussion of the potential contribution of economists to systems analyses.

available for analyzing problems of allocating scarce resources, for evaluating merits and costs of alternative programs in terms of diverse objectives. Yet these tools, concepts, models, criteria, as yet are least developed to deal with uncertainty. And in those very fields where pre-decision analysis is at its highest premium—fields like foreign aid and military research and development, where major current investments and commitments must be made to further national objectives in a distant future—uncertainty is the central fact: uncertainty as to the future environment, as to the eventual performance of alternative programs launched today, even as to the operative national objectives in that environment and time and hence the future evaluation of performance.[1]

Ambiguity is extreme, by any of its indices: relevant information sparse, or obviously unreliable or contradictory; wide differences in the expressed expectations of different individuals; low confidence expressed in available estimates. In general, a useful model of ambiguity in the mind of a single decision-maker is the analogy of an intelligence panel advising the President on Soviet military inventory, each member giving a precise, definite probability distribution, each distribution different. In the high, practical realms we consider here, that situation of opposed, expert prediction is no metaphor but a familiar experience. For the decision-maker himself, one who must act in tumult and semi-blindness, the question: "How is it reasonable to choose . . . given what I know, what I must guess or doubt, and what I cannot know?" has more than philosophical or heuristic interest. It is a *cri du coeur*, it is for him *the* relevant question.

But what, after all, might it mean?

Shackle's response is stark:

> If we ask what in such a case it is rational to do there is no answer, if rationality means choosing the most preferred amongst a set of attainable ends. For he does not know what ends are attainable with the means at his disposal, indeed, in the face of this ignorance, his powers of action are not properly described as "means" at all.[2]

> . . . I conceive the nature of expectation itself, as an act of creative imagination and not of "rational" calculation; for calculation is impossible when the data are incomplete, and in face of ignorance, rationality is a mere pretense.[3]

---

[1] See Ellsberg, "The Crude Analysis of Strategic Choices," *American Economic Review*, Vol. 61, 1961, pp. 472–478.

[2] Shackle, *Uncertainty in Economics*, p. 9.

[3] *Ibid.*, p. 74.

These somber reflections seem too ominously relevant to the very circumstances upon which this study focuses to be dismissed; it would be well to keep them in mind in what follows, to guard against demanding or accepting too-ambitious answers. Yet neither is it necessary to dismiss the decision-maker's question, when even modest guidance could be helpful. Let us turn to consider what to expect of a theory of "reasonable" behavior.

THE NATURE AND USES OF NORMATIVE THEORY

Decision theory applies to statistical problems the principle that a statistical procedure should be evaluated by its consequences in various circumstances.[1]

Even before the widespread growth of "systems analysis," with its demands for criteria of action under uncertainty, statisticians had confronted that requirement in their own work of inference, experimental design, description, and more than occasionally, recommendation. Although the relevance of their findings to decision-making had long influenced statistical practice, it was only relatively recently that statisticians had come to analyze their work *as* decision-making in itself: that is, to formalize their problems in terms of abstract models of decision-making behavior and to examine, criticize and select statistical practices on the basis of very general criteria and intuitive insights on general decision-making processes. Since uncertainty is the very subject-matter of their discipline, they could scarcely be tempted to adopt for this purpose familiar models of choice that abstracted from all uncertainties, whatever the promised gains in simplicity add rigor. They were forced to develop new tools and criteria and in so doing made advances whose implications extend far beyond the statistical problems that originally motivated the inventors. (We shall, in fact, be litte concerned below with the direct application of these notions, or of others to be advanced in this study to statistical practice).

However, long after notions of alternative acts, consequences corresponding to different states of nature and a payoff function over consequences had been introduced in a statistical setting, much statistical literature still emphasized the peculiarities of the problems facing statisticians and made no strong effort to justify proposed decision criteria in terms of

---

[1]D. Blackwell and M. A. Girshick, *"Theory of Games and Statistical Procedures,* New York, 1954, p. vii. The authors note that this principle was first clearly emphasized by Neyman and Pearson in their theory of testing hypotheses, and then extended to all statistical problems by A. Wald; see Wald, "Contributions to the theory of statistical estimation and testing hypotheses," *Annals of Mathematical Statistics,* Vol. 10, No. 4 December, 1939, pp. 299–326.

general standards of rational choice. In particular, in the absence of a well-defined concept of personal probability and proposals for measuring it, and for other reasons not analyzed here, criteria were sought that would evaluate alternative procedures and determine choice among them in terms of the payoff *value* of their consequences in various circumstances, without requiring estimates of relative *probability* of the different circumstances. The resulting criteria were open to challenge as arbitrary, unmotivated, either unsystematic or unreasonably constraining.[1] Even the proponents of such rules tended to be diffident about the basis for accepting them. In Wald's last paper on statistical decision theory, he offers the rather tentative motivation for the minimax criterion: "It is *perhaps not unreasonable* to judge the merit of any particular decision rule entirely on the basis of the risk function [i.e., payoff function] associated with it."[2]

This modest claim did not, needless to say, deter critics from asserting that in many circumstances it seemed to them *quite* unreasonable to do so. Likewise for other decision rules that ignored the factor of opinion, or partial belief. Several of these had been suggested, conflicting with each other, having at least (and perhaps at most) the merit that, given knowledge of payoffs only, they were meaningful and could generate systematic choices even under conditions of extreme uncertainty. Yet few denied that action consistent with any of these rules would, in some situations, be inconsistent with what seemed reasonable standards of behavior, in the light of

---

[1] The prime example of such a criterion was Wald's minimax principle, described by Savage in an important early review of Wald's *Statistical Decision Functions* (New York, 1950): "The general rule by which the theory of statistical decision functions proposes to solve all decision problems . . . is the only rule of comparable generality proposed since Bayes' was published in 1763." ("The Theory of Statistical Decision," *Journal of the American Statistical Association*, Vol. 46, No. 253, March, 1951, pp. 58–59). He expressed significant reservations about the rule at that time; but ten years' experience with it led to final tones of disillusionment, which, though colored by his new "Bayesian" views, are probably widely shared: "The minimax theory, too, can be viewed as an attempt to rid analysis almost completely of subjective opinions, though not of subjective value judgments. From this point of view, the minimax theory of statistics is, however, an acknowledged failure. The minimax rule has never been taken seriously as a philosophic principle for inductive behavior, and even as a rule of thumb little of any good has been found in it." ("The Foundations of Statistics Reconsidered," p. 578.)

[2] A. Wald, "Basic Ideas of a General Theory of Statistical Decision Rules," *Proceedings of the International Congress of Mathematics*, Cambridge, 1950, Vol. 1, p. 233; (italics added).

one's true preferences and beliefs. There were grounds for pessimism that the discussion would ever be advanced beyond this point.

The break in this atmosphere came with a new attitude toward the possible meaning and role of probabilities to be assigned to statistical hypotheses. The older attitude was expressed by Wald:

> In many statistical problems the *existence* of an a priori distribution, i.e., a probability distribution over statistical hypotheses prior to a given experiment cannot be postulated, and in those cases where the existence of an a priori distribution can be assumed, it is usually *unknown* to the experimenter.[1]

The notion that probabilities might or might not meaningfully "exist," and that if they existed might or might not be "known" to the experimenter reflected operational concepts of probabilities as having "objective" magnitude, independent of the opinions of a particular experimenter, and measured by experimental or logical operations applicable only to certain classes of events or propositions: available, then, at most only occasionally to a particular experimenter to guide inference on the basis of Bayes' Theorem. In the new approach, as Bruno de Finetti pointed out:

> If the "*a priori* probabilities" are not meant to be mysterious objective entities that are known or not, but are expressions of one's own belief, which *cannot be unknown to oneself,* the validity of Bayes' rule becomes absolutely general.[2]

Whether one's belief is always known to oneself in the form of a definite, unique probability distribution is an issue we shall examine later; but a more general limitation of the approach, from the earlier point of view, is that:

> It does not contend that the opinions about probability are uniquely determined and justifiable, [i.e., for all persons]. The probability does not correspond to a self proclaimed "rational" belief, but to the effective personal belief of anyone . . . it is necessary to give up the aim of a rational uniquely defined criterion.[3]

---

[1] Wald, *Statistical Decision Functions,* p. 16; (italics added).

[2] Bruno de Finetti, "Recent Suggestions for the Reconciliation of Theories of Probability," *Proceedings of the Second Berkeley Symposium on Mathematical Statistics and Probability,* Berkeley, 1951, p. 220; italics added.

[3] *Ibid.,* p. 218.

Thus, it is *not* one of the tests of an individual's "reasonableness" in the approach we shall be examining, that he be "right," in some impersonal, "objective" sense. However desirable it might be to give a definitive answer to the decision-maker's plea, "What is it reasonable to do?" without, in principle, having to interrogate him further on what it is he, personally, *wants* to accomplish and what he *believes* the consequences of various actions to be, the postulates of the "neo-Bayesian" school do not lead, in any case, to "objective" recommendations or to any guarantee of "correct" or objectively "best" choices.

Savage notes that one source of a demand for such definitive answers is:

> by false analogy with the 'objectivity' of deductive logic, whatever the correct philosophical analysis of this latter kind of objectivity may be. Some principles of rational behavior seem to have this kind of objectivity, and the theory of utility and personal probability is based on them. For example, a man prepared to make a combination of bets that is logically certain to leave him worse off is 'objectively' irrational. It is perhaps thinkable that enough of these principles exist to eliminate all but one set of opinions as irrational. The main point for us here is that no such attempt has yet succeeded, so we must do the best we can with what we are sure of.[1]

The principles one may feel "sure of", from this point of view, are guides not to "truth" but to *consistency:* consistency among beliefs, among values, among actions, and between beliefs, values and actions. When actions are believed to lead with certainty to given consequences, certain rules of consistent choice have been accepted (particularly, among economists) as defining reasonable thought. No such logic-like behavior rules for choice under extreme uncertainty have found comparably general acceptance. It is this lack, and nothing more spectacular, that the "neo-Bayesians" purport to remedy. This does not minimize the impact of their achievement, if accepted; the canons of logical consistency among beliefs, preferences, and actions that they propose would invalidate nearly all of the decision criteria alluded to above, and a great deal of current statistical practice as well.

These consequences for statistics follow from the point of view that any special decision criteria proposed for use by statisticians should be compatible with fundamental, general criteria of rational decision-making under uncertainty, and that the latter must inevitably take into account, despite prejudices against explicit "subjectivity," differing degrees of belief.

---

[1]Savage, "The Subjective Basis of Statistical Practice," University of Michigan, July 1961, (hectographed), p. 2.10.

Thus, I. J. Good addressed the statistical profession, at the outset of a "Bayesian" article on "Rational Decisions":

I am going to discuss the following problem. Given various circumstances, to decide what to do. What universal rule or rules can be laid down for making rational decisions? My main contention is that our methods of making rational decisions should not depend on whether we are statisticians. This contention is a consequence of a belief that consistency is important. The resolution of inconsistencies will always be an essential method in science and in cross-examinations. There may be occasions when it is best to behave irrationally, but whether there are should be decided rationally.[1]

This passage suggests both the boldness and the restraint in the approach toward rules of rationality that we shall be discussing: on the one hand, rules are sought with universal application; on the other, the rules are to ensure consistency only, not to dictate choice in specific, isolated situations (and, as Good and Savage make clear, they are explicitly to allow for individual variation). In other words, the functions of the "logic-like criteria of consistency in decisions" we shall examine are to be as limited— and as pervasive, and as potent—as those of more familiar logics.

Savage notes that the principal value of logic "is in connection with its normative interpretation, that is, as a set of criteria by which to detect, with sufficient trouble, any inconsistencies there may be among our beliefs, and to derive from the beliefs we already hold such new ones as consistency demands."[2] Analogously, he asserts that the principal use he would make of the postulates he proposes is "normative, to police my own decisions for consistency and, where possible, to make complicated decisions depend on simpler ones."[3]

The latter use of the theory, to assist in reducing complex decision problems, by analysis, into a set of sub-problems more readily soluble, is particularly stressed by such "neo-Bayesians" as Robert Schlaifer and

---

[1] I. J. Good, "Rational Decisions," *Journal of the Royal Statistical Society*, Series E, Vol. 14, No. 1, 1952, p. 107. The *limitations* of a policy or theory that ensures consistency only are well expressed by Ramsey: "We put before ourselves the standard of consistency and construct these elaborate rules to ensure its observance. But this is obviously not enough; we want our beliefs to be consistent not merely with one another but also with the facts: nor is it even clear that consistency is always advantageous; it may well be better to be sometimes right than never right." (Ramsey, *op. cit.*, p. 191).

[2] Savage, *Foundations of Statistics*, p. 20.

[3] *Ibid.*, p. 20.

Howard Raiffa. As they put it, when the decision-maker has reduced his problem to choice within a well-defined set of contenders, he will wish "to choose among these contenders in a way that will be logically consistent with (a) his basic preferences concerning consequences, and (b) his basic judgments concerning the true state of the world."[1]

THE VALIDATION OF NORMATIVE PROPOSITIONS

The usefulness of a *satisfactory* extension of logic into the realm of decision is obvious. *But how will we know when we have one?* By what tests may we distinguish a satisfactory theory from a bad one? Consistency, after all, is not so hard to achieve if we are uncritical of the "laws" with which we force ourselves to be consistent. If consistency is a necessary attribute of reasonable behavior, it is scarcely sufficient. It is well known that alternative axiomatizations, sometimes contradictory, are available for important physical theories and even for fundamental areas of logic and arithmetic (e.g., the postulate systems for "Euclidean" vs. "non-Euclidean" geometries); though conflicting, each may be useful, perhaps in different applications and for different purposes. It might well be the case, on this analogy, that *several* quite different sets of norms, each internally consistent but perhaps mutually contradictory, could be established as "reasonable"; and that many others are conceivable that could be regarded neither as reasonable nor useful. What is it that lends significance to a *particular set* of logical axioms proposed as normative criteria? More generally, how are any propositions about norms to be validated, or rendered operationally meaningful?

There are a number of ways in which such statements about norms may be operationally grounded so as to be potentially refutable upon analysis or empirical observation. First, it might be stated that a given set of norms are internally consistent and capable of providing an unambiguous classification of behavior as conforming or not conforming. Second, it might be asserted that a set of meaningful propositions expresses norms that *do* decisively influence the behavior of specified people: or at least, characterize that part of their behavior that represents deliberation, reflection, calculation. It is this hypothesis—that certain norms *are* intuitively compelling—upon which our discussion will focus, so we shall discuss it in more detail presently. Third, the immediate or long-run *consequences* (in some "objective" sense, independent of the actor's expectations or desires) of obeying certain norms or disregarding others under specified circumstances may be hypothesized. Fourth, the logical relationship of the given norms to specified "super-criteria," or their pragmatic relationship in the

---

[1]Raiffa and Schlaifer, *Applied Statistical Decision Theory*, p. 3. Note comments below on the use of the phrase "logical consistency" in this context.

light of given "objective" consequences, may be examined. The modes of *test* for these different sorts of propositions clearly differ from one to the other; hence also, in a vague sense, their "testability." A final sort of proposition is much less easy to confront with empirical data than any of these: it is the subjective evaluation of certain norms or their predicted consequences in terms of one's own "super-criteria," or the estimated evaluation by someone else in terms of *his* "higher norms." Such evaluation is undoubtedly important; even essential in the "selection" of appropriate norms for one's own formal behavior or for an organization. And there is no doubt that such judgments are often *expressed*, sometimes with firm conviction; thus they may be "observed" and serve as data testing propositions about "higher norms" in the way that propositions of the second sort mentioned above are tested. But in comparison to the latter propositions about the norms that given people *do* accept in practice, propositions about the norms in terms of other, "higher" criteria, (often vaguely specified or wholly implicit) are one step further removed from the basic and relatively accessible data on their "actual" preferences and beliefs.[1]

I shall follow L. J. Savage in concentrating upon the problem of discovering postulates or decision rules that *are* normative criteria for specified people: for "you," for me, for all those people who accept as normative criteria the customary rules of logic and arithmetic when appropriate

---

[1]A discussion of some rather idiosyncratic, "super-criteria" is furnished by a passage from an unpublished paper by Paul Samuelson, cited by Alan S. Manne; it may not be a fair representation of the considered views of its author (an article by Samuelson in the same issue of *Econometrica* has quite a different tone), but it serves to illustrate the above remarks, and to set the sharply diverging viewpoint we shall adopt in useful contrast.

"Having successively stripped the Bernoulli theory of its (1) *empirical*, (2) *normative*, and (3) *deductive* supremacy, what have I left to justify its interest and importance?. . . The new significance of the Bernoulli theory to me is of an *aesthetic* and *semantic* character. The problem that I have in mind is not how people behave, nor how they ought to behave, nor what axiomatic systems logicians should formulate and analyze. It is rather: Given the ancient usages with respect to how a 'rational man' behaves, and given the modern economist's reduction of the rational behavior concept down to little more than 'consistent' preference behavior, what strength of axioms must 'naturally' fits in with usage?"

(Paul Samuelson, "Utility, Preference, and Probability," hectographed abstract of paper given before the Conference on Les Fondements et Applications de la Theorie du Risque en Econometrie, March 15, 1952; quoted in Alan S. Manne, "The Strong Independence Assumption—Gasoline Blends and Probability Mixtures," *Econometrica*, Vol. 20, No. 4, October 1952, p. 8).

Manne notes that this seems to reduce the problem to one of applied aesthetics.

or are otherwise considered "reasonable." We shall later give secondary attention to the question: What criteria *should* one accept as normative, and what "higher" criteria and evidence are relevant to this judgment? As noted above, it is not impossible to give operational meaning to this question but it is much harder than for the first, and the two questions are fairly distinct (both, of course, being quite distinct from the question that dominates investigation of behavior aiming at prediction or description: How *do* people tend to behave, when they act without reflection?).

Savage supplies a clear operational meaning to the proposition that certain rules *are* normative guides, *for you*, and his test will be the one relied upon throughout this study:

> When certain maxims are presented for your consideration [as "rational"], you must ask yourself whether you try to behave in accordance with them, or, to put it differently, how you would react if you noticed yourself violating them.[1]

The question is not whether you do conform to these maxims invariably in your day-to-day, unreflective behavior—whatever the maxims, and whoever you are, Savage predicts that you will not do that—but whether, when contradictions are brought to your attention and you are given time to reflect on all the implications of your choices, you conclude that you wish to persist in your "violations," or whether, on the other hand, you tend to discover that some of your earlier choices were over-hasty "mistakes" which you are glad to "correct."

Thus the proposition that certain people *do accept* given normative principles (in contrast to the proposition that certain rules *should be accepted* by them) involves definite empirical predictions as to how a "violator's" behavior will *change* when he is made aware of conflicts with the principles. In principle, one might allow the violator "a couple of years to brood over his answers"[2] before recording the experimental result: if one wanted to protect the theory from practical test, which is far from Savage's intention. Unlike some writers (discussed later) who purport to derive principles similar to Savage's directly from "super-criteria" (such as "long run success" or avoidance of victimization), Savage in *The Foundations of Statistics*, consistently encourages his readers to confront his hypothesis that certain postulates represent *their own* normative criteria with the relevant empirical data: i.e., their own intuition, soberly consulted, on the way they would *wish* to behave in given situations.

---

[1] Savage, *Foundations of Statistics*, p. 7.

[2] Samuelson, "Probability, Utility, and the Independence Axiom," *Econometrica*, Vol. 20, No. 4, October 1952, p. 678.

In general, a person who has tentatively accepted a normative theory must conscientiously study situations in which the theory seems to lead him astray; he must decide for each by reflection—deduction will typically be of little relevance—whether to retain his initial impression of the situation or to accept the implications of the theory for it.[1]

Thus, Savage exposes his own theory to empirical "refutation" by a given reader. This is admirable; it is by such risk-taking that science advances. To the extent that his theory is valid for his own decisions, Savage doubtless feels that there are grounds for arguing that it is "better" than competing normative theories and that others "should" follow it, but he spends little time attempting to persuade anyone who does not. He seeks "principles as *acceptable* as those of logic itself"[2] and dares to make crystal clear what he means by "acceptance":

If, after thorough deliberation, anyone maintains a pair or distinct preferences that are in conflict with [a given normative principle] he must abandon, or modify, the principle; for that kind of discrepancy seems intolerable in a normative theory.[3]

I have emphasized this point of view so strongly, and propose to adopt it as the basis for criticism of Savage's own work, not because of a mean desire to snare him in his own devices or because his theory is peculiarly vulnerable to this test, but because I agree with Savage that it is perfectly appropriate to his purposes. I respect and share his purposes; they are worthy standards by which to measure his achievement, and mine. I believe that in certain situations of "extreme" uncertainty, many of the readers whom Savage is addressing in the passages quoted will find, after thorough deliberation, that they wish to "maintain distinct preferences" in conflict with certain of the Savage postulates;[4] and that they must therefore be wary, to say the least, of using these postulates uncritically in their own decision-making, I shall propose certain other criteria, intended for the same purposes as the Savage postulates but, I conjecture, less likely to be confronted with deliberate and persistent violation by these persons: i.e,, more likely to be "accepted" as (approximations to) norms of their behavior. This hypothesis is put forward in the same spirit, and to the same ends, as Savage's; I invite the same tests.

---

[1] Savage, *Foundations of Statistics*, p. 102.

[2] *Ibid.*, p. 6; italics added.

[3] *Ibid.*, p. 102. The specific principle referred to is the "Sure-thing Principle" discussed below.

[4] In particular, with the "Sure-thing Principle."

Daniel Ellsberg

To assert that such introspective exercises are appropriate tests for the propositions to be considered, or that a persistent discrepancy between deliberated preferences and the implications of a proposed normative theory is "intolerable" is to *define* in operational terms the nature and goals of a normative logic of choice. Perhaps it would be most useful to interpret such a logic as: *A theory of one's own deliberated preferences:* a theory of the logical relationships among those choices that one has opportunity to base upon "mature consideration." As such, it would appear as an empirical, predictive/descriptive theory that could be true or false, or rather, more or less realistic. The test would be whether or not one did find that his deliberated choices, perhaps in contrast to his initial, hasty choices, were in good agreement with the implications of the theory.

From this point of view the tests suggested by Savage emerge clearly as the relevant ones. Moreover, the goals of the approach may appear in a sharper light. A reliable, tested theory of the logical patterns inherent in one's "best", most conscientious and deliberate decision-making would enable one to approach similar standards expediently in more urgent or less formal decision-making. The various propositions, axioms, postulates to be examined might all be regarded as hypotheses on the way one would act if one had time, as Ramsey puts it, to "stop to think."[1]

THE UTILITY AXIOMS AS NORMS

These same issues arose earlier in connection with the allegedly normative character of the "von Neumann and Morgenstern utility axioms" (which can, in fact, be deduced as theorems from the Savage postulates), and it is instructive to recall some of that discussion. Von Neumann and Morgenstern themselves did not propose a normative interpretation of their axioms, even to the extent of conjecturing that many people actually accepted them as norms. Their strongest claims were that it is "reasonable," "plausible," "legitimate" to hypothesize that some people actually behave this way, while making no commitment as to the advisability, "rationality"

---

[1]Among Ramsey's notes, under the heading "Logic as Self-Control", are some comments on the value of a logic of consistency: "Self-control in general means either (1) not acting on the temporarily uppermost desire, but stopping to think it out; i.e., pay regard to all desires and see which is really stronger; its value is to eliminate inconsistency in action; or (2) forming as a result of a decision habits of acting not in response to temporary desire or stimulus but in a definite way adjusted to permanent desire. The difference is that in (1) we stop to think it out but in (2) we've thought it out before and only stop to do what we had previously decided to do." Ramsey, "Further Considerations," *op. cit.*, p. 201.

or "optimality" of the presumed behavior.[1] However, most subsequent expositions, critiques, and elaborations of their approach took it for granted that the axioms defined "rational choice." In particular, articles of that period by Jacob Marschak stressed the dual aspect of such theories:

> The theory of rational behavior is a set of propositions that can be regarded either as idealized approximations to the actual behavior of men or as recommendations to be followed[2]

but concentrated upon the normative aspects. An article with the challenging title, "Why 'Should' Statisticians and Businessmen Maximize 'Moral Expectation'?" began:

> The word 'should' in the title of this paper has the same meaning as in the following sentences: "In building a house, why should one act on the assumption that the floor area of a room is the product and not the sum of its length and width?"; "If all A are B and all B are C, why should one avoid acting as if all C were A?". People may often act contrary to these precepts or norms but then we say that they do not act reasonably. To discuss a set of norms of reasonable behavior (or possibly two or more such sets, each set being consistent internally but possibly inconsistent with other sets) is a problem in logic, not in psychology. It is a normative, not a descriptive, problem.[3]

This paragraph expresses concisely several notions that are central to our discussion. But it is essential to be quite clear that *the question whether a certain internally consistent set of behavior norms actually does enjoy the same measure of acceptance, the same general "authority," as familiar rules of logic and arithmetic is not a normative but a descriptive problem.*

It is not simply to be asserted. Internal consistency is not an adequate test (as the reference to the possible existence of conflicting, rival sets of norms should indicate; one might also ponder the actual existence of competing logical systems, such as the rival axiomatizations of geometry); still less are aesthetic considerations of form, style, and semantic usage. *Does* action contrary to the given behavior principles evoke the same attitudinal response in an individual, or in general, as does a gross blunder in deduction or division?

---

[1] von Neumann and Morgenstern, *The Theory of Games*, Princeton, 1947, pp. 17–29 and 617–632.

[2] Jacob Marschak, "Rational Behavior, Uncertain Prospects, and Measurable Utility," *Econometrica*, Vol. 18, No. 2, April 1950, p. 111.

[3] *Proceedings of the Second Berkeley Symposium on Mathematical Statistics and Probability*, University of California Press, 1951, p. 493.

We must be careful to distinguish between the meaningful, and respectable, *aspiration* to "'prolong' logic and arithmetic into the realm of decision"[1] and the demonstrated *achievement* of that goal. It is, I maintain, premature to claim of any currently discussed set of behavior norms relating to uncertainty that action violating them:

> . . . is important to economics in the same way in which . . . inability to measure, to imagine, to remember, are important. We treat it in the same way that we treat the fact that people make mistakes of arithmetic and infringe upon the rules of conventional logic.[2]

Similarly, it can be quite misleading to describe, without careful qualification, any of the sets of behavior postulates currently under discussion as embodying the requirements of "logical consistency." Raiffa and Schlaifer use this phrase in the passage cited earlier and elsewhere in their book in connection with axioms equivalent to the Savage postulates, though less intuitively appealing; they frequently refer to these axioms as "basic assumptions concerning logically consistent behavior."[3] They do, at least at one point, advance the subjective judgment that these principles are "eminently reasonable in our opinion." But *since they never mention the possibility of alternative, conflicting, "logics" of behavior*, it is very easy to form the impression (perhaps correct) from their work that they regard these principles not just as "eminently" but as *uniquely* reasonable, as ordinary rules of logic are commonly regarded by the unsophisticated. This is, to say the least, debatable. It is, in fact, the very point at issue in the present discussion; we shall certainly not begin by assuming the matter settled. It is simply not true that the sole desire to be reasonable, consistent, or "logical" inevitably commits one to obey, i.e., to force one's behavior to "be consistent with", this specific set of principles (or any other set that has been proposed or that I shall advance). Such a commitment must depend ultimately upon individual judgment (which may or may not be reasoned and explicit), not upon traditional "logic."

In general, the importance of any *a priori* reasoning is that it picks out the variables on which the analysis is to rest.[4] Any empirical success in

---

[1] Marschak, "Rational Behavior . . .," *op. cit.,* p. 112; the reference is to the von Neumann-Morgenstern utility axioms.

[2] Marschak, *ibid.,* pp. 139–140. I would have little quarrel with this statement if the word "we" were replaced by "I."

[3] Raiffa and Schlaifer, *op. cit.,* p. 24; also pp. 16, 23.

[4] James S. Duesenberry, *Income, Saving, and the Theory of Consumer Behavior,* Cambridge, 1949, p. 10.

basing predictions upon observations of these particular variables and no others reveals a kind of "consistency" in behavior; consistency with the hypotheses. The more of it the better, from the point of view of the theorist; but his professional interest may make him suspect as an advisor.

The man who is out of step with a given normative theory may "hear a different drummer": may see distinctions, or the relevance of certain variables, that the theorist guarding the simplicity of his theory would prefer to see ignored. As I. M. D. Little has said of a man whose preferences among outcomes are observed to be intransitive (over time):

> What are we to say about a consumer who insists on being illogical? The answer is simply that we say he is illogical, which means nothing more than that our system of logic does not apply to him. It does not mean that he is irrational, or silly or mad.[1]

With this reassurance, I may state that so far as my own judgment is concerned, I no longer happen to agree with the authors cited above that the particular axioms they mention are "eminently reasonable" in *all* situations. Their rules, in certain situations, would compel me to make a set of choices which I would regard, taken as a whole, as *unreasonable;* they would force me to overlook certain aspects and types of data, certain differences between situations, which I regard, upon reflection, as vitally relevant to reasonable decision-making and which would, in fact, strongly influence my choices in ways that would conflict with their system of logic. In these situations, I could be "logically consistent" with *their* principles only at the cost of being *inconsistent* with my own true, deliberated preferences. These personal comments are included in this introduction only to point up the nature of the judgments which the reader will later be invited to make for himself.

In an article written while still skeptical himself of the compelling quality of the von Neumann-Morgenstern axioms, Paul Samuelson once recorded the stand of a man who spoke for all rebels:

> The most rational man I ever met, whom I shall call Ysidro, determined his own ordinal preference pattern. . . .

> When told that he did not satisfy all of the von Neumann-Morgenstern axioms, he replied that he thought it more rational to satisfy his preferences and let the axioms satisfy themselves.[2]

---

[1] I. M. D. Little, *A Critique of Welfare Economics* (Oxford, 1950), p. 16.

[2] Paul Samuelson, "Probability and the Attempts to Measure Utility," *Economic Review, Tokyo University of Commerce* (Hitotsubashi University), Vol. 1, July 1950, pp. 169–170.

Speaking, apparently, directly to this reported critic, Savage commented:

> I don't see how I could really controvert him, but I would be inclined to match his introspection with some of my own. I would, in particular, tell him that, when it is explicitly brought to my attention that I have shown a preference for f as opposed with g, for g as compared with h, and for h as compared with f [where f, g, h are actions] I feel uncomfortable in much the same way that I do when it is brought to my attention that some of my beliefs are logically contradictory. Whenever I examine such a triple of preferences on my own part, I find that it is not at all difficult to reverse one of them. In fact, I find on contemplating the three alleged preferences side by side that at least one among them is not a preference at all, at any rate not any more.[1]

This hypothetical prediction on one's own behavior exemplifies precisely the operational content of an assertion that one finds certain rules of choice normatively acceptable or compelling. The issues are thus met fairly: it is to be a match of introspection.

That conscientious deliberation *can* lead to changes in one's stated beliefs was demonstrated by Samuelson himself, who subsequently, after two years of "brooding" over Savage's "Sure-Thing Principle," announced himself a "fellow traveler" of the Savage approach.[2]

With a backward glance at Ysidro, who presumably no longer looked so rational as before, Samuelson covered his retreat from earlier views (or "advance in another direction") by pointing out:

> In short: it is anything but a casual thing to have and know one's complete ordering or set of indifference curves; and if you ask a casual question, you must expect to get a casual answer.[3]

NORMATIVE THEORY AND EMPIRICAL RESEARCH

Men try to act reasonably, and sometimes succeed. So, at least, economists tend to presume; it is their major heuristic device. In every field of their

---

[1] Savage, *Foundations of Statistics*, p. 21.

[2] Paul Samuelson, "Probability, Utility, and the Independence Axiom," *Econometrica*, Vol. XX, No. 4, October 1952, pp. 672, 677.

[3] *Ibid.*, p. 678. This notable willingness to reverse himself in public is, of course, admirable; but scarcely more impressive than the acuity and foresight shown in selecting, *two years earlier*, the Economic Review of Hitotsubashi University as a vehicle for views he was later to repudiate.

interest, it has suggested important variables, framed processes of measurement and test, generated fruitful hypotheses and supported useful recommendations.

The emphasis on intuition, introspection, reflection, and norms in our earlier discussion may have given a misleading impression of the of the separation between the tasks of designing useful normative principles and the more usual business of economic theory, creating and testing hypotheses on actual behavior. Progress in the latter activity often depends upon and interacts with successful effort in the former, to a degree that tends to be underrated in recent times. This interdependence is particularly marked in the early, exploratory phase of theoretical investigation; and regrettably, though it is not always recognized, that is the phase in which the investigation of decision-making behavior under uncertainty still finds itself.

In the first place, to the extent that we expose, or invent, decision criteria that are accepted by given decision-makers as normatively valid for their behavior—i.e., as characterizing patterns of consistency which they *wish* to achieve—these criteria may serve as an empirical theory of their actual, unreflective behavior. Such a theory, from the point of view of prediction and description, will generally be crude and approximate at best. Yet in the early stages of an investigation, it has often proved a great improvement over hypotheses reached from alternative starting-points.

Rules of deductive logic can be interpreted as an empirical theory in just the same way, and with the same sharp limitations. Thus, Savage notes that his logic-like postulates of rational behavior:

> can be interpreted as a crude and shallow empirical theory predicting the behavior of people making decisions. This theory is practical in suitably limited domains, and everyone in fact makes use of at least some aspects of it in predicting the behavior of others. At the same time, the behavior of people is often at variance with the theory.[1]

But even when it does not lead directly to satisfactory empirical theories of behavior, the notion of "reasonableness" has nevertheless been of great value to empirical research. It has served to suggest certain hypotheses to an economist, certain questions to ask at the outset of an investigation of behavior: "What are the objectives of this behavior?"; "What relative values are placed upon various outcomes?"; "What actions are regarded as available, and what outcomes are expected, to follow them, with what assurance?" One reason this approach has proved particularly fruitful in the exploratory phase of an investigation is that it suggests the relevance of a body of data that may lie close to hand, the product of intuition, common sense, common

---

[1]Savage, *Foundations of Statistics*, p. 20.

observations and experience. It leads the economist to seek initial answers to his questions by substituting questions that may be easier to answer: "What would *I* do if I wanted this, and believed that?"

To think that this line of inquiry is too obvious, self-evident, to be dignified as a formal heuristic principle or be associated with a particular discipline would, I think, be quite mistaken. Savage describes the "Bayesian theory," which follows from what he calls, with justice, the "economic-theoretic approach to statistical problems," as being "but an elaboration of common sense";[1] but in reporting his understandable exhilaration at the clarifying, simplifying, unifying effect of applying economic analysis to statistical problems ("Those of us who adhere to this movement feel that it represents a great step forward and the breaking of a log jam")[2] Savage notes the paradox posed by such advances: "It would seem reasonable to suppose that a generation of bright people working in the subject would not overlook major opportunities to exploit common sense, but the unreasonable seems to have happened."

If this "normative" approach no longer characterizes the whole of economic analysis or even of exploratory research, there are still few important hypotheses or accepted results in economics to which it has not contributed. Yet in economics proper, prior to the developments in statistical decision theory, the whole heuristic machinery of the approach had faltered in the presence of uncertainty; the economist would ask his usual question of himself, and get no clear reply.

The cost of this failure to generate useful, convincing concepts of reasonable behavior under uncertainty has, in fact, been a relative impoverishment of every aspect of the investigation of actual behavior under uncertainty. The relative underdevelopment of this field would be gravely underestimated if we marked only the scarcity of "finished," fully tested, complex and reliable theories and recommendations. More immediate and troublesome are the lack, even, of exploratory questions; of meaningful concepts, testable hypotheses; of useful and accepted processes of measurement and test; of accepted bodies of data. Workers in this field have lacked agreement not merely on definitions but on the relevance of basic variables and observations; they lack agreement even on a common language in which to disagree.

The most glaring example of such controversy, of course, concerns the concept of "probability." A great deal of debate on the relevance or the exact bearing of "probabilities" upon problems of choice is rendered sterile by failure of the participants individually to specify, let alone to agree

---

[1] Savage, "The Foundations of Statistics Reconsidered," p. 583.
[2] Savage, "Bayesian Statistics," p. 2.

on, any operational definition of the term "probability." Statements as to how people behave, or should behave, when probabilities are "known" or "not known" are typically unaccompanied by any indication of the sort of observation on which this distinction might be based, or the operational tests by which such statements could be refuted or supported.

A considerable amount of economic theorizing has by now been constructed utilizing, among other materials, magnitudes labelled "subjective probabilities": apparently in the optimistic belief, or hope, that a substructure of measurement procedures and actual results would be designed and installed by the time the structure was ready for occupancy. Such theorists owe the "neo-Bayesians" a significant debt of gratitude for providing, none too soon, a collection of techniques for measuring subjective probabilities; thus making a large body of theory meaningful at last, whether or not it proves to be realistic and useful. The doubts I shall raise about the *general* validity or feasibility of these techniques cast me more in the thankless role of troublemaker with respect to these theories; but doubtless it will turn out, as always, that better theories are possible, designed to be meaningful in terms of data that *are* available.

The "neo-Bayesian" approach seems beyond question to have clarified these conceptual discussions enormously. Its proponents have been exemplary in their precision of language and qualification and their devotion to the principles of operational definition. They have shown unmistakably the possibilities, in principle, of useful measurement and the relevance of certain types of observations.

C. West Churchman has expressed a point of view that stresses the limitations but also suggests the promise that such an analysis of normative principles holds, in general, for empirical investigation:

> Decision theory is or will be a science constructed from certain observables. Postulational methods in decision theory are agreements—or "preconstructions"—on what is to be observed, what the observables are to be called, and how they are to be used to define optimal decision patterns.

> Suppose we simply say that postulational decision theory is a set of agreements concerning the measurements of behavioral properties like "value," "probability" and the like. Postulational decision theory represents a prolegomenon to measurement, not a theory of decisions as such.[1]

---

[1]C. West Churchman, "Problems of Value Measurement for a Theory of Induction and Decisions," *Third Berkeley Symposium on Mathematical Statistics and Probability*, Vol. V, Berkeley, 1956, pp. 55–56.

The theories to be discussed are, in fact, more ambitious than this would suggest, but the comment expresses the *minimum* contribution such methods are likely to make. I believe, however, that a major shortcoming of the Ramsey / de Finetti / Savage approach is that it omits important variables, important aspects of "what is to be observed," considerations, recognized in some earlier discussions, which are essential to the understanding both of reasonable and of actual behavior under uncertainty.[1] At the same time, their approach has shown clear possibilities for measuring the effects of these other variables; since the measurements that they do propose are essential to this process, the next three chapters will be devoted to the conceptual basis for the measurement, where feasible, of definite subjective probabilities and utilities.

If my argument is accepted that the effects of these omitted factors upon reasonable, deliberate decision-making are measurable and important, a natural extension would be to frame and test corresponding hypotheses on actual behavior, just as Savage's work has already led to experimental measurement of the variables he considers.[2] Such empirical work should strongly complement and interact with the continuing analysis of normative principles.

For the remainder of this study we shall be concerned with the problem of designing normative decision-making criteria—rules of a personal logic of choice—that may be more helpful to certain decision-makers, reflecting more faithfully the nature of their uncertainties and their own definite, underlying preferences among gambles, than other criteria currently

---

[1] To anticipate later discussion, the considerations alluded to here are subjective judgments and impersonal data on the relative "adequacy" and inherent "ambiguity" of available information, judgments of relative precision and confidence in estimates of degree of belief, and situational and personality differences affecting response to these factors. Measurements of the degree and influence of these factors may be possible on the basis of gambling behavior (of a sort that some "neo-Bayesians" would ignore or reject as "non-rational," since it contradicts certain postulates) or statements (of a sort these "neo-Bayesians" would regard as irrelevant).

[2] The recent publication of the hypotheses to be considered here in detail, in "Risk, Ambiguity, and the Savage Axioms," *Quarterly Journal of Economics,* Vol. LXXV, No. 4, November 1961, pp. 654–656, led, I am happy to say, without delay to an experimental investigation by Professor Selwyn Becker (an experimental psychologist) and Frederick Brownson of the University of Chicago, in which some 34 subjects made paired comparisons among gambles for real money. Though their work has not yet been published, they allow to say that their results tend very strongly to support the hypotheses and assertions in my article.

available for the task of evaluating important, complex alternatives subject to extreme uncertainty. Whether or not their behavior, as reflected in appropriate decision rules, can be considered "optimal" in terms of various "super-criteria" is a matter that will receive secondary consideration.

The fact that certain patterns of chosen, deliberated behavior may conflict with particular axioms of "rational" decision-making that at first glance appear reasonable could not, in any case, foreclose the question of optimality. As we have just discussed, empirical research, and even preliminary speculation, about the nature of actual or "successful" decision-making under uncertainty is still too young to give us confidence that *any given postulates* are not abstracting away from vital considerations. This would be true even in the absence of specific counterexamples to given postulates of the sort we shall consider; and, of course, it applies with equal force to any proposed decision rules that I shall advance in the present study, even if these rules are admitted to be realistic and useful in terms of the behavior of given individuals. Indeed, empirical findings, as, hopefully, they begin to appear in more abundance, will undoubtedly change the views of every party to the current discussion in important ways now unforeseeable. As Churchman has remarked:

> Now, any agreements reached prior to measurement are not binding and serve as devices to guide progress, not rules to limit it. We don't know how to measure the values of decision today, and until we do, it would be foolish to agree to any commitment once and for all.[1]

---

[1]Churchman, *op. cit.,* p. 56.

2

THE BERNOULLI PROPOSITION

IN MUCH RECENT theorizing on "reasonable" decision-making under uncertainty the following proposition, first associated with Daniel Bernoulli, plays a central role as hypothesis, theorem, or recommendation:

For a reasonable decision-maker, there exists a set of numbers ("von Neumann-Morgenstern utilities") corresponding to the uncertain outcomes of any given risky proposition or "gamble," and a set of numbers (numerical probabilities)[1] corresponding to the events determining these outcomes, such that the ranking of mathematical expectations of utility computed for various gambles on the basis of these numbers will reflect his actual, deliberated preferences among these gambles.[2]

---

[1] A probability measure on a set S is a function P(B) attaching to each $B \subset S$ a real number such that (where $\cup$ = union, "and/or;" $\cap$ = intersection, "and;" 0 = empty set):

(1) $P(B) \geq 0$ for every B.

(2) If $B \cap C = 0$, $P(B \cup C) = P(B) + P(C)$.

(3) $P(S) = 1$.

(See L. J. Savage, *Foundations of Statistics*, p. 33)

Thus, the probability number attached to a union of several events within a set of events, S (e.g., the union of all events that a particular action associates with a given outcome) equals the sum of the probability numbers attached to the separate events in the union. It is asserted that *at least one* probability distribution exists (possibly more than one, for a finite set of gambles) satisfying the proposition.

[2] Let us assume that a finite set of distinct outcomes is associated with any set of actions. A "von Neumann-Morgenstern utility function" over outcomes is a function, U, associating real numbers with outcomes in such a way that, if x_i represent the distinct outcomes ($i = 1 \ldots, n$) of action I, and p_i the probabilities attached

As stated, this "Bernoulli proposition" may seem neither empirically plausible as a description of all significant, deliberate behavior, nor intuitively compelling as a general standard of reasonableness in choice. What has made it, in recent years, the focus of widespread interest, controversy, energetic analysis and advocacy has been its derivation as a *theorem* from various sets of axiomatic propositions which have themselves, in considerable degree, both these appealing properties. This approach, begun by Frank Ramsey in 1926 and developed most fully by L. J. Savage, has demonstrated that any pattern of choice contradicting the "existence assertion" above must also violate certain proposed canons of reasonable behavior that are, undeniably, far more persuasive as normative criteria than is the "Bernoulli proposition" itself.[1]

In one of the earliest presentations of his approach, Savage described these canons as:

---

to them, and if y_j and p_j represent the outcomes and probabilities, respectively, of action II (j = 1 . . ., m), then the individual "does not prefer" I to II if and only if

$$\sum_{i}^{n} p_i \cdot U(x_i) \le \sum_{j}^{m} p_j \cdot U(y_j)$$

The above "Bernoulli proposition" asserts that for a reasonable individial, there exists a probability measure over the set, S, of events that affect the consequences of his acts and hence over the separate outcomes of a given act, and a "von Neumann-Morgenstern utility function" over his outcomes with respect to the given probability measure.

If a particular real-valued function of outcomes, U, is a "von Neumann-Morgenstern utility function" for the individual, then $U' = aU + b$, where a, b are any real numbers, $a > 0$, is *also* a "von Neumann-Morgenstern utility function" for him; i.e., substituting utility numbers corresponding to U' in the calculations above will not affect the ranking of the mathematical expectations of utility for the various gambles. There will thus be an infinite family of appropriate utility functions, any pair of which will be related by an increasing linear transformation.

If U and U' are utilities such that, for some outcomes, x, y, x or referred to y, $U(x)$ = U' (x) and U(y) = U' (y), then U and U' are identical, i.e., they assign the same numbers to every outcome. Thus, if two utility numbers are assigned arbitrarily (reflecting order of preference) to two outcomes, *at most one* "von Neumann-Morgenstern utility function" will exist for an individual, corresponding to that assignment. Hence, fixing two numbers determines the "von Neumann-Morgenstern utility function" uniquely, corresponding to an arbitrary choice of unit and origin of the utility scale. (See Savage, *Foundations of Statistics*, pp. 72–75.)

[1] Frank P. Ramsey, "Truth and Probability" (1926), *The Foundations of Mathematics*, New Jersey, 1960, pp. 156–198. L. J. Savage, *The Foundations of Statistics*, New York, 1954.

. . . certain principles of conduct or of decision that I would like, at least so it seems to me, never to violate. I think, naturally, if not modestly, that no one would want deliberately to violate them. That suggests, in fact, that the actual behavior of individuals would be sometimes in good accord with the principles and their consequences, a conclusion which could be of value in empirical tests, in certain cases.[1]

One of the logical consequences of these principles of conduct is the "Bernoulli proposition." In fact, Savage commented on that occasion, he had made no other use of the axioms than to "justify" that "existence theorem"; that task accomplished, the axioms themselves could be forgotten.[2] The principles of conduct proposed by Ramsey, Savage and others, and the conclusions based on them, seem to me, as to their authors, sufficiently compelling to place the burden of argument currently upon those who would claim—as I do—that patterns of deliberate choice violating these principles are to be expected in certain circumstances and may, in those situations, be defended as reasonable.

Such an argument could attack the realism or universal acceptability of one or more of the proposed axioms; but this would not necessarily invalidate the conclusion, since several alternative sets of axioms lead to that same theorem.[3] However, it is possible to test the "Bernoulli proposition" itself directly. Even in its general form of existence assertion, before any specification of the processes by which utility and probability are to be measured, it is operationally meaningful; it places definite restrictions on any body of deliberated choices that could be said to conform to it. An

---

[1] L. J. Savage, "Une Axiomatisation de Comportement Raisonnable Face a L'Incertitude," *Colloque International d'Économétrie*, 12–17 May 1952, on "Fondements et Applications de la Théorie du Risque en Économétrie," Paris, Centre National de la Recherche Scientifique, 1953, p. 29; my translation.

[2] Savage, *ibid.,* p. 33; my translation.

[3] Widespread interest in the derivation of the "Bernoulli proposition" from axioms on choice among risky propositions began with the discussion in *The Theory of Games and Economic Behavior* by John von Neumann and Oskar Morgenstern (Princeton, 1943, pp. 17–29; and Appendix, 2d edition, 1947, pp. 617–632) of the possibility of deriving an appropriate *utility* function from choices, obeying certain axioms, among gambles with *known probabilities.* Somewhat different axioms with this consequence were then presented by Jacob Marschak ("Rational Behavior, Uncertain Prospects, and Measurable Utility," *Econometrica*, April 1950, pp. 111–141; and, "Why 'Should' Statisticians and Businessmen Maximise 'Moral Expectation'?", *Proceedings of the Second Berkeley Symposium on Mathematical Statistics and Probability* (Los Angeles, 1951); and by Paul Samuelson ("Utilité, Préférence et Probabilité," *Colloque International d'Econométrie,* 12–17 May 1952, on "Fondements et

assertion that a given decision-maker or a given body of preferences is "reasonable" in the sense of this test *could be refuted* by specifiable data on choices; for there are patterns of preference among gambles that could *not* correspond to a ranking of their mathematical expectations of utility based upon *any* hypothetical probabilities or utilities, however determined.

To illustrate this, let us consider an example that we shall subsequently examine in a broader context. Suppose that an individual is confronted with a choice between the following pair of actions, where A, B, C are specified, mutually exclusive and exhaustive events (i.e., one and only one will occur) and *a, b* are any two outcomes such that the individual prefers *a* to *b*:

		Events			
		A	B	C	
Actions	I	a	b	b	Fig. 2.1a
("Gambles")	II	b	a	b	

Since there are only two possible outcomes to each action, the same two for each, it is clear that whatever utility numbers should be assigned to these outcomes, that action will have the higher mathematical expectation of utility that offers the *higher probability of the preferred outcome, a.* The "Bernoulli

"Applications de la Théorie du Risque en Économétrie," Paris, Centre National de la Recherche Scientifique, 1953, pp. 141–150).

All of these axioms can be derived from the Ramsey or Savage axioms, already cited. Other axiom-sets leading to existence-proofs both for utility and probability, similar in spirit but not equivalent to those of Ramsey or Savage, have been presented by P. Suppes and D. Davidson (*Decision-Making*, Stanford, 1957; "A Finitistic Axiomatization of Subjective Probability and Utility," *Econometrica*, XXIV, 1956, pp. 264–275).

All of these sets are fairly closely related, in that behavior violating one set is almost sure to violate the others. But quite different axioms have been proposed in which choice is presumed to be "stochastic" (the assumption that actions are subject to a complete ordering, Savage's Postulate 1, is dropped), yet which still lead to the "Bernoulli proposition" (see, for example, R. Duncan Luce, "A Probabilistic Theory of Utility," in R. D. Luce and H. Raiffa, *Games and Decisions*, New York, 1957, pp. 371–384).

We shall give explicit attention only to the Savage axioms, which have the clearest *normative* interpretation and deal most directly with probabilities; however, both the counterexamples and the counterargument to be presented with respect to the Savage approach bear directly on the "Bernoulli proposition" and hence apply fully to all of the other treatments mentioned.

proposition" asserts that for a reasonable man, a probability measure exists over the events A, B, C such that the action he actually prefers will be the one with the higher probability of the preferred outcome according to this measure.[1]

Suppose that the individual decides, after deliberation, that he definitely prefers action I. Not merely one, but infinitely many probability distributions "exist" that are compatible with this choice in the sense of the "Bernoulli proposition": all those in which $p_A > p_B$.

Now suppose that we confront the same individual with another pair of actions, where A, B, C, a, b are the same as before.

	A	B	C
III	a	b	a
IV	b	a	a

Fig. 2.1b

For any given probability distribution, the probability of outcome a with action III is $p(A \cup C) = p_A + p_C$. The probability of outcome a with action IV is $p(B \cup C) = p_B + p_C$. Let us suppose he decides that he prefers action IV in this case. For this to be "reasonable" in the sense of the "Bernoulli proposition," there must exist at least one probability distribution, such that the mathematical expectation of utility is higher for I than for II, and higher for IV than for III. This means there must be a probability distribution, p_A, p_B, p_C $(0 \le p_i \le \Sigma p_i = 1)$, such that $p_A > p_B$ *and* $p_A + p_C < p_B + p_C$. But *there is none.*[2]

Thus, the "Bernoulli proposition" has empirical content; *it rules out the pattern of choices above.* That is, it asserts that a "reasonable man" will never deliberately make such choices; in effect, it denies the "reasonableness" of

---

[1] If an appropriate von Neumann-Morgenstern utility function over consequences exists for our individual, we can assign two values arbitrarily to determine origin and scale; let us assign values 1, 0 to a, b. Then whatever probability distribution may be assigned, the *expected utility* for action I is p_A; for action II, p_B.

[2] Following the assumptions of the preceding footnote, the *expected* utility of action III is $p_A + p_C$; the expected utility of action IV is $p_B + p_C$. The "Bernoulli proposition" implies the existence of a probability distribution (the utilities being fully "given" in this example involving only two distinct outcomes) such that the ranking of expected utilities corresponds to the actual preference ranking of actions. But as indicated in the text, no such probability distribution exists, given the preferences hypothesized.

such behavior. Moreover, since this proposition is implied by the Savage postulates, it must be the case that this pattern of choices violates at least one of those postulates. And so it does: Postulate 2, the embodiment of what Savage calls the "Sure-Thing Principle."[1]

The formal statements of Savage's postulates in *The Foundations of Statistics* are quite general, so as to apply to actions whose consequences are continuous functions of infinite sets of events, but the sense of Postulate 2 is as follows: If for certain events the consequences of two actions "agree" (i.e., if they have the *same* consequences for the given events), then one's preference between the two actions should not be affected by the *value* of the consequences for those events. As it applies to this example, the "Sure-Thing Principle" requires that one's preference between two actions should not change if the value of the payoffs in a *constant column* (a column of outcomes all with the same value) is changed. Since the only difference between the pair of actions I, II and the pair III, IV is the change in the value of the "constant column" corresponding to event C, an event for which the consequences of I, II and of III, IV "agree," the order of preference among actions "should" be the same between the two pairs. Thus, if the individual deliberately chooses I in preference to II, Postulate 2 (hence the "Bernoulli proposition") requires that he prefer III to IV as well. To prefer IV over III is to contradict both postulate and proposition.

So much to establish the operational meaningfulness of the postulates and the "Bernoulli proposition." How *useful* are they? How well do they satisfy the various purposes of a general theory of "reasonable" behavior? Is it true, as Savage conjectured in the passage cited earlier, that no one would want, in any circumstances, deliberately to choose behavior of the sort they rule out?

That is the central issue in this thesis, and I shall not attempt to develop the case for my own—negative—opinion fully until we have discussed in greater detail the implications of the postulates and the "Bernoulli proposition" within the situations where they *are* presumed to apply. However, to put that discussion in better perspective, let us anticipate the later critique to the extent of a single example.

A POSSIBLE COUNTEREXAMPLE: ARE THERE UNCERTAINTIES THAT ARE NOT RISKS?

Let us suppose that "you" are confronted with a decision problem essentially equivalent to the abstract example above. Specifically, you are to imagine an urn known to contain 30 red balls and 60 black balls and yellow balls; you are not told the proportion of black to yellow. One ball is to

---

[1] Savage, *Foundations of Statistics*, pp. 21–23.

be drawn at random from the urn. An observer sets out to determine your adherence to the "Bernoulli proposition" by observing your choices. among various gambles; let us assume that you are convinced *he knows no more about the contents of the urn than you do*. Without indicating in advance all the alternatives he will offer, he asks you to choose between the following two gambles:

	30		60
	(A)	**(B)**	**(C)**
	Red	**Black**	**Yellow**
I	$100	$0	$0
II	$0	$100	$0

Fig. 2.2a

Action I stakes a $100 "prize" on the occurrence of a red ball; II stakes the same prize on a black. Which do you prefer; or are you indifferent?

Now the observer offers you the following two actions, under the same circumstances (prior to a drawing):

	30		60
	Red	**Black**	**Yellow**
III	$100	$0	$100
IV	$0	$100	$100

Fig. 2.2b

Action III stakes the prize on "red or yellow" (i.e., you will "win" if either of these colors is drawn). Action IV stakes the prize on "black or yellow." Which of these do you prefer; or are you indifferent?

A very common (in my experience and in some others',[1] the most common) pattern of responses to these hypothetical alternatives is: action I pre-

---

[1] Ellsberg, "Risk, Ambiguity, and the Savage Axioms," *Quarterly Journal of Economics*, Vol. LXXV, November 1961, No. 4, pp. 654–656. See Howard Raiffa's report in the same issue of experiments with his graduate students in statistics ("Risk, Ambiguity, and the Savage Axioms: Comment," *ibid.*, pp. 690–694) and, also in the same issue, William Fellner's results in similar (independent) experiments ("Distortion of Subjective Probabilities as a Reaction to Uncertainty," *ibid.*, pp. 686–689). An earlier, independent experiment by John Chipman reproduces virtually equivalent alternatives to those above (although Chipman was testing a stochastic theory

ferred to II, and IV preferred to III. A closely related pattern often encountered is, I indifferent or very slightly preferred to II, IV definitely preferred to III (tests of "degree of preference" will be discussed later). A third, infrequent pattern is II preferred to I, III preferred to IV. Since the situation is equivalent to the one we have already analyzed, it is clear that all three patterns violate the behavior implied by the "Bernoulli proposition" and the "Sure-Thing Principle." Thus, there is evidence that behavior patterns that cannot be described as maximizing the probability of a preferred outcome, or more generally, as maximizing the mathematical expectation of utility, are not merely *conceivable;* they actually occur.

Are these patterns characteristic, also, of more *deliberate* decision-making? Or would these same "violators"—including "you"?—eventually choose to change their behavior, upon reflection, to a pattern that does not conflict with the "Bernoulli proposition" (such as I indifferent to II, III indifferent to IV)?

If so, then the *importance of analysis* based upon the postulates and the "Bernoulli proposition," in terms of "improving" unreflective behavior, is magnified by such evidence that "mistakes" are likely in the absence of reflection.[1] If not, then it will be important to determine for such people the circumstances, if any, under which the "Bernoulli proposition" *does* repre-

---

of choice similar to that of Luce, *op. cit.*); his results, under carefully controlled experimental conditions and subjected to statistical analysis, accord fully with the above pattern. (J. S. Chipman, "Stochastic Choice and Subjective Probability," in *Decisions, Values and Groups,* ed. D. Willner [New York, Pergamon Press, 1960]). Finally, a recent experimental investigation of the hypotheses and assertions in "Risk, Ambiguity, and the Savage Axioms" has been conducted by Frederick Brownson and Selwyn Becker of the University of Chicago; though their results have not yet been published, they have permitted me to say that the above assertion was strongly supported.

The Chipman, Fellner, and Brownson and Becker results all relate to observed behavior; subjects were not particularly encouraged to deliberate, nor were violations of any postulates brought to their attention. Hence, the findings do not test fully hypotheses on self-conscious, "formal," deliberated decision-making, which is our main concern here. At the least, however, they do indicate an area of *systematic* deviation from the "Bernoulli proposition," to the extent that the latter is interpreted as a "crude empirical theory" of actual behavior; it will be argued below that such deviations do correspond to deviating patterns of *deliberated* behavior which must be interpreted in terms of different *norms* from those that underlie the "Bernoulli proposition."

[1] This is the conclusion drawn by Howard Raiffa, *op. cit.*, p. 691, after observing behavior of the sort described above: in himself, among others.

sent an acceptable normative guide for them, and to provide them with a more acceptable normative theory covering circumstances when it does not. Following Savage's example, I may speak for one individual—myself—on this point. I find that I would conform, in this particular case, to the first pattern mentioned: I preferred to II, IV preferred to III. My reasons will be discussed later, in more extended discussion of this and related examples; it is, no doubt, intuitively evident that the circumstances such examples will share involve a degree of "vagueness" or "ambiguity" in the available information, and some sensitivity in one's preferences to the relative "definiteness" of the relative payoff probabilities in various gambles. I may say that my preferences in this case have persisted through some years of reflection, although I have had full benefit of prolonged and thorough analysis of the implications of this behavior by sophisticated proponents of the view that it is unreasonable. Nor do I find myself alone.

I have introduced this brief, anticipatory discussion of an evident "counter-example" not, at this point, to persuade or even to indicate all the important issues, but to support a certain point of view about the theories advancing the "Bernoulli proposition": namely, that these theories need not be regarded, as so often they seem to be, as stating virtually self-evident principles, universally applicable, beyond criticism, modification or improvement relative to their aims; but as *hypotheses* on desired or deliberated behavior, and specifically, hypotheses that may be realistic and useful in *some* circumstances but not (or not so much) in others.

This point of view, and the argument by which I shall try to support it, is closely analogous to the approach taken by Daniel Bernoulli himself, in launching the "Bernoulli proposition." It may provide historical perspective, as well as useful introduction to several issues, to recall his exposition here.

VULGAR EVALUATIONS OF RISK

Bernoulli's paper of 1738 entitled "Exposition of a New Theory on the Measurement of Risk" began by characterizing the *old* theory. "Ever since mathematicians first began to study the measurement of risk," he observed, "there has been general agreement" that the expected *value* of a risky proposition, or gamble, should be computed by multiplying each possible gain by its probability and taking the sum of these products; where the gains were measured by their *money* values and the probabilities by the ratio of "favorable" to "unfavorable" events among an exhaustive set of mutually exclusive, equi-probable events. This was to be regarded as the "reasonable" evaluation of the gamble.[1]

Thus, a money sum equivalent to this weighted average of money gains from the gamble should be regarded as having value equal to that of the gamble. It would represent a "fair" or "reasonable" trade in exchange for the risky proposition; a reasonable person should be indifferent between the two alternatives, preferring any larger sum of money to possession of the gamble, and the gamble to any lesser sum. There was, then, "general agreement" that in choosing among risky propositions (including sure outcomes), the reasonable man would choose that gamble with the highest weighted average of money gain. He would *maximize the mathematical expectation of money.*

Bernoulli noted that this rule depended only upon money gains and "known" probabilities, presumed the same for all prospective gamblers; to base upon it recommendations for all persons in all circumstances would imply that "no characteristic of the persons themselves ought to be taken into consideration." The size of the stakes relative to the gamblers' "specific financial circumstances," the gamblers' attitude toward risk: these were regarded as differences between situations that, so far as reasonable behavior were concerned, should make no difference. Yet to Bernoulli they seemed *relevant:* not only to prediction but to advice.

To make this clear it is perhaps advisable to consider the following example: Somehow a very poor fellow obtains a lottery ticket that will yield with equal probability either nothing or twenty thousand ducats. Will this man evaluate his chance of winning at ten thousand ducats? Would he not be ill-advised to sell this lottery ticket for nine thousand ducats? To me it seems that the answer is in the negative. On the other hand I am inclined to believe that a rich man would be ill-advised to refuse to buy the lottery ticket for nine thousand ducats. If I am not wrong then it seems clear that all men cannot use the same rule to evaluate the gamble. The rule established [above] must therefore be discarded.[2]

For future reference, let us cast his example into the framework of our earlier illustration. Bernoulli confronts two hypothetical subjects with the following gambles, where the payoffs are in ducats and E is an event with

---

[1] Daniel Bernoulli, "Specimen Theoriae Novae de Mensura Sortis," *Commentarii Academiae Scientiarum Imperialis Petropolitanae,* Tomus V (Papers of the Imperial Academy of Sciences in Petersburg, Vol. V), 1738, pp. 175–192; translated by Dr. Louise Sommer, as "Exposition of a New Theory of the Measurement of Risk," *Econometrica,* Vol. 22, No. 1, January, 1954, pp. 23–26; quotation from p. 23.

[2] *ibid.,* p. 24.

	(Heads) E ($\frac{1}{2}$)	(Tails) $\bar{E}$ ($\frac{1}{2}$)
I	20,000	0
II	10,000	10,000
III	9,000	9,000

Fig. 2.3

"known" probability equal to that of not-E (e.g., consider E the occurrence of Heads on a single toss of a coin believed to be fair): *Will* the pauper, asks Bernoulli, be indifferent between I and II? Will he really prefer gamble I if the payoff to II is reduced, say, by one ducat? Would he be foolish or ill-advised if he actually *preferred II to I*, to such a degree that he even preferred III—with a payoff 1,000 ducats less—to gamble I?

To all of these questions, Bernoulli suggests, the answer is "No." A "very poor man" might well make choices that conflicted with the accepted theory, deliberately, advisedly. And he should not be considered unreasonable for doing so: for finding its implied recommendation (to hold out for 10,000, not a ducat less) in conflict with his true preferences, and acting contrary to it. Nor should a theory of reasonable behavior require of everyone identical preferences among gambles. In the same situation, a man with different resources or requirements might reasonably make different choices. One whose fortune was large compared to the stakes at issue would be well-advised to follow the traditional principle; whereas, Bernoulli suggests later, a rich prisoner who needs no less than 20,000 ducats to repurchase his freedom might pay even *more* than 10,000 for a 50-50 chance to win his ransom.[1]

It does not seem to stretch Bernoulli's argument to read into it the same test of acceptability of a normative theory as that proposed by Savage, and implied by the discussion of my example earlier. If *he* were poor, Bernoulli can be interpreted as saying, he could imagine himself under certain conditions violating the traditional normative principle, even after full reflection on the implications of his choices; and he conjectures that the reader's introspection (and empathy) will correspond. Hence the traditional rule is *not* an acceptable normative guide for Bernoulli; nor for the reader, if he agrees; nor for the poor man they hypothesize. That is, it will not serve the purposes of a personal logic of choice; it will not permit the "deduction" of ultimately acceptable decisions in complex situations

---

[1] *Ibid.*, p. 25. I believe this is a fair inference from Bernoulli's example, though strictly speaking what he says is that the rich prisoner will place a higher value on a gain equivalent to his ransom than would another man who had less money. In my interpretation, Bernoulli allows for "increasing marginal utility of money" in such special cases, though he says "they represent exceedingly rare exceptions."

from more familiar, simpler choices, nor will it reveal "inconsistencies" in judgment of a sort one will be anxious to "correct." For such purposes another, more acceptable theory must be found. And Bernoulli proceeds to advance one.

> Anyone who considers the problem with perspicacity and interest will ascertain that the concept of *value* which we have used in this rule may be defined in a way which renders the entire procedure universally acceptable without reservation. To do this the determination of the *value* of an item must not be based on its *price*, but rather on the *utility* it yields. The price of the item is dependent only on the thing itself and is equal for everyone; the utility, however, is dependent on the particular circumstances of the person making the estimate.[1]

The pauper's choice may be explained, Bernoulli argues, by supposing that the "utility" of 9,000 ducats is greater for him than for the rich man (equal, perhaps, to that of 10,000 for the latter). In general, the effect of introducing the variable "utility" is to enable the observer, or decision-maker, to make a *distinction*, for purposes of action or advice, between two situations in which the money stakes and probabilities are the same. Because the "utilities" may be different, "it may be reasonable for some individuals to invest in a doubtful enterprise and yet be unreasonable for others to do so"; it may be as wise for one man to buy insurance as for another to sell it, even when the buyer knows he is reducing his expected money wealth and increasing the seller's; and a given insurance premium, against a given risk, may be worthwhile for one man but too costly for another.

In an appendix to his paper, Bernoulli attributed priority for the notion of "utility," and its application to the now-famous St. Petersburg Paradox (so-called from the journal in which Bernoulli's paper appeared) to the Swiss mathematician Gabriel Cramer, whose comments on the paradox he quoted:

> For the sake of simplicity I shall assume that A tosses a coin into the air and B commits himself to give A 1 ducat if, at the first throw, the coin falls with its cross upward; 2 if it falls thus only at the second throw, 4 if at the third throw, 8 if at the fourth throw, etc. The paradox consists in the infinite sum which calculation yields as the equivalent which A must pay to B. This seems absurd since no reasonable man would be willing to pay 20 ducats as equivalent. You ask for an explanation of the discrepancy between the mathematical calculation and the vulgar evaluation. I believe

---

[1] *Ibid.,* p. 24.

that it results from the fact that, *in their theory,* mathematicians evaluated money in proportion to its quantity while, *in practice,* people with common sense evaluate money in proportion to the utility they can obtain with it.[1]

The Cramer/Bernoulli solution is to enter "utilities" into the same formula as before, in place of money gains. For each gamble the "mean utility" or "moral expectation" can be computed by summing the products of the probability and the utility of each possible money gain. Bernoulli lays down the "fundamental rule" that the value of a risky proposition should be taken to be the money profit equal in utility to the mean utility or moral expectation of the gamble. The following proposition is then proposed as "universally acceptable without reservation." Between two risky propositions, the reasonable man will prefer that with the higher moral expectation; he will act so as to *maximize the mathematical expectation of utility.*

Though measurement problems for both probability and utility remain (for discussion in the next chapter), we have virtually arrived at the original "Bernoulli proposition." The most significant modern reinterpretation of the proposition is to allow not only the utilities of the outcomes but their *probabilities* to vary subjectively between two persons evaluating a given gamble. This extension, too, was referred to common experience: the difference of opinion that makes horse races. In one of the earliest papers suggesting the measurement of differing subjective probabilities by bets, Emile Borel observed:

It has been said that, given two bettors, there is always one thief and one imbecile; that is true in certain cases when one of the two bettors is much better informed than the other, and knows it; but it can easily happen that two men of good faith, in complex matters where they possess exactly the same elements of information, arrive at different conclusions on the probabilities of an event, and that in betting together, each believes . . . that it is he who is the thief and the other the imbecile.[2]

---

[1] *Ibid.,* p. 33. Cramer's comments are quoted from a letter to Bernoulli's cousin, Nicholas Bernoulli (1728). Cramer goes on to resolve the paradox by arguing that utility is bounded, so that moral expectation is reduced drastically: by his calculation for himself, to the equivalent of about 13 ducats.

[2] Emile Borel, "A Propos D'Un Traite De Probabilites," *Revue Philosophique,* t. 98, 1924, pp. 321–336; reprinted in *Valeurs Pratique des Probabilites,* Gauthiers-Villars, Paris, 1939; quotation on p. 137; my translation. I am indebted to L. J. Savage for this reference, which is of particular interest for antedating Frank Ramsey's paper in several respects (see next chapter).

The Ramsey/Savage introduction of subjective probabilities into the Bernoulli formula, just like Bernoulli's introduction of subjective utility, has the effect of *admitting a wider range of individual behavior as "reasonable": of recognizing, accepting, and measuring the influence of variations in individual circumstances, information, and personality upon reasonable behavior.* Each recognized the earlier theory, which ignored certain of these variations or treated them as irrelevant to reasonable choice, as a special case; acceptable, or approximately so, in restricted circumstances.

My intention is no different. Like the theories those authors found and criticized, the theories that currently support the "Bernoulli proposition" seem to me approximations, good for most men in some situations, for some, perhaps, in most: and quite inadequate for many men in some important circumstances, for which they need, and probably can find, better approximations. These recent theories are, I maintain, theories that apply to *decision-making based on definite opinions,* and to the measurement of definite opinions. Within that sphere (which can be operationally defined) they are both valid and important, and flexible enough to encompass a broad range of individual behavior. Yet still they abstract from important informational and personality variables that influence deliberate decision-making when opinions are indefinite or conflicting. In such circumstances procedures designed for measuring definite opinions may give inconsistent results (just as measurement procedures presuming linear utility will often fail). But this is nothing new, nor need it lead to chaos. New theories can find order in the phenomena and provide measurements of new variables.[1]

A theory that ignores such variables buys simplicity at the price of what Cramer described as a "discrepancy between the mathematical calculation and the vulgar evaluation." To paraphrase Cramer,[2] I believe that such discrepancies—whose existence and extent will be discussed below—"result from the fact that, in their theory, mathematicians evaluate" gambles

---

[1] As Norman Dalkey has pointed out to me, the axiom of "Archimedean ordering" was for some time regarded as indispensable to the foundations of utility measurement, as laid down by Ramsey and von Neumann and Morgenstern; yet when consideration of the possibility of "lexicographic ordering", and other considerations, motivated an attempt to bypass it, a richer theory was found to be possible on simpler foundations (see M. Hausner, "Multidimensional Utilities," and R. M. Thrall, "Applications of Multidimensional Utility Theory," Chapters XII and XIII in *Decision Processes,* ed. R. M. Thrall, C. H. Coombs, R. L. Davis, New York, 1954, pp. 167–186). Anxiety over the prospect of decision theory without the "Sure-Thing Principle," Dalkey joins me in conjecturing, may be just as premature.

[2] Cramer, quoted in Bernoulli, *op. cit.,* p. 33. Compare Savage's comment on the principle of maximizing that mathematical expectation of *money:* "The principle

in terms of precise probabilities and utilities, "while, in practice, people with common sense" take reasonable account, in their behavior, of their degree of ignorance of both.

It is true that the vulgar evaluations I seek to "rationalize" encounter closely-reasoned and persuasive arguments that they violate "self-evident" principles of reasonable decision-making. Yet I am encouraged to challenge what is becoming a new orthodoxy of opinion by the thought that the theory of expected value defeated by Cramer and Bernoulli—so easily, it now seems to us, with their introspective exercises—appeared to generations of subtle minds as just as unshakable, as intuitively and logically compelling, as uniquely "right," as does the "Sure-Thing Principle" today to the truest believer.[1]

---

was at first so categorically accepted that it seemed paradoxical to mathematicians of the early eighteenth century that presumably prudent individuals reject the principle in certain real and hypothetical situations." (*The Foundations of Statistics*, p. 92.)

[1] I am indebted to L. J. Savage for suggesting this analogy, in conversation (which is not to say that his assessment of its import is identical with mine).

3

THE MEASUREMENT OF DEFINITE OPINIONS

THE ADVICE OF the "neo-Bernoullian" school to decision-makers who must choose among actions with uncertain consequence is to act "as if" they assigned definite utilities to consequences, definite probabilities to events, and maximized moral expectation. In principle, they might attain the required quasi-logical structure, or "consistency," in their body of decisions without ever having either probabilities or utilities consciously in mind.[1] But it is clear that if one were *trying* to achieve this sort of consistency, by far the most convenient way to ensure it would be to discover for oneself an appropriate set of probabilities and utilities and to use these numbers in calculating preferred choices. In fact, it is rather hard to imagine a body of decisions among complex alternatives exhibiting the nice consistency required by the theory unless it did reflect just this sort of calculation; in any case, it is the very possibility of subjecting complex decisions to reasoned, systematic, explicit *calculation,* that is the chief appeal of the approach. It is easy to see that a decision-maker who accepts the argument, as phrased seductively by Raiffa and Schlaiffer, that:

---

[1]Indeed, even when calculations are explicit, Raiffa and Schlaiffer take pains to reassure those statisticians trained in the "objectivist" school—who might experience anxiety or guilt to find themselves attaching probabilities to statistical hypotheses—that those numbers they are being urged to assign to events need not be regarded as "probabilities" in any forbidden sense, but as a "mere weighting device required to arrive at a reasoned choice"; for purely technical reasons, the "weights" happen to obey the axioms of classical probability theory (Raiffa and Schlaiffer, *Applied Statistical Decision Theory,* p. 16).

a few basic principles of logically consistent behavior—principles which
are eminently reasonable in our opinion—*compel* one to choose among
[actions] *as if* one used such a weighting function,[1]

has every reason to make the measurements of his own utilities and probabilities that will enable him to use the simple formula of moral expectations in his later decision-making.

But how to get the numbers?

To the extent that the "Bernoulli proposition" applies to a person's
actual behavior, it can be proven that appropriate numbers can be derived
directly from data on his actual preferences among certain gambles.[2]
Given a particular pattern of choice, certain assignments of numbers to

---

[1]*Ibid.*, p. 16; italics in original.

[2]Although Bernoulli himself is not specific as to how he proposed to measure
the utility used in the calculation of moral expectations, it has generally been
assumed (with some basis in his exposition) that the supposed the possibility of an
introspective or "empathetic" measurement involving no actual or hypothetical
comparison of risky propositions. Nevertheless, it is a logical consequence of the
"Bernoulli proposition" that a consistent measurement of utilities and probabilities
can be derived from choices among gambles *if* those choices are consistent with the
principle. These numbers would not necessarily correspond—i.e., in the case of utilities, be related by a linear transformation—to those derived from any other process
of measurement; but a discrepancy could arise only if the latter numbers were *not*
used to calculate the moral expectation of gambles and so to determine choice
among gambles. Any utility numbers that *were* used thus, in accordance with
Bernoulli's recommendation, would have the properties of a "von Neumann-
Morgenstern utility function"; no matter how they had been measured initially,
they could be ascertained by observation of the person's choices among risky
propositions. Utility numbers that did *not* have these properties, though they might
be perfectly meaningful in terms of operations not involving risk-choices and more
useful than von Neumann-Morgenstern utilities in areas where the latter are not
directly relevant—e.g., welfare comparisons or choices among certain outcomes—
would not necessarily be relevant at all to risk-choices: certainly not in terms of
Bernoulli's "fundamental rule."

It is noteworthy that Bernoulli himself does not use his presumed measurements of "numerical utility" for any other purpose than to predict or advise choices
among gambles. If he had been shown the possibility of measuring utility by
observing such choices, given that the person choosing were following his fundamental rule, it seems plausible that Bernoulli would have acknowledged this process
of measurement as the most convenient and appropriate for his purposes. In this
he would contrast with, say, Marshall or Jevons, who hoped to make more extensive use of the concept of "utility" and would not have accepted "von Neumann-
Morgenstern utility"—even if it could be definitely determined—as necessarily

outcomes and events can be ruled out as incompatible with the theory; and for certain patterns of choice, only one assignment of probability numbers (or for utilities, an assignment unique up to a linear transformation) would be consistent with the theory.[1] Thus, the decision-maker who wishes to determine numbers measuring his beliefs and values, as an aid in choosing among complex alternatives, need only "watch himself bet"— or ask himself how he would choose among alternative, hypothetical gambles—in situations involving simpler or more familiar alternatives among which he found it easier to choose. The consistency demanded by the theory implies that any numbers determined by such choice will, or "should," be pertinent to his harder decisions.

To the extent that such self-interrogation reveals no inconsistency with the "neo-Bernoullian" postulates, or no inconsistencies he is unwilling to eliminate upon reflection, it *can* yield definite, precise numerical values for the utilities and probabilities of the outcomes and events involved in the comparisons. I find the arguments of current proponents of the "Bernoulli proposition" entirely persuasive as to the possibility of establishing these definite measurements for any reasonable decision-maker I can imagine, for *some* events and outcomes. My present quarrel is with their assertion that one must, to behave reasonably, so act as to make possible equally definite measurements of probability with respect to *every* conceivable event. But even if some limitations were accepted, this would scarcely detract from the importance of their demonstration that the notion of a definite degree of belief *can* be made operationally meaningful and given meaningful, precise numerical expression. Moreover, we shall see that it is most

---

relevant. It was precisely because Marshall expected divergence between their "von Neumann-Morgenstern utility function" and their "real" utilities for many people— those who would accept bets whose expectations of money gain was zero or negative (implying a "von Neumann-Morgenstern utility function" concave upward, whereas their "true" utility function was presumed always to be concave downward)—that he would have rejected measurements of utility based on this "irrational" behavior (see Alfred Marshall, *Principles of Economics* [London, 1925], Mathematical Appendix, Note IX, p. 843).

For a full discussion of the relation, in operational terms, of "von Neumann-Morgenstern utility" to earlier concepts of "measurable utility," see: Ellsberg, "Classic and Current Notions of 'measurable Utility,'" *Economic Journal*, Vol. LXIV, No. 255, September 1954, pp. 528–556.

[1]If the theory is obeyed, there will always be *at least one* set of numbers compatible with any given body of decisions. But, as we have already seen, for some patterns of choice *no* consistent assignment of numbers is possible; in such cases— which I believe will be frequent and important in bodies of reasonable and deliberated decisions—this sort of observation will not yield definite measurements of probability and utility.

convenient to delimit and express the "vagueness" of less definite opinions by comparing them with degrees of belief to which it is possible meaningfully to assign numbers. Let us proceed, then, to explore the conceptual basis[1] of the numerical measurement of opinions and values, in terms of risk-choices, under those conditions in which the "Bernoulli proposition" or the postulates leading to it *are* obeyed.

VON NEUMANN-MORGENSTERN UTILITIES

It is clear that if one of the two variables that figure in Bernoulli's fundamental rule were "known" or assumed "given" in terms of relevant measurements, it would be a straightforward process to deduce appropriate values of the other from observed choices. In Bernoulli's own critical example, values for the relevant probabilities and the objective outcomes (in ducats) were given:

	E (prob. $\frac{1}{2}$)	E (prob. $\frac{1}{2}$)	
I	20,000	0	
II	10,000	10,000	Fig. 3.1
III	9,000	9,000	
IV	12,000	12,000	

For each of the hypothetical subjects, numerical utilities for the money stakes could be derived from their choices: in particular, from actual indifference between two actions. Since utility is determined by this process only up to a linear transformation, we could start by assigning, for each subject, values to two of the outcomes simply reflecting order of prefer-

---

[1]We shall not go into the problems and subleties of actual, experimental procedures designed to determine numerical probabilities or utilities for given subjects; for discussions of modifications in theory needed to resolve certain ambiguities or allow for inevitable inconsistencies in responses, see the works by Suppes and Davidson, Luce and Chipman already cited. However, notice that most of their difficulties arise from trying to interpret non-verbal behavior of subjects who were acting hastily, making decisions that were at best of minor importance to them, and who had no special motivation to be "consistent".

The problem of a decision-maker who is trying to determine *his own* attitudes and beliefs in a definite form for help in making practical decisions of importance, with ample time for analysis and reflection, is entirely different. It still may not be easy, but the relatively straight-forward procedures discussed below should be more directly relevant.

ence. For convenience in comparison, let us assign the same numbers, say, 1 and 0, to the same two outcomes, 20,000 ducats and 0 ducats respectively, for each of the subjects. This effectively fixes scale and origin of the utility function for each person.

Suppose that the rich man were exactly indifferent between gambles I and II (for these stakes, he obeys the pre-Bernoullian principle; his utility is linear on money). Only *one* utility number for the outcome 10,000 ducats is simultaneously compatible with: (a) this indifference; (b) the assumption that he conforms to the "Bernoulli proposition"; (c) the two numbers already assigned arbitrarily. Given all these premises, we must assign for him: $U(10,000) = \frac{1}{2}$.

Following Bernoulli's argument, the pauper might well *prefer* II to I; by the same assumptions. The number assigned to $U(10,000)$ for him must be greater than $1/2$. If he should be indifferent between I and III, we can assign a definite number to $U(9000)$ for the pauper: $1/2$. As for the rich prisoner who needs a minimum of 20,000 ducats to complete his ransom, he might place a *lower* value than this rich, free colleague on 10,000 ducats sure, *relative to gamble I*. The prisoner might prefer I to any of the other options, except, let us say, IV; indifference between I and IV would indicate that a *50% chance* of gaining his freedom was equivalent in value for him to 12,000 ducats certain. We express precisely this by assigning: $U(12,000) = \frac{1}{2}$.

The differences in the relative utilities assigned to various outcomes for the different persons reflect only the differences in their observed preferences among gambles, and would be the basis for varying predictions or recommendations on their future choices.[1] But either to make or to use this measurement it would be necessary to "know" or to presume given the numerical probability of at least one event.

PROBABILITY AS PRICE

On the other hand, if relevant *utility* values were presumed known, the same observed choices could be used to infer appropriate probability values, i.e., to "measure probability." In particular, the pre-Bernoullian principle of maximizing the mathematical expectation of *money* implied that relevant utilities were known as soon as money outcomes were known; it assumed, in effect, that "von Neumann-Morgenstern utility" was equivalent to money, up to a linear transformation. Though Bernoulli rejected this rule as applying to all

---

[1] Interest in measuring utility for actual subjects, by this method and for the purpose of describing risk-behavior, was aroused by the discussion in von Neumann and Morgenstern, op. cit.; hence the term, "von Neumann-Morgenstern utilities." The earliest application was by Frederick Mosteller and Phillip Nogee, "An Experimental Measurement of Utility," *Journal of Political Economy*, October, 1951.

reasonable people under all circumstances, he noted that it could "continue to be considered approximately valid in games of insignificant moment" (i.e., when the greatest possible gain or loss is insignificant relative to total resources).[1] The assumption results in a great simplification of the process of measuring probabilities, under circumstances when it can be considered valid. For Bernoulli (and the more recent "neo-Bernouillians")[2] this would mean that the decision-maker using this method in self-interrogation must limit the stakes in his hypothetical gambles to relatively small amounts (though here, as Ramsey points out,[3] the measurement may be spoiled by "reluctance to bother about trifles"). Others, both before and after Bernoulli, have made implicit use of the assumption in measuring probabilities, without apparent awareness of the pitfalls indicated by Bernoulli.

Thus, in the same essay in 1763 that introduced "Bayes' Theorem," Thomas Bayes defined probability as follows:

> The probability of any event is the ratio between the value at which an expectation depending upon the happening of the event ought to be computed, and the value of the thing expected upon its happening . . . By chance I mean the same as probability.[4]

---

[1] Bernoulli, op. cit., p. 27.

[2] Schlaifer, who more or less takes for granted the unique reasonableness of the "Bernoulli proposition" in general, recommends that the decision-maker in business take advantage, in measuring his own utilities, of the fact that businessmen tend to "act in accordance with expected monetary value when the amounts at stake are not too large"; they "tend to treat acts which must have one or the other of just two possible consequences as being 'really worth' the expected monetary value as long as the worst of the two consequences is not too bad and the best of the consequences is not too good." Therefore, in a complex problem with many possible consequences, Schlaifer suggests that the businessman decide "whether or not he should use expected monetary value as the basis of his evaluation by looking only at the best and the worst of the consequences and asking himself whether he would act in accordance with expected monetary value if these were the *only* possible consequences." (Schlaifer, *Probability and Statistics for Business Decisions,* p. 28.) If the answer is "Yes" for some consequences, he can use hypothetical gambles involving those stakes to measure his subjective probabilities, even if the answer is "No" for the larger problem in which he is directly interested.

[3] Ramsey, *op. cit.,* p. 176.

[4] Thomas Bayes, "An Essay Towards Solving Problems with Optimum Chances," *The Philosophical Transactions,* 1763; cited in R. A. Fisher, *Statistical Methods and Scientific Inference,* London, 1956, p. 376.

Though writing 25 years after Bernoulli, Bayes took for granted the traditional, pre-Bernoullian principle of maximizing the mathematical expectation of money. If we accept this provisionally as valid at least for Bernoulli's "rich man," it would follow that if he were evaluating expectations as he "ought," his presumed indifference between gambles I and II above would imply a probability of winning the 20,000 ducat stake in gamble I equal, "by definition," to $10,000/20,000 = 1/2$. If the event in question were the occurrence of Heads on a toss of a fair coin, presumably he would likewise be indifferent between 10,000 ducats certain and an alternative gamble offering the 20,000 ducats on the occurrence of Trails (not-Heads) on the same toss. This would lead to the measurement of the probability of Tails as $1/2$, supporting the interpretation of these two ratios as probabilities, since: prob(Heads) + prob(Tails) = 1.

The same approach is followed, and greatly elaborated by Bruno de Finetti, in his paper (1931), "La Prevision: ses lois logiques, ses sources subjectives," which had in other respects a strong influence on Savage's work. Like Ramsey and Savage, de Finetti argues that a "quantitative, numerical" measurement of the degree of probability attributed by an individual to a given event is "revealed by the conditions under which he would be disposed to bet on this event"; but he gives a definition of probability equivalent to that of Bayes, assuming (implicitly) that utility is linear on money:

> Let us suppose that an individual should be obliged to evaluate the price p for which he would be disposed to exchange the possession of any sum S whatever (*positive or negative*) conditional on the occurrence of a given event E with the possession of the sum pS; we will say by definition that the number p is the measure of the degree of probability attributed by the individual considered to the event E, or more simply, that p is the probability of E.[1]

Thus, if an individual is indifferent between gambles I and II below, for any S, where the payoffs are in money, de Finetti tells us to define the probability of the event E as p:

	E	Ē
I	S	0
II	pS	pS

Fig. 3.2a

---

[1]Bruno de Finetti, "La Prevision: ses lois logiques, ses sources subjectives," *Annales de l'Institut Henri Poincare*, 7 (1937), p. 6, my translation, italics added.

Likewise, if he is indifferent between gambles III and IV below, for any S, we may measure the probability of $\bar{E}$ as q:

	E	$\bar{E}$
III	0	S
IV	qS	qS

Fig. 3.2b

Though eschewing this definition in the *Foundation of Statistics*, because of the questions it raises concerning utilities, Savage has employed it in a recent exposition of his views, because it is "the most colorful and easy definition to comprehend when one first hears about the subject, and it is easy to employ."

> Let us, to begin with an example, consider what you think about the weight of that chair. There is no trickery; it is the kind of chair it seems to be, and it weighs something. Suppose (overlooking some points of law) that I were to write a contract on a slip of paper promising the bearer 10 dollars if this chair weighs more than 20 pounds and offer the contract up for auction. Why would you bid for it? If you would bid as much as 5 dollars I would say, roughly speaking, that you regard it as at least an even money bet that the chair weighs more than 20 pounds. If you pay just 9 dollars, I would take this as meaning, by definition, that the probability of this event is exactly 9/10 for you. In short, the personal probability of an event for you is the price you would pay for a unit payment to you in case the event actually obtains. In other words, a probability is the price you would pay for a particular contingency.[1]

There are certain things we must ask of this definition, as of any other operational definition of probability: (a) are probabilities well-defined by this method; or is it, for example, necessary to specify the sums of money involved? (b) do the numbers arrived at by this method obey the classical axioms of probability? On both counts, as Savage points out, "There is a little flaw in this definition of personal probability. It collides with the facts of life about large sums of money, that is with utility phenomena."[2]

Both Bayes and de Finetti simply assume that there exists a *fixed* price p for a unit payment staked on E, *whatever* the size of the unit stake; to this assumption, which takes for granted the pre-Bernoulli principle of reasonable behavior, Bernoulli's counterexamples apply with full force.

---

[1] Savage, "Bayesian Statistics," lecture at the Third Symposium on Decision and Information Processes, Purdue University, April 1961 (to be published in *Decision and Information Processes*, Macmillan; pp. 4–5).

[2] *Ibid.*, p. 5.

Even for Bernoulli's "very poor man," a stake of two ducats might be sufficiently small relative to his resources that he would calculate the value of a contingency involving this amount by the traditional rule based on the mathematical expectation of money; he might bid 1 ducat for a stake of 2 ducats contingent on the event: Heads on a single toss of a fair coin. We would then estimate the probability of Heads for him as 1/2, or the same number determined by the rich man's bid of 10,000 ducats for a 20,000 ducat stake on the same event.

But Bernoulli supposes that the pauper might reasonably estimate the value to himself of a risky proposition offering 20,000 ducats on Heads as no higher than 9,000 ducats; i.e., he would be happy to sell it for any greater amount. This would lead, by the above definition, to the assignment of 9/20 as the probability of Heads for him. Moreover, since presumably his choices would not be affected if he were told that the risky proposition paid off on Tails, not on Heads after all, we would assign 9/20 probability to Tails for him. At this point, several shortcomings of the definition would have emerged (aside from any feeling of uneasiness that might be associated with assigning different numbers to the probability of Heads for the rich man and the pauper): 1) it leads us to assign different numbers to the probability of the same event for the pauper, depending upon the size of stake associated with it; probability is not well-defined for him by this method independently of the payoffs; 2) the numbers corresponding to p and q do not "act like probabilities": they do not sum to 1.

If we were measuring the probability of Heads or Tails for Bernoulli's "rich prisoner" by his presumed willingness to pay, say, 12,000 ducats for 20,000 ducat contingent on either, we would find, $p = q = 12/20$, and $p + q = 6/5 > 1$. In either of these cases, the results would be incompatible with the interpretation of the given numbers as probabilities, let alone with their use in calculating moral expectations.

There are two ways in which we could avoid these difficulties and still preserve this straightforward definition, at least in special circumstances. First, if the stakes in question were restricted to amounts so small that you acted "as if" utility were a linear function of money within that range of outcomes, we might derive unambiguous estimates of your probabilities, which could then be applied in calculations involving larger sums. This assumes that there is such a range of outcomes for you. Second, it might be possible to express the payoffs in the gambles not in terms of money but in terms of your "real" von Neumann-Morgenstern utilities, (possibly not linear on money) measured for you by observing your choices among *other* gambles (in which the relevant probabilities were "known").

Thus, when we assumed we "knew" that the probability of Heads was 1/2, we had no difficulty in assigning the utility value 1/2 to 9,000 ducats for Bernoulli's pauper, as the only number simultaneously compatible with: (a) the assumption that he obeys the "Bernoulli proposition" (or postulates implying it); (b) his indifference between 9,000 ducats for certain and 20,000 ducats contingent on Heads; (c) the arbitrary assignment of 1,0 as utilities corresponding to 20,000 ducats and 0 ducats. Likewise, on similar grounds we assigned the utility number $1/2$ to 10,000 ducats for the rich man and 12,000 ducats for the rich prisoner. Now, suppose that we offered each of them a choice between I and II below, where the payoffs are in utilities (so that the money outcome to action II is 9,000, 10,000 or 12,000 for the poor man, rich man or rich prisoner, respectively) and E is some *different* event whose probability has not yet been measured.

	E	E̅
I	1	0
II	$\frac{1}{2}$	$\frac{1}{2}$
III	0	1

Fig. 3.3

For any one of these individuals, indifference between I and II would lead to the measurement, prob(E) $= \frac{1}{2}$, as the only probability number compatible with these premises.

But the question would remain: How did we "know," to start this process off, that the probability of Heads was $1/2$ for these subjects? Frank Ramsey, in his essay on "Truth and Probability" provides a possible answer: a given E may be assigned probability $= 1/2$ for a given individual on the assumption that he obeys the "Bernoulli proposition" in all his choices and the observation that he is indifferent between gambles I and III above, where the arbitrary utility numbers 1 and 0 represent *any* two outcomes a, b, such that a is preferred to b.

Assuming that at least one ("ethically neutral") event can be found such that the individual is indifferent "between betting one way and betting the other for the same stakes," or between staking a given prize "on" or "against" the event, for any prize, then one numerical probability $(1/2)$ can be determined for use in calculating moral expectations. Ramsey then proposes to derive utilities for outcomes other than the initial a, b by observing choices among gambles with other outcomes involving the event E, prob (E) $= 1/2$; just as we found, e.g., the utility of 9,000 ducats for the pauper earlier. On the basis of this utility scale, based upon actual, observed choices (assuming the choices to be consistent with the existence of such a scale), we could end by assigning, on the basis of *other* observed choices, numerical probabilities other than $1/2$ to other events.[1]

---

[1]Ramsey, *op. cit.*, pp. 177–182.

Without assuming that a reasonable individual will obey the "Bernoulli proposition" in all his choices, and hence without conceding that the above measurement of prob(E) = 1/2 would be appropriate with respect to *every* event E for which he might be indifferent between I and III above, it is possible to assume that there is *some* event E such that (1) a reasonable individual will be indifferent between I and III above, for any money stake, and (2) he chooses consistently with the "Bernoulli proposition" in all his choices among gambles in which that event or its complement are the only relevant events. Those assumptions would imply that for any individual under discussion it should be possible to measure his "von Neumann-Morgenstern utilities" for all outcomes, even though we knew his subjective probability for only one event.[1]

Without making it part of the *definition* of "reasonableness," let us assume henceforth that these assumptions are valid for any of the reasonable individual under discussion: i.e., for "you" (and me). This amounts to assuming that the "Bernoulli proposition," the von Neumann-Morgenstern axioms, the Ramsey-Savage postulates, or equivalent hypotheses, are satisfied *at least* by your choices among some large set of gambles, involving any outcomes and certain events (at least, one particular event and its complement). It will simplify a good deal of the discussion, and help us to focus upon the problems of uncertain opinion (rather than values) that are our major concern, if we thus assume that we *can* always express payoffs in the form of "von Neumann-Morgenstern utilities" for a given individual. No conclusions will depend upon this assumption, but it is not incompatible with any conclusions I shall propose; nor do I believe it to be unrealistic.

From now on, then, we shall assume that it is always possible to express payoffs in terms of numbers such that your pattern of preferences and indifferences among given gambles will be unaffected if the number u_{ij} corresponding to each outcome is subjected to the transformation, $a \cdot u_{ij} + b$, $a > 0$. In special cases—typically, when money outcomes are small—money outcomes may be one of the appropriate scales of utility for you; i.e., utility may be a linear function of money. But, instead of simply assuming this to be true in the fashion of Bayes or de Finetti, we shall suppose any such assertion to be based upon observation of your choices among gambles in circumstances under which you *did* obey the "Bernoulli proposition."

We can now represent the definitions cited above by Bayes, de Finetti and Savage, in terms of the following choices, where the payoffs are "von Neumann-Morgenstern utilities":

---

[1]The experimental measurement of utilities by Suppes, Davidson and Siegel, reported in *Decision Making*, follows this schema, first suggested by Ramsey: discovery of a single event with probability $= \frac{1}{2}$, by Ramsey's test; measurement of utilities; measurement of other probabilities.

	E	$\bar{E}$
I	1	0
II	p_o	p_o
III	0	1
IV	q_o	q_o

Fig. 3.4a

The amount, say, of money corresponding to the payoff 1 above may be 1,000 ducats, or $10, or 1 shilling, with some smaller amount corresponding to the payoff 0. The number corresponding to any other outcome represents its "von Neumann-Morgenstern utility" for you in a utility scale corresponding to the first two, arbitrary assignments; it is presumed that there exists *some* event with respect to which you obey the "Bernoulli proposition," and that in gambles in which the given outcome is staked upon that event you act "as if" you assigned to it the given utility number. Thus, if you are indifferent between actions I and II above, you will be assumed to be indifferent between V and VI below, and between VII and VIII; since the payoffs to any one pair are related to those of another by an increasing linear transformation:

	E	$\bar{E}$
V	0	-1
VI	p_o^{-1}	p_o^{-1}
VII	10	0
VIII	$10p_o$	$10p_o$

Fig. 3.4b

If these actions were all offered as alternatives, the same utility function over outcomes would be presumed for all; the differences among outcomes would be such as to be represented by the "von Neumann-Morgenstern utilities" shown (thus, the amount of money represented by $10p_o$ might be more or less than 10 times the amount of money represented by p_o). But if one pair were offered in isolation, we could not tell from the payoffs alone whether this were the case or whether, the objective outcomes being the same as in another pair of actions, the scale and/or origin of the utility function had been changed.

For a given individual, a given utility function, and a given event E, p_o is to be understood as the *largest* payoff such that he will not prefer II to I. Let us assume that when the payoff to action II is exactly p_o the individual is indifferent between II and I. In Savage's terms (but with payoffs now in utilities—which *may* correspond to money outcomes, especially if the stakes are small), p_0 is "the price you would pay for a unit payment to you in case the event actually obtains." Likewise, q_0 is the largest payoff such that the same individual does not prefer IV to III, the maximum price he would pay for a unit payment in case the event E does *not* obtain (a unit payment contingent on not-E).

Now, assuming that these numbers do represent "von Neumann-Morgenstern utilities" for you, it is clear that the only probability numbers for E and $\bar{E}$ compatible with the assumption that you obey the "Bernoulli proposition" are, in the light of these preferences: $prob(E) = p_0$, $prob(\bar{E}) = q_0$. But while the assignment of numbers in this case follows tautologically from the latter assumption, that assumption itself is far from tautological. Whether or not the numbers so assigned to a large set of events *are* "probabilities" in the sense of obeying the classical axioms of probability is an empirically meaningful question, the answer depending upon whether or not you do conform, in all your choices, to the "Bernoulli proposition."

It is useful to consider separately two questions on these properties. Is it true that: (1) $prob(E) + prob(\bar{E}) = 1$ for every event E (i.e., will $p_0 = 1 - q_0$, as defined above, for every E); and is it true that (2) for every set of mutually exclusive events, E, F, . . . G, $prob(E \text{ or } F \text{ or } . . . G) = prob(E) + prob(F) + . . . prob(G)$? The first property is a necessary but not sufficient condition for the second.

If conditions can be stated, and fulfilled, for which both these questions can be answered "Yes"—for a certain class of events E—then the Bayes/de Finetti/Savage definitions cited above will have led, at least for those events under the given conditions, to a meaningful, quantitative measurement of opinions, or degrees of belief, in the form of numerical probabilities. One meaningful answer will have been supplied to the query: How to compute numbers suitable for the calculation of moral expectations?

As we have already indicated, both the above questions *will* be answered "Yes" *for all events* if one's "von Neumann-Morgenstern utilities" are known and the "Bernoulli proposition" is assumed satisfied. But none of the writers on the subject in this century have been content simply to take, for example, adherence to the "Bernoulli proposition" as a primitive, self-evident condition of reasonable behavior.

"COHERENCE" AND "DEFINITENESS" OF PROBABILITY-PRICES

Two, basically different lines of argument have been proposed to justify the belief that observation (in particular, self-observation) of "reasonable" betting behavior will lead to consistent measurements of a unique probability distribution over *all* events for a given person. The Ramsey/Savage postulates represent an approach which, unlike the definitions above, has the advantage of making no initial assumptions about utilities; we shall consider them in the following chapter. The second approach, initially presented in detail by Bruno de Finetti, supports the definitions discussed above; it requires assumptions about utilities but, as Savage has recently commented, it "seems much easier to apply introspectively."[1]

Although both of these approaches purport to specify conditions of reasonable behavior in general, which have the effect of ensuring that numerical probabilities can be assigned uniquely to *all* events for a reasonable individual, it is useful to interpret these conditions of choice as defining circumstances under which probabilities *can* meaningfully be assigned to *some* events, without committing ourselves in advance to the assumption that these conditions will always be satisfied with respect to every event. We can then begin to consider circumstances in which, though the conditions implied above are violated, it is possible to give quantitative expression (in the form of numerical *boundaries*) to opinions, or degrees of belief, which cannot be assigned definite numerical probabilities on the basis of observed betting behavior.

The de Finetti approach continues along the lines of regarding probability as a "price" (for purposes of measurement), but without reliance upon the explicit assumption that you obey the "Bernoulli proposition." Instead, two separate assumptions guarantee that the observed betting ratios will satisfy the two properties listed above and will correspond in general to a unique probability measure.

The first is contained in his definition of the degree of probability, cited earlier; it is the requirement that the price p at which one is indifferent between possession of the sum pS and the possession of a gamble offering S contingent on event E, be constant for any S *positive or negative*. This does not follow merely from the assumption that S is expressed in terms of "von Neumann-Morgenstern utility," since it is understood that the payoff if E does not occur remains fixed at O as S varies. If S, interpreted as a utility payoff, were positive initially, p_oS should be a fixed ratio of S for any positive S, the other payoff remaining O; but a negative number for S contingent on E, with O payoff to not-E (the *order* of these payoffs thus changing) could

---

[1]L. J. Savage, "Subjective Probability and Statistical Practice," SRC-910235I4, University of Chicago, mimeographed; to be published in 1962 in *The Foundations of Statistical Inference*, L. J. Savage and others, Methuen, London. For expository reasons, Savage has actually relied upon the definition of personal probabilities in terms of "prices of gambles" or betting odds, and justification in terms of "coherence"— i.e., the de Finetti approach—in his recent writings rather than the approach he used in *The Foundations of Statistics*, though referring to the latter for resolution of problems associated with utilities. (See, for example: "The Subjective Basis of Statistical Practice," University of Michigan, July 1961; "Bayesian Statistics," which contains the passage already quoted on probability as the "price of a contingency.")

never be obtained by a transformation $a \cdot U + b$ with a positive. In other words, action V below could not be obtained from action I merely by a change in origin or scale of the utility function. Having defined p_0 (the payoff to action II, where II is indifferent to I) as the value to you of gamble I, let us *define* p^o as the payoff for which action V is indifferent to action VI below:

	E	$\bar{E}$
I	1	0
II	p_0	p_0
III	0	1
IV	q_0	q_0
V	-1	0
VI	$-p^o$	$-p^o$

Fig. 3.5

    If we take the origin of the utility scale arbitrarily to correspond to the "no bet" or "status quo" outcome, then negative payoffs represent required *payments* by you. In any case, as noted above, it does not follow from the assumption that these payoffs represent your "von Neumann-Morgenstern utilities" that indifference between I and II and between V and VI implies $p_0 = p^o$. What the assumption on utility *does* imply is that $-p^o = q_0 - 1$; or, $p^o + q_0 = 1$. This follows from the relation between the payoffs for the pair V, VI and the pair III, IV; the payoffs for these two pairs *are* related by an "admissible" transformation of the utility function, i.e., a transformation that does not affect preference or indifference between actions. The payoffs to action V represent the payoffs to action III "shifted downwards by one unit," i.e., with one unit subtracted from each payoffs: in effect, a translation or shift in origin of the utility scale upwards by one unit. Therefore, if VI is indifferent to V, the payoff to VI, $-p^o$, must be equivalent in value to the payoff to IV shifted downwards one unit: $-p^o = q_0 - 1$, or $p^o = 1 - q_0$.

    De Finetti's definition contains the implicit *assumption* that $p_0 = p^o$. This *implies* that $p_0 = 1 + q_0 = 1$. To repeat, the assumption is not contained in the (weaker) assumption that p_0 is constant for any *positive* utility sum S, or that $-p^o$ is constant for any *negative* utility sum $-S$, or in de Finetti's other assumption that utility is an increasing linear transformation or money. Nor is the assumption that $p_0 = p^o$ derived in any way, by those writers that make explicit and essential use of it,[1] from more fundamental (or more intuitively plausible) assumptions.

---

[1] See Abner Shimony, "Coherence and the Axioms of Confirmation," *Journal of Symbolic Logic*, Vol. 20, No. 1, March 1955, p. 7 ("for ease in mathematical considerations, S is allowed to be either positive or negative"); R. Sherman Lehmann,

Before arguing with the general applicability of this assumption, it is important to see clearly its significance in situations when it *does* apply. When action I is indifferent to II, and III is indifferent to IV, respectively, and these preferences are maintained for any increasing linear transformation of the payoff function (so that III indifferent to IV implies V indifferent to VI), then p_o, q_o and p^o ($= 1 - q_o$) are well-defined utility values. *If it is true* that $p_o + q_o = 1$ (so that $p_o = p^o$), then the only probability numbers satisfying the "Bernoulli propositions," given these preferences, are $\text{prob}(E) = p_o = p^o$ and $\text{prob}(\bar{E}) = q_o = 1 - p_o$. In other words, when these preferences occur—and there is no general reason why they should *not* (occasionally, or frequently) be observed—there is a solid basis for the assignment of a definite number, $p = p_o = p^o$, as representing the magnitude or "your" degree of belief in the occurrence of the event (truth of the proposition) E. The statement "your degree of belief in E is p" conveys, in these circumstances, a definite operational meaning as to your betting behavior, or the value to you of (the maximum price you will pay for) gambles such as I, III or V.

The intuitive justification of calling p, under these circumstances, a *definite* degree of belief same clear; a more technical definition of "definite" will be introduced later. "Indefiniteness" of your degree of belief could be associated with $p_o \neq p^o$, i.e., $p_o \neq 1 - q_o$. The explicit assumption ruling this inequality out as a possibility for reasonable behavior seems fairly gratuitous; at least, I cannot see that it has any direct intuitive appeal, although it would follow as a theorem from the Savage postulates (discussed in the next chapter).

It is possible, on the other hand, to develop a theory of statistical inference and decision, making important use of the notion of personal probability as defined and measured by betting behavior, *without* assuming the existence of a definite numerical degree of belief, corresponding to $p_o = 1 - q_o$, for *every* event. The recent, highly significant paper by C. A. B. Smith already cited, "Consistency in Statistical Inference and Decision," goes far toward

---

"On Confirmation and Rational Betting," *Journal of Symbolic Logic*, Vol. 20, No. 3, September 1955, p. 253; John G. Kemeny, "Fair Bets and Inductive Probabilities," *Journal of Symbolic Logic*, Vol. 20, No. 3, September 1955, p. 267 (Kemeny assumes directly that $p_o = 1 - q_o$).

These writers all derive measures of "degree of confirmation" equivalent to determinate subjective probabilities for propositions, following the argument of de Finetti (which is suggested by Ramsey, *op. cit.*, pp. 180, 182–183, in effect as an alternative to his axiomatic approach). The crucial role of the above assumption—and its lack of explicit justification—in all these expositions is pointed out by Cedric A. B. Smith in "Consistency in Statistical Inference and Decision," *Journal of the Royal Statistical Society*, Series B, Vol. 23, No. 1, 1961, pp. 6, 9.

developing just such an approach: which shall also be our present goal. Smith "accepts" and analyzes (without specifically "rationalizing") certain patterns of behavior which will be the focus of our attention in subsequent chapters; and he introduces concepts highly useful for describing them.

Smith's exposition is mainly in terms of acceptable betting odds rather than prices of contingencies offering a unit stake, but since these notions are isomorphic, propositions on p_o and $p^o = 1 - q_o$ follow immediately from his discussion. He neither assumes, implies, nor argues that *equality* must hold in every case between p_o and p^o; in contrast to de Finetti, Ramsey, Shimony, Lehmann and Kemeny, "this seems a more definite expression of opinion than I would be prepared to make."[1] Smith explicitly allows the possibility that a reasonable man may set prices for contingent stakes on certain events such that $p_o + q_o < 1$, so that $p_o < p^o$ $(=1 - q_o)$.

From this point of view, $p_o = p^o = 1 - q_o$ is still possible as a special case, in which the common value may be designated prob(E) and interpreted as a definite numerical probability. But in general your degree of belief concerning E must be represented by *two* numbers, $p_o(E)$ and $p^o(E)$. The fact that (on an argument discussed below) $p_o(E) \leq p^o(E)$ justifies the terms, "lower" and "upper" "betting probabilities" respectively. Since the two numbers cannot be presumed in general to be equal, it would be necessary in every case to make an absolute minimum of *two* observations (or for you to ask yourself a minimum of two questions) concerning a given event, one concerning the price you would pay for a unit stake *on* the event and one as to the price you would pay for a unit staked *against* the event. The latter establishes q_o, hence p^o $(= 1 - q_o)$.

If the "Bernoulli proposition" were obeyed in every case (or the various sorts of assumptions implying it) there would be no need to measure q_o, since it would be determined by p_o $(= 1 - q_o)$; in principle, a single observation, determining p_o, would be sufficient to determine all your betting behavior concerning bets *on or against* that event. This is the result assumed or implied by Bayes, de Finetti, Ramsey and Savage. Under Smith's assumptions, prediction/prescription of all such bets would likewise be possible, but *two* independent measurements would be necessary for each event, as specified above.

Smith does use an argument, one that is central to de Finetti's exposition and mentioned by Ramsey, which has the effect of ruling out $p_o + q_o > 1$ as unreasonable (thus requiring that $p_o + q_o \leq 1$, $p_o \leq p^o$). This argument involves the notion of "coherence" of a system of betting odds or announced prices for contingencies. After assuming, in effect, that a definite numerical degree of belief $p = p_o = p^o$ is assigned by a reasonable individual to every event, de Finetti expresses the requirement of "coherence" as follows:

---

[1]Smith, *op. cit.*, p. 6.

When an individual has evaluated the probabilities of certain events, two cases can occur: either it is possible to place bets with him in such a way as to assure oneself of winning in any event [i.e., to ensure that *he* will suffer a net loss whatever event occurs]; or this possibility does not exist. In the first case one must say, obviously, that the evaluation of probability given by this individual contains an incoherence, an intrinsic contradiction; in the other case, we will say that the individual is coherent. It is precisely this condition of *coherence* which constitutes the sole principle from which one could deduce the whole calculus of probabilities; this calculus then appears as the ensemble of rules to which the subjective evaluation of the probabilities of different events by the same individual must be subjected if one does not wish there to be a fundamental contradiction among them.[1]

On the *assumption* (not emphasized by de Finetti) that $p_o = 1 - q_o$ for *each* event E, de Finetti demonstrates that the requirement that these *definite* degrees of belief be *coherent* implies that they must obey strictly the classical axioms of probability.[2] However, what is of interest here is the effect of the latter requirement in the absence of the former assumption. As Smith demonstrates, the requirement of "coherence" by itself implies, with respect to p_o and q_o as we have defined them, only that $p_o + q_o \leq 1$.

The nature of the argument can be seen clearly in terms of our example. Suppose that you announce you are willing to pay "up to" a utility value p_o for the gamble above (a stake of 1 unit contingent on E), and that you are willing to pay up to q_o for gamble III above (a stake of 1 contingent on $\bar{E}$). Arguments based on the notion of "coherence" contain, implicitly (except for Smith's discussion), the special, additional assumption that under these circumstances you will be willing to pay *both* prices, i.e., the sum $p_o + q_o$, to possess both gambles simultaneously. Assuming this to be true, let us suppose that $p_o + q_o > 1$. Then a "cunning better," as Ramsey puts it, could "make a book against you"; he could offer you a set of bets, each of which would be acceptable to you according to your announced offers, but which together would assure you of a net loss no matter what event occurred.

---

[1] de Finetti, *op. cit.*, p. 7; my translation. For an extensive discussion of the "coherence" argument, its relation to "definiteness," and its expression in terms of *odds*, see Appendix to this chapter.

[2] *Ibid.*; see also demonstrations in the papers cited by Lehmann and Shimony; Smith, who alone emphasizes the crucial role of *both* assumptions, derives this result for (what he considers) the special case in which they both apply, *op. cit.*, pp. 6–12.

Specifically, he could offer you gamble I at the price p_o and gamble III at the price q_o. For this combination of gambles you would pay $p_o + q_o > 1$; if E occurred you would receive the stake of 1 unit, and likewise if $\bar{E}$ occurred. Thus, "in either event" you would *lose* the amount $p_o + q_o - 1 > 0$. As Smith puts it, you "will be a fool to allow this."[1] If you are to avoid it, while remaining willing to accept any combination of bets at stated prices (a requirement whose compelling nature is not intuitively obvious to me), you must adjust your announced prices so that $p_o + q_o \leq 1$.

On the other hand, the coherence requirement does not rule out the possibility that $p_o + q_o < 1$; i.e., that $p_o < 1 - q_o = p^o$. For suppose that this is the case. It would not be remarkably cunning for an opponent to force gambles I and III upon you at these prices (the highest you will pay), since he would then be committed to pay you 1 "in any event," for a certain net *loss* of $1 - p_o - q_o > 0$. In other words, he could only succeed in *making a book against himself.*

If we accept the cogency of the coherence requirement, then, we can assume that for a reasonable bettor, $p_o \leq p^o$ ($= 1 - q_o$) for every event, justifying the names, "lower" and "upper" "betting probabilities" for p_o (E), $p^o(E)$[2] respectively. If, furthermore, p_o strictly less than p^o were accepted as reasonable—as Smith's discussion suggests it might be—we could represent one's degree of belief in a certain proposition or event in general by an interval of numbers between 0 and 1, with "definite" degrees of belief ($p_o = p^o$) being represented by unique points.

A system of degrees of belief defined in terms of intervals, some of positive length, would not determine a simple ordering of events in terms of probability (i.e., a qualitative probability relationship $\leq \cdot$), since intervals might overlap, or one might even enclose another. In such cases, particularly the latter, it would be impossible to say without ambiguity, in terms of this definition alone, either that one of the two events was "more probable than" the other, "less probable," or "equally probable." Yet a *partial ordering* of events (transitive but not connected) *in terms of probability* would still be possible; e.g., even when the degree of belief in neither of two events is "definite," the "upper betting probability" of one might be lower than the "lower betting probability" of the other. Moreover, one could postulate the existence of a complete ordering of events in terms of "lower betting probabilities," and *another* in terms of "upper betting probabilities." Neither of these orderings would correspond to a qualitative probability relationship $\leq \cdot$, since neither lower nor upper betting probabilities "combine" for unions of events in the strictly additive fashion required of

---

[1] Smith, *op. cit.*, p. 5; Ramsey, *op. cit.*, p. 182.

[2] Smith suggests, instead, the term "lower and upper *picnic* probability" (from Latin, *pignus* = bet), op. cit., p. 5. I do not think this will catch on.

numerical probabilities; but under certain conditions, very similar laws of combination can be stated for them, based on inequalities rather than equalities.[1] The attractiveness of such a *system of partially ordered intervals as a mathematical model for a subjective system of degrees of belief some of which are "indefinite"* (as opposed to a model consisting of the real *numbers* between 0 and 1) may be immediately evident, though we shall postpone a detailed exploration.

We shall return to this subject after discussing further counter-examples to the Savage postulates and introducing the closely-similar concept of "upper and lower intuitive probabilities" discussed by Koopman and Good. But this brief discussion may have suggested one way in which the notion of degrees of belief that are *within limits* "indefinite" might be given fairly precise operational meaning. After examining it in the light of the Savage postulates and other criteria, we may or may not conclude that behavior leading to differential "upper" and "lower" betting probabilities in the Smith sense is "reasonable"; but we have already seen that it can be orderly, predictable and describable, *consistent with the existence of a meaningful, von Neumann-Morgenstern* utility function (since the utility axioms, which are applicable with respect to "definite" degrees of belief, do not suffice to rule out "indefiniteness" behavior with respect to all events), and need not expose the individual to the risk that someone can, in an *objective* sense, "make a fool of him" by making a book against him.

The "indefiniteness" implicit here is to be distinguished from a sort of "vagueness" frequently mentioned by Savage. In his discussion, cited above, of personal probability as the price of a contingency, Savage points out that it cannot really be determined precisely by you, *any more than any other price:* "Who can say exactly what he would give or take for a particular contingency?"[2] This is to say that when you ask yourself the exact, maximum price p_0 you would pay for a unit stake contingent on E, there is bound to be a certain degree of arbitrariness in any precise answer; this might show up in indecision between two very close estimates, or in some shifting between them on separate occasions. Likewise for your estimate of q_0. Thus, even with the most "definite" degree of belief, there might in practice be some discrepancy between your initial estimates of p_0 and $1 - q_0$.

However, it is implicit in the de Finetti/Ramsey/Savage discussions that in such cases there should be *acceptable* estimates both of p_0 and q_0 (i.e., estimates within the haze of "fuzziness" or "vagueness" surrounding each price) such that $p_0 + q_0 = 1$. The behavior suggested by Smith, and exhibited in connection with the counterexamples to be discussed, may have a character quite distinct from this, such that no such values of p_0 or q_0 may

---

[1] See Smith, *op. cit.*, pp. 6–12; and Appendix to this chapter.
[2] Savage, "Bayesian Statistics," p. 5.

exist, within the fuzzy range of prices all of which may seem "approximately acceptable"; it may be that $p_o < 1 - q_o = p^o$ for *any* values acceptable to you. In terms of Savage's example (assuming utility linear on money), you might not be able to say exactly the most that you would pay for a stake of $10 contingent on E's occurring; but you might feel quite sure that $5 was too much, and at the same time feel quite sure that $5 was too much to pay for the same stake contingent on E's *not* occurring. This would imply p_o "definitely" $< 1/2$. Thus, the following comment by Savage, referring explicitly to Smith's work, seems to miss a vital point:

> Some of the ideas that have been invoked [to "give a realistic account of *vagueness and indecision*"] are those of partial order and of unknown probabilities. One defect of some theories is that in an effort to provide a *zone of indecision* they create a zone with sharp edges. . . These are at least as objectionable as the unrealistic sharpness that the modified theory is supposed to remove.[1]

If p_o (E) or q_o (E) have been treated in our discussion as "sharply" estimated or known, that is, of course, an idealization of reality. But the "zone of indefiniteness" that is implied by Smith's approach and by my counterexample discussed above is quite distinguishable, both conceptually and behaviorally, from any "zone of indecision" surrounding the *edges* of the former zone.

To put this another way, you might feel quite sure that, so far as the maximum bids you were prepared to make were concerned, $p_o(A)$ was for you distinctly lower than $p_o(B)$, and $p^o(A)$ (= $1 - q_o$ (A)) distinctly higher than $p^o(B)$ (= $1 - q_o$ (B)), even though you could determine none of these values precisely in your own self-interrogation. In other words, you might be able to say *definitely* that the upper and lower betting probabilities for event A enclosed those for event B (we might say: the "range of indefiniteness" was distinctly greater for A than for B) even though you definitely could not compare "the probability" of A to that of B nor even determine

---

[1] Savage, "The Subjective Basis of Statistical Practice," p. 2.14 (italics added). I shall comment later on the implications of the fact that Savage virtually always links "vagueness" and "indecision" in his discussion; in other words, he suggests that "vagueness" is associated with violations of Postulate 1, complete ordering of actions. The phenomenon in which I am interested, and which I believe Smith is considering, seems to me to be associated with violations of Postulate 2, the Sure-Thing Principle, not *necessarily* with indecision, intransitivities, or inconsistencies on repeated trials. We shall consider this problem at length below; I am not sure that Smith would agree with me in every case on this matter, but I believe that he would in this context.

exactly the boundary-values of probability for either. And you might make choices, in choosing among gambles involving both A and B, that definitely violated Postulate 2, whether or not your "vagueness" concerning the exact values of $p_o(A)$ and $p_o(B)$ resulted in "indecision" (i.e., violations of the postulate of complete ordering of actions).

If such patterns of decision are, on the contrary, to be rejected as unreasonable, this cannot be on the grounds of the "coherence" requirement alone, nor (I conjecture) *by any comparably "objective" argument*. In fact, there would seem to be no way to justify a *general* requirement that $p_o = 1 - q_o = p^o$ (i.e., that all degrees of belief be "definite") unless it can be derived from introspective standards of "consistency" that have claims to general acceptability.[1] The postulates of choice in Savage's *Foundations of Statistics,* to which we turn in the next chapter, offer themselves in this light; and they have this consequence.

---

[1] And it would seem, upon grounds that bear a closer intuitive relationship to "reasonableness" than the requirement laid down by de Finetti, Shimony, and Lehmann, that pS be constant for any S positive or negative.

J. G. Kemeny, in "Fair Bets and Inductive Probabilities" (*Journal of Symbolic Logic,* Vol. 20, No. 3, September 1955) takes an approach which does lead to a justification of this requirement; but at the price of introducing, it seems to me, criteria that bear no direct relation to "reasonableness" in decision-making. He concentrates upon the concept of "fairness" in betting, an interest which he attributes— mistakenly, I believe—to these other authors ("The question of what constitutes fairness in betting quotients has been studied by Ramsey, de Finetti, and Shimony. Thanks to their combined efforts we now have a satisfactory definition of fairness. . . . The term 'coherent' is used by previous authors for what is here described as 'fair' or 'strictly fair.' The present terminology is preferred because it is more suggestive . . .," *op. cit.,* p. 263, 264n.). (See Appendix for further discussion of their approach.)

He describes a set of betting quotients as *fair* if there is no betting system which will guarantee a profit; it is clear from his analysis that this requirement implies that *neither* of two players betting with each other should be able to make a book against the other. "The condition of fairness is violated if some betting system assures the gambler that, no matter what actually happens, he will *profit,*" (p. 264; my italics). This assertion shows clearly the actual gulf between Kemeny's requirement of "fairness" and the requirement of "coherence" that we have been discussing, which specifies that the reasonable gambler must not expose himself to certain *loss;* it is scarcely in the spirit of the latter approach to forbid him any opportunity to guarantee himself a *profit.*

The investigation of the conditions of "fairness," in Kemeny's traditional sense, is interesting in itself; in fact, this notion was prominent in the *pre-Bernoullian* analyses that led to concentration upon the principle of maximizing the mathematical

Appendix to Chapter 3

ON MAKING A FOOL OF ONESELF: THE REQUIREMENT OF COHERENCE

ALTHOUGH HE DOES not mention the notion of "coherence" in *The Foundations of Statistics,* Savage has come to rely upon it heavily in more recent expositions:

> It isn't quite the opinions of just anybody that make probabilities. When we theorize about probabilities, we theorize about a coherent person. By a coherent person I mean pretty much a person who does not allow a book to be made against him, a person such that if you offer him various contingencies you can not, by some sleight of hand, sell him such a bill of goods that he will be paying you money no matter what happens.

> Should you offer 5 dollars for this contingency, 6 for that, 3 for the other, and so on in such concatenation that when all the chips are down you will have to pay me something, net, no matter what happens, then you have made a mistake. Of course, real people do make mistakes. We make mistakes all the time; we can not hope to avoid them entirely. We can, however, deplore mistakes and try to hold them to a minimum. So we look into the conditions of coherency for a system of probabilities. By a system

---

expectation of money, as does Kemeny's own analysis (see Bernoulli, *op. cit.,* pp. 23–24). But such considerations have nothing to do with the motivations or the decision procedures of either of the players individually. Kemeny seems not to notice the difference in focus between his approach and that of the other authors he cites. "Whatever else reasonableness may imply, it certainly implies fairness" (p. 264). Surely not! However one might choose to stigmatize the gambler who permits himself to make a book against an opponent, "unreasonable" does not seem the *mot juste.*

of probabilities I mean what you would offer for all contingencies under discussion in a given context.

Easy theories show that if you are consistent, your probability function, the probability that you associate with each event, is a mathematical probability in the ordinary sense. That is, the probability is nonnegative, the probability that two and two make four is 1. The probability that one of two mutually incompatible events will occur is the sum of the two probabilities. . . .

You now have the bare bones of the theory of personal probability. It pertains to events and to an idealized, or coherent person. Nothing in the theory says that all coherent people are the same, but it does say that there are certain rules, breach of which is incoherence. And presumably you don't want to be incoherent. I don't.[1]

I have cited these comments at length because they are typical of a number of passages by various authors which give a considerably misleading impression of the strength of the coherence assumption *by itself.* The statement by de Finetti, cited above, that "It is precisely this condition of *coherence* which constitutes the sole principle from which one could deduce the whole calculus of probabilities;" is a prime example of this tendency.[2] As a matter of fact, even when we grant the various special assumptions that are necessary to make the notion of coherence at all meaningful and sensible, it is *not true* that a requirement that the system of announced "betting prices" be coherent is enough in itself to guarantee that these betting prices correspond to *definite* degrees of belief: i.e., that $p_o + q_o = 1$ for any given event E. The latter result must be given as an independent assumption, or implied by other fundamental assumptions independent of the notion of coherence; as Smith's discussion demonstrates (and our later discussion will corroborate), it cannot be taken for granted as a self-evident or inescapable condition of reasonable behavior.

---

[1] Savage, "Bayesian Statistics," pp. 7, 9.

[2] de Finetti, *op. cit.,* p. 7; my translation. See also papers cited by Shimony and Lehman.. Similarly, see Savage: "The theory of subjective probability is only a theory of coherence. . .," ("The Subjective Basis of Statistical Practice," p. 4.29); "Roughly speaking, it can be shown that such a probability structure Pr, and one only, exists for every person who behaves coherently in that he is not prepared to make a combination of bets that is sure to lose" ("Subjective Probability and Statistical Practice," p. 5).

Although both conditions are *implied* by the Ramsey/Savage postulates, either one by itself rules out certain types of behavior violating those postulates but not others. Thus, it is distinctly possible to satisfy the requirement of "coherence" alone (for what that is worth; I will question its cogency later) while violating, for example, Savage's Postulate 2, the Sure-Thing Principle: thus preventing the inference even of an unambiguous *ordering* of all events in terms of probability, on the basis of observed choices. In the light of such possibilities, one must guard against the natural tendency to read into statements such as those quoted above hints that the "theory of personal probability" consists *solely* of "rules, breach of which is incoherence," or that "the whole calculus of probabilities" can be deduced from the "sole principle" of coherence, or that, in effect, adherence to the "Bernoulli proposition" is not only sufficient but also *necessary* for "coherence." Any such inference would be invalid.

The distinction between these two conditions, of "definiteness" and "coherence," appears clearly in Ramsey's discussion (from which I have drawn the concept of "definiteness"). Having deduced the classical laws of probability as a consequence of his definitions and axioms, he comments:

> Any *definite* set of degrees of belief which broke them would be inconsistent in the sense that it violated the law of preference between options. . . . If anyone's mental condition violated these laws, . . . he could have a book made against him by a cunning better and would then stand to lose in any event. . . .

> Having any *definite* degree of belief implies a certain measure of consistency, namely willingness to bet on a given proposition at the same odds for any stake [i.e., positive or negative], the stakes being measured in terms of ultimate values. Having degrees of belief obeying the laws of probability implies a *further* measure of consistency, namely such a consistency between the odds acceptable on different propositions as shall prevent a book being made against you.[1]

The relation between these two sorts of consistency requirements can be seen in terms of my example from the previous chapter, concerning an urn known to contain 30 Red balls and 60 Yellow or Black balls in undisclosed proportion, one ball to be drawn from the urn. Instead of asking you to state preferences between pairs of actions, we might use the maximum "price" you would pay for each action, considered *separately* (assuming that we, or you, have previously measured your "von Neumann-Morgenstern utility function").

---

[1]Ramsey, *op. cit.*, pp. 182–183; italics added.

Fig. 3.6

	30	60			(a)	(b)	(c)	(d)
	Red	Yellow	Black					
I	1	0	0	$p_o(R)=$	1/3	1/3	1/3	1/3
II	0	1	0	$p_o(Y)=$	5/12	1/6	1/3	1/6
III	0	0	1	$p_o(B)=$	5/12	1/6	1/3	1/6
IV	1	1	0	$q_o(B)=$	5/6	5/6	2/3	1/2
V	1	0	1	$q_o(Y)=$	5/6	5/6	2/3	1/2
VI	0	1	1	$q_o(R)=$	2/3	2/3	2/3	2/3

The four columns on the right indicate four sets of hypothetical "bids" that you might make for these individual gambles (let us assume, for reasons that will be discussed later, that you make these bids sequentially, without foreknowledge of the full set of gambles on which you will be asked to bid). It is assumed in all four cases that you assign, in effect, a "definite" probability = 1/3 to the drawing of a Red ball, and that your bids for a unit staked on Yellow or on Black (or on not-Yellow and not-Black) are equivalent.

The first two columns (a) and (b) represent "incoherent" sets of "bids," though in the second column (b) all degrees of belief shown are "definite." The sets of bids in the second two columns (c) and (d) are "coherent," though only those in (c) represent "definite" degrees of belief.

By the assumptions underlying the notion of "coherence," if you announced the set of "bids" (a), an "opponent" could sell you gambles I, II and III together, for the combined price of 14/12; he would have to pay you 1 whichever color were drawn from the urn, so that you would be certain to suffer a net loss of 1/6 "in any event."

Case (b) illustrates the fact that if all of your degrees of belief are "definite" ($p_o = 1 - q_o$) but they do not obey the axioms of probability, your system of degrees of belief will be "incoherent." In this particular case, your opponent could make no profit off you by offering you I, II and III together, but by selling you IV, V and VI at a combined price of 14/6, he would assure himself a profit (and you a loss) of 1/3, since he would pay out only 2 whichever event occurred. If all your degrees of belief are "definite" in terms of Ramsey's first measure of consistency, $p_o = 1 - q_o$, then the additional requirement that it be impossible to "make a book against you" implies that these numbers must satisfy the laws of probability; e.g., in this case, it must be true that prob(Red) + prob(Yellow) + prob(Black) = 1. Given, in this case, prob(Red) = 1/3 and prob(Yellow) = prob(Black), this means that the two conditions together dictate the unique set of "bids" in column (c).

However, the "coherence" requirement alone does not dictate the set (c), nor any other set having the characteristics of a probability distribution, if the requirement is dropped that $p_o + q_o = 1$. Thus, the pattern of bids in column (d) is "coherent" although it does not imply "definite" degrees of belief for Yellow or Black. It would not be terribly cunning for your opponent in this case to force you to accept gambles I, II and III together at your announced combined price of 2/3, since *he* would then end up with a net loss of 1/3 whichever event occurred; he would have allowed you to make a book against *him*. Likewise, if he forced IV, V and VI together on you, for 5/3, thereby committing himself to pay out 2 in any event. No other combination is any more promising for him; he cannot make a book against you at these announced prices.

The set of bids in case (d), of course, corresponds exactly to the pattern of preferences among gambles of those individuals who would (like myself) prefer gamble I to II if that were the only pair offered, and IV to III, if that pair were offered instead.[1] It is of interest to see here that such a pattern of bids is not ruled out by the requirement of "coherence." We have already seen that such preferences *do* violate other proposed criteria of reasonable choice, e.g., Savage's Postulate 2, the Sure-Thing Principle; the Savage postulates thereby demonstrate themselves to be *stronger* than the "coherence" requirement (they are sufficient but not necessary for "coherence"), not, as the quotation above by Savage and other passages may seem to imply, equivalent to it.

We could not infer for you (nor could you infer for yourself) a definite degree of belief, for example, for Yellow from your bids in case (d), since $p_o(Y) + q_o(Y) = 5/6 < 1$. Yet, following Smith, we could still give meaningful quantitative expression to your opinion concerning Yellow; we could describe $p_o(Y) = 1/6$ as the "lower betting[2] probability" for Yellow and

---

[1] See "Risk, Ambiguity and the Savage Axioms," pp. 653–668 for a possible rationale of such choices and a decision rule that would generate such a pattern of "bids." A similar decision rule is suggested, *ibid.*, p. 633, which generates bids corresponding to those in case (b), reflecting the pattern of preferences, II preferred to I, III preferred to IV; these bids, unlike those in case (d) *would* violate the requirement of "coherence," as usually interpreted. Thus, that requirement can be regarded as ruling out some forms of behavior violating the Savage postulates, but not others.

The discussion in the reference above will be found, in expanded and modified form, in subsequent chapters of this thesis. In particular, we shall consider arguments which would support the reasonableness even of a pattern of bids as in (b): thus, in effect, rejecting the requirement of "coherence" entirely.

[2] Smith offers, instead, the term "lower *pignic* probability" (from Latin, *pignus* = bet), *op. cit.*, p. 5. I do not think this will catch on.

$p^o(Y) = 1 - q_o(Y) = 1/2$ as the "upper betting probability" for Yellow (where $q_o(Y)$ is the "lower betting probability" for not-Yellow, the highest acceptable price for a gamble staking a unit *against* Yellow).

If this sort of behavior were accepted as reasonable—as Smith's discussion suggests it might be—we might find it useful to represent a degree of belief in general by an *interval* of numbers between 0 and 1, with certain "definite" degrees of belief being represented by unique numbers. In the case of the set of bids (d) above, we would find the interval corresponding to your degree of belief in Yellow, defined by the lower and upper betting probabilities 1/6, 1/2, *enclosing* the "degenerate interval" corresponding to the definite degree of belief in Red (both upper and lower probabilities for Red = 1/3).[1]

Fig. 3.7

	$p_o(Y)$	$p(R)$	$p^o(Y)$	$p(\bar{R})$	
0	1/6	1/3	1/2	2/3	1

A system of degrees of belief defined in terms of intervals, some of positive length, would not determine a *complete ordering* of events in terms of probability, since cases like this could arise in which one interval enclosed another; it would be impossible to say, in terms of this definition alone, either that Red was "more probable than" Yellow, or "less probable," or "equally probable." But a *partial* ordering would still be possible. There is no ambiguity in describing Red, in this case, as "less probable than" not-Red; and even when the "degrees of belief" of two events are not "definite," but are defined by intervals, one can be said to be definitely "less probable than" the other if its *upper* betting probability is lower than the *lower* betting probability of the other. Moreover, although lower betting probabilities will not, in general, combine according to the axioms of

---

[1] The Sure-Thing Principle rules out such a relationship between "degrees of belief" by banning such patterns of choice as gamble I preferred to II, IV preferred to III: a pattern which implies $p_o(R) > p_o(Y)$ and $q_o(R) > q_o(Y)$, hence $p^o(R) < p^o(Y)$. If all degrees of belief were represented by intervals of positive length, $p^o - p_o > 0$, Savage's Postulate 2 would rule out the possibility that one interval might enclose another, but it would not rule out "overlapping" intervals: $p_o(A) < p_o(B)$, $p^o(A) < p^o(C)$, where $p_o(A) < p^o(A)$ and $p_o(B) < p^o(B)$. However, if to every rational number there corresponds an event with that *definite* probability, comparisons with such events will ensure, in the light of Postulate 2, that all events have definite probabilities, since Postulate 2 implies that no event can have upper and lower betting probabilities that *enclose* those of another event.

probability, under certain conditions (e.g., coherence) very similar laws of combination can be stated for them, based on inequalities rather than equalities. Two examples would be: for $E \cap F = 0$, (a) P_o (E or F) $\geq p_o(E) + p_o(F)$; (b) p^o (E or F) $\leq p^o(E) + p^o(F)$.

ACCEPTABLE ODDS: DEFINITE, COHERENT, AND OTHERWISE

It does not seem worthwhile to go through our whole discussion again in terms of betting odds rather than "prices," but this approach is worth some mention, since it offers an alternative, and somewhat more familiar, definition of a "definite" degree of belief. In Ramsey's words:

> . . . the probability of 1/3 is clearly related to the kind of belief which would lead to a bet of 2 to 1. . . . The old-established way of measuring a person's belief is to propose a bet, and see what are the lowest odds which he will accept.[1]

Ramsey points out that this definition runs into problems connected with utility—"Clearly mathematical expectations in terms of money are not proper guides to conduct"[2]—but he introduces the concept of what we have called "von Neumann-Morgenstern utility" ("Ramsey utility" would be historically correct) to surmount this obstacle. This utility measure of "goods and bads," he asserts,

> allows validity to betting as means of measuring beliefs. By proposing a bet on [a proposition] p we give the subject a possible course of action from which so much extra good will result to him if p is true and so much extra bad if p is false. Supposing the bet to be in goods and bads instead of in money, he will take a bet at any better odds than those corresponding to his state of belief; in fact his state of belief is measured by the odds he will just take. . . .[3]

> . . . This amounts roughly to defining the degree of belief in p by the odds at which the subject would bet on p, the bet being conducted in terms of differences of value as defined.[4]

This point of view is easy to relate to our previous one, now that we have introduced the notion of utility payoffs. Consider the following actions:

---

[1] Ramsey, *op. cit.*, p. 172.
[2] *Ibid.*, p. 183.
[3] *Ibid.*, p. 176.
[4] *Ibid.*, p. 180.

	E	Ē
I	1	0
II	1/3	1/3
III	2/3	-1/3
IV	0	0
V	2	-1
VI	0	0

Fig. 3.8

The payoff to Action II represents the highest utility payoff such that you do not prefer II to I; i.e., p_0 (E) = 1/3. But the payoffs to the next two pairs of actions are related to the payoffs in this pair by increasing linear transformations; it follows that you must be indifferent between III and IV, and between V and VI, as well. The payoffs in III and IV are related to those in I and II by the transformation: $U' = U - 1/3$; those in V and VI are related to those in I and II by $U'' = \dfrac{U-1/3}{1/3}$. Either III or V could now be described as "a bet on E at 2:1 odds on E against Ē." Indifference between III and IV, or between V and VI, would indicated that 2:1 were the lowest odds on E at which you would find a bet on E acceptable; at "worse" or "less favorable" odds (e.g., 1:1 or 1/2:1) you would prefer *not to bet*, i.e., to choose IV or VI, if available. Then, if we had observed III and IV, or V and VI, *instead* of I and II, we could have deduced P_0 (E) just as well from this knowledge of acceptable odds, by applying the necessary transformation to transform III and V into the form of action I, and noting the corresponding (transformed) payoff to IV or VI.

The condition necessary to ensure that a degree of belief defined in terms of "prices" will be "definite" ($p_0 + q_0 = 1$) has its exact counterpart in terms of odds. *If* this condition is satisfied, then I' will be indifferent to II' below (assuming I indifferent to II above), III' indifferent to IV', and V' indifferent to VI'.

	E	Ē
I'	0	1
II'	2/3	2/3
III'	-2/3	1/3
IV'	0	0
V'	-1	1/2
VI'	0	0

Fig. 3.9

Thus, the requirement that your degrees of belief be "definite" amounts in this case to the requirement that the lowest acceptable odds at which you will bet on $\bar{E}$ (or *against* E) are $1/2{:}1$ on $\bar{E}$. In general, if w_o are the lowest odds at which you will accept a bet at w:1 on E, and W_o are the lowest acceptable odds for a bet on $\bar{E}$ (against E), the necessary condition for your degree of belief to be "definite" in Ramsey's sense (corresponding to $p_o + q_o = 1$) is: $w_o \cdot W_o = 1$, or $w_o = 1/W_o$.

But, again, this equality does *not* follow merely from the assumptions with respect to utility; and the notion of "coherence" rules out only one inequality,[1] $w_o \cdot W_o < 1$. Again following Smith's discussion, if "coherence" is required but not the "definiteness" of every degree of belief, we allow the possibility that $w_o > 1/W_o$ (with the familiar implications for "upper" and "lower" betting probabilities).

It follows from the conditions guaranteeing the "definiteness" of degrees of belief that if I is indifferent to II below, then III must likewise be indifferent to II (and I) (when payoffs are "von Neumann-Morgenstern utilities; compare II below to III' in the previous example):

	E	$\bar{E}$
I	2	–1
II	0	0
III	–2	1
IV	–1	2

Fig. 3.10

If it is the case that you are indifferent between I, II and III, we would indeed, following Ramsey, ascribe to you a definite degree of belief in E, prob(E) $= 1/3$ (prob($\bar{E}$) $= 2/3$).[2] And if we assumed conditions guaranteeing that all your degrees of belief were definite, we would not even need the evidence that you were indifferent between II and III (i.e., that prob(E) $= 2/3$); we would *infer* that, from the evidence that you were indifferent between I and II in each case.

---

[1] In most of the mathematical literature, statements on odds are translated into words in a different fashion from that adopted here, with the effect of reversing the inequalities mentioned. It seems to me that my usage is somewhat easier to relate to ordinary speech; it makes no difference which is used so long as a given discussion is internally consistent.

[2] We recall Ramsey's definition: "Having any definite degree of belief implies a certain measure of consistency, namely willingness to bet on a given proposition at the same odds for any stake, the stakes being measured in terms of ultimate values" (Ramsey, *op. cit.*, p. 182). Gambles I and III above will each be indifferent to II (i.e., be "barely acceptable bets") *if and only if both* I is indifferent to II

But Smith would "allow" you to *prefer* II, or "not betting," to III; you might, instead, be indifferent between IV and II, where IV is clearly preferable to III. In other words, you might demand 2:1 odds on E before you would accept a bet on E; and you would demand 2:1 odds (or at any rate, odds better than 1/2:1) on $\bar{E}$ before you would bet on $\bar{E}$; assuming that you had, in either case, the option of *not betting*. This behavior is clearly not compatible with the assignment of "definite" degrees of belief for you. Yet it does not conflict either with the requirement of "coherence" or the assumptions on your utility function. And it can be described in an orderly fashion in terms of "upper and lower betting odds" or "upper and lower betting probabilities" corresponding here to: $p_0 (E) = 1/2$, $p^0 (E) = 1 - 1/3 = 2/3$.

In general, the "Bernoulli proposition," or any set of postulates or criteria implying it, rules out the possibility that action II below—"not betting"— can ever be preferred *both* to gambles I and III (where payoffs are "von Neumann-Morgenstern utilities," as measured in other gambling choices, and E is any event):

	E	$\bar{E}$
I	X	-Y
II	0	0
III	-X	Y

Fig. 3.12

Action I can be described as a bet on E at X:Y odds on E; action III is a bet on $\bar{E}$ at Y:X odds on $\bar{E}$ (or, a bet against E at X:Y odds against E). The "Bernoulli proposition," or, for example, the Ramsey/Savage postulates, or the requirements of "definiteness and coherence," permit the possibility that you are indifferent between I, II and III, in which case we define your definite degree of belief: prob(E) = Y/X + Y. Or, at the given odds, you may prefer I to II to III, or III to II to I. But these hypotheses do not permit you "reasonably" to *prefer not to bet than to take either side* of the bet at these given odds, whatever the odds may be.[1] Smith does.

---

below *and* III is indifferent to IV (when all payoffs are "von Neumann-Morgenstern utilities"):

	E	$\bar{E}$
I	1	0
II	1/3	1/3
III	–1	–1
IV	–1/3	–1/3

Fig. 3.11

[1] If you satisfy the "Bernoulli proposition" or any of the equivalent axiomatizations, there exist numerical probabilities for E and $\bar{E}$ in terms of which your

As a commentator on Smith's paper has observed, "His development of a theory of subjective probability based on hypothetical betting differs from some previous theories" in part, "in allowing, in effect, an individual the option at a particular level of betting neither on A nor on not-A."[1] Such "reluctance to gamble"—when a no-risk option, "not betting," is available—seems intuitively to correspond to recognizable behavior-patterns associated with circumstances in which opinions are exceptionally "indefinite." Nor does the requirement of "coherence"—prominently utilized by Smith—tend to discredit it.

If this behavior were to be accepted as reasonable (we are merely raising the question at this point), certain of the Savage postulates, as we shall see, would have to be modified or rejected; yet the actual effect on the process of inference and measurement of degrees of belief would not seem radical. The notion of "definite degree of belief" would still be perfectly meaningful; but it would be defined, as would a less definite degree of belief, by a *dual* condition, relating to the price you would pay for a unit stake *on* a given event *and* the (independent) price you would pay for a unit stake on its complement.

---

preferences among actions correspond to their moral expectations. Let prob(E) = p and prob $(\overline{E})$ = (1 − p). If you *preferred* action II *both* (a) to action I and (b) to action III, this would imply:

$$\text{(a)} \quad p \cdot X - (1 - p) \cdot Y < 0,$$
and $$\text{(b)} -p \cdot X + (1 - p) \cdot Y < 0; \text{ or,}$$
$$\text{(a)} \ X < \frac{(1 - p)}{p} \cdot Y \text{ and (b) } X > \frac{(1 - p)}{p} \cdot Y$$

But this is a contradiction; there exist no numbers X, Y, p, $0 \le p \le 1$, that satisfy these conditions.

For proof from the Savage postulates of a closely related constraint, see Theorem 3, Appendix to Chapter Five.

[1] D. R. Cox, "Discussion on Dr. Smith's Paper," (Smith, "Consistency in Statistical Inference and Decision") *Journal of the Royal Statistical Society*, Series B, Vol. 23, No. 1, 1961, p. 27. Cox remarks that he considers the change an improvement; both his interpretation and evaluation are seconded by I. J. Good in the same discussion, p. 28.

It is clear that the behavior suggested here by Smith is closely related in motivation and pattern to behavior associated with my counter-examples to the Sure-Thing Principle discussed above and in "Risk, Ambiguity and the Savage Axioms" (see other examples discussed below). However, in a number of respects the hypotheses and decision rules I shall propose for situations in which degrees of belief are "indefinite" seem to differ significantly from Smith's; in particular, as will be discussed, I do not propose to rely upon the notion of "coherence" nor to imply any necessary randomness in decision.

We do not affect Ramsey's meaning at all—we merely make it explicit, and suggest that it may apply to a somewhat special case—if we paraphrase the statement cited earlier: "The probability of 1/3 is clearly related to the kind of *definite* belief which would lead indifferently to a bet of 2 to 1 *on* an event, *or* 1 to 2 *against* it." If one but not both bets were barely acceptable to you, then we could not infer from your preferences a definite degree of belief; which still need not mean, so far in our discussion, that you were mad, or beyond the reach of systematic theorizing.

If, on the other hand, such behavior is to be characterized as unreasonable, it must clearly be upon other grounds than "coherence."

I have emphasized this point, because "coherence" does seem, in some ways, to be more intuitively compelling as a criterion of reasonable behavior than most others, such as the Ramsey/Savage postulates we shall be considering: For one thing, it has the appearance of being an "objective" test.

The postulates, on the other hand, seem explicitly concerned with introspective phenomena. What reason is there to believe that individuals will obey the Ramsey/Savage postulates; and why should they? The main answer given is the intuitive *reasonableness* of the postulates themselves. In other words, it is predicted that a person who finds himself violating one of the postulates will experience an intellectual tension, unease, discomfort, of the same sort that he experiences when he finds himself making a mistake in arithmetic or an inconsistency in logical deduction;[1] and that he will wish to correct his "mistake." On the other hand, if he does *not* happen to feel this pressure to remove an "inconsistency," there is nothing much more for proponents of the postulates to say to him, except that their theory will not be useful to him in his decision-making; the postulates provide no obvious basis from which to *criticize* his idiosyncratic behavior, or even to encourage him to change it, if it already reflects conscientious reflection on his part.

An argument based on "coherence" appears more powerful, independently of the whims and tastes or intuitive responses of the individual decision-maker. Whether or not violation of the proposed postulates makes a decision-maker *feel* "foolish," this argument goes, such violation

---

[1] At least, Savage predicts this for himself; *Foundations of Statistics*, pp. 21, 102–103. There has recently been increasing interest in the field of social psychology in the effect of a desire for *consistency* in one's opinions and attitudes upon behavior; see Leon Festinger, *A Theory of Cognitive Dissonance*, Illinois, 1957 (where "dissonance" refers to the emotional and motivational aspects of perceived inconsistency).

will result in his *being* foolish, in an important, "objective" sense. It will be possible to "make a fool of him."[1]

It is asserted that it is possible to deduce all postulates necessary to demonstrate the "Bernoulli proposition," and thus to establish the comparability of all events in terms of numerical probabilities, simply from the requirement that it *not* be possible to "make a fool of" the decision-maker, in a specific sense. This sense is defined at the outset of one article:

> The purpose of this paper is to analyze rational betting. In particular, we concentrate on one necessary feature of rational betting, the avoidance of certainty of losing to a clever opponent. If a bettor is quite foolish in his choice of the rates at which he will bet, an opponent can win money from him no matter what happens.

> This phenomenon is well known to professional bettors—especially bookmakers, who must as a matter of practical necessity avoid its occurrence. Such a losing book is called by them a "dutch book." Our investigations are thus concerned with necessary and sufficient conditions that a book not be "dutch."

> De Finetti has started with the same idea and used it as a foundation for the theory of probability.[2]

The advantages of this approach as a basis for exhortation are obvious: "Presumably you don't want to be incoherent," Savage remarks pointedly; "I don't."[3] It is not hard to understand why proponents of the "Bernoulli proposition" are anxious to derive it solely, if possible, from this single, transparent, inexorable requirement. It excuses them from theorizing, in a normative context, about those benighted individuals who violate their postulates:

> There are good reasons for holding that someone whose decisions are not consistent with the view that he is attempting to maximize expected utility

---

[1] "A no less fundamental source of the notion of objectivity in empirical matters (that is, in induction) is by false analogy with the 'objectivity' of deductive logic, whatever the correct philosophical analysis of this latter kind of objectivity may be. Some principles of rational behavior seem to have this kind of objectivity, and the theory of utility and personal probability is based upon them. For example, a man prepared to make a combination of bets that is logically certain to leave him worse off is 'objectively' irrational." (Savage, "The Subjective Basis of Statistical Practice," p. 2.10.)

[2] R. Sherman Lehmann, "On Confirmation and Rational Betting," *Journal of Symbolic Logic*, Vol. 20, No. 3, September 1955, p. 251.

[3] Savage, "Bayesian Statistics," p. 9.

does not have a rational pattern of preferences and expectations. Such a person has, in effect, a "Dutch book"; it would be possible for a clever better to make a book against him such that he would lose in every eventuality. For such a person, the concept of optimum strategy as defined in game theory, and the theorems of statistical decision theory generally, have little application.[1]

Such deviants can, in other words, be cast, discredited, into outer darkness, along with advocates of full-cost pricing; while on the positive side:

In fact, a person who succeeds in conforming to the principles of coherence will behave as though there were a probability measure associated with all events, in terms of which his preference among statistical procedures is such as to maximize expected utility under this measure.[2]

Yet, as we have seen, these assertions must be regarded either as misleading or mistaken. It is possible to announce a set of betting quotations that is comfortably "coherent," precluding any danger of falling prey to a Dutch book, yet which is *not* consistent with the existence of a definite probability measure over all events, with respect to which the better maximizes expected utility. Such patterns of behavior are ruled out for a "coherent" set of "betting probabilities" only when it is the case that *each* "betting probability" is "definite," in the sense that $p_o = 1 - q_o$.

One author has described the latter condition—on the basis of which the "coherence" requirement leads to numerical probabilities—as fulfilled "When a person X has a set of beliefs precise enough to determine decisions in betting."[3] But it is precisely this inference that is pernicious. Situations in which degrees of belief can meaningfully be regarded as "definite" and

---

[1] D. Davidson and P. Suppes, *Decision Making*, p. 2.

[2] Savage, "The Foundations of Statistics Reconsidered," p. 579. This and some similar assertions might be valid if the "principles of coherence" were defined broadly enough: so as to be equivalent to the postulates in *The Foundations of Statistics*. But when "coherence" is explicitly defined, by Savage or anyone else, it has always been in terms of the single principle of avoiding the possibility of certain loss.

[3] Shimony, "Coherence and the Axioms of Confirmation," p. 5. Shimony defines a degree of belief in proposition E = r when an individual would accept a bet on E on the following terms, or on terms more favorable to himself than these: (a) to pay rS and collect nothing for a net gain of – in case E is false: (b) to pay rS and collect S, for a net gain of $(1 - r)S$, in case E is true. S is known as the "stake" and r, which is the ratio between the amount risked and the stake, is called the "betting quotient." [For positive S, r corresponds to p_o.] "For ease in mathematical considerations, S is

precise undoubtedly exist. But none of the arguments examined in this chapter seems persuasive that such circumstances exhaust the realm of reasonable decision-making behavior: or exhaust the area in which systematic theorizing on decision-making, or explicit and helpful decision criteria, or decisive and reasoned choice are possible. As Smith's discussion indicates and as I shall argue repeatedly in other contexts, beliefs that must be treated as "indefinite" within limits can still be precise enough to determine decisions in betting, and susceptible of quantitative expression in terms of inequalities, even though the pattern of decisions determined does not permit the inference of unique numerical probabilities.

allowed to be either positive or negative." (*Op. cit.*, p. 7.) But this latter condition amounts precisely to the requirement that the individual should be equally willing to bet at the quotient r *on* E, or at the quotient (1 − r) on not-E, i.e., *against E*. It would be less misleading to state this as an explicit requirement, instead of making casual remarks about positive and negative stakes.

4

OPINIONS AND ACTIONS: WHICH COME FIRST?

"PHILOSOPHY MUST BE of some use, and we must take it seriously; it must clear our thoughts and so our actions." So begins the last of Frank Ramsey's posthumous papers.[1] But in his brilliant and pathbreaking essay, "Truth and Probability,"[2] he reversed this order of program; he chose to develop a philosophy of consistent action, from which rules of consistent thought might be inferred. Later, L. J. Savage was to follow this same route.

For Savage, this emphasis on behavior rather than belief represents a direct approach to his goal: a "theory of consistent *decision* in the face of uncertainty."[3] But for Ramsey, who (like Keynes) defined the subject of his inquiry as "the logic of partial belief,"[4] it might seem roundabout. Ramsey is certainly correct in stating that partial belief, or degree of belief, "has no precise meaning unless we specify more exactly how it is to be measured."[5] But why should it be measured in terms of preferences among actions, which depend not only on degrees of partial belief but on values of outcomes? Why not simply *ask* a person to compare his degrees of belief in two propositions or possible occurrences and to tell us his judgment?

In some circumstances, it is precisely a person's degrees of belief, or state of uncertainty, concerning some propositions that is the focus of our

---

[1] Frank P. Ramsey, "Philosophy," *The Foundations of Mathematics,* Littlefield, Adams & Co., New Jersey, 1960, p. 263.

[2] Ramsey, *op. cit.,* pp. 156–198.

[3] Savage, *Foundations of Statistics,* p. 27; italics added.

[4] Ramsey, "Truth and Probability," *op. cit.,* p. 166.

[5] *Ibid.,* p. 167.

interest; we may not be at all concerned to predict or recommend his behavior or his preferences among outcomes. For example, a decision-maker (or "commander") may call upon the services of an expert for certain forecasts (an "intelligence estimate"), on which he intends to rely in calculating his own best course of action. He may not be basically interested in which course of action the expert himself would choose, for he may suspect the consultant does not share precisely his goals, or his judgment of the acceptability of risks or the availability of alternatives. The commander wishes to be able to choose, not the action the expert would prefer, but the action that the expert would prefer if he were exactly like the commander in all these *latter* respects. What he wants to know are the expert's opinions about probabilities (not about values or alternatives), his degrees of partial belief. Why not simply ask for them?

To this Ramsey and Savage would reply that their method of interrogation, which amounts to asking the person "not how he feels, but what he would do in such and such a situation"[1] can reveal, just as effectively as a direct question, which of two events he considers more probable. They would go on to argue that their method of questioning is much *better*, even for the above purposes.

It is not necessary to go into their argument here; it has overtones of a "behaviorist" position, a strong sense of the desirability of non-verbal behavior as data, though this is undercut by Savage's willingness to accept verbal reports of hypothetical choices. They both take the point of view that *judgments of preference among actions* are somehow more fundamental, more "reliable" or constant, more clear-cut and accessible to introspection, than direct *judgments of relative degree of belief*.[2] Others have an opposite opinion; *the fact is that theories of probability can be built upon either sort of data.* And whatever the merits of the Ramsey/Savage case, certain theories of probability which start immediately from intuitive judgments of belief have a marked advantage for my particular purposes: as noted in Chapter One, they make it possible to talk precisely about vagueness.

As I have indicated, I wish particularly to consider problems of decision-making under conditions of *"extreme* uncertainty, ambiguity, vagueness, confusion," situations in which one's opinions are not sharply defined. But there is *no way to characterize such situations meaningfully* within the framework of the Ramsey/Savage approach. Either a person obeys the Ramsey/ Savage postulates under given circumstances or he does not. If he does, we can infer *definite* probabilities over events for him. If he does not:

---

[1] Savage, *Foundations of Statistics*, p. 28.

[2] See Ramsey, *op. cit.,* pp. 169–172; Savage, *Foundation of Statistics*, pp. 27–28. "In many cases, I think, our judgment about the strength of our belief is really about how we should act in hypothetical circumstances" (Ramsey, *op. cit.,* p. 171).

then he lies outside the theory, and no inferences are made about the possible, subjective reasons or objective circumstances for his "unreasonable" behavior. For a person who obeys the postulates, we can distinguish between situations in which he assigns roughly uniform probabilities to a large set of events and those in which he does not; but in the former case, the data assumed in this approach allow no inference as to the "definiteness" of his opinions, the "confidence" with which he holds them, or the amount, quality, and unanimity of the information on which he bases them. It is possible to *assume* that these are "differences that do not make a difference." But I, obviously, have not chosen to start with such an assumption, and the Ramsey / Savage concepts and data suggest no means of measuring such differences at all. In fact, from the data they presume available, there is no way to identify situations of the sort in which I am interested.

On the other hand, in the approaches of B. O. Koopman and I. J. Good, evidence of the vagueness of opinions emerges naturally and directly. It is even possible to give quantitative expression to the notions of *relative* vagueness or ambiguity. With these measurements in mind, we shall be in a better position to judge whether or not such concepts are relevant to behavior. We shall describe the Koopman / Good notions briefly here and again at the end of this chapter, after discussing the Ramsey / Savage postulates.

THE LOGIC OF DEGREES OF BELIEF

We have already noted I. J. Good's definition of a "body of beliefs" as "A set of comparisons between degrees of belief of the form that one belief is held more firmly than another one, or if you like a set of judgments that one probability is greater than (or equal to) another one."[1] A fundamental premise of the theories of "the logic of partial belief" that we shall consider—by Keynes, Good, and B. O. Koopman—is that such comparisons can *sometimes* be made; i.e., that questions as to the relative probability of two propositions will be regarded as having an unambiguous meaning, and will at least sometimes evoke a definite, non-arbitrary answer. A set of such answers will constitute a body of beliefs; a theory of probability specifies rules of consistency between such stated comparisons, meant to maintain a scrupulous awareness that "all probabilities are conditional," that any degree of belief in a given proposition at a given moment is contingent upon certain presumed "evidence," information, data, or hypothesis.

Two phrases in the above quotation, which I have italicized, are particularly significant; Koopman refers to a "(partial) ordering" of eventualities, and mentions the possibility that an individual may be "non-committal"

---

[1] I. J. Good, "Rational Decisions," p. 109.

as to the truth or falsity of the proposition: a/h <· b/k. In other words, while Koopman makes the bold assumption that, under the conditions he specifies, the question, "Do you judge that a/h <· b/k?" . . . "conveys a precise meaning" to the listener, he does *not* assume that the individual questioned will at every moment and for all *a, b, h, k, be able or willing to give it a definite answer.* All three of the authors cited allow for, and expect, frequent inability to assert a definite comparison of intuitive probability between given propositions, on given presumptions; such *lacunae* in the responses of a reasonable person ensure that his responses will *at most* establish only a *partial* ordering over all eventualities.

Koopman continues:

> The position of acceptance, rejection, or *doubt*[1] taken with regard to a/h <· b/k may vary from individual to individual and from moment to moment with the same individual, depending as it will upon his entire state of mind. Nevertheless, if a certain individual at a certain moment subscribes to both of the following: a/h <{ b/k, b/k <{ c/l, he *must* at the same moment subscribe to a/h <{ c/l, [*Axiom of Transitivity*] and also he must subscribe to each of ~a/h {> ~b/k, ~b/k {> ~c/l. [*Axiom of Antisymmetry*]. For otherwise he will be in a condition of mental incoherence of the same nature as logical inconsistency. We thus come to a second essential in the thesis of intuitive probability, namely, that its comparisons obey fixed laws which, like the laws of intuitive logic to which they are akin, are axiomatic, and owe their authority to man's awareness of his own rational processes.[2]

> When the intuition exerts itself upon a situation involving uncertain events, it is capable of performing two tasks: firstly, it may assert comparisons in probability; and secondly, it may state laws of consistency governing such comparisons . . . From the laws of consistency a theory may be constructed (and this is our present object) with the aid of which, comparisons in probability (and indeed, values of numerical probability) can be deduced from others which are hypothesized: but beyond this, the laws of consistency do not allow one to go.[3]

Koopman proceeds to state nine "intuitively evident laws of consistency governing all comparisons in probability," of which the two cited above are important, though simple, examples. Of some of the others, Koopman cannot pretend that they are *immediately* intuitively evident; "in

---

[1] Italics added.

[2] Koopman, *op. cit.*, p. 271. Axioms cited in brackets are stated on p. 276. ~*a* symbolizes "not-*a*," the negation or logical complement of *a*.

[3] *Ibid.*, p. 271.

some cases, to be sure, the full understanding of their meaning may offer some difficulty: the only claim is that, their meaning once being apprehended, their truth will be granted."[1] Or as Good sums up Koopman's system more tersely: "Although it is complicated it is convincing if you think hard."[2] I agree with both judgments.

There seems no need to launch into a full discussion of the sort of "truth" or the meaning of "convincing" implied in the above statements, since the remarks in the opening chapter on the meaning, verification, and functions of normative theories apply fully here. Although Koopman speaks of his axioms as "intuitively given," we can regard them as tentative hypotheses until we have tested their own validity, for ourselves, as "theories of the structure of our body of beliefs" (just as axioms on choice can be tested as "theories of the structure of our deliberated preferences").

I think that the axioms of Koopman or Good on consistent beliefs are quite likely to pass this test, as their authors expect. These axioms are much weaker than those of Ramsey or Savage; they could, in fact, be deduced from the Ramsey / Savage postulates, but not vice versa. This follows from the fact that the Koopman axioms (and the Good axioms along with Good's rules of application) yield only a partial ordering over events, and do not necessarily lead to numerical probabilities for any events, whereas Ramsey / Savage axioms in their entirely lead to numerical probabilities for all events, and even in a reduced form yield a complete ordering of all events.

The difference between the strength (and in my opinion, the plausibility) of the two sorts of results corresponds to different attitudes as to what constitutes a "satisfactory" theory of probability. According to Ramsey,

A satisfactory system must in the first place assign to any belief a magnitude or degree having a definite position in an order of magnitudes . . . But to construct such an ordered series of degrees is not the whole of our task; we have also to assign numbers to these degrees in some intelligible manner.[3]

In his discussion Ramsey seems to assume that a satisfactory theory must assign numbers to *all* events. Savage makes an even stronger statement, in *defining* a relation between events as a "qualitative probability" if and only if, among other requirements, it is a "simple ordering" (i.e., connected and transitive) over *all* events.[4] With such relationships

---

[1] *Ibid.*, p. 275. For formal statement of axioms, see Appendix to this chapter.

[2] I. J. Good, "Subjective Probability as the Measure of a Non-Measurable Set," *Proceedings of the International Congress of Logic, Mathematics and the Philosophy of Science*, Stanford, 1960, to be published.

[3] Ramsey, *op. cit.*, p. 168.

[4] Savage, *Foundations of Statistics*, p. 32.

as their objective, both Ramsey and Savage construct axioms of "reasonable" behavior which imply the existence of a numerical probability function over all events considered.

In contrast, far from making such a requirement part of their definition of a probability relationship, or even seeking axioms that would imply it in general, Keynes, Koopman and Good promote what they regard as adequate and useful theories of probability which have no such general implication. In fact, all three of these authors argue strongly that the application of an appropriate idealized, normative theory to the sort of judgments they accept as data will *not*, even frequently, lead to a complete ordering of events for a given individual. Nor does such a "failure," in their view, cast doubt either upon the reasonableness of the individual or the usefulness of the theory.

If called upon to comment on this difference in goals and results,[1] Ramsey and Savage would doubtless cite it as an advantage of their own "decision-centered" theory, which calls upon judgments of preferred choice rather than judgments of comparative belief, and which derives the stronger and more comprehensive inferences about beliefs from *axioms of choice that purport to be no less intuitively compelling than the weaker axioms of "intuitive probability."* From the point of view of a theory of decision, this attitude would be justified if we should conclude (a) that their axioms of choice were indeed normatively compelling, and (b) data on beliefs, including evidence of indecision, doubt, or inability to compare degrees of belief, were neither necessary nor useful to explain deliberate decision-making behavior that could be considered "reasonable." I shall argue, along with Keynes, Koopman and Good, that conscientious "non-committal" responses on questions of belief, these preventing the inference of a complete ordering over events for the individual, are data on the individual's state of uncertainty fully as valid and significant as are his most definite statements of relative probability. Moreover, I shall argue that such data are highly relevant to a theory of decision as well as a theory of intuitive probability; that it is on the basis of such data that one can predict specific patterns of *violation* of the Savage axioms (thus complementing or improving the Ramsey/Savage theory as an empirical, predictive, theory); and

---

[1] It is rather remarkable that neither Ramsey nor Savage seem to discuss, in their major works on the subject, the *possibility* of an axiomatization of partial belief that might lead only to a partial ordering. Although Savage, in *The Foundations of Statistics*, refers frequently to Keynes and Koopman, and once to Good (when he comments that Koopman and Good express "personalistic views that tend to ignore decision, or at any rate keep it out of the foreground"; p. 60), he never, so far as I can discover, mentions the notion on which they all place great emphasis: that definite judgments of relative probability are not always possible and that a probability relationship must therefore be regarded as a partial ordering.

that in circumstances evoking these responses such violations can be regarded as *reasonable,* so that a better normative theory must (and can) be found.[1] (See Chapters Six and Seven.)

With this critical introduction, let us now consider the Savage theory of decision.

OPINIONS THAT MAKE HORSE RACES

If I offer to pay you $10.00 if any one horse of your choosing wins a given race, your decision tells me operationally which you consider to be the most probable winner.[2]

With this sentence Savage sums up an approach that is at the heart of his *Foundations of Statistics*. It is an extension of Ramsey's operational definition of probability = 1/2 to the comparison and, in special cases, numerical measurement of probabilities other than 1/2, without assuming either utility known as a linear function of money or prior measurement of the utility function. The trick is to consider only choices among gambles all offering the same two outcomes, these being associated with various different subsets of events. So long as one of the outcomes is definitely preferable to the other, it is not necessary even to attach conventional utility numbers to them to infer from your choices the relative subjective probabilities you attach to these subsets of events. For in these circumstances the principle of maximizing the mathematical expectation of utility reduces to the principle of *maximizing the probability of the preferred outcome.*

If we assume that you obey the "Bernoulli proposition," at least in your careful, deliberated choices, then by knowing which outcome you prefer and which events you prefer to stake it on, we can infer which events you regard as "more probable than" others. Thus, this approach to the measurement of your probabilities simply abstracts from all the "utility" difficulties considered in the last chapter, though it requires observation of choices from a more restricted, specially designed set of gambles.

But Savage also provides a set of postulated constraints upon your choice-behavior (under all circumstances, not merely for these special choices that serve to measure your probabilities) that imply the "Bernoulli proposition" as a theorem. If you find that these postulates characterize your own intuitive standards of "consistency" in choice among gambles— i.e., if you, like Savage, conclude that you would like never to violate these

---

[1] Keynes and Koopman do not commit themselves as to the impact of "vagueness" upon decision-making. Good has some highly pertinent comments, discussed below, that are consistent with these assertions.

[2] Savage, "The Foundations of Statistics Reconsidered," p. 581.

principles—and if you succeed in conforming to them, it follows that you *will* obey the "Bernoulli proposition" with respect to all events in all your choices. A subset of the postulates (1–5: see below) suffices to ensure that you can *compare* the relative probabilities of all events or propositions, merely by asking yourself, "Which horse would I back? On which event would I prefer to stake a given prize?" among a given field of alternatives. To some events it will be possible, on the basis of such questions, to assign numerical probabilities, and by comparing other events to these, it is possible to assign numerical boundaries to the probabilities of those others. Finally, Postulate 6 or a similar postulate ensures that there is a sufficiently rich sequence of events with numerical probabilities available for comparison so that (to any given degree of approximation) numerical probabilities can be assigned uniquely to every event.

Thus, these principles of choice assure the possibility of numerical measurement of probabilities: hence of utilities also, since the von Neumann-Morgenstern utility axioms, which apply to gambles with numerical probabilities attached to events, are implied by the Savage postulates. But even if measurement were not a primary objective, the postulates, as canons of consistent behavior, purport to guide and restrict your pattern of choices; in many situations, they tell you *what to do*, or what not to do, if you are to be "reasonable" and "consistent" with certain other choices. Whether this advice reliably mirrors your own honest, deliberated preferences is, as Savage emphasizes, for you to decide; he offers no demonstration that if you follow preferences that lead you into conflict with his postulates, you will eventually suffer for it. As quoted earlier, Savage points out:

> In general, a person who has tentatively accepted a normative theory must conscientiously study situations in which the theory seems to lead him astray; he must decide for each by reflection—deduction will typically be of little relevance—whether to retain his initial impression of the situation or to accept the implications of the theory for it.[1]

In the following chapter, we shall consider some situations in which the theory seems, in the light of my own preferences (shared by others), to lead me astray. But in any case, we can examine the postulates as conditions of choice behavior that do ensure, when they are satisfied, the measurability of all probabilities and utilities. They deserve attention in this role even if we should end by concluding that they are not universally and uniquely "reasonable," since they are unquestionably more plausible than the equivalent conditions (including the constancy of betting "prices" for positive or negative stakes) considered in the last chapter.

---

[1]Savage, *Foundations of Statistics*, p. 102.

Let us use the symbol $\leq$· to mean, alternatively, "not preferred to" or "not more probable than," depending on whether it connects actions (gambles) or events, respectively. Since actions or gambles will be represented by Roman numerals and events by capital letters, the usage should not be ambiguous in context. Correspondingly, $\{\geq$ will mean "preferred or indifferent to" or "not less probable than." The meanings of $<\{, \{>, \doteq$ will be derived from the basic symbols in the usual manner.

To return to Savage's operational test, let us suppose that there are three horses entered in a given race, named unevocatively A, B, C, and for simplicity we assume you regard it as certain that one and only one of these will be declared the winner (this assumption is *not* implicit in or required by Savage's definition; it merely simplifies the following exposition). We offer you the chance to stake a $10 prize alternatively on a win by A, B, or C.

	A	B	C
I	$10	$ 0	$ 0
II	$ 0	$10	$ 0
III	$ 0	$ 0	$10

Fig. 4.1

If you choose action I (when actions I, II, III are available), Savage proposes to infer that you regard the probability of winning the $10 stake with that action to be higher (or at least, not lower) than with any of the others. His operational test of your subjective probabilities, applied to pairwise comparisons, can be expressed:

$$I \{\geq II <=> A \{\geq B; I \{\geq III<=>A \geq C.$$

Thus, a set of observed choices among alternative actions of this sort will lead to a set of inferred comparisons among events, of the form: A $\{\geq$ B, or A $<\{$ B, or A $\doteq$ B. But under what conditions will it be possible to infer a "qualitative probability relationship," or even stronger, a numerical probability measure, over all events, on the basis of the latter comparisons? And what reason do we have to expect these conditions to be fulfilled, in general or in an individual case?

A "qualitative probability relationship" must be a weak ordering over at least some events;[1] but it must have certain additional properties.

---

[1] Savage and Ramsey require a probability relationship (even a "qualitative" or non-numerical one) to be a simple ordering over all events; i.e., the relationship $\leq\{$ must be "connected", so that for *any* two events, A, B, either A $\leq\{$ B or B $\leq\{$ A. As

Savage defines a relation ≤· between events as a qualitative probability if and only if, for all events B, C, D within a set of events S (where O represents a "vacuous event" containing *no* states of the world as elements, and B̄ means "not-B"):[1]

1. ≤{ is a simple ordering; i.e., it is connected (for all B, C, either B ≤{ C or C ≤{ B) and transitive (if B ≤{ C, C ≤{ D, then B ≤{ D).
2. B ≤{ C if and only if B ∪ D ≤{ C ∪ D, providing B ∩ D = C ∩ D = 0.
3. 0 ≤{ B, 0 ≤{ S.

These basic, defining properties imply many others; e.g.,

4. If B ≤{ C, then C̄ ≤{ B̄.
5. If B ≤{ B̄ and C {≥ C̄, then B ≤{ C; equality holding in the conclusion, if and only if it holds in both parts of the hypothesis.

It is easy to imagine patterns of *choices among gambles* such that the inferred *comparisons among events* based upon them would fail one or more of these conditions for a qualitative probability; *a fortiori*, it would be impossible to assign a numerical probability measure to events that would correspond to such actual choices. It is possible, on the other hand, to specify constraints on the pattern of choices that would ensure that the conditions for a qualitative probability would be met. The Ramsey or Savage postulates on reasonable choice state such constraints; they rule out (as "unreasonable") those patterns of behavior which would contradict the logic-like "consistency" requirements on which the inferences of probability comparisons are based. As stated in *The Foundations of Statistics*, the Savage postulates[2] do not, of course, apply merely to actions with two con-

---

will be discussed later, in the works of J. M. Keynes, B. O. Koopman, and I. J. Good, a probability relationship is presumed to be, in general, only a *partial* ordering; the possibility is admitted that certain pairs of events, e.g., C, D, exist such that for a given individual, *neither* C ≤{ D *nor* D ≤{ C. C and D are said to be "incomparable" with respect to relative probability for this individual, written C ịD.

This difference in attitude toward the "essential requirements" of a probability relationship corresponds to a difference in emphasis on the problem of "vagueness" or "ambiguity" in the perception of probability relationships, which will receive central attention in our later discussion.

[1] L. J. Savage, *Foundations, of Statistics*, pp. 32–33.

[2] There seems no convenient way to refer to the postulates on reasonable choice under uncertainty to be found in L. J. Savage's *Foundations of Statistics* (1954) other than as the "Savage postulates." In view of Savage's feelings, expressed in conversation, that identification of theoretical positions with personalities contributes to undue commitment and controversy, I must apologize for this practically inescapable usage.

sequences only; they apply, in fact, to actions whose consequences are continuous functions of events, assuming infinite sets of states of the world. But these formal statements, though general and rigorous, are regrettably opaque, making scarcely any direct appeal to intuition. Since the contradictory behavior I wish to examine in the next chapter involves violation of the postulates, primarily Postulate 2, under very general circumstances including the ideally simple ones represented by two-consequence gambles, it will not be necessary for our purposes to confront the postulates at all in their full generality.[1] It is enough to consider their impact upon the set of "acceptable" choices in Savage's horse-race example. This will indicate their separate roles and importance in the theory, i.e., the effect of violating them upon the possibility of inferring probabilities from such choices.

Suppose we offer a choice between actions I and II above: the chance to stake a $10 prize either on horse A or on B. If we are to infer which of these you consider the more probable winner, we must always be able to conclude from your behavior either that you "prefer" action I to action II, or II to I, or that you are indifferent between them. Behavior that could not be interpreted as any one of these, if possible given our operational rules of interpretation associating your behavior with preference or choice, would leave A and B "incomparable" with respect to probability.

Moreover, if your behavior indicates (under our rules of interpretation) that you prefer I to II, and II to III, but that between I and III you prefer III, your implied comparisons of events would lack the required transitivity. Another, less obvious, form of "troublesome" behavior that must be ruled out is the following: suppose that, in choosing among actions I, II, or III you would choose action I; but that if you were limited to the alternatives I and II (even though horse C were still running) you would prefer action II. This sort of behavior (which could result from the criterion of "minimaxing regret," discussed later) would make it impossible unambiguously to state your preference between actions I and II, and hence the relative probability of A and B, without specifying the whole set of alternatives available in a given case.

All of these patterns of behavior are ruled out by Savage's Postulate 1: *The relation ≤{ is a simple ordering among acts.*[2] That is, for every pair of acts, I, II, either I ≤{ II or II ≤{ I; and for every I, II, III, if I ≤{ II, and II ≤{ III, then I ≤{ III.

---

[1] For a summary of the formal statements, see Appendix to this chapter.

[2] Savage expresses reservations about this postulate, as an idealization of reality, more frequently than about the others; apparently because he believes that "vagueness" of probabilities, or lack of definiteness concerning one's own opinions, will be reflected in behavior through violation of this postulate: i.e., through inability to decide on which of two horses to place the stake, or through changing one's

Obviously, if Savage's test is to lead to any inferred inequalities between probabilities, there must exist some prize you consider worthwhile. Savage defines preference among consequences in terms of preference among *constant* acts, i.e., acts whose consequences are independent of the state of the world; consequence *a* is preferred to consequence *b* if and only if for any constant actions I, II offering the consequences *a*, *b* respectively, I is preferred to II. Postulate 5 asserts: *There is at least one pair of consequences, a, b, such that a is preferred to b.* We have been assuming implicitly that $10, $0 satisfy this test; the assumption seems, as Savage puts it, "innocuous."

Also, if we are going to use the same two outcomes, associated with different events by different gambles, to measure your probabilities, your preference between these two outcomes must not depend upon the events with which they are associated. Postulate 3 asserts that if two actions I, II have the *same* outcome for some set of states of nature, and that if for some "non-null"[1] states of nature for which they do not have the same outcome, I has outcome *a* and II has outcome *b*, then I {≥ II if and only if *a* {≥ *b* (i.e., regardless of the states of nature for which the actions offer these outcomes). This is obviously a special form of the familiar principle of "admissibility," or non-domination

---

choice in two closely-repeated trials with the same alternatives, or through intransitivities. He even mentions a "temptation to explore the possibilities of analyzing preference among acts as a *partial ordering* . . . admitting that some pairs of acts are incomparable. This would seem to give expression to introspective sensations of indecision or vacillation, which we may be reluctant to identify with indifference. My own conjecture is that it would prove a blind alley losing much in power and advancing little, if at all, in realism . . ." (*op. cit.*, p. 21.)

Like Savage, I am willing to adopt the idealization of behavior implied in the assumption that an individual employs determinate decision rules in his decision-making, which determine a definite choice (or strict indifference) for any set of alternatives. And the rules I shall consider all generate a *simple ordering of actions*, i.e., they satisfy Postulate 1, although my central interest is in phenomena associated with vagueness in opinion. This reflects my own conjecture that such phenomena are not necessarily reflected in "indecision or vacillation" in choice but, frequently, in simply ordered choices that violate Postulate 2 and hence are incompatible with an inferred qualitative (or numerical) probability relationship over events.

[1] An event or state of the world is said to be "null"—in effect, "impossible" or "of negligible probability"—when, for any two actions I, II that differ in payoff only under that event, I = II, whatever the actual difference in payoff. In other words, the values that acts take on states of the world comprising that event are irrelevant to all decisions. See Savage, *Foundations of Statistics*, p. 24.

of preferred acts.[1] One act is said to *dominate* another if its outcome is preferred or indifferent to the corresponding outcome of the other for each state of nature, and strictly preferred for at least one state of nature. A slightly stronger form of Postulate 3 would be:[2] *If action I dominates action II, I* {≥ II.

All the decision rules that have been proposed in recent literature for decision-making under uncertainty—and all that I shall consider or propose below—satisfy Postulate 3, in either its weaker or stronger form. That is, it has been agreed virtually universally that if the outcome to one action is better than or indifferent to that of another "in any event" (no matter how finely subdivided the set of events), and better in some, you should not prefer the second action to the first. Recognition of this criterion has the useful consequences: (1) you can reject certain ("dominated") actions from further consideration, thus narrowing your search for "preferred" actions, on the basis of your preferences among consequences alone, without bothering to ask yourself questions on your relative probabilities; in certain sets of actions, this process might leave only one ("undominated") candidate for choice; (2) if two people differ in their subjective probabilities but agree in their preferences for consequences and accept this criterion, they must agree in their preferences among certain acts.

Next, suppose that you preferred to stake a $10 prize on horse A rather than horse B; but that if the prize in question were $100, or $1, you would prefer to stake it on B. We would not be able to infer which horse you considered "a better bet to win;" or at least, we would have to state your probability relationships relative to a specified stake. This behavior is ruled out by Savage's Postulate 4, which essentially ensures the independence of probability comparisons and preferences among outcomes. In choices among gambles all offering the same two outcomes, *a, b,* Postulate 4 requires that preference among gambles be independent of the values of *a* and *b,* given their ordering. As Savage puts it, it is "the assumption that *on which of two events the person will choose to stake a given prize does not depend on the prize itself.*"[3] Thus, if, on due reflection, you definitely prefer I to II

---

[1] See Luce and Raiffa, *Games and Decisions*, p. 287. An act is said to be "admissible" within some set of actions if it is not dominated by any act within that set.

[2] This requirement is equivalent to Postulate 3 in the presence of Postulates 1 and 2. It is assumed in this definition that states of the world have been sufficiently well defined, with respect to a given set of actions, so that no further analysis of a given state into distinguishable states of the world would reveal a new "difference" in payoff between two actions. This condition distinguishes Postulate 3, or equivalent postulates relative to "domination," from any form of Postulate 2, the "Sure-Thing Principle," below.

[3] Savage, *Foundations of Statistics*, p. 31. Savage notes that in practice a person "might reverse himself in going from a penny to a dollar, because he might not have

below, you must prefer III to IV, where $X represents any given (positive) amount of money.

	A	B	C
I	$10	$ 0	$ 0
II	$ 0	$10	$ 0
III	$ X	$ 0	$ 0
IV	$ 0	$ X	$ 0

Fig. 4.2

All the decision rules I shall consider or propose subsequently obey Postulates 1, 3, 4, and 5 under all circumstances when they are applicable. But if you obey these postulates, when applicable, in all your choices among gambles, we can infer a *simple ordering of events* from your choices. If we introduce a relational symbol ⓢ between events such that A ≤ B means "You do not prefer to stake a given prize[1] (of whatever magnitude) upon event A rather than upon event B," then we can establish that: (a) for any two events A, B, either A ⓢ B or B ⓢ A; and (b) if A ⓢ B and B ⓢ C, then AⓈ C.

However, this relationship ⓢ, based upon your (possibly self-) observed choices, *will not necessarily have the characteristics defined earlier of a qualitative probability relationship* ≤·. Your ordering of events might lack the

---

found it worth his trouble to give careful consideration for too small a prize," but that it would "seem unreasonable" for him to reverse his decision "if the prize were reduced from a dollar to a penny." (*op. cit.*, p. 30). This is the sort of practical consideration we have not been considering in detail in this discussion because of our assumption that we are considering only decisions that already reflect careful deliberation. However, in subsequent discussion I shall argue that it is when the stakes are "important," not when they are trivial, that *deliberate* choices violating the Savage postulates are most likely. This could mean that in going back again from important to trivial sums, reverses in decisions might appear. However, let us assume henceforth that we are considering only problems in which decision rules designed for "important" choices are used.

[1]As we have already been using it, by the phrase, "To offer a prize upon A" we mean: to make available an action with consequence *a* if A occurs, (or "obtains") and *b* if A does not occur (i.e., if Ā, not-A, occurs, where *a* is preferred to *b*. For you to "stake a prize upon A rather than B," when someone has offered you alternatively a given prize on A or on B, is to choose the former action.

sort of structure associated with "additivity." That is, even though you obeyed all the above postulates, it might not be true for all A, B, C, such that A ⊜ B, and A ∩ C = B ∩ C = O, that (A ∪ C) ⊜ (B ∪ C). And specifically, relationships among various events and their complements might not have the required properties. Even though you had a consistent (i.e., connected and transitive) ordering among A, $\bar{A}$, B, $\bar{B}$, that ordering might take, for example, the form B ⊜ A ⊜ $\bar{B}$ ⊜ $\bar{A}$, whereas a qualitative probability relationship requires: B ≤· A <=> $\bar{B}$ ·≥ $\bar{A}$.

Thus, suppose you preferred I to II, and IV to III, below:

	A	B	C
I	$10	$ 0	$ 0
II	$ 0	$10	$ 0
III	$10	$ 0	$10
IV	$ 0	$10	$10

Fig. 4.3

Let us suppose that you never chose from this whole set of alternatives, but that you are offered one pair of actions at a time, without being told what pairs will subsequently be offered. Action III offers the prize on the event, "$\bar{B}$" or equivalently, "A or C;" IV offers the prize on "B or C", or "$\bar{A}$." From II <· I, I <· III, III <· IV, these preferences being transitive, we could define: B ⊜ A ⊜ $\bar{B}$ ⊜ $\bar{A}$. But as noted above, this would conflict with the interpretation of ⊜ as a qualitative probability relationship ≤·.

Likewise, from III <· IV we would define: (A or C) ⊜ (B or C), where A ∩ C = B ∩ C = O. But from I ·> II we would have B ⊜ A. Again, we would be unable to interpret B ⊜ A as equivalent to A ·> B, or "A is more probable than" B. On the basis of these observed choices, we could make no inference *either* of the form "A is not less probable than B" or "B is not less probable than A." In other words, Savage's basic operational definition of relative probability, cited at the beginning of this chapter, would not lead to valid inferences. And since, given these choices, we could not even make valid comparisons of the probabilities of A and B, *a fortiori* we could find no probability *numbers* to assign to A, B, C in terms of which you could be described as obeying the "Bernoulli proposition," or maximizing the mathematical expectation of utility (for any utility numbers we might assign to $10 and $0; see the discussion of a similar example in Chapter Two).

POSTULATE 2: THE "SURE-THING PRINCIPLE"

Such choices (which are "consistent with" Postulates 1, 3, 4, and 5) are defined as "inconsistent" and are forbidden by Savage's Postulate 2, which Savage offers as the expression of what he terms the "Sure-Thing Principle." To repeat our earlier description of this postulate, it requires that the choice between two actions should be affected only by the payoffs corresponding to events for which the two actions offer *different* payoffs. The choice should be independent of the values of payoffs for events on which the two actions "agree," i.e., for which they offer the same payoffs; hence, it should not be affected if these values are changed.

Since actions I and II above "agree" in their payoffs to event C, both offering $0, your preference between them should not be affected if the payoff under C for each of them is changed from $0 to $10 (or to any other common outcome). If you prefer I to II, you must prefer III to IV, since the "relevant" payoffs in the two pairs are equivalent, the only difference between the pairs being the value of payoff for events on which the two actions in each pair "agree."

The implications of violating Postulate 2, in terms of the possibility of inferring additive probabilities from your choices, have been indicated above; what are the arguments for obeying it? Savage offers the following rationale. Suppose that you would not prefer II to I if you *knew* that horse C would not win; if, on the other hand, you knew that C *would* win, you would still not prefer II to I, whatever the payoff under C, given that the payoffs were identical for the two actions. So, since you would not prefer II to I "in either event"— i.e., either knowing that C obtained or knowing that not-C obtained—you should not prefer II when you *do not know whether or not* C will win.

Referring to this particular argument as the "Sure-Thing Principle," Savage asserts that although it is seldom that a definite decision can be determined by this principle alone: "except possibly for the assumption of simple ordering, I know of no other extralogical principle governing decisions that finds such ready acceptance."[1] However, he notes that the principle, as stated in this form:

> cannot appropriately be accepted as a postulate in the sense that P1 is, because it would introduce new undefined technical terms referring to knowledge and possibility that would render it mathematically useless without still more postulates governing these terms. It will be preferable to regard the principle as a loose one that suggests certain formal postulates well articulated with P1.[2]

---

[1] Savage, *Foundations of Statistics*, p. 21.
[2] *Ibid.*, p. 22.

The substance of the formal postulate that Savage offers as expressing, intuitively, the same constraints upon behavior as the "Sure-Thing Principle," has been presented in our discussion of the example above.[1]

Savage's verbal statement of the "Sure-Thing Principle" could be used as well to justify Postulate 3, which requires essentially that a preferred action must be non-dominated. The wording would have to be changed to apply to pairs of actions such that you would not prefer the first to the second either knowing that *any given state of the world* (rather than: some one, given *event*) obtained or knowing that it did not obtain. But the two principles are unquestionably similar in spirit. It is possible to describe Postulate 2

---

[1] Three slightly different, though logically equivalent, formal statements of this postulate appear in *The Foundations of Statistics:* in the end-papers of the book, on p. 23, and on p. 87. Since we will be concerned only with violations of this postulate that can be exhibited in terms of simple examples such as the one above, it does not seem worth the space required to introduce the special notions and symbolism necessary to reproduce intelligibly any of these formal expressions here. See Appendix to this chapter for an unannotated statement of the postulates reproduced from the end-papers to *The Foundations of Statistics*.

In other axiomatizations of probability and utility leading to the "Bernoulli proposition," the logical role played by Savage's Postulate 2 in ensuring additivity of probabilities is taken by other, closely-related postulates: e.g., "Rubin's Postulate" (see Herman Chernoff, "Rational Selection of Decision Functions," *Econometrica*, Vol. 22, No. 4, October, 1954, p. 431; or Luce and Raiffa, *Games and Decisions*, p. 290); or Milnor's "column linearity" postulate (see John Milnor, "Games Against Nature," in *Decision Processes*, ed. Thrall, Coombs, and Davis, p. 51; or Luce and Raiffa, *Games and Decisions*, p. 290; for an equivalent postulate, see D. Blackwell and M. A. Girshick, *Theory of Games and Statistical Decisions*, New York, 1954, p. 117, postulate L_3).

All of these require concepts or information beyond those required to define Savage's Postulate 2. Rubin's Postulate requires the notions of definite probabilities and von Neumann-Morgenstern utilities; Milnor's postulate, which implies that adding a constant to a column of utility payoffs should not change the preference ordering among acts, requires that the latter numerical operation should have some explicit operational meaning in terms of behavior. However, since the rationale presented for each of these postulates is somewhat different and one may carry more intuitive appeal for a given reader than the others, we shall consider them explicitly in a later chapter (see Chapter Eight).

If numerical probabilities were assumed known for *all* relevant events, so that the subject was dealing explicitly with "known risks," Savage's Postulate 2 and these others would amount to Samuelson's "Special Independence Assumption" ("Probability, Utility and the Independence Axiom," *Econometrica*, Vol. 20, October. 1952, pp. 670–78; discussed together with the other postulates in a later chapter) on which Samuelson relies heavily in his derivation of "von Neumann-Morgenstern utilities."

as the extension of the principle of dominance or admissibility as repre-sented by Postulate 3 to gambles that have other gambles as "prizes;" though the two postulates remain conceptually distinct so long as we pre-serve the distinctions between states of the world and events, and between consequences and actions or gambles.

But whereas I would take no exception to Savage's comment on the general "ready acceptance" of the verbal argument for the "Sure-Thing Principle" as it applies to Postulate 3 (this postulate will not come up for challenge in any of our later discussion), I shall argue that Postulate 2 must be discarded as a general condition of reasonable choice. I believe, in other words, that for many decision makers, a proposed logic of consistent deci-sion that defines patterns of choice violating Postulate 2 as "unreasonable" *under any circumstances* will not serve their purposes. Consequently, it is important to keep in mind that Postulate 2 (which we will identify with the "Sure-Thing Principle") and Postulate 3 (which may be identified with the notions of "domination" or "admissibility") are quite separate require-ments, as indicated by Savage's use of two separate postulates.[1]

Though we have not yet heard every argument that can be offered in favor of obeying the Savage postulates in all deliberate choices, we have now seen various ways in which these postulates, if accepted, do constrain

---

[1] In recent published comments on alleged counterexamples to the Savage pos-tulates (Howard Raiffa, "Risk, Ambiguity, and the Savage Axioms: Comment," *Quarterly Journal of Economics*, Vol. LXXV, No. 4, November, 1961, p. 694), Howard Raiffa describes one action as better than another "by strict dominance" although it is by no means true that the outcome to the first is preferred or indifferent to the outcome of the second for every *relevant state of the world*. It is clear in context that what is involved is Postulate 2, or some form of the Sure-Thing Principle or Samuel-son's Independence Axiom, not Postulate 3 or any equivalent requirement of admissibility using the notion of "domination" in a strict, traditional sense.

Similarly, Raiffa and Schlaifer, in *Applied Statistical Decision Theory*, describe one of their assumptions (which seems, in fact, to correspond to admissibility, or Savage's Postulate 3) as "the so-called sure-thing or dominance principle" (p. 24). Except for these two passages, I am unaware of any references in the literature of statistical decision theory that treat these two notions as synonymous. Of the authors cited in the preceding footnote, not only Savage, but Chernoff, Milnor, Luce and Raiffa, and Blackwell and Girshick, all represent the two requirements by two distinct postulates, despite their similarity.

Since I wish to draw attention to differences in their respective vulnerability to counterexamples, and in fact to question the acceptability of *one* of these require-ments as a general criterion of reasonable choice, I must object to language that blurs the distinction between them.

choices among simple, two-outcome gambles. It is clear that a pattern of choices obeying the postulates will avoid the particular "inconsistencies" described that would invalidate inferences as to an underlying probability distribution. What is less obvious, but can be proved,[1] is that these postulates alone are sufficient to rule out *all* inconsistencies that have such effect.

It is still to be expected that casual, hasty choices among gambles will result in frequent violations of the postulates. But for an individual who *wishes* not to violate these principles in his important, deliberated choices, and who takes the time to discover and eliminate "inconsistencies" among his initial choices, his preferences among two-outcome gambles will determine a meaningful relationship over all events having the properties of a qualitative probability relationship (and not merely a general, simple ordering ⩾ of events, which follows from these postulates even in the absence of Postulate 2). It is indeed plausible that such individuals exist. Whether such behavior is to be regarded as, in all circumstances, uniquely reasonable, remains at issue; but even that position, though I shall dispute it, seems far from absurd.

Postulates 1–5 alone are still insufficient to ensure the possibility of establishing a numerical probability measure on the set of all events. In Savage's words, a probability measure on a set S is a function P(B) attaching to each B ∈ S a real number such that:

1. P(B) ≥ 0 for every B.
2. If B ∩ C = 0, P(B ∪ C) = P(B) + P(C).
3. P(S) = 1.

The probability measure P(S) is said to *agree with* the qualitative probability over S, if for every pair of events B, C, P(B) ″ P(C) if and only if B ″· C.[2]

What is most important in our discussion is to understand the conditions under which numerical probabilities can be assigned meaningfully to *some* events. In our horse race example, if it should happen that you prove *indifferent* between staking a given prize on horse A, B, or C, and if you are known to conform to the Savage postulates in all your choices, then we can assign the probability numbers 1/3, 1/3, 1/3 to the events A, B, C respectively. Moreover, these are the *only* numbers with the characteristics of a probability measure that agree with the qualitative probability relationship implied by your preferences.

To say that these numbers represent a probability measure that agrees with your qualitative probabilities must be to say that you regard all events

---

[1] Savage, *Foundations of Statistics*, p. 32.

[2] *Ibid.*, pp. 33–34. Savage makes a distinction between "strictly agreeing" and "almost agreeing" that is not important for our purposes.

assigned, by implication, the number 2/3 as "equally probable;" i.e., you must be indifferent between actions IV, V, and VI below.

	A	B	C
I	$10	$ 0	$ 0
II	$ 0	$10	$ 0
III	$ 0	$ 0	$10
IV	$10	$ 0	$10
V	$ 0	$10	$10
VI	$10	$10	$ 0

Fig. 4.4

But this will follow by direct application of Postulate 2, given your presumed indifference between I, II, and III. Moreover, it must be true—as it is here—that for each event; prob (E) + prob ($\bar{E}$) = 1.

The principle here is, of course, the same used by Ramsey in measuring a probability = $\frac{1}{2}$. Now we have found events with probability = 1/3; and by giving you the opportunity to stake a given prize on a horse in this race or on the occurrence of some quite *different* event E, we can give operational meaning to the statement that, for example, the probability of E is greater than 1/3 for you. If we can find, say, *six* mutually exclusive and exhaustive events—for example, the six sides of a die that may land uppermost in a single toss—on which you are equally willing to stake a given prize, we can measure probabilities precisely equal to 1/6, and proceed to make finer comparisons.

This approach to numerical probabilities, by comparisons with subsets or elements of sets of equi-probable events, is closer to de Finetti's procedures (1931) than to those of Ramsey or Savage; but the earliest discussion known to me is in a review of Keyne's *Treatise on Probability* by Émile Borel. Since I know of no account of Borel's contribution in English (and only one reference, by Savage), the passage deserves quotation:

> There is a simple example, well-known to economists, of magnitudes which, despite their complexity can be subjected to a linear numerical evaluation; this is the case of everything that can be bought and sold. . . . Well, it appears that the method of betting permits, in most cases, a numerical evaluation of probabilities which has precisely the same character as the evaluation of prices by offers to trade. If one wishes to know the price of a

ton of coal, it is enough to propose successively higher and higher sums to the one who holds the coal; at a certain figure, he will decide to sell; conversely, if the holder of coal offers his coal, he will end by finding a buyer if he lowers his demands sufficiently. There will be naturally a little deviation between the prices thus fixed; I have no need to present here a theory of average prices; what is certain is that in practice, in normal periods of economic activity, these average prices are well defined and fairly stable.

Similarly, I can offer someone who expresses a judgment susceptible of verification a bet on his judgment. If I wish to avoid having to take account of attraction or repugnance toward betting, I could give a *choice between two bets offering the same profit in case of a win*. Paul claims that it will rain tomorrow; I admit that we agree on the precise meaning of this assertion and I offer him, at his preference, the chance to receive 100 francs if his prediction is verified, or to receive 100 francs, if a throw of a die brings the point 5 or the point 6. In the second case, the probability that he will receive 100 francs is equal to one-third; if therefore, he prefers to receive 100 francs if his meteorological prediction is correct, it must be that he attributes to this prediction a *probability greater than one-third*. The same method may be applied to all verifiable judgments and permits one to evaluate probabilities with a precision entirely comparable to the precision with which one evaluates prices.[1]

To fit this passage into our present approach, we must read into it the assumption that you will be indifferent between staking a given prize on one outcome or another of a single toss of a die, so that the basis of assigning probability $1/3$ to the outcome (5 or 6) is not left unspecified.

If we now imagine a well-shuffled pack of, say, 100 cards numbered on their faces 1 to 100, you might be willing to stake a given prize indifferently on any given number between 1 and 100 as the next card to be drawn. If you obeyed the Savage postulates, we could then construct for you an event corresponding to any numerical probability $r/100$, $0 " r " 100$. You should be indifferent between staking a given prize on one or another sets of r specified cards out of the 100, the prize to be won if one of the r cards specified were to be drawn; you should *prefer* to stake the prize on any set of $r+1$ cards than on any set of r cards, and prefer the latter to any set of $r-1$ cards.[2]

---

[1] Émile Borel, "A Propos d'un Traite de Probabilitiés," Revue Philosophique, t. 98, 1924; reprinted in, *Valeurs Pratique des Probabilitiés*, Gauthiers-Villars, Paris, 1939, p. 143; my translation, italics added. I am indebted to L. J. Savage for this reference.

[2] In principle, the set of all sequences of a given length of repeated "independent" trials of a random event, such as the 2^n sequences of n tosses of a "fair" coin, should likewise provide a set of equi-probable events, whose probabilities are thereby numerically measurable.

Although "mistakes" in the calculation of complex probabilities would be natural, it seems plausible that with events of this peculiar sort the postulates should be generally acceptable as precise normative guides, serving to indicate "inconsistencies" that, once discovered, would be painless to eliminate.

Moreover, once unambiguous probabilities are assigned to this large set of events, comparisons with quite different events can, in principle, establish *their* numerical probabilities within 1%. Thus, if you would rather stake a prize on event E than on the possibility of drawing a card whose number is between 1 and t, inclusive, but you would prefer the drawing if the winning numbers were between 1 and $t + 1$, then the (only) numerical probabilities for E compatible with your preferences are between $t/100$ and $(t+1)/100$. This might seem an extraordinarily precise judgment, but

---

Thus, I. J. Good's neat statement: "Numerical probabilities can be introduced by imagining perfect packs of cards perfectly shuffled, or infinite sequences of trials under essentially similar conditions. Both methods are idealizations, and there is very little to choose between them. It is a matter of taste: that is why there is so much argument about it." (Good, "Rational Decisions," *Journal of the Royal Statistical Society*, Series B, Vol. XIV, No. 1, 1952, p. 110).

Savage seems, in his published writings, to favor the latter notion, following de Finetti; he suggests that a postulate asserting *that S can be partitioned into an arbitrarily large number of equivalent subsets—which is what is at issue here—"could be made relatively acceptable by observing that it will obtain if, for example, in all the world there is a coin that the person is firmly convinced is fair, that is, a coin such that any finite sequence of heads and tails is for him no more probable than any other sequence of the same length; though such a coin is, to be sure, a considerable idealization."* (Foundations of Statistics, p. 33).

Though the point, as Good observes, is not an essential one, I suspect rather strongly that this particular idealization is considerably further from realization for most people than the notion of equi-probability in a single drawing from large packs of shuffled cards or well-mixed balls in an urn. How many people are really prepared to be convinced, or to bet as if they believed, that 17 heads in a row, tossing any given coin, are no less likely than any other given sequence of 17 outcomes? Try this on your wife. Many psychological experiments have shown implicit notions of serial correlations, positive or negative, between repetitive trials, and skepticism of the existence of "independence" to be very deeply ingrained in the prior probabilities of most people: possibly as the result of considerable experience outside of psychological laboratories. (See J. S. Bruner, J. J. Goodnow, and G. A. Austin, *A Study of Thinking*, Chapter 7, "On categorizing with probabilistic cues," which includes many references; J. J. Goodnow, "Determinants of choice-distribution in two-choice probability situations," *American Journal of Psychology*, Vol. 68, pp. 106–116; H. Hake and R. Hyman, "Perception of the statistical structure of a random series of binary symbols," *Journal of Experimental Psychology*, Vol. 45, pp. 64–74.)

adherence to the Savage postulates implies the possibility in every case of just this degree of precision: and more, when the postulate is added (Postulate 6) that *the set of all events can be partitioned into events of arbitrarily small probability*, or the weaker (de Finetti) postulate is used, that *S can be partitioned into an arbitrarily large number of equivalent subsets*. These latter postulates, or others with equivalent effect,[1] assure the existence of a probability measure assigning a precise numerical probability to every event in S.

The problems we shall be exploring in subsequent chapters, however, arise long before the measurement process reaches a high degree of refinement. In fact, they concern the possibility of asserting meaningfully that a reasonable individual regards one event as "not less probable than" another in every case of a comparison: let alone the possibility of assigning numerical probabilities to each event, accurate to several significant figures. It is plausible and certainly convenient to assume that fairly precise numerical probabilities can be assigned to *some* events by the various methods described above; at any rate, that assumption will not be questioned here. The question to be discussed is whether it is realistic to suppose this to be possible for *all* relevant events, even given the careful, deliberated, highly calculated decision-making we have been assuming.

Savage himself, in writings subsequent to *The Foundations of Statistics*, has given considerable emphasis to the "vagueness" of many personal probabilities, as a practical problem to be expected in any application of the theory.

> In principle, anyone can, by asking himself how he would bet, elicit his own subjective probability distribution for the velocity of neon light in beer. But no one is really prepared to do so with much precision. . . .[2]

However, Savage has continued, in these writings, to be regrettably vague as to the precise manner in which he expects "vagueness" to be manifested in choice-behavior, particularly with respect to conformity with his postulates (though frequent linkages with "indecision" suggest violations of Postulate 1, at least).

In the last chapter we considered one way in which the "indefiniteness" of certain probabilities might be given numerical limits in terms of "upper" and "lower" betting probabilities, corresponding to the maximum "prices" you might be prepared to pay for a unit utility staked, respectively *on* and *against* the occurrence of a given event. It would be appropriate to consider here corresponding behavior in choices between staking a given

---

[1] Savage, *Foundations of Statistics*, pp. 33–40; e.g., P6′: If B< {C, there exists a partition of S the union of each element of which with B is less probable than C (p. 38).

[2] Savage, "Subjective Probability and Statistical Practice," p. 11.

prize on a given event E or upon a certain event with numerical probability r/t (the disjunction of r out of t disjoint, equi-probable events). We could define r_o as the greatest r (for given t, e.g., 100) for which you would *not* prefer to stake a given prize upon an event with probability r/t, rather than upon the event E; you would prefer to stake the prize on any event with numerical probability r'/t, $r' > r_o$, than upon the event E. Similarly, R_o can be defined as the greatest r for which you would *not* prefer to stake a prize on an event with numerical probability r/t, than upon the event $\bar{E}$, i.e., on "not-E" or, *against* E).

Let $r^o = t - R_o$. It can be shown that if the interval $r^o - r_o$ is significantly large (> 2), your pattern of choices violates Postulate 2; and it would be easy to relate such a phenomenon to the pattern of choices that would indicate $p^o > p_o$, as previously defined. Moreover, just as it would be possible conceptually to distinguish between "fuzziness" of the "betting probabilities" p_o and p^o (perhaps revealing itself in indecision, vacillation or a feeling of arbitrariness near those boundary-values), and the "indefiniteness" of opinion concerning E reflected in an interval $p^o - p_o$ of definitely positive length, so we might distinguish between "fuzziness" of the values, r_o and r^o, associated with violations of Postulate 1, and behavior leading to a definite estimate of $r^o - r_o > 0$, associated with violation of Postulate 2.

This is precisely the behavior hypothesized by William Fellner in his stimulating article, "Distortion of Subjective Probabilities as a Reaction to Uncertainty."[1] Like Borel, Fellner assumes the existence of what he calls a "standard process," like our pack of cards, providing a set of events to which an individual assigns "definite" numerical probabilities. Suppose that this individual proves indifferent between staking a given prize on some event E in a "non-standard process" and staking the identical prize on a standard-process event which, say, has the probability .3 (thus $r_o/t = .3$). Fellner then conjectures that this individual might likewise be indifferent between staking the prize *against* E (i.e., on $\bar{E}$) or on the same standard-process event with probability .3 (i.e., $R_o/t = .3$, so that $r^o/t = 1 - R_o/t = .7$).[2] Fellner suggests that such behavior might well be considered reasonable, when associated with what would be called here "vagueness" or

---

[1] *Quarterly Journal of Economics*, Vol. LXXV, 1961, pp. 670–689. Fellner's work, done quite independently of mine reported in the same issue ("Risk, ambiguity and the Savage Axioms") lends most encouraging support to the conjectures advanced in the latter paper and in the present study.

[2] *Ibid.*, p. 673. It is clear that Fellner is focusing upon the same phenomenon, in terms of behavior pattern, circumstances of information and subjective conditions of uncertainty, that is the subject of this study. However, his formalization of the behavior pattern and his hypotheses as to the underlying decision criteria seem to differ significantly from mine, as advanced in the following chapters.

"ambiguity" concerning the relative probability of E between the limits .3 and .7 (he does not relate the behavior directly to the Savage postulates, or to any other formal, normative decision-making criteria). The pattern is, of course, essentially the same as that imagined by C. A. B. Smith (*op. cit.*).

Recognizable as such behavior might seem to be, it does involve violation of Postulates 1 and/or 2. Referring to the Borel example, suppose that Paul, who says that it will rain tomorrow, is virtually indifferent between the offer of 100 francs if a throw of a die brings the point 6, and an offer of 100 francs if there is *no* rain tomorrow; he would definitely prefer to see the prize on 5 or 6 than to stake it *against* rain. Having already concluded that Paul attributes a probability greater than 1/3 to his prediction of rain, Borel would now conclude that his probability must be approximately 5/6. But that might be hasty; for, when the prize is again staked *on* the occurrence of rain, Paul might profess himself close to indifference between that offer and 100 francs if the die turns up 1, 2 or 3: and, definitely to prefer staking the prize on 1, 2, 3 or 4 than on his prediction.

If one merely has a practical interest in discovering, roughly, Paul's confidence in his prediction, these results might be quite adequate; Borel might say, "Well, that's what I mean by a precision entirely comparable to the precision with which one evaluates prices." But within the "neo-Bernoullian" framework, such a pattern of preferences constitutes a challenge and an enigma, for it inevitably entails violation of the Savage postulates. Giving Paul the benefit of the doubt, his "unreasonable" preferences might be assumed to be hasty, unconsidered; but the "neo-Bernoullian" approach provides no hints for inferring from these "inconsistent" choices what his "real" preferences might prove to be, nor what considerations might have led to just these choices, nor when to expect such choices. *Explanations* in terms of "vagueness" of probabilities within certain limits are not strictly available to the "neo-Bernoullian," since it seems impossible to interpret such notions operationally in terms of choices consistent with the postulates, whereas the theory provides no basis whatever for explaining, describing or predicting, let alone "rationalizing" choices that conflict with the postulates.

INTUITIVE PROBABILITIES AND "VAGUENESS"*

The Koopman/Good approach, described at the beginning of this chapter, would find itself less at a loss to analyze Paul's behavior hypothesized

---

*This section, which discusses an abstract approach alternative to that of Ramsey/ deFinetti/Savage, may be regarded as an appendix and omitted at first reading: or postponed till after Chapter Five, since it provides a general theoretical foundation for concepts discussed less formally in Chapters Six and Seven.

above. Paul's *opinions* on tomorrow's weather might or might not be compatible with the Koopman axioms on consistent partial beliefs, but these observed preferences among gambles would not be conclusive either way.

If Paul, upon being *asked* (or, upon *asking himself*) to compare his degrees of belief in certain propositions, should assert that he definitely judged "rain tomorrow" to be *less probable than* "1, 2, 3 or 4 on the next toss of this die," and at the same time asserted that he definitely judged "no rain tomorrow" to be less probable than "5 or 6 on the next toss of of this die" (i.e., "*not* 1, 2, 3 or 4"), then his state of mind would fall outside the Koopman theory of consistent opinions, just as his choices already fall outside the Savage theory of consistent decisions. The above pair of definite comparisons would violate Koopman's Axiom of Antisymmetry: if proposition *a* (on the presumption *h*) is judged *less* probable than proposition *b* (on the presumption *k*), then *not-a* is *more* probable than *not-b* (on the same presumptions).[1] If the laws of consistency that seem to Koopman to govern his definite comparisons of probability (both comparisons and laws being derived intuitively, the latter from his "awareness of his own rational processes") applied to Paul, then from Paul's judgment that "rain tomorrow" was definitely less probable than "1, 2, 3 or 4 on this die" it should be possible to *infer* that he would judge "no rain" as definitely more probable that "5 or 6." Failure of this prediction would imply, from Koopman's point of view, that Paul's mind was in "a condition of mental incoherence of the same nature as logical inconsistency."[2]

However, Koopman would allow Paul to say instead, as between "rain tomorrow" and "1, 2, 3 or 4 on this die": "I don't know [I'm not sure; I can't say] that one is more probable than the other." Or, if questions were being put to Paul (e.g., by himself) as to whether he definitely judged the first contingency (a) more probable, (b) less probable, or (c) equally probable compared to the second, Koopman's theoretical system (and that of I. J. Good) would allow for his answering "No" to all three questions. From such assertions—either explicitly expressing doubt, or denying any definite comparisons—neither Koopman nor Good would attempt to infer any definite probability comparisons concerning other pairs of propositions; on

---

[1] The interpretation of the "contingencies" *a* and *b* is clear in this example; the "presumption" *h* might be, "in terms of certain, specified measurements, it will either rain or not rain tomorrow"; the presumption *k* might be, "this die will be thrown, and will show either 1, 2, 3, 4, 5 or 6 spots on its uppermost face." Either presumption might also specify, in more or less detail, "and my information bearing on the matter is. . . ."

[2] Koopman, "The Axioms and Algebra of Intuitive Probability," p. 271. For Koopman's formal statements of his actions see Appendix of this Chapter.

the contrary, their axioms would require that Paul must, "consistently," be equally "vague" in comparing the probabilities of "no rain" and "5 or 6."

Even when Paul balked at asserting definite comparisons between the two propositions in each of these pairs, both Koopman and Good assume that Paul would be willing to assert definite comparisons between each of these propositions and *some* other propositions. Given the existence of what Koopman calls an "*n*-scale" it would be possible to express his uncertainty concerning any one of them in terms of numerical inequalities. An *n*-scale is defined by Koopman as any non-null set of *n* mutually exclusive propositions which a given individual judges definitely to be equally probable, on the presumption that one of them is true.

Propositions concerning the various possible outcomes of a single toss of Borel's die *might* prove to be a 6-scale for Paul; another *n*-scale might relate to the drawing of a card numbered from 1 to *n* from a pack of *n* well-shuffled cards, or the *n* sequences of Heads, Tails, resulting from $log\ n$ tosses of a fair coin.[1] Given definite judgments of equal probability for all propositions specifying a particular outcome from the *n* possible outcomes, then one and only one numerical probability distribution over the *n* propositions will "agree with" these judgments and all the other judgments then implied by the axioms: a function assigning probability $/n$ to each proposition (given that one of them is true) and probability m/n to any proposition of the form "One of the following *m* propositions belonging to this *n*-scale is true." Thus, for the members of such a set of propositions and for compound propositions derived from them, the Koopman axioms do imply the possibility of meaningful numerical measurement; and by comparing *other* propositions to propositions based upon an *n*-scale, *numerical inequalities* can be stated regarding the probabilities of these other propositions (even if definite comparisons cannot always be asserted *among* the other propositions).[2]

---

[1] Koopman, "The Axioms and Algebra of Intuitive Probability," p. 283. Since definite, subjective judgments of equal probability are required, a set of *n* propositions that constitutes an *n*-scale for one person need not qualify as such for another; and it is an empirical proposition to assert that a given set of propositions satisfies these conditions for a given person. No assertion is made by Koopman that any given set of propositions, or any set defined purely by its "objective" (impersonal) properties, should

[2] It is not implied by the Koopman axioms on intuitive probability that *even one* n-scale of propositions will exist for a given individual; none of the axioms involves the notion that two probabilities are judged to be strictly equal (only the relation ≤ { signifying "equally or less probable than" is employed). Prior to introducing the notion of an n-scale, Koopman demonstrates that it is not necessary to the development of a powerful theory of intuitive probabilities to suppose that a given

If we assume that for each integer n there exists an n-scale for Paul (e.g., relating to a pack of n cards, perfectly shuffled), then for each rational number $x = m/n$ ($m < n$) there exist propositions G and H, such that Paul may be said to assign the numerical probability x to the eventuality G/H. With this extra assumption, Koopman deduces from his axioms on comparisons numerical theorems concerning what he christened "upper and lower probabilities" p. and p* for a given eventuality.[1] The lower probability of the eventuality a/h, written p.(a,h), may be defined as the least upper bound of numbers x such that "you" judge *definitely* that the eventuality a/h is equally or *more* probable than an eventuality G/H to which the numerical probability x may be assigned. The upper probability of a/h, p*(a,h), is defined as the greatest lower bound of numbers x' such that you judge *definitely* that a/h is equally or less probable than an eventuality G'/H'. On the assumption that indefinitely large (i.e., "fine") n-scales exist for you and that you obey the axioms on comparisons, Koopman proves[2] that *limits* p.(a,h) and p*(a,h) as n increases always exist, and that they satisfy the relation: $O \le p.(a,h) \le p^*(a,h) \le 1$.

The statement of this relationship in terms of inequalities is highly significant. *The Koopman axioms on intuitive probabilities do not imply that, in general, p.(a,h) = p*(a,h)*. This is in striking contrast to the implications of the Ramsey/de Finetti/Savage theory of consistent choice among gambles. It would obviously be easy to define concepts within the latter approach corresponding to the notions of an "n-scale" and of "upper and lower probabilities"; but conformity to the Savage postulates would demand that the

individual *ever makes* a judgment of equal probability; for example, he presents thirteen theorems concerning comparisons, or *judged inequalities* between the probabilities of different eventualities, prior to introducing the notion of an n-scale. Thus, the presumed existence of even one n-scale, or even one judgment of equal probability between two non-certain and non-null propositions, is neither a requirement of "reasonableness" or "consistency," nor a prediction concerning typical bodies of belief, nor a proposition put forward as "intuitively evident" in the spirit of the axioms. Rather, the existence of an n-scale—and the stronger notion that at least one n-scale may be regarded as existing for a given individual, for any positive integer n—is "assumed" solely for the purpose of exploring its implications in the light of the axioms and theorems (it is closely similar in spirit and effect to the various forms of Savage's Postulate 6).

[1] C. A. B. Smith bases his notion of "upper and lower pignic[betting] probabilities" (*op. cit.*) upon the concepts of "upper and lower intuitive probabilities" introduced by Koopman. I have used the notation p_0 and p^0 to distinguish the former "betting probabilities" from Koopman's "intuitive probabilities," for which I preserve Koopman's symbols, p. and p*.

[2] Koopman, *op. cit.*, p. 285; Theorem 15.

"upper" and "lower" probabilities determined for any given event on the basis of deliberate choices among gambles be *equal.* The consequences of the Koopman axioms are, in this sense, less "strong." Yet this difference does not follow from any evident desire on Koopman's part to allow for empirically-relevant but "unreasonable" patterns of belief, or to forego any constraints that in his eyes appropriately define "reasonableness."

The axioms proposed by Koopman are described by him as *"the* intuitively evident laws of consistency governing all comparisons in probability";[1] it is implied that no additional axioms justifying stronger inferences qualify, in his opinion, for assertion with the same intuitive force. Of course, as Savage points out with reference to his own postulates, the statement of any theory based upon such personal standards is never necessarily complete; "there is no telling when someone will come upon still another postulate that clamors to be adjoined to the others."[2] However, it is noteworthy that Koopman evidently felt no urgent *need* to search his intuition for further constraints. In his opinion, these axioms "form a *sufficient* basis for what we envision as the legitimate role of a theory of intuitive probability"[3] (i.e., "to develop the rules for the derivation of comparisons in probability from other comparisons in probability previously given"[4]). Yet the strongest inferences that his axioms and theorems, together with the assumption of the existence of all n-scales, permit us to draw in general about the relationship of upper and lower probabilities for a given eventuality are the inequalities stated above. Thus, $p^*(a,h) = p^*(a,h)$ is not a criterion, in Koopman's approach nor in the closely similar approach of I. J. Good,[5] of a "reasonable" or "consistent" body of beliefs.

---

[1] Koopman, *op. cit.,* p. 275; italics added.

[2] Savage, *Foundations of Statistics,* p. 60. Compare Herman Chernoff's remark on his own proposed axiom system: "My intentions were not to give as brief an axiom system as possible. In the main, except for trivial cases, axioms were included if and only if they struck me as being reasonable requirements for 'rational' selection" ("Rational Selection of Decision Functions," *Econometrica,* Vol. 22, 1954, p. 440n). A set so determined is liable to expand or contract over time; there is not even a guarantee that a set of criteria will be judged "intuitively compelling" that are mutually incompatible, i.e., that *no* pattern of belief or decision can satisfy simultaneously. Someone who found the Luce and Raiffa axioms 1 to 11 all equally imperative in certain circumstances would be in that unhappy position (see *Games and Decisions,* p. 296).

[3] Koopman, *op. cit.,* p. 275; italics added.

[4] *Ibid.,* p. 271.

[5] In Good's abstract approach in *Probability and the Weighing of Evidence* he assumes for simplicity that probabilities can always be represented by numbers, but emphasizes that "full use is never made of the assumption," since Good, like

Koopman's acceptance of this limited result reflects his initial conception (shared by Good) that an intuitive probability relationship over propositions or events may properly be regarded as a *partial ordering*, allowing for the incomparability of certain pairs of propositions. The nature of a partial ordering in terms of probability, when upper and lower probabilities are not in general identical, appears from Koopman's *Theorem 16: The relation* $a_1/h_1 \leq \cdot\; a_2/h_2$ *implies both* p· $(a_1,h_1) \leq$ p·(a_2,h_2) *and* $p^*(a_1,h_1) \leq p^*(a_1,h_2)$. *And* $p^*(a_1,h_1) < $ p·(a_2,h_2) *implies the relation* $a_1/h_1 \leq \cdot\; a_2/h_2$.

The meaning of both assertions in this theorem is to be understood in terms of the sorts of *judgments* they are and are not ruling out (in the light of the axioms and assumptions of the theory). The first rules out the *definite judgment* that one proposition is equally or *less* probable than another when, at the same time, comparisons of each to propositions defined in terms of an *n*-scale would indicate that either: (a) the upper and lower probabilities of either proposition were *enclosed* by the upper and lower probabilities of the other; or (b) both the upper and lower probabilities, respectively, of the first proposition were *greater* than the upper and lower, respectively, of the second. The second, very important, proposition is that comparisons revealing the *upper* probability of one proposition to be less than the *lower* probability of another justify the inference that the first is judged to be less than or equally probable to the second. I.e., the individual should be willing to make such a judgment ("should" in the sense of obedience to the axioms of the theory), both *non-committal* attitudes and definite judgment that the first is more probable than the second being ruled out.

At the same time, it is important to notice the variety of relationships that these two propositions do *not* rule out; for neither proposition is it true that the *reverse* implications from the ones stated follow from the theory.

Thus, in terms of Paul's hypothetical comparisons above, it might be that (if we drop the "presumptions" from the notation, bearing in mind that all probabilities are conditional on certain evidence and assumptions) his lower and upper probabilities for "rain tomorrow" are: p·("rain") = 1/2,

---

Koopman, regards probability judgments as leading to a partial ordering only and stresses problems of vagueness and incomparability. In "Subjective Probability as the Measure of a Non-Measurable Set," he describes his earlier approach as adopted "in order to avoid the complications of Koopman's approach" and presents a new set of axioms that lead to Koopman's theorems (and some others) on upper and lower probabilities. I have followed the latter paper by Good in some of my exposition, above, of Koopman's system; Good's paper is as yet unpublished and I am greatly indebted to him for furnishing me with a manuscript copy (it is forthcoming in the *Proceedings of the International Congress for Logic, Methodology and Philosophy of Science,* Stanford, 1960.

p*("rain") = 5/6. To say this is to imply that with respect to *any* eventuality whose upper and lower probabilities both lie *between* 1/2 and 5/6—perhaps, the eventuality, "1, 2, 3, or 4 will occur on a toss of this fair die"—Paul is unable to judge definitely (even in response to his own question) either that he regards "rain tomorrow" as "more probable," or "less probable," or "equally probable."

Another important constraint is implied by Koopman's *Theorem 17*: p.(a,h) + p*(~a,h) = 1. It follows immediately from this that: p.(a,h) + p.(~a,h) ≤ 1 and if p.(~a,h) < p*(~a,h) then p.(a,h) + p.(~a,h) < 1. Moreover, since Theorem 17 may also be written: p.(~a,h) + p*(a,h) = 1, it follows that p*(a,h) = 1 − p.(~a,h).

Thus, "lower probabilities" do not conform to the properties demanded of a "probability measure": the "lower probabilities" of an exhaustive set of mutually exclusive propositions need not sum to unity (nor will the lower probability of a union of several disjoint propositions equal, in general, the sum of their separate, lower probabilities). The same is true for upper probabilities.[1]

Theorem 17 implies that it should be possible to *infer* your upper and lower probabilities for a given eventuality by determining your upper and lower probabilities for the complementary eventuality. Thus, given Paul's presumed upper and lower probabilities for "rain tomorrow," his upper and lower probabilities for "no rain tomorrow" should be, respectively, 1/2 and 1/6. With these values, Theorem 16 would rule out a definite judgment by Paul that "rain tomorrow is less probable than not." If the lower probability for "rain" were, instead, slightly greater than 1/2 and the upper probability for "no rain," correspondingly lower than 1/2, Paul should be able to judge definitely that "rain tomorrow is more probable than not." On the other hand, if the intervals for "rain" and "no rain" overlapped, Theorem 16 would neither compel nor rule out the latter definite judgment.

Like the other theorems, Theorem 17 states a rule of consistency among comparisons of probability that follows from the Koopman axioms. In practice, frequent inconsistency is to be expected; what is claimed for the theory is that when inconsistencies are detected, it will be found possible

---

[1] However, a number of theorems can be proven from the Koopman/Good axioms asserting *inequalities* relating the upper and lower probabilities for unions or intersections of eventualities to the sums or products of the component eventualities. See I. J. Good, "Subjective Probability as the Measure of a Non-Measurable Set,"; also, Good, "Discussion of Dr. Smith's Paper," pp. 28–29. The addition theorem may be stated:

If E and F are mutually exclusive given H, then:

P.(E/H) + P.(F/H) ≤ P.(E or F/H) ≤ P.(E/H) + P*(F/H) ≤ P*(E or F/H) ≤ P*(E/H) + P*(F/H).

(hopefully, easy) in the course of mature consideration to "correct" one or more of the conflicting comparisons without doing injustice to one's intuitive judgments.

In an actual application of the theory, the equality relationship specified in Theorem 17 would be expected to hold, at best, roughly on the basis of initial judgments, since the values of the variables are determined by quite different sets of comparisons which are not themselves precise. But in the light of the theorem, the *absence* of equality implies a body of comparisons of belief that is inconsistent, in some respects, with one or more of the Koopman axioms. If those axioms are "intuitively evident" to a given individual, in the sense of being normatively compelling (and I believe they will be to most people who can and will, as Good says, "think hard"), he will be motivated to eliminate the inconsistency. To the extent that "fuzziness" of the values of $p.(a,h)$ and $p^*(a,h)$ is at fault—which might typically be the problem—he should find it easy to "adjust" them within small margins until he reached values that were consistent both with his beliefs and, in the sense of this theorem, with each other. Indeed, if the theory is functional, he should feel that this process of reconsideration and adjustment had led him closer to registering his "true" beliefs in his responses. (If he could *not* "conscientiously" register responses compatible with the theorem, after full reflection, he would then have to reconsider the acceptability of the theory.)

"Definite" probabilities can emerge in the special case in which $p.(a,h) = p^*(a,h)$; or equivalently, in which $p.(a,h) + p.(\sim a,h) = 1$. In this case the eventuality a/h is said to be appraisable, and the common limit

$$p(a,h) = p_*(a,h) = p^*(a,h)$$

may be called the (numerical) probability of a/h.

It follows from Theorem 16 that if a_1/h and a_2/h are both appraisable, then the inequality $p(a_1,h_1) < p(a_2,h_2)$ implies the relation $a_1/h_1 <\{ a_2/h_2$. Moreover, for *such* eventualities (which include, for example, all members and unions of members of an n-scale) the usual axioms of a classical probability measure will follow from the Koopman axioms. For example, if a_1 and a_2 are mutually exclusive given h, and a_1/h and a_2/h are both appraisable, then $(a_1 \text{ or } a_2)/h$ will be appraisable, and:

$$p(a_1 \text{ or } a_2, h) = p(a_1, h) + p(a_2, h).$$

Koopman makes the important remark that if the set of all eventualities were *completely* ordered by $\leq$· (assuming the existence of n-scales for all n) every eventuality would be appraisable.

However, given the possibility for a given individual of "incomparability" between certain pairs of propositions, there might be a significant *gap* between $p.(a,h)$ and $p^*(a, h)$ [$=1 - p.(\sim a, h)$]. This might be true even if, on the basis of "mature consideration" he had settled on a set of judgments that were compatible with the normative theory in the sense that p·(a, h) + p*(~a, h) = 1. Moreover, the positive length of this interval between p· and p* might differ quite obviously and significantly between one proposition and another. Such an interval is, then, a form of "vagueness" that is quite distinct from the vagueness or fuzziness, the zone of arbitrariness or imprecision or inconsistency between repeated trials, that must surround the individual estimates of such variables as p· (a, h) or p* (a, h) in any empirical application, *as it must surround any measurement of a subjective variable.* The *former* vagueness, evidenced and perhaps approximately *measured* by p* (a, h) - p· (a, h) [>0], is allowed for in the Koopman theory even when, in an idealized discussion, *imprecisions* of measurement and judgment are ignored.

Suppose, now, that Paul's expressed comparisons among probabilities lead to the inference (contrary to earlier hypotheses) that his lower and upper probabilities for "rain tomorrow" are 1/3 and 5/6, respectively; and that his lower and upper probabilities for "no rain tomorrow" are, correspondingly, 1/6 and 2/3 respectively. Thus:

Fig. 4.5

Should Paul carry his umbrella tomorrow?[1] How might he reasonably *bet* on the weather, today? How is he to act upon such "vague" opinions?

As quoted earlier, Keynes suggests for occasions when our expectation of rain is neither more or less likely than not, nor as likely as not, that it is "an arbitrary matter to decide for or against the umbrella . . . though it will be rational to allow caprice to determine us and to waste no time on the debate." Should Paul's choice be random, then; or might certain determinate decision rules serve him better as normative criteria?

As for his betting behavior, it is clear that the notions of "upper and lower intuitive probabilities" are *formally* similar to those of "upper and lower betting probabilities". There is no need to assume that the values of p· and p* would be identical, for a given proposition, with p_o and p^o (the two pairs of numbers reflect quite different introspective questions or observations). However, a variety of decision rules could be imagined, taking "intuitive probabilities" as argument and leading to observable "betting

---

[1] No doubt a "neo-Bernoullian", pondering Paul's state of mind, would lay odds he would not come in out of the rain.

probabilities" (or, if such a decision rule were known or guessed, "intuitive probabilities" could be inferred from observed, or introspected,
"betting probabilities").

Some of these hypothetical rules would lead to "definite" "betting
probabilities" even when the "intuitive probabilities" were *not* appraisable;
indeed, *no other rules could be "reasonable" in the light of the Savage postulates,*
or in terms of any other approach leading to the "Bernoulli proposition."
In fact, if we were sure that all behavior in which we were interested (e.g.,
our own) conformed invariably to the Savage postulates, we would hardly
be interested in Koopman's question, "Do you judge X to be more probable than Y, or less probable, or equally probable; or are you unable to
judge?" For that line of questioning might yield only a partial ordering of
probabilities, whereas Savage's question, "Which would you rather stake
a prize on, X or Y, or are you indifferent?" would, *if* his postulates were
always obeyed, yield a *simple ordering;* as Koopman would put it, all eventualities would be comparable and all probabilities appraisable. The concept of "vagueness" might still be meaningful, in terms of Koopman's concepts, but it would not evidently be *relevant* to betting behavior.

On the other hand, on the basis of given upper and lower intuitive
probabilities for various events—or more generally, *a given set of probability distributions over events which are compatible with all your "definite" comparisons of probability*[1]—certain decision rules could generate various patterns of behavior systematically *violating* the Savage axioms. In particular,
with respect to events whose "intuitive" probabilities were "non-appraisable" such rules might lead to choices among gambles such that their "betting probabilities" would not be "definite." For example, a simple rule
leading to the betting behavior hypothesized by C. A. B. Smith[2] and by Fellner, above, for choices among two-payoff gambles would be: *Maximize the
lower "intuitive" probability of the preferred outcome.*

Some such theory, arguing from non-appraisable intuitive probabilities to non-definite betting probabilities via a specified decision rule, might
account usefully for the phenomena related to "vagueness" which even
"neo-Bernoullians" describe as limiting application of their approach. In
Chapters Six and Seven we shall consider a variety of decision rules that
might meaningfully be defined for circumstances in which your definite
intuitive judgments of relative probability do not determine a unique probability distribution over propositions/events.

---

[1]This *set* of "reasonably acceptable" probability distributions—all those distributions that are not ruled out by your definite probability judgments in a given
state of mind—will later be symbolized Y^0 (Chapter Seven).

[2]*Op. cit.;* see discussion in Chapter Three and its Appendix. This rule would be
an application of what is termed in Chapter Seven the "restricted minimax criterion."

However, rather than to carry out further exercises entirely in the abstract, it is time to confront some illustrations which, if still hypothetical, are more concretely realized and may challenge your intuition more productively. The examples in the next chapter have been constructed to evoke, intuitively, responses associated with "vagueness" or (limited) "indeterminacy" of personal probabilities. Thus, before spending effort at devising methods for measuring "vagueness" or theories for guiding and describing behavior in such circumstances, we may try to establish the scope and importance of such phenomena.

We face the question: Are violations of the Savage postulates—associated with the "vagueness," "fuzziness," "ambiguity," or "incomparability" of opinions—phenomena from which an idealized theory of *decision* must, and may usefully, abstract? Must we, that is, accept Savage's conclusion, at once reassuring and fatalistic: "Some people see the vagueness phenomenon as an objection; I see it as a truth, sometimes unpleasant, but not curable by a new theory."[1] Or is this phenomenon of such importance that the purposes of a normative logic of choice demand a theory that takes account of it explicitly?

We shall consider, in the following chapter, some of the behavior with which such a theory might have to deal.

---

[1] Savage, "Bayesian Statistics," p. 6.

Appendix to Chapter Four

SAVAGE SUMMARIZES, IN a form slightly altered from his text and somewhat more concise, his postulates and definitions on the end-papers of *The Foundations of Statistics*. I reproduce his summary here (with his page references to the fuller versions in his text), without annotation, mainly for the convenience of those already familiar with Savage's exposition, who may wish to compare assertions in my discussion with his formal, general statements. [I have changed his symbols for acts, the relationships "not preferred to" and "not more probable than," and not-E, to conform to my notation.]

The formal subject matter of the theory

The states, a set S of elements s, s', . . . with subsets A, B, C, . . . (page 11).

The consequences, a set F of elements f, g, h, . . . (page 14).

Acts, arbitrary functions I, II, III, . . . from S to F (page 14).

The relation "is not preferred to" between acts, $\leq\{$ (page 18).

The postulates, and definitions on which they depend

P1   The relations $\leq\{$ is a simple ordering (page 18).

D1 $I \leq\cdot II$ given B, if and only if $I' \leq\{ II'$ for every I' and II' that agree with I and II, respectively, on B and with each other on $\cdot\overline{B}$ (page 22).

P2   For every I, II, and B, $I \leq\{ II$ given B or $II \leq\{ I$ given B (page 23).

D2 $g \leq\{ g'$; if and only if $I \leq\{ I'$, when f(s) = g, f'(s) = g' for every $s \, _\epsilon \, S$ (page 25).

D3   B is null, if and only if $I \leq\{ II$ given B for every I, II (page 24).

P3   If f(s) = g, f'(s) = g' for every s ε B, and B is not null; then $I \leq\{ I'$ given B, if and only if $g \leq\{ g'$ (page 26).

D4 $A \leq\cdot B$; if and only if $I_A \leq\{ I_B$ or $g \leq\{$ for every I_A, I_B, g, g' such that: $I_A(s) = g$ for s ε A, $I_A(s) = g'$ for s ε $\overline{A}$, $I_B(s) = g$, for s ε B, $I_B(s) = g'$ for s ε $\overline{B}$ (page 31).

P4   For every A, B, $A \leq\{ B$ or $B \leq\{ A$ (page 31).

P5   It is false that, for every f, f', f ≤{ f' (page 31).

P6* Suppose it false that I ≤{ II; then, for every f, there is a (finite) partition of S such that, if I' agrees with I and II' agrees with II except on an arbitrary element of the partition, I' and II' being equal to f there, then it will be false that I' ≤{ II or I ≤{ II' (page 39).

D5   I ≤· g given B (g ≤{ I given B); if and only if I ≤{ II given B (II ≤{ I given B), when h(s) = g for every s (page 72).

P7** If I ≤{ g(s) given B (g(s) ≤{ I given B) for every s ε B, then I ≤· II given B (II ≤{ I given B) (page 77).

Luce and Raiffa (*Games and Decisions,* p. 303) states the two main theorems that follow from these postulates:

Theorem. There exists a unique real-valued function P defined for the set of events (subset of S) such that
   (i) $P(E) \geq 0$ for all E,
   (ii) $P(S) = 1$,
   (iii) If E and E' are disjoint, then $P(E \cup E') = P(E) + P(E')$,
and
   (iv) E is not more probable than E' if and only if $P(E) \leq P(E')$.

P is called the personalistic probability measure reflecting the individual's reported feelings as to which of a pair of events is more likely to occur.

Theorem. There exists a real-valued u defined over the set of consequences having the following property: If E_1, where i = 1, 2, . . ., n, is a partition of S and A is an act with consequence c_i on E_i, and if E_i', where i = 1, 2, . . ., m, is another partition of S and A' is an act with consequence c_i' on E_i', then A * A' if and only if

---

* A slightly different, somewhat simpler form is given in the text: If I <{ II, and *f* is any consequence; then there exists a partition of S such that, if I or II is so modified on any one element of the partition as to take the value *f* at every s there, other values being undisturbed; then the modified remains less than II, or I remains less than the modified II,as the case may require (pp. 39–40).
This implies a weaker postulate which is all that is required for the measurement of probability: P6': If B <{ C, there exists a partition of S the union of each element of which with B is less probable than C (p. 38).
** P7, which I have not discussed, is required in order to guarantee the existence of a utility function over acts with an infinite set of consequences (it is not needed for purposes related to probability measurement).

$$\sum_{i=1}^{n} u(c_1)P(E_1) \ge \sum_{i=1}^{n} u(c_1{}')P(E_1{}').$$

Koopman Axioms of Intuitive Probability
[B. O. Koopman, "The Axioms and Algebra of Intuitive Probability," *Annals of Mathematics, Vol. LXI, 1940, pp. 275–276; for slightly different formal statement see "The Basis of Probability," Bulletin* of the American Mathematical Society, Vol. LXVI, 1940, pp. 766–767.

Symbols: a, b, h, k, $\le\cdot$ defined in text, Chapter Four; ~denotes negation, (or mere juxtaposition) denotes conjunction or logical product, and denotes disjunction or logical sum. The identically false proposition is denoted by O and is regarded as coinciding with every a ~ a. "The symbol for identity = and material implication $\subset$ (a $\subset$ b meaning "a implies b") are used here rather than ≡ and $\supset$ in order to bring out the parallel with the mathematical theories of sets and algebras."].

V. *Axiom of Verified Contingency.*
  $a/h <\{ k/k.$

I. Axiom of Implication.
  If $a/h \ge k/k$, then h$\subset$a.

R. Axiom of Reflectivity.
  $a/h \le\{ a/h.$

T. Axiom of Transitivity.
  If $a/h \le\{ b/k$ and $b/k \le\{ c/1$, then $a/h \le\{ c/1.$

A. Axiom of Antisymmetry.
  If $a/h \le\{ b/k$, then ~ $a/h \{\ge$ ~ $b/k.$

C. Axioms of Composition.
  Let $a_1b_1h_1 \ne 0$ and $a_2b_2h_2 \ne = 0.$
  C_1. If $a_1/h_1 \le\{ a_2/h_2$ and $b_1/a_1 h_1 \le\{ b_2/a_2h_2$, then $a_1b_1/h_1 \le\{ a_2b_2/h_2.$
  C_2. If $a_1/h_1 \le\{ b_2/a_2h_2$ and $b_1/a_1h_1 \le\{ a_2/h_2$, then $a_1b_1/h_1 \le\{ a_2b_2/h_2.$

D. Axioms of Decomposition (Quasi-Converses of C).
  Let $a_1b_1h_1 \ne 0$, $a_2b_2h_2 \ne 0$, and $a_1b_1/h_1 \ne\cdot a_2b_2/h_2$ Then if either of the eventualities
  (i) a_1/h_1, b_1/a_1h_1, has the supraprobable relation ($\{\ge$) with either of
  (ii) a_2h_2, b_2/a_2h_2, it will follow that the remaining eventuality of (i) will have the infraprobable relation ($\le\{$) with the remaining one of (ii).

P. Axiom of Alternative Presumption.
  If $a/bh \le\{ r/s$ and $a/~ bh \le\{ r/s$, then $a/h \le\{ r/s.$

S. Axiom of Subdivision.
  For any integer n let the propositions $a_1, \ldots, a_n, b_1, \ldots, b_n$ be such that $a_ia_j = b_ib_j = 0$ (i ≠ j) i, j = 1, . . ., n; a = a_1 . . . $a_n \ne 0$; b = b_1 . . . $b_n \ne 0$; $a_1/a \le\{ \ldots \le\{ a_n/a$; $b_1/b \le\{ \ldots \le\cdot b_n/b$; then $a_1/a \le\{ b_n/b.$

5

UNCERTAINTIES THAT ARE NOT RISKS

LET US NOW consider some hypothetical experiments in which the quality of your information varies between one event and another and from one gamble to the next.

Let us imagine that an observer sets out explicitly to discover your subjective degrees of belief concerning certain events by interrogating you as to your preferences in various pairs of gambles. He has no other interest in your choices, nor in the outcome of a gamble, than to learn your opinions; the prize money at risk is, in his eyes cheap payment for this information.

We suppose, to begin, that you confront two urns containing red and black balls, from one of which a ball will be drawn by a process you regard as random. For you to "stake a prize on Red$_I$" will mean that the ball will be drawn from Urn I and that you will receive a prize a (say, $100) if a red ball is drawn ("if Red$_I$ occurs") and a smaller amount b (say, $0) if a black is drawn ("if not-Red$_I$ occurs").

You have the following information. Urn II contains exactly 50 red and 50 black balls, randomly mixed; you are allowed to verify this. Urn I is guaranteed to contain 100 red and/or black balls, but you are not told the proportion nor allowed to inspect them; so far as your explicit information goes, there may be any number of red balls from 0 to 100. You are not told by whom, or by what process, or for what purpose the composition of Urn II was determined (except that it was *not* determined, or revealed, to the observer who is offering you gambles). However (to exploit the flexibility of introspective experiments), you are urged to consider your preferred choices below in the light of a *range* of possible circumstances that might influence your guesses or assumptions on these matters.

In particular, you might try to imagine circumstances that would convince you that the person offering you gambles *knows no more about the contents of Urn II, or how they were determined, than you do*, so that his offers convey to you no "information" on those contents. In fact, it would be quite appropriate to the purposes of this exercise *to imagine that the "observer" is yourself.*

The very essence of the "neo-Bernoullian" approach in every practical application (indeed, the essence of any application of normative decision-making criteria) is to discover your own preferences and beliefs in the context of artifically simple choice-situations—generally hypothetical and introspective—so that you may "deduce" or "calculate" decisions that will be ultimately acceptable to you among complex or unfamiliar alternatives. This involves turning away, momentarily, from the complex problem, to construct and contemplate some simpler models of decision problems, with respect to which you "ask yourself" your preferences among various actions, or gambles. If the models have been well chosen for the purpose, your answers may be immediate, sharply defined, and *relevant* to your decision in the complicated problem. There is an art to conducting this self-interrogation fruitfully, though the "neo-Bernoullian" postulates, for example, provide a systematic framework. Robert Schlaifer's *Probability and Statistics for Business Decisions* is an excellent "neo-Bernoullian" handbook for businessmen, to guide them through the process of choosing useful models with which to explore their own, obscurely-relevant intuitive preferences.[1]

Thus, you may think of the present problem as having been abstracted from another, more complex problem, or hypothetically imagined by yourself, for the very purpose of asking yourself how you would bet on these particular events: the answers, if they come quickly and unambiguously, to be applied in certain of your *other* decisions (e.g., the "three-color urn" example to be considered next).

The "observer"—whoever he is—presents you with one choice at a time, without indicating what subsequent choices you may be offered:

1.   "On which would you prefer to stake the prize, Red$_I$ or Black$_I$: or are you indifferent?" That is, if a ball is to be drawn from Urn I, on which "event" do you prefer the $100 stake, Red or Black: or do you care?

---

[1]See, for example, pp. 26–49, for the self-analyses of Mr. A, Mr. B and Mr. C. Raiffa and Schlaifer's *Applied Statistical Decision Theory,* which is much more technical, is oriented somewhat more to the needs of the statistician, but with the same end: to enable the decision-maker practically and systematically to exploit his intuitive preferences and beliefs to simplify his choice-problem among complicated alternatives.

2. "On which would you prefer to stake the prize, Red_{II} or $Black_{II}$? Or are you indifferent?"

Neither the Savage axioms, nor any arguments I shall propose, prescribe your answers to these question. There are those who would claim that you "must" or "should" be indifferent in one or both of these choices, but no such proposition is at issue here. In particular, the conditions of the experiment are not intended to ensure "complete ignorance"—if such a state is ever meaningful—of the proportion of red balls in Urn I. If you have had much experience with psychological testing before, you may feel you can bring a good deal of information and intuition to bear on the problem of the contents of Urn I; feel free to do so.

"What is the likelihood that the experimenter [whoever *he* is] has rigged this urn, rather than choosing the proportion at random?" you might ask yourself. "If he deliberately chose a certain number of red balls, what number did he probably pick? If my interrogator is trying to trick me, how is he going about it? What other bets is he going to offer me? What sort of results is he after?" (*Most* people would not worry about these last three points if, as I have suggested they might be, they themselves are their own "interrogators". Some people are naturally suspicious, anyway; I do not want to foreclose any considerations that you may think are pertinent. But a side question may prove relevant, when we analyze your choices: When you ask yourself questions like these, *how sure* are you of your answers, and how clear-cut are they?) Depending on your answers, you may decide you prefer one color or the other in Urn I (or in Urn II, for that matter); or that you are indifferent in one or both cases.

Let us suppose, for the moment, that you are indifferent within each pair of bets. This is typically[1] the case. It need not mean that you feel "completely ignorant" or that you could think of no reason to prefer one bet to the other; it does indicate that your reasons, if any, to favor one color or the other balanced out subjectively (perhaps because they applied symmetrically to either color). If you happen, on the contrary, to be one of those who feel that "Balls usually turn out to be mostly red in experiments like these,"

---

[1]Here we see the advantages of purely hypothetical experiments. In "real life," facing real balls in a laboratory, you would probably turn out to have a subtle color preference that would invalidate the whole first set of trials, and various other biases that would show up one by one as experiment after experiment ended inconclusively.

However, the experiments by Chipman and by Becker and Brownson discussed later did reveal indifference in bets essentially similar to the ones considered here.

we will attend to your case later. By "indifference" we mean, as usual, that if 10¢ were added to the stake on one color you would prefer that bet to its alternative.

Now the observer offers a third pair of alternatives:

3. "On which would you prefer to stake the prize, Red_I or Red_{II}? Or are you indifferent?" In other words, if a red ball represents a "win," which urn would you choose to draw from, I or II?

When you have answered this, he asks finally:

4. "On which would you prefer to stake the prize, $Black_I$ or $Black_{II}$?"[1]

By the time we have reached the third question, a test of the Savage axioms impends; they did not constrain your first choices, but given those, they dictate your third and fourth. It is now possible, in other words, that you have violated the axioms. I would bet that you have.

Judging from a large number of responses, under absolutely non-experimental conditions,[2] your answers to these last two questions—still assuming you were indifferent in the first two cases—are likely to fall into one of three groups. You may still be indifferent within each pair of options. But if you are in what seems a larger group, you will report that you prefer to stake the prize on Red_{II} rather than Red_I, and $Black_{II}$ rather than $Black_I$. The preferences of a small minority run the other way, preferring prizes staked on Red_I to Red_{II}, and $Black_I$ to $Black_{II}$.

If you are in either of these latter groups, you are now in trouble with the Savage axioms.

Suppose that, betting on Red, you preferred to draw out of Urn II. The observer, applying the basic notion of the Ramsey/Savage approach, would infer tentatively that you regarded Red_{II} as "more probable than"

---

[1]Note that in no case are you invited to choose both a color and an urn freely; nor are you given any indication beforehand as to the full set of gambles that will be offered; nor do you ever choose from the full set of gambles. If these conditions were altered (as in some of H. Raiffa's experiments with students, to be discussed later), you could employ randomized strategies, such as flipping a coin to determine what color to bet or in Urn I, which might affect your choices; see Chapter Eight.

[2]E.g., faculty seminars at Harvard, Chicago, Yale and Northwestern Universities, the Interdisiplinary Colloquium on Mathematics in the Behavioral Sciences (UCLA), the St. Louis meetings of the Econometric Society (December, 1960), and several seminars at The RAND Corporation.

Red$_I$. He then observes that you also prefer to bet on Black$_{II}$ rather than Black$_I$. Since he cannot conclude that you regard Red$_{II}$ as more probable than Red$_I$ and, at the same time, not-Red$_{II}$ as more probable than not-Red$_I$, he cannot infer a definite "qualitative probability relationship" between Red$_I$ and Red$_{II}$ that is consistent with your choices. This is not merely an obstacle to his assigning probability *numbers* to these events for you; you are not acting "as if" you had a definite, weak *ordering* of these events in terms of probability. You are inevitably violating Savage axioms (specifically, P1 and/or P2, complete ordering of actions and the Sure-Thing Principle) (See Theorem 1, Appendix to this chapter).

The same applies if you preferred to bet on Red$_I$ and Black$_I$, respectively, rather than Red$_{II}$ or Black$_{II}$. (Norman Dalkey, for example, asserts these preferences: so long as the possible loss *b* is not large and negative.) Moreover, if you fall into either of these patterns, you can be convicted of violation either on your last *two* choices alone (as above) or on your first three alone. Given your indifference in the first two choices, adherence to the axioms would imply that Red$_I$ is "equally likely" to not-Red$_I$, and Red$_{II}$ is equally likely to Red$_{II}$ (or to Black$_{II}$), and any preference for drawing a particular color from one urn over the other leads to a contradiction.[1]

Lloyd Shapley has pointed out that the nature of the third choice in the sequence, between bets on Red$_I$ and Red$_{II}$, might in itself affect your guesses about the contents of Urn I; suspicion of the experiment might lead you to stake your money on the urn whose contents you had checked. The suggestion at the outset, that you attempt to imagine conditions that would persuade you effectively that your questioner had no more, or no better, information than you, was intended to forestall such suspicions; it seems to be easier for some people than for others to imagine such conditions. In particular, you are encouraged to ask yourself how you would bet if you were putting all these offers to yourself, hypothetically. But even in the distracting presence of a second-party interrogator (as, at a seminar) we can test for the effect of "suspicion:" ask yourself if you would, if offered the chance *after* the third question, now prefer to bet on Black$_I$ rather than Red$_I$ in the second comparison? After the fourth question? If you would *remain indifferent between bets on the two colors* in Urn I—and many people report that they would—the contradiction remains.

It is sometimes objected that the extreme paucity of information about the contents of Urn I creates an artificial, unrealistic situation in which responses are unrelated to normal patterns. This is arguable; while it is perhaps never true that one can be said to have "*no* information" or relevant experience concerning the consequences of an action, one surely encounters situations no richer in pertinent cues than this one. Nature does not

---

[1]See Theorem 1, Appendix to this chapter.

always give hints; learning processes must *start* somewhere, and sometimes the subject starts "cold."

However, the behavior I am seeking to expose should not be sensitive to the *precise* amount or form of information. Let us suppose instead that you have been allowed to *draw a random sample of two balls* from Urn I, and that you have drawn one red and one black. Or a sample of four: two red and two black. People often claim that this change conditions affects their *feelings* of uncertainty about Urn I considerably, and certain experiments (described in the next example) can register resulting changes in their behavior. But not the simple choices we have considered so far. The new information does not seem to change the observed pattern of responses appreciably.[1] The same conflicts with the axioms appear; many who preferred Red$_{II}$ to Red$_I$, Black$_{II}$ to Black$_I$ before, still do. And their preference is tenacious, despite their observations. Lowering the prize on Red$_{II}$ by one

---

[1]Although we are primarily concerned with individual, deliberated, self-conscious decision-making in the light of explicitly proposed normative criteria—i.e., with the results of "your" own reflection upon these examples—this happens to be one of the rare instances in which you can compare your intuitive responses to some empirical, descriptive data that is directly relevant. In 1957 John Chipman conducted a carefully controlled and exhaustively analyzed experiment investigating the choices of ten subjects in several hundred paired comparisons between gambles equivalent to those considered above. (John Chipman, "Stochastic Choice and Subjective Probability," in *Decisions, Values and Groups* (New York, 1960) pp. 70–95, ed. D. Willner. Chipman's experimental design was conceived entirely independently, indeed prior to my notions in this field; and intended for somewhat different purposes, namely, to construct a stochastic theory of choice and to test certain "strong stochastic transitivity postulates").

For "urns," Chipman used large kitchen match boxes, containing broken match pieces in various known or *unknown* proportions of heads to stems. Certain (varying) odds in small amounts of money would be specified, along with a winning event (the drawing of a head, or a stem); the subjects would then choose which of two specified boxes they would prefer for the drawing. Each subject confronted each *pair* of boxes used six times in the course of the experiment, so that he had an opportunity to change his choice, which frequently happened; "preference" was measured by his "majority" choice within a given pair, "indifference" by a frequency of choice = 1/2.

One comparison was virtually identical to our example above. The choice was between a box known (and verified by the subject) to contain exactly 50 heads and 50 stems, and a box whose contents were not inspected, but from which an allegedly random sample had been drawn (in the subject's presence) yielding 5 heads and 5 stems. *Seven* out of his ten subjects distinctly preferred to draw from the

dollar or several, relative to the prize on Red_I, will not reverse it; neither will removing one red ball (or adding a black one) from Urn II.

THE "THREE-COLOR URN" EXAMPLE

The following example yields a direct test of one of the Savage postulates; we have discussed it earlier, but this time you are invited to brood on your own choices. Imagine an urn known to contain 30 red balls and 60 black balls and yellow balls; you are not told the proportion of black to yellow. (Alternatively, imagine that a sample of two drawn from the black and yellow balls has resulted in one black and yellow.) All earlier comments on "experimental" conditions apply here, e.g., you may, if you wish, think of the various "offers" as having been formulated by *you*, to define your own degrees of belief for use in some *other* decision problems. One ball is to be drawn at random from the urn; the following actions are considered:

	30 Red	60 Black	Yellow
I	–$100	$0	$0
II	$0	–$100	$0

Fig. 5.1

Action I offers a prize on Red, II offers the same prize on Black. Which do you prefer? Or are you indifferent?

Now consider the following two actions, under the same circumstances:

	30 Red	60 Black	Yellow
III	–$100	$0	–$100
IV	$0	–$100	–$100

Fig. 5.2

"known" 50-50 box; five out of these, in their 30 comparisons, *never* chose the 5-5 box over the 50-50 (*ibid.*, Table VIII, p. 88). One subject was indifferent (i.e., chose the 5-5 box half the time); the other two subjects, who *preferred* to draw from the 5-5 box, *also preferred* a 6-4 (sampled) box to a 60-40 (known) box, and a 4-6 box to a 40-60 box. (The latter preference, under certain circumstances, for bets upon a more "ambiguous" event, can also be found for many individuals, I believe, in their *deliberated* decision-making and must be reflected in their normative criteria; examples that illustrate this pattern and decision rules that express it will be discussed at length in Chapter Seven).

Action III offers a prize on "Red or Yellow;" IV offers a prize on "Black or Yellow." Which of these do you prefer? Are you indifferent? Take your time!

If your preferences run, I over II, and IV over III: you are normal, to judge by most of the responses I have observed.[1] That you are also reasonable, a "neo-Bernoullian" would dispute (though I will defend); like the minority who prefer II to I and III to IV, you are violating the Sure-Thing Principle, P2. The two pairs of actions differ only in their third column, which is constant for each pair; P2 requires the ordering of I to II (whatever it is) to be preserved in III and IV.

The more common pattern above implies that the subject prefers to stake a prize on Red rather than on Black; and he also prefers to stake the prize *against* Red rather than against Black. An attempt to infer between Red and Black the relationship "not less probable than" on the basis of the Ramsey/Savage operational definition would fail, since his choices would indicate that he regarded Red as more probable than Black, but not-Red as also more probable than not-Black. Moreover, he would be acting "as if" he regarded Red as more likely than Black, but "Red or Yellow" as less

---

[1]This pattern of responses is also reported as typical by Howard Raiffa ("Risk, Ambiguity, and the Savage Axioms: Comment," *Quarterly Journal of Economics*, Vol. LXXV, pp. 690–694; see quotation below, this chapter, and discussion in Chapter Eight), who has presented the above examples (some in modified form) to his classes in graduate statistics, Harvard University, to his students at the Harvard Business School and to "a few seasoned business executives—'men of experience'" (*ibid.*, p. 691).

Since publication of "Risk, Ambiguity, and the Savage Axioms," Selwyn Becker and Frederick Brownson of the University of Chicago have conducted as systematic experimental investigation of gambling choices, involving "real money," related to the example above. Their results are not yet published; however, they have permitted me to say that they found marked, consistent patterns corresponding to those described.

As in the case of Chipman's experiment, the Becker and Brownson experiment relates directly to undeliberated behavior, not necessarily conforming to normative criteria that the subjects would endorse explicitly. On the other hand, Raiffa's experience, like my own, though lacking in experimental controls, fulfills some of the important conditions of a test of proposed normative criteria: highly self-conscious and deliberated (though hypothetical) decision-making, with opportunity to revise choices and full exposition of the implications of various patterns of choice in the light of various criteria.

likely than "Black or Yellow," though Red, Yellow and Black were mutually exclusive.[1]

Once again, it is impossible, on the basis of such choices, to infer even qualitative probability relationships for the events in question (specifically, for events that include Yellow or Black, but not both). *A fortiori*, given any values of the payoffs, it is impossible to find *any* probability numbers in terms of which these choices could be described—even roughly or approximately—as maximizing the mathematical expectation of utility: as was demonstrated in Chapter Two.

Again, we might check to see whether a choice of I over II, and IV over III, represents a "true" preference. If these would be your choices: would you change your mind if the prize on Red were reduced by 10 cents? Or if, instead, one Red ball were removed from the urn? Some state they would shift their choices under these conditions; they demonstrate themselves to be close to indifference. But many others do not. To get a quantitative indication of the *degree* of their preference, we may ask a slightly more complex question: "How many Red balls would have to be removed before you would prefer to bet on Black than to bet on Red (i.e., prefer II to I)?" Alternatively: "What reduced stake on Red would make you indifferent between betting on Red and betting on Black, with $100 prize on Black?"[2] For each question, the answers will vary for different people; and for a given person, the answer to either question will typically vary with the amount of information presumed available. Thus, the *larger the sample* postulated of Yellow and Black balls

---

[1] In the spirit of the above example, Kenneth Arrow has suggested the following one:

| | 100 | | 50 | 50 |
	R_I	B_I	R_{II}	B_{II}
I	$100	100	$ 0	0
II	100	0	100	0
III	0	100	0	100
IV	0	0	100	100

Fig. 5.3

Urn I and Urn II, from our first experiment, have here been dumped into a common urn. Let us assume that you are indifferent between I and IV, and between II and III. Suppose, as many people do, you prefer I to II; what is your ordering of III and IV? If III is not preferred to IV, P2, the Sure-Thing Principle is violated. If IV is not preferred to III, P1, complete ordering of actions is violated. If III is indifferent to IV, both P1 and P2 are violated.

[2] Becker and Brownson, in the experiment cited above, found that subjects who stated preferences such as I preferred to II, or IV to III, were willing to pay a significant premium to back their preferred gambles in many bets.

(showing equal proportions), the *less* the proportion of Red, or the stake on Red, must be reduced before the preference for I over II is eliminated.

Returning to our first example, we can ask similar questions, or we can ask: "*How much would you pay* to draw a ball from Urn II (known to contain 50 Red and 50 Black) to draw a ball from Urn II, with a prize of $100 on a Red ball? How much would you pay if the same prize were on drawing a *black* ball from Urn II? What is the most you would pay to draw from Urn I, with a $100 stake on Red? On Black?" We must appeal here both to your intuition and your honesty; but to reduce the strain on both, we could observe your maximum bids for these gambles in the context of an *auction*, with safeguard against collusion.

If your bids are consistent with your former choices in the light of P1, complete ordering of actions, you will offer equal amounts for the first two gambles, and equal amounts for the second two; but the last two bids will be less than the first two. This is merely a new way of demonstrating your violation of the postulates: this time with a quantitative aspect we shall exploit in later chapters. For the postulates imply that for *any* event such that you are equally willing to stake a given prize *on* or *against* the event, you should be willing to pay an amount for either of these gambles dependent only on the size of the prize; for gambles offering identical prizes on two different events of this nature, your best offer should be the same in each case.[1]

If you were among those who violated the postulates (or if you think you can project yourself into that frame of mind) you might now test whether the symmetry of information concerning some of the variables was critical to your preferences. If you prefer to stake a prize on Red_{II} rather than on Red_I when you know there are to be 50 Red and 50 Black balls in Urn II, would your preference eventually shift if the known proportion of colors in Urn II were to be shifted against Red sufficiently far, say to 40 Red_{II}; 60 $Black_{II}$ or lower? Many people report that it would, and that there would be some proportion, very roughly defined, at which they would be indifferent between staking the prize on Red_{II} and Red_I.[2] But at *that proportion* in Urn II, would you now be indifferent, as the postulates

---

[1]See Theorem 2, Appendix to this chapter.

[2]Assuming that the known proportion $r/100$ in Urn II determines for you a "definite" probability that a Red ball will be drawn from Urn II, this critical proportion at which you are indifferent establishes r_0 for Red_I for you, as defined in the last chapter. Typically, for $r/100$ within a certain region you will find it "hard to decide" or "an arbitrary decision" on which event to stake the prize; this is the phenomenon of "fuzziness" noted by Savage and others. Yet you may find it *easy* to choose R_{II} when $r/100$ is $1/2$ or *moderately* lower. When this is true also with respect to staking the prize on $Black_{II}$ or $Black_I$, we have the phenomenon of "indefiniteness" of betting probabilities, r_0 definitely $< r^o (= 1 - R_o)$ (See Fellner, *op. cit.*, p. 673).

require, between staking a prize on Black$_I$ or on Black$_{II}$? If Black$_{II}$ at this point constituted 60–70 per cent of Urn II, it is hard to imagine an initial preference for Black$_{II}$ not being intensified.

Similar tests could be conducted, and similar results are to be expected, if instead of varying the known proportion in Urn II we imagined asymmetric results favoring Red$_I$ in a small sample drawn from Urn I.[1]

Likewise, in the three-color urn example, if you preferred initially to stake a prize upon Red than upon Yellow (knowing there to be precisely 30 Red balls out of 90), we might find by removing Red balls sequentially from the urn that we reached a point at which your preference was reduced to indifference: say, when 10 or 15 Red balls had been removed. Similarly, if instead of lowering the number of Red balls we biased the results of a small sample of Yellow and Black in favor of Yellow. If Savage's basic inference were valid for you, we would say at this point that your personal probabilities for Red and Yellow were equal. But this would (would it not?) run up against the fact that your preference for staking a prize on (Yellow or Black) rather than (Red or Black), or on not-Red rather than not-Yellow, was now even stronger than before.

---

[1]In the Chipman experiment, not only did his subjects markedly *prefer* to draw from (i.e., to stake a prize on an event in) the 50-50 box than from the 5-5 box, but the 50-50 box was chosen in 1/6 of the comparisons with a 7-3 (sampled) box, and similarly a "known" 60-40 box was chosen in 1/3 of the comparisons with the 7-3 box (although the 7-3 box was chosen in a majority of the latter two comparisons). In contrast to this "indecision," in virtually all choices between the 60-40 box and the 50-50 box, all subjects preferred the former; in the case of two exceptions, "both subjects promptly remarked 'that was a stupid thing to do' (even though one of them had won)" (*op. cit.*, p. 84).

These results confirmed a conjecture by Chipman that even though an individual might "generally" choose to stake a prize on drawing a black ball from an urn, with "unknown" proportion of black to white, from which a sample of 7 black and 3 white had been drawn, than from urns with "known" proportions 60:40 or 50:50 black to white, and even though he might virtually *always* prefer to draw from the 60:40 rather than the 50:50 urn, still "in occasional—infrequent but still not rare—moods of extreme caution" both of the latter might be preferred to the former (*ibid.*, p. 77; such behavior would conflict with the "strong stochastic transitivity postulate" of Marschak and Davidson, "Experimental Tests of Stochastic Decision Theory," *Cowles Foundation Discussion Paper* No. 22, Yale University, 1957).

One of our tasks in the chapters immediately following will be to discover or invent explicit normative criteria that *could* generate choice-patterns appropriate to such "moods of caution:" for use in those circumstances, frequent or infrequent, when only such choice-patterns would correspond to a decision-maker's true, deliberated preferences.

Finally, if a small sample from Urn I in the two-urn example should be slightly biased in favor of one color, e.g., Red_I, presumably the maximum price you would pay for a $100 prize on Red in a drawing from Urn I would be somewhat higher than your maximum price for the same prize staked upon Black.[1] But how high would it be: relative to the price you would pay for the prize staked on Red_{II}? If in the absence of the sample, or having seen a small, symmetric sample from Urn I, you would have bid less for a stake on Red_I, or on $Black_I$ if that were offered alternatively, than for the same stake on Red_{II} or $Black_{II}$, it might well be that your maximum bid for either of the former gambles would *still* be less than for either of the latter. That is, you might still prefer to stake the prize on Red_{II} than on Red_I, even after the asymmetric sample results, and you might indicate this by bidding higher for the former gamble.[2] But the postulates, to the contrary, rule out the possibility in any case that you might bid higher for a prize staked on an event E than on an event F, and simultaneously be willing to bid higher for a prize staked on $\bar{E}$ than on $\bar{F}$, if the latter pair of gambles were offered alternatively.

In fact, the postulates have a powerful consequence in this context. If E is any event (for example, Red_{II}) such that you are equally willing to stake a given prize, say $100, on E or on $\bar{E}$, and if you are willing to pay to a certain price, say $40, for $100 staked on E (or on $\bar{E}$), then for *any* event F whatsoever, and its complement $\bar{F}$, either you must be indifferent between options offering $100 staked on F and $100 staked on $\bar{F}$, in which case you must be willing to pay $40 for either, or else you must be willing to pay *more* than $40 for *one* of these options. The possibility that you might not be willing to pay *as much as* $40 for either of these options, if only one were offered, is ruled out by the postulates.[3] Is it ruled out, as well, by your intuition as to the choices on bids you might make in these hypothetical situations? My own conscience is permissive on this point, as on the others that have been raised.

---

[1] I.e., p_o (Red_I(, as defined in Chapter Three, would now be higher than p_o ($Black_I$) = q_o (Red_I). The following discussion also applies to those who *started* with vague feelings that "Balls tend to be red in experiments like this."

[2] I.e., you might indicate that p_o (Red_I) < p_o (Red_{II}) and q_o (Red_I) < q_o (Red_{II}), hence p^o (Red_I) > p^o (Red_{II}). This would constitute a case in which the "upper and lower betting probabilities" for Red_I *enclosed* those Red_{II}, which, as noted in Chapter Three, is ruled out by Postulate 2 (or by the assumption that all degrees of belief are "definite," $p_o = p^o = 1 - q$. See discussion of the hypothetical set of bids (d) in Fig. 3.6, Chapter Three. The discussion of the three-color urn example also applies directly here.

[3] See Theorem 3, Appendix to this chapter. The possibility that you might be willing to pay *more* than $40 for each option is likewise ruled out.

VULGAR EVALUATIONS OF AMBIGUITY

Although we have devoted most of the discussion above to patterns of choice that appear to reflect some reluctance to bet on "ambiguous" events—such patterns seem commonly associated with these particular examples—we shall consider in Chapter Seven some examples and choice-pattern in which the factor of relative information seems to enter in a more complex fashion.[1]

Earlier I suggested a possible relationship between the two examples considered in this chapter. Suppose that the "real" problem demanding your decision was that represented in Fig. 5.1, between actions I and II in the "three-color urn" example. Which to stake the prize on, Red or Yellow? This is the sort of choice with respect to which Chipman's subjects exhibited some "indecision" (in the form of switching their choices on successive occasions): involving a comparison between an event concerning which information is scanty (in Chipman's case, and let us say, in this, the information consisting of a small sample) and one about which much more

---

[1]In choosing between a box with a given, "known" proportion of "winning" match pieces and a box with the same sample proportion, *seven* out of the ten subjects in Chipman's experiment conformed to the following pattern: (a) 60-40 box preferred to 6-4 box; (b) 50-50 box preferred to 5-5 box; (c) 4-6 box preferred to 40-60 box (*op. cit.,* p. 88; three of these subjects each displayed "indifference" with respect to *one* of these comparisons). Of the three remaining subjects, one *always chose* the box with "known" proportion (i.e., in 18 choices, 6 for each pair), and the other two subjects always *preferred* the sampled box.

Chipman's main hypothesis covering the observed behavior is that individuals tend: "to bias unknown probabilities towards one-half. That is, when information is favorable the alternative with greater information is preferred, whereas if information is unfavorable the alternative with less information is preferred." This covers preferences (a) and (c) above; however, it fails totally to explain the strong preferences (b), since it would imply strict indifference in the 50-50:5-5 comparison. As Chipman points out: "When information is no more unfavorable than favorable (i.e., when frequencies are one-half) there is a marked tendency to prefer situations with greater information; curiously enough the above tendencies do not appear to be balanced off in this intermediate case."

Data on the latter choice alone, Chipman remarks, "suggest that a minimax principle is at work; however, the data on the other two choices strongly suggest a Bayesian principle with uniform *a priori* probabilities of heads and stems. The combined data suggest that a lexicographic principle may be at work." (*ibid.,* pp. 87–88). In Chapter Seven we shall, indeed, analyze a decision criterion combining Bayesian and minimax principles (the "restricted Bayes/Hurwicz criterion") which can generate *all* the choice patterns exhibited by Chipman's subjects (his data cannot, in fact, be represented adequately by a lexicographic principle).

is known. Let us imagine that the choice is not easy for you. To make it easier, you might investigate your preferences in some other situations which,
if not simpler, do not present this particular contrast.

First, ask yourself (you *are*, unequivocally, your own interrogator now)
how you would choose if you were offered the following two gambles:

60

	Yellow	Black
V	$100	$0
VI	$0	$100

Fig. 5.4

In other words, you are to construct a hypothetical choice-situation
equivalent to Urn I in our first example, for the purpose of measuring your
relative degrees of belief for Yellow and Black. Let us suppose that you find
yourself "definitely" indifferent between V and VI.

Next, you might imagine an urn similar to Urn II in our first example,
but now containing exactly 30 Red, 30 Yellow and 30 Black balls. First, check
to see if you are indifferent between staking a prize on any one of these colors. Then ask yourself on which you would prefer to stake a prize: "Yellow
or Black" in this hypothetical, modified "Urn II" or "Yellow and Black" in
the urn that "really" concerns you (i.e., action IV in Fig. 5.2). Again, let us
say, you find it easy to conclude that you are indifferent between these
hypothetical offers. Finally, you ask yourself whether you are indifferent
between staking a prize upon Red in the hypothetical "Urn II" or in your
"real" problem; let us suppose that you are.

Now, from many different points of view, the results of your reflection
upon these particular hypothetical choices would be, in some degree, *relevant* to your choice in your "real" problem. But would they be *sufficient* to
make your course clear in the latter case?

"Yes," the "neo-Bernoullian" would say; "your problem is solved.
Since you are indifferent between V and VI, you regard 'Yellow' and
'Black' as *equally probable.* But from your other answers, we can deduce that
you assign probability 2/3 to 'Yellow or Black' and 1/3 to Red in your 'real'
problem. Ergo, you assign probability 1/3 to Yellow, the same as to Red.
So you should be indifferent between staking the prize on Red or on Yellow. I am assuming, of course, that you wish to be consistent (i.e., with the
Savage postulates). Incidentally, in case you should run into the problem
of betting on 'Red or Black' versus 'Yellow or Black,' you've managed to
solve that one for yourself at the same time; you should be indifferent
between those offers, too. As a matter of fact, now that you stop to think
about it in the light of the other preferences you've stated, you *are* indifferent in both these cases, aren't you really?"

Well, are you?

I am not, in this particular example, or I might not be, even though my introspective answers in the "hypothetical" cases might have been those assumed above. After very considerable reflection on this point, it seems to me that in many imaginable circumstances my clear preferences in those particular hypothetical comparisons *would not be a reliable basis for predicting* my deliberated preference between staking a prize on Red or on Yellow in the postulated "real" problem. Moreover, if I were confronted with a choice between staking a prize on "Red or Black" ("not-Yellow") versus "Yellow or Black," ("not-Red") my deliberated preference, in general, could not reliably be inferred (by me, or by you) from knowledge alone of my preference for staking a prize on Red or on Yellow. In other words, after conscientious deliberation upon specific examples, I have concluded that I do *not* always wish to act "as if" the relative probabilities of any two events for me were "definite" (e.g., Red versus Yellow, Yellow versus not-Yellow, in this example).

In contrast, the "neo-Bernoulli" theory presumes one's deliberate choices among gambles that stake prizes *on* various events always to be strictly predictable from his deliberate choices among gambles that stake prizes *against* those events; that, in essence, is the operational content of the requirement that personal probabilities be "definite." Such a theory of one's deliberated preferences is evidently not to be relied upon for my own decision-making. If an adequate normative theory is attainable for me (and I believe it is; see Chapter Seven) it must be a different one.

As for "you": if at any point in these hypothetical exercises you have found your initial choices at variance with the Savage postulates, you might now pause to reconsider. Impulsive violations of a systematic sort (as in the Chipman, or Becker and Brownson experiments) deserve close attention, but they are far from conclusive, in themselves, as to your fundamental standards of consistent decision-making. If, in fact, you should quickly repent of your discrepancies—if you should decide that your choices implying conflicts with the axioms were "mistakes" and that your true preferences, upon reflection, involve no such inconsistencies—you confirm that the Savage postulates are indeed acceptable to you as *normative criteria* in these situation. (You may join, in reliance upon the Savage postulates as instruments and guides of your decision-making, those individuals who are scarcely tempted[1] in any of these examples to depart from the "Bernoulli proposition"). But this is very far from a universal reaction.

---

[1]This sizeable group ranges from those who, as one put it, "feel the pull" of the counterexamples—who "see the difference" between the options in the various pairs but conclude it does not, or should not, "make a difference" to their decision-making—to those who insist that they cannot distinguish any difference whatever

After rethinking all their "offending" decisions in the light of the postulates, it seems fair to say that a number of people who otherwise appear not only sophisticated but reasonable decide that they wish to persist in their choices. Their moods concerning this conclusion vary. Some violate the axioms cheerfully, even with gusto: others sadly though decisively, having looked into their hearts, found conflicts with the axioms and decided, in Ysidro's phrase, to satisfy their preferences and let the axioms satisfy themselves. Among the latter are individuals who previously felt committed to the axioms, many of them surprised and some dismayed to have discovered that they wished, in certain situations, to violate the Sure-thing Principle.

To a thoroughly convinced "neo-Bernoullian" such attitudes on the part of others bespeak only the frailty of human reason, of which he is inclined to be tolerant; indeed, if he is a teacher of statistics, they present a stimulating challenge, an assurance of how much he is needed.

The latter point of view has been ably articulated by Howard Raiffa, who is not reluctant to affirm that "it is not hard to elicit from most people (and I include myself in this category) a set of mutually inconsistent responses to questions or to observe in their actions inconsistent behavior."[1] Quite specifically, after exposing the "three-color urn" example above to the intuition of numerous students of mathematical statistics and classes in the Harvard Business School, under circumstances in which all "inconsistencies" were helpfully pointed out and discussed, rules of thumb for avoiding them suggested, and subjects given every opportunity and encouragement to revise their choices, Raiffa reports:

> I concur with Ellsberg that most subjects choose act I over II and IV over III [Figures 5.1, 5.2], thus violating the Savage Axioms. Also I admit that many of these subjects are reluctant to change their choices when it is pointed out to them that their behavior is inconsistent with the Sure-thing Principle. Many are also not very impressed with the argument that *no* partition of the sixty (black, yellow) balls would lead to the pattern I over II and IV over III.[2]

---

in the nature of their uncertainty, or even the state of their information, concerning, say, Urn I versus Urn II, or Red versus Yellow. With these latter individuals (not at all with the former) I find it peculiarly hard to communicate. My private feeling toward them (after becoming convinced that they are sincere) is that they simply lack certain faculties of discrimination, as in color-blindness. *They* think I am hallucinating.

[1]Raiffa, "Risk, Ambiguity, and the Savage Axioms: Comment," p. 690.

[2]*Ibid.*, p. 694. Raiffa goes on to present an argument which he uses—with what success, he does not report—to "undermine further [sic] their confidence in their initial choices." This argument is discussed at length in Chapter Eight.

But this experience evokes from Raiffa the same response as his discovery, which he also reports, of his *own intuitive* desire to violate the Surething Principle in this example: it arouses in him "renewed respect for the importance of the Savage theory."

> I wish to reaffirm . . . that Savage's theory is not a descriptive or predictive theory of behavior. It is a theory which purports to advise any one of its believers how he *should* behave in complicated situations, *provided* he can make choices in a coherent manner in relatively simple, uncomplicated situations.

> The fact that most people can be shown to be inconsistent in their manifest choice behavior cuts two ways: First, it emphasizes the difficulties encountered in putting into practice a model which demands in each application that the decision-maker assign a set of preferences to a host of simple problems which are internally consistent. Second, it clearly demonstrates how important it is to have a theory which can be used to aid in the making of decisions under uncertainty. If most people behaved in a manner roughly consistent with Savage's theory then the theory would gain stature as a descriptive theory but would lose a good deal of its normative importance. We do not have to teach people what comes naturally. But as it is, we need to do a lot of teaching . . .[1]

Raiffa's general comments are quite valid, for anyone whose *deliberated* preferences, in contrast to his hasty, unreflective choices, are in good accord with the Savage theory: for example, for Raiffa himself, who asserts that after reflection and analysis, though not before, "I find that I would want to behave in a manner consistent with Savage's normative prescriptions of behavior" in the given example.[2] But what of those who are "reluctant to change their choices" to conform to the Savage theory, with which, upon reflection, they are "not very impressed"? Initial, intuitive desire to violate a proposed normative theory may be, as Raiffa suggests, a necessary condition for the theory to be "important" to a given decision-maker, but it is scarcely a sufficient one. The fact that widespread, systematic discrepancies can be observed in the behavior of given people in certain circumstances means that the theory is *either important for them or it is useless and misleading for them* in those circumstances: depending upon the extent

---

[1] *Ibid.*, pp. 690–691.

[2] *Ibid.*, p. 690. Raiffa makes similar comments with respect to the related examples cited by William Fellner, "Distortion of Subjective Probabilities as Reaction to Uncertainty," *Quarterly Journal of Economics,* Vol. LXXV, 1961, pp. 670–689.

to which deliberation in the light of the theory finally induces them to change their courses.

Certain "neo-Bernoullians" (among those who admit the "pull" of certain counterexamples) have expressed to me the view, in conversation: "But I *must* have a logic of choice, to help me analyze complex alternatives in terms of simple ones; and *what other theory is there?*" This attitude seems disturbingly similar to that of a gambler who plays poker with a dealer he knows to be crooked, because "It's the only game in town."[1]

There *are* alternatives to the Savage theory (we shall consider several in the next two chapters, still others exist, and many more, no doubt, await construction); but "you" are not likely to find one—or even to look for one—better suited to your preferences unless you remain critical at all times of the appropriateness, for you, of any given theory in given circumstances.

An *inappropriate* theory of the structure of your deliberated preferences will lead you to "deduce," from your choices in certain, simple situations, decisions among important, complex alternatives that would appear *contrary* to your own clear, deep-felt preferences in the latter circumstances if you "stopped to think."[1] You may, in general, need a normative logic of choice, but not that badly; at least, you do not need that one.

---

[1] As a graduate student I was once engaged as a consultant, on the recommendation of Wassily Leontief, to a speculator in cotton futures who wanted instruction in "game theory." In the course of the first session, I inquired and finally learned his motivations; he suspected his *broker* of cheating him, and he wanted to learn minimax principles to protect himself. I advised him, without fee, to look for a new broker. There are, I suspect, strict "neo-Bernoullians" at this moment who might profitably be looking for a new theory.

[2] Suppose that your "real" problem were to choose between a *given pair* of the alternatives below, where payoffs are expressed in your "von Neumann-Morgenstern utilities," previously measured:

	30	60	
	Red	Yellow	Black
I	0	0	0
II	100	0	−100
III	100	100	−200
IV	0	−100	100

Fig. 5.5

If your self-interrogation (see Figure 5.4 and subsequent discussion) revealed (a) that you were indifferent between staking a given, *positive reward* either on Yellow or on Black, and (b) that you assigned, in effect, probability = 1/3 to Red, then

In the following chapters we shall turn to the question, whether it is possible to give a coherent, formal description of the way the "violators" described above *are* behaving, and a sensible account, that may be acceptable to them, of *why* they behave as they do. If you are one of those who feel you would *not* wish to disobey the Savage postulates in any of the situations we have discussed, you may yet change your mind.

---

the "neo-Bernoullian" advice (or inference on your deliberated preferences) would require *indifference* between any given pair of the actions above; in particular, the gambles II, III and IV should each be "barely acceptable," or indifferent to the option of "not gambling," action I.

The "restricted Hurwicz criterion" introduced at the end of Chapter Six and the "restricted Bayes/Hurwicz criterion" discussed in Chapter Seven could account for such contrary, deliberated preferences (simultaneously with preferences [a] and [b] above) as: I preferred to II, III, or IV; and/or II preferred to III or IV. Neither such tastes for "insurance" when information is ambiguous, nor the opposite preferences, need contradict the assumption that the payoffs specified represent your "von Neumann-Morgenstern utilities" (see discussion of Rubin's axiom in Chapter Eight). To *deduce* these preferences, such criteria would require data such as your independent choices with respect *both* to Fig. 5.1 and to Fig. 5.2.

Appendix to Chapter Five

IN ORDER TO relate the assertions in the text clearly to the postulates, let us change the experimental setting slightly. Let us assume that the balls in Urn I are each marked with a I, and the balls in Urn II with a II; the contents of both urns are then dumped into a single urn, which then contains 50 Red$_{II}$ balls, 50 Black$_{II}$ balls, and 100 Red$_I$ and Black$_I$ balls in unknown proportion (or in a proportion indicated only by a small random sample, say, one Red and one Black). Alternatively, as in the text, we could keep the urns separate and regard the choice of urn as an "event" controlled by the questioner, to be "given" in any one comparison of gambles. The following proofs, stated informally, would apply, given the specified premises, if R$_I$, B$_I$, R$_{II}$, B$_{II}$ were replaced by any four mutually exclusive, exhaustive events.

THEOREM 1:

The following actions are to be considered:

	50 R$_{II}$	50 B$_{II}$	100 R$_I$	B$_I$
I	a	b	b	b
II	b	a	b	b
III	b	b	a	b
IV	b	b	b	a
V	a	a	b	b
VI	b	b	a	a

Let us assume that a person is indifferent between I and II (between betting on R$_I$ or B$_I$), between III and IV and between V and VI. It would then follow from Postulates 1 and 2, the assumption of a complete ordering of actions and the Sure-Thing Principle, that I, II, III and IV are all indifferent to each other.

For suppose, to the contrary, that I is preferred to III (the person prefers to stake a prize on R_I rather than on R_{II}), despite our premises. Postulates 1 and 2 imply that certain transformations can be performed on this pair of actions *without affecting their preference ordering;* specifically, one action can be replaced by an action indifferent to it (P1—complete ordering) and the value of a constant column can be changed (P2—Sure-Thing Principle).

Thus starting with I and III and performing such "admissible transformations" it would follow from P1 and P2 that the *first* action in *each* of the following pairs should be preferred:

	R_{II}	B_{II}	R_I	B_I	
I	a	b	b	b	
III	b	b	a	b	
I'	a	b	b	a	
III'	b	b	a	a	P2
I''	a	b	b	a	
III''	a	a	b	b	P1
I'''	b	b	b	a	
III'''	b	a	b	b	P2
I''''	b	b	a	b	
III''''	a	b	b	b	P1

Contradiction: I preferred to III, and I'''' (equivalent to III) preferred to III'''' (equivalent to I).

LEMMA 1:

If $a \geq c > b$, and you are indifferent between actions I and II below, then by Postulate 4 you must be indifferent between III and IV below; the reverse implication is also valid. That is: $I \doteq II \Longleftrightarrow III \doteq IV$.

	A		B	
	R_{II}	B_{II}	R_I	B_I
I	a	a	b	b
II	b	b	a	a
III	c	c	b	b
IV	b	b	c	c

Proof: follows directly from Savage's statement of Postulate 4 (*Foundations of Statistics*, p. 31, or end-papers; see Appendix to Chapter Four, above). Note that: I, II, III, IV; A, B; a, b, c; are such that

1. $b < a, b < c$.
2a. (The payoff to) I = a, III = c for $s \in A$
    " I = b, III = b for $s \in \bar{A}$
2b. " II = a, IV = b for $s \in B$
3. I $\doteq$ II " II = b, IV = b for $s \in \bar{B}$

Thus by Postulate 4: III $\doteq$ IV.

THEOREM 2:

Given the following actions I–IX: if you are indifferent between I, II, III, and likewise between V, VI, VII, and between VIII and IX; then by Postulates 1, 2 and 4 you will be indifferent between all the actions I–VII, and, by Postulate 3, between the payoffs c and c'.

[In our example, c is the maximum "price" you would pay for a stake of a on R_{II}, or on B_{II} *given* that drawing will be from balls marked II (payoff b if you fail to "win" in either case.) c' is the maximum price you would pay for a stake of a on R_I or on B_I, *given* that the drawing would be from balls marked I (b if you fail to "win"). Given indifference between placing a stake on R_I or B_I, and between placing a stake on R_{II} or B_{II}, Theorem 2 states that c $\doteq$ c'.]

	R_{II}	B_{II}	R_I	B_I
I	a	b	b	b
II	b	a	b	b
III	c	c	b	b
IV	b	b	c	c
V	b	b	c'	c'
VI	b	b	a	b
VII	b	b	b	a
VIII	a	a	b	b
IX	b	b	a	a

Proof: (a) VIII $\doteq$ IX => III $\doteq$ IV by Postulate 4 (see Lemma 1).
(b) I $\doteq$ II, VI $\doteq$ VII, VIII $\doteq$ IX => I $\doteq$ II $\doteq$ VI $\doteq$ VII by Theorem 1 (Postulates 1 and 2).
(c) Hence IV $\doteq$ V ($\doteq$ I $\doteq$ II $\doteq$ III $\doteq$ VI $\doteq$ VII) by Postulate 1.
(d) Hence c $\doteq$ c', by Postulate 3 (see Appendix to Chapter Four).

THEOREM 3:

If you are indifferent between I, II, III, IV below, then by Postulates 1, 2 and 4, you must not prefer action IV *both* to V and to VI. That is, given I $\doteq$ II $\doteq$ III $\doteq$ IV, then either IV $\leq$ V or IV $\leq$ VI, or both (in which case IV $\doteq$ V $\doteq$ VI). Or: either V $\cdot$> IV $\cdot$> VI or VI $\cdot$> IV $\cdot$> V or V $\doteq$ IV $\doteq$ VI. [In our example, c is the maximum price you would pay for a stake of a on R_{II}, or on B_{II}, b if you "lose." Note that we make no assumption here that V $\doteq$ VI; R_I and B_I may be thought of as *any* two events for which the other premises hold. Under those conditions, I $\doteq$ II $\doteq$ III, the von Neumann-Morgenstern utilities must be such that U(c) = U(a) + U(b)/2. c cannot; if Postulates 1, 2, 4 are obeyed, be both "too much to pay" for a stake of a on R_I *and* "too much to pay" for a stake of a on B_I, if that were offered alternatively, *given* that one of R_I, B_I must occur.]

	R_{II}	B_{II}	R_I	B_I
I	a	b	b	b
II	b	a	b	b
III	c	c	b	b
IV	b	b	c	c
V	b	b	a	b
VI	b	b	b	a

Proof: Suppose, to the contrary, that IV $\cdot$> V *and* IV $\cdot$> VI. Then the first action in each pair below must be preferred to the second.

	R_{II}	B_{II}	R_I	B_I	
IV	b	b	c	c	
V	b	b	a	b	
	a	a	c	c	P2
	a	a	a	b	
	c	c	a	a	P1 and
	a	a	a	b	Lemma 1
	b	a	a	a	P2 and
	a	a	a	b	P1
	b	b	b	a	
	a	b	b	b	P2
VI	b	b	b	a	
IV	b	b	c	c	P1

Contradiction (to hypothesis that IV $\cdot$> VI).

6

WHY ARE SOME UNCERTAINTIES NOT RISKS?

INDIVIDUALS WHO WOULD choose action I over II and IV over III in the three-color urn example below are simply not acting "as if" they assigned definite numerical (or even qualitative) probabilities to the events in question and maximized the mathematical expectation of utility. Though this is a special, simple situation in which each gamble offers the same two outcomes, they are not acting "as if" they sought to maximize the probability of the preferred outcome; for whatever definite probabilities are assigned to the relevant events, their pattern of choices is inconsistent with that assumption. There are, it appears, other ways for them to act. But what *are* they doing?

	30 Red	Yellow	60 Black
I	$100	$0	$0
II	$0	$100	$0
III	$100	$0	$100
IV	$0	$100	$100

Fig. 6.1

Are they choosing at random? Is their behavior entirely outside the context of the careful, deliberated, self-conscious decision-making which is the focus of our discussion? On the contrary; their choices appear neither hasty nor careless, and they seem to persist after considerable reflection on the fact that they are violating the "Sure-Thing Principle." Many of the people in this category are, by other standards and to all outward appearances,

155

emininently reasonable; and they tend articulately to insist that they *want* to behave this way, even though they may be generally respectful of the Savage postulates. There are strong indications, then, that the Savage postulates are not acceptable to them as a normative theory; the postulates, taken as a whole, do not serve their needs for a logic of choice under uncertainty corresponding to their own preferences.

This is quite apart from the question whether or not their behavior is "foolish" in terms of some impersonal super-criteria. One may always conjecture, after any given length of time has elapsed, that someone who still persists in an initial choice violating given postulates has simply not yet attained that enlightened self-awareness that marks the truly "rational" man. But if we are to accord the proposition that a given postulate is an acceptable normative guide for a given individual the status of a meaningful, refutable hypothesis, there must come a point when we regard it as being refuted. As Savage makes unequivocally clear:

> If, after thorough deliberation, anyone maintains a pair of distinct preferences that are in conflict with the sure-thing principle, he must abandon, or modify, the principle; for that kind of discrepancy seems intolerable in a normative theory. Analogous circumstances forced D. Bernoulli to abandon the theory of mathematical expectation for that of utility.[1]

If, indeed, the proponents of postulates leading to the "Bernoulli proposition" claimed to be bringing ultimate moral guidance to earth, to be ignored at the risk of loss and disgrace, such a statement as the above would make no sense; it would seem undue tolerance or false kindness, like encouraging a child to persist in his own, idiosyncratic rules of addition. But there is nothing paradoxical about it when "normative theory" is interpreted modestly, as it is throughout *The Foundations of Statistics,* as: *a theory of one's own deliberated preference patterns.* If a theory built on the Sure-thing Principle will not work for you—*because it leads to wrong predictions of the choices you wish to make when you "stop to think"*—then you need a different theory.

Suppose you confronted the "complex" alternatives III and IV in the three-color urn example (the choice between staking $100 on "Red or Black" or on "Yellow or Black"); imagine that your preference is not at once intuitively obvious. An advocate of the "Sure-thing Principle" might suggest: "Ask yourself which you would prefer between actions I and II (staking the prize on "Red" or on "Yellow"); even though no one has offered you those, you may find it easier to decide. Then, if you're sure you would prefer I to II, take action III instead of IV; you won't regret it, when you stop

---

[1] Savage, *Foundations of Statistics,* p. 102.

to think." Here indeed is a theory leading to just the *sort* of advice that is wanted; it tells you how to infer your choices "logically" in complicated or unfamiliar situations from other choices you can make more confidently, on the basis of intuition or, perhaps, earlier analysis. Only: is it *true* that these inferences will not conflict with the choices you would make if you did take time to know your own mind in the more complex case? That needs checking; and in this particular case, for a good many people, it would not be true. The Sure-thing Principle, then, is not available to them as a convenient device for "calculating" acceptable decisions in one situation from their own prior decisions in another. We must consider the problem of devising a logic of choice for them that would better meet these goals.

A first question is whether the other normative principles proposed by Savage are, like Postulate 2, invalidated for these decision-makers by their choices in the given examples. So far, the answer would appear to be: No. The individuals in question state preference or indifference definitely, without evident vacillation or indecision. So far as we have yet seen, their preferences among actions are "connected" and transitive: for example, IV $\cdot \geq$ III $\cdot \geq$ I $\cdot \geq$ II (based on pairwise comparisons). Thus, Postulate 1 is preserved. Postulate III, non-domination of preferred actions, has not been violated, though tested: e.g., III $\cdot \geq$ I and IV $\cdot \geq$ are consistent with it.

To test Postulate IV, we must check whether any of the announced preferences would change if the $100 prize were changed to $1,000, or to $1. Here we may find some violations. Some individuals who prefer IV to III and I to II at large stakes claim that their preference fades to indifference as the stake becomes trivial; likewise, some of those who claim indifference between I and II and between III and IV when the prize is (hypothetically) $100 assert that their attitude would change if the "no-win" payoff were lowered from $0 to –$1,000 (or to some non-monetary "bad" outcome, e.g., bodily harm). Thus, variations in the psychological "importance" of the prize may lead to some variation in announced preferences violating Postulate 4.[1] However, for a given individual let us assume there is a level of prizes (including possible "negative" payoffs to "no-win") sufficiently "important" to bring into play decision-making rules and procedures reserved for important decisions; and if we consider only such decision problems, there is no indication yet that Postulate 4 will meet with violations.

There is generally no problem in demonstrating preference for $100 over $0 for all these individuals, so Postulate 5 is safe. Postulate 6 meets no

---

[1] Though apparently not, as conjectured by Savage, in the direction of increased adherence to the postulates, including Postulate 2, as stakes increase and decision-making grows more "careful." See Savage, *Foundations of Statistics*, p. 30.

test in this context. Moreover, all of these conclusions seem to apply equally well to the other examples considered in Chapter Five: e.g., the two-urn case. So far, Postulate 2 is the only obvious casualty.

But if we tentatively conclude that Postulates 1, 3, 4 and 5 hold for the individuals in question, it follows from our discussion in Chapter Four that we could establish for them not only a complete ordering of actions but a complete ordering of events in terms of the relationship ??211??, where A ??211?? B means the individual "does not prefer to stake a given prize upon event A rather than upon event B" (where A and B may be any two events, not necessarily disjoint). Thus, these postulates would imply a considerable amount of order, structure, or "consistency"—hence, predictability— in their pattern of choices, even though it would be impossible to infer from them a definite qualitative probability relationship over events. If we had previously measured "von Neumann-Morgenstern utilities" for them, we could investigate their "upper and lower betting probabilities"; and even if we had not, we could establish inequalities for these variables, given that Postulates 1, 3 and 4 were obeyed. Thus, the pattern of choices: IV $\cdot$> III $\cdot$> I $\cdot$> II should correspond to the following pattern of "betting probabilities," or "bids for a unit utility stake": $p_o(\text{Yellow}) < p_o(\text{Red}) < q_o(\text{Yellow}) < q_o(\text{Red})$, or $p_o(\text{Yellow}) < p_o(\text{Red})$ and $p^o(\text{Yellow}) > p^o(\text{Red})$;[1] i.e., the upper and lower betting probabilities for Yellow enclose those for Red.

DECISION CRITERIA FOR "COMPLETE IGNORANCE"

The assertions by many of the individuals concerned that they *wish* to persist in just these choices suggest strongly that the apparently reliable patterns of behavior exhibited reflect the operation of definite normative criteria—evidently differing from those considered in Chapter Four—to which these people are trying to conform. The most direct route to discovering these rules (which may not be wholly conscious or explicit) would be to interrogate the decision-makers themselves; but first let us narrow the set of hypothetical rules in terms of which we might interpret their answers. We can identify, even with these few observations, a number of candidate rules which they are *not* following.

Since they are not even behaving "as if" they assigned any definite numerical probabilities to events and maximizing the mathematical expec-

---

[1] See the corresponding, hypothetical set of bids, case (d) in Fig. 3.6, Appendix to Chapter Three, where utilities are assumed known: $p_o(\text{Red} = p^o(\text{Red}) = 1/3$, $p_o(\text{Yellow}) = p_o(\text{Black}) = 1/6$, $p^o(\text{Yellow}) = p^o(\text{Black}) = 1/2$. Note that: (a) this system of "betting probabilities" is "coherent"; it would be impossible for an opponent to make a book against it; (b) it implies a "definite" degree of belief for Red, though not for Yellow.

tation of utility, we can, of course, rule out the possibility that they *are*, consciously and explicitly, doing precisely that. The most familiar *alternative* decision rules are those that have been proposed for the case of "complete ignorance" in "games against Nature": i.e., decision problems in which the relevant events are regarded as strategies by a fictitious player, Nature, about whose objectives or likely choice of strategy there is "absolutely no information." Whether these circumstances are adequately defined is open to question; i.e., there is a problem of specifying *when in general* any one of these decision rules might be appropriate. But our only interest here is to discover whether one of them could describe the patterns of behavior associated with our particular examples; i.e., whether we could say that any of the individuals violating Postulate 2 acts "as if" he applied one of these criteria, of which the best-known are the four discussed by John Milnor in his paper, "Games Against Nature."[1]

Assuming the game formulation, in which payoffs u_{ij} are expressed in terms of "von Neumann-Morgenstern utilities," your actions are represented by rows in a matrix in which the columns represent events ("strategies by Nature"), these criteria are described and labelled by Milnor respectively:

1. *Laplace.* Choose a row for which the average payoff $(u_{i1} + \ldots + u_{in})/n$ is maximized. (This amounts to acting "as if" equal probabilities were assigned to the different events.)
2. *Wald* (Minimax principle). Choose a row for which the minimum payoff $\text{Min}_j\, u_{ij}$ is maximized. If mixed strategies are allowed, choose a probability mixture $(\xi_1, \ldots \xi_m)$ of the rows so that the quantity $\text{Min}_j\, (\xi_1 u_{1j} + \ldots + \xi_m u_{mj})$ is maximized. (This leads to the same results as assigning the "least favorable probability distribution" $(\zeta_1, \ldots \zeta_n)$ over events; i.e., considering *all possible* probability distributions over events, assigning that one for which $\text{Max}_i\, (\zeta_1 u_{i1} + \ldots + \zeta_n u_{in})$ is minimized.)
3. *Hurwicz.* Let α, $0 \le \alpha \le 1$ represent your "optimism" coefficient, let a denote the smallest component and A the largest component in each row; choose a row for which $\alpha A + (1 - \alpha)a$ is maximized. (For $\alpha = 0$ this reduces to the Wald criterion.)

---

[1] In *Decision Processes*, ed. R. M. Thrall, C. H. Coombs, R. L. Davis (New York, 1954), pp. 49–59. See also the excellent discussion of the same four criteria in Luce and Raiffa, *Games and Decisions* (New York, 1957), pp. 278–286; and the discussion of alternative criteria including three of the four here (excluding the "Hurwicz criterion") by Herman Chernoff, "Rational Selection of Decision Functions," *Econometrica*, Vol. 22, No. 4, October 1954, pp. 422–443.

4. *Savage* (Minimax Regret).[1] Define the regret matrix (r_{ij}) by $r_{ij} = \text{Max}_k\, u_{kj} - u_{ij}$ (i.e., r_{ij} is the amount that has to be added to u_{ij} to equal the maximum utility payoff in the *j*th column). Now apply the Wald criterion to the matrix (r_{ij}). Choose a row for which $\text{Max}_j\, r_{ij}$ is minimized; or if mixed strategies are allowed, choose a probability mixture $(\xi_1, \ldots \xi_m)$ such that $\text{Max}_j\, (\xi_1 r_{1j} + \ldots + \xi_m r_{mj})$ is minimized.

It is unnecessary to proceed here to any elaborate analysis of the logical relationships among these rules or their individual merits and limitations,[2] since the fact is that *none* of them could, in the form considered, generate the patterns of choice in which we are interested. Any one of these rules would lead to *indifference* between the "pure strategies" I and II, and between III and IV: the Wald and Hurwicz rules because both members of each pair have identical maxima and minima; the Laplace rule because both members have the same average payoff; the Savage Minimax Regret rule because both members have the same maximum regret.[3] We shall consider choices among probability mixtures of actions, or mixed strategies, in the next chapter; however, consideration of mixed strategies here would

---

[1] r_{ij} measures the difference between the payoff you could attain if you were able to act with the certain knowledge that E_j obtained and that which you will attain if (without certain knowledge) you decide on action *i* when E_j does in fact obtain. Savage regards the term "regret" regrettable, since it seems to him "charged with emotion and liable to such misinterpretation as that the loss necessarily becomes known to the person" (i.e., that he always learns with certainty which E_o actually does obtain). (*Foundations of Statistics*, p. 163.) However, such terms as "loss" or "risk" introduce confusion with criterion (2). Savage would regard it as no loss simply to suppress criterion (1) from discussion, since he does not consider it worthy of serious consideration in those contexts in which the two criteria would give differing results. We shall find, on the contrary, that a modification of criterion (2) will give us one solution to our problem, unlike any modification of criterion (4); therefore we must preserve the distinction.

It should be mentioned that criterion (4) is identified with Savage because he introduced it in a review of Wald's work, "The Theory of Statistical Decision," *Journal of the American Statistical Association*, Vol. 46, 1951, pp. 55–67. Although it is discussed at length in *The Foundations of Statistics* (pp. 158–219) in connection mainly with problems of *group* decision, it is quite distinct from Savage's "neo-Bayesian" decision criteria, and in fact, conflicts with Savage's Postulate 1, complete ordering of actions; Savage would not currently defend it for individual decision-making.

[2] For this, see the discussions cited above by Milnor, Luce and Raiffa, and Chernoff.

[3] The "regret" matrix for *each* of the two pairs, assuming 0, 1 utility payoffs, is:

not affect the conclusion that none of these rules could lead to the choices, I preferred to II and IV preferred to III (or, vice versa).[1]

It is not too surprising that none of the individuals considered in Chapter Five are acting "as if" they obeyed any one of these four decision rules, since these are generally associated (as in Milnor's discussion) with situations of "complete ignorance," where that notion is defined operationally in terms of behavior patterns satisfying two conditions:[2]

(a) the preference ordering of the actions is independent of the labelling of the states of nature; i.e., the ordering of rows (actions) is the

	Red	Yellow	Black
I (III)	0	1	0
II (IV)	1	0	0

Fig. 6.2

Note that no one whose decisions were based upon a "regret" matrix could violate the Sure-Thing Princi ple as applied to the original payoffs, since all constant columns of payoffs would transform to a column of 0's in terms of "regret," so that changes in the payoff value in a constant value could not affect decisions. However, such a person might (e.g., if he followed the Minimax Regret rule) violate Postulate 1, complete ordering of actions; though that would not show up in this example.

[1] If mixed strategies were considered, a $\frac{1}{2}:\frac{1}{2}$ probability mixture of actions I and II would be preferred either to I or to II as "pure strategies" or to any other mixture, in terms of the Minimax Regret rule, since, utilities of 0, 1 corresponding to the outcomes $0, $100, the maximum regret would be reduced from 1 to $1/2$; a $\frac{1}{2}:\frac{1}{2}$ probability mixture of III and IV would be optimal with respect to these two components, in terms of the Minimax Regret rule, the Wald rule, and the Hurwicz rule for any α, $0 \leq \alpha < 1$ (the latter two because the minimum payoff would be raised from 0 to $\frac{1}{2}$). Either of the "pure strategies" I, II would be preferred to any proper probability mixture in terms of the Hurwicz rule with $\alpha > 0$, since the maximum payoff would be reduced.

[2] The two conditions appear as "axioms" 2 (Symmetry) and 8 (Column duplication), respectively, in Milnor's treatment; *op. cit.,* pp. 51–52; or as "axioms" 10 and 11, respectively, in Luce and Raiffa, *op. cit.,* pp. 294–296. These authors fail to draw attention to the fact that these axioms, quite unlike the others they consider, are obviously intended to apply to special circumstances only. In particular, you will violate the second condition if you act "as if" you assigned "at least" some positive probability $\in$ to *each* of the events shown ($n \geq 3$).

same for any permutation of the columns of payoffs, or for any association of a given column of payoffs with a particular state of nature;

   (b)   the ordering is not affected if a new column, identical with some old column of payoffs, is adjoined to the matrix; or conversely, it is not affected if a "repetitious" column is deleted (i.e., two states which yield identical payoffs for all payoffs are collapsed into one).

These postulated conditions of choice-behavior have typically been presented as "axioms," equivalent to the Savage postulates,[1] but it is obvious that they are not proposed, as are the Savage postulates, as characterizing "rational" preferences under all circumstances of uncertainty. Neither pattern of choice would seem appropriate (i.e., "reasonable") if the decision-maker definitely believed (by any conceivable operational test, including verbal assertion) one given state of nature "more likely" to be the true state than another. (This does not mean that these conditions imply that *equal probabilities* are assigned to every state of nature; on the contrary, the second condition, in combination with the first, conflicts with the possibility of assigning any definite probabilities at all in accordance with the "Bernoulli proposition").

It would be difficult, if not impossible, in the recent literature in statistical decision theory to find a defense of any of these four rules as "reasonable" in circumstances where neither of the above conditions is satisfied.[1] And it is clear that none of the postulated behavior in connection with our example satisfies these conditions taken together. The two conditions would imply that action I is indifferent to action IV, since the payoffs to one are a permutation of the payoffs to the other when the second and third columns (one of which is "repetitious") are collapsed into one (see Fig. 6.1):

	30	60	
		not-Red	
	Red	**Yellow**	**Black**
I	$100	$ 0	
IV	$ 0	$100	

Fig. 6.3

---

[1]The second condition above would imply violation of the Laplace rule, unless that criterion were modified to apply to a set of acts only after deletion of all "repetitious" columns; in this modified form, the criterion would not lead to a complete ordering of acts, since it would fail the condition of "independence of irrelevant alternatives" (see Luce and Raiffa, *op. cit.*, p. 296).

   Neither those individuals who violate Postulate 2 nor those who obey it would be indifferent between these two actions, or fail to prefer action IV, given the known 2/3 proportion of "not-Red" balls in the urn. Without developing G. L. S. Shackle's analysis in full here, we might take note of the fact that his hypotheses on behavior, as applied to this situation, would amount to a generalization of the "Hurwicz criterion" and would fail, for the same reason as that criterion, to correspond to the postulated behavior. By Shackle's description of circumstances in which the "potential surprise" of a given event may be greater than zero, neither the drawing of a Red ball, a Yellow ball, or a Black ball should occasion positive surprise; in terms of the information given, each of these must be regarded as "perfectly possible." In such a situation Shackle assumes that one's decision will reflect only two "focus outcomes" for each act, its maximum and minimum payoffs.[1]

   Although Shackle would allow preference between actions to be a more general function of these pairs of related maximum and minimum payoffs than the Hurwicz rule implies (the Hurwicz rule corresponds to a special case in which the indifference sets in Shackle's "gambler's indifference map" are parallel straight lines, with slope dependent on α), his hypothesis would still imply that action I must be indifferent to II and III to IV—in fact, that I, II, III, IV must all be indifferent to each other—since they all have identical maxima and minima.

   The relationship of Shackle's work to other proposals and axioms related to decision criteria has not, to my knowledge, been examined in any published writings, and I shall not take space to do so here, except to conjecture that his most distinctive hypotheses are best applied to situations in which the two conditions above, characterizing "complete ignorance," are satisfied. This follows almost tautologically from the nature of Shackle's hypotheses; but I would further conjecture that these postulated conditions are much less generally realistic than Shackle's discussion would suggest. At any rate, it is clear that neither these conditions nor Shackle's hypotheses are satisfied for typical individuals in connection with the examples we have been discussing.

   In other words, virtually no one tends to act "as if" he were "completely ignorant" of the relative probabilities of Red and not-Red in the three-color urn example, either in the technical sense above or in any other sense (such as both being indistinguishably, "perfectly possible"). On the contrary, an individual is likely to exhibit "definite" degrees of belief for

---

[1]See G. L. S. Shackle, *Expectation in Economics* (Cambridge, 1952), Chapter II, "The Nature of Expectation," and appendices to Chapter II. I am not aware that this relation between Shackle's hypotheses and the Hurwicz criterion has been remarked in print elsewhere.

the drawing of a Red ball in this case, by any of the operational tests discussed in Chapters Three and Four, if ever he does: whether or not his degree of belief in the drawing of a Yellow ball, or a Black, is equally "definite" by those tests. If we imagine "von Neumann-Morgenstern utilities" to have been measured, and utilities 1, 0 assigned arbitrarily to the outcomes \$100, \$0, we would expect very generally maximum bids of $1/3$ for the gamble I and $2/3$ for the gamble IV; i.e., as defined in Chapter Three, $p_o(\text{Red}) = 1 - q_o(\text{Red}) = p^o(\text{Red}) = 1/3$. Or, using the "Borel" test from Chapter Four, we would expect any given individual to be indifferent between staking a given prize on the drawing of a Red ball from this urn or on the occurrence of one out of three disjoint, equi-probable events (given that one of them will occur); *and* likewise to be indifferent between staking a prize on "not-Red" or on the union of any two of the three events.

On the other hand, for at least some individuals, those who violate Postulate 2, we cannot assign "definite" probabilities to the drawing of a Yellow ball (or a Black). As we have already conjectured, they would pay *less* than $p_o(\text{Red})$ for a unit utility staked on Yellow, and *also less* than $q_o(\text{Red})$ [$= p_o(\text{"not-Red"})$] for a unit utility staked on "not-Yellow"; i.e., typically, $p_o(\text{Yellow}) < p_o(\text{Red}) = p^o(\text{Red}) < p^o(\text{Yellow})$, and similarly for Black. Likewise, assuming that they would be indifferent between staking a given prize on Red or on any event whose probability has been *measured for them* at $30/90$ (say, drawing a card numbered 1 to 30 from a well-shuffled pack of 90 cards), and between staking the prize "against" Red or on any event with probability for them $= 60/90$, it appears that they prefer to stake a prize on one of the former events (probability $= 1/3$) than on Yellow, yet also prefer to stake it on one of the latter events (probability $= 2/3$) than against Yellow.[1]

Thus, *none* of the familiar criteria for predicting or prescribing decision-making under uncertainty corresponds throughout to their pattern of choices. Although their behavior is consistent with the "Bernoulli proposition" with respect to *some* events (Red, not-Red), permitting measurement of "definite" degrees of belief for those events and ruling out hypotheses that they are consistently obeying the minimax, Hurwicz, Shackle or minimax regret decision rules, it still does not enable us to infer that they regard Yellow as "less probable than" Red, or "more probable," or "equally probable."

Why not? The time has come to seek some insights into their behavior by listening to their verbal comments on it. Supposing "you" to be one of those who violate Postulate 2 in this example: What do you think you are doing? What are you *trying* to do? Why don't you act as if you were seek-

---

[1] In terms of the notions introduced at the end of Chapter Four, $r_o(\text{Yellow})$ $< r_o(\text{Red}) = t - R_o(\text{Red}) < t - R_o(\text{Yellow}) = r^o(\text{Yellow})$.

ing the highest probability of winning the prize? If you think, for some reason, that Red is "more probable" than Yellow, why don't you also act is if "Red or Black" is "more probable" than "Yellow or Black"?

The last question may bring the response: "But I *don't know* whether Yellow is less probable than Red, or more probable." We then point out that "you" choose action I over II. A common reply would be: "But not because I think Yellow is less probable; I *don't know* which is more probable. *That's* why I prefer I to II; I know that with action I the *probability of winning the prize* is 1/3, 1:2, and I *don't know what it is* with action II; it could be better or worse, anything from 0 to 2/3. I *know* that action IV gives me a 2:1 chance to win the prize, 2/3 probability, whereas the probability of winning with action III might be only 1/3. That's why I prefer action IV."

Such a statement (familiar to anyone who has interrogated those who violate Postulate 2 in this example) seems to reflect some sort of calculation, some personal logic underlying choice. Yet it is not self-evident that this "logical calculation" is based on much reflection, or is any way "reasonable." A skeptic, versed in the postulates of personal probability, might ask of the "reasons" advanced for the choices made: "So what?" Even before that, it is virtually obligatory to ask: "What do you *mean*, you don't know probabilities?" At first hearing, statements about "ignorance of probabilities" seem operationally meaningless from the Ramsey/de Finneti/Savage point of view, since nothing within their approach has prepared us to relate such a notion to betting behavior. If, as de Finetti puts it, probabilities are to be understood only as "expressions of one's own belief, which cannot be unknown to oneself,"[1] what are we to make of an announcement that you "aren't sure" what probability to assign to Yellow? Do you mean you don't know your own mind? And even if we were to admit that possibility as a recognizable, transient state of affairs, how do you pretend to deduce positive preferences for actions from your confusion?

There is, in fact, a way of interpreting the quoted statements that makes them meaningful within the Ramsey/de Finetti/Savage, or "neo-Bernoullian"[2] approach; though the interpretation does not make the behavior allegedly based upon the stated judgments any more reasonable in

---

[1] de Finetti, "Recent Suggestions for the Reconciliation of Theories of Probability," p. 220.

[2] I shall use this term henceforth to denote this dominant wing (apparently including, for example, Raiffa and Schlaifer) of the "neo-Bayesian" school, which insists upon inferring probability from betting behavior alone and demands that "reasonable" behavior be consistent in every case with definite, uniquely-defined numerical probabilities; as distinguished from less exacting "neo-Bayesians" such as I. J. Good (see Chapter Eight) and myself.

"neo-Bernoullian" terms, it helps to expose the differences at issue. While the "neo-Bernoullian" school cannot accept the meaningfulness of statements that you are "uncertain of the probability" of Yellow, they have no difficulty in understanding the assertion that you are uncertain of the proportion of Yellow balls in the urn (i.e., of the number of Yellow balls, given that 60 out of 90 balls are Yellow or Black); especially when it is understood that this proportion, if known with certainty, would determine a definite probability distribution for you over the drawing of a Red, Yellow or Black ball. Statements that you are "sure" that the probability of drawing a Yellow ball is "less than 2/3" can then be translated: you are certain that, as guaranteed, there are *no more than* 60 Yellow balls in the urn.

Let us now assume (a) that you obey the von Neumann-Morgenstern utility postulates (hence, the Savage postulates) for some subset of events to which you assign "definite" probabilities; (b) that the drawing of a single ball of specified color from an urn with *known* proportions of colors would constitute such an event; (c) that your "von Neumann-Morgenstern utilities" for outcomes have been measured by previous observation of your choices among such gambles, and the values 1, 0 assigned arbitrarily to the outcomes $100, $0. This amounts to assuming that we (and "you") know how you would evaluate the given actions and choose among them if you were certain of the proportion of Yellow (Black) balls in the urn, *or if you assigned any definite probabilities to the various possible proportions.* Assuming you regard all proportions of Yellow between 0 and 2/3 as "possible," the utility values of each action are shown in the diagram below as a function of this proportion (assumed to vary continuously, allowing for all possible "expected values" of the proportion between 0 and 2/3):

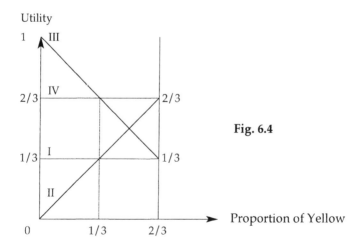

Fig. 6.4

Given our assumptions as to how you would choose if you "knew" the number of Yellow balls in the urn, this diagram makes it easy to relate your choice to your uncertainty, your opinions or partial beliefs, concerning that number. (You are, of course, equally uncertain as to the number of Black balls, but since that is constrained to be 60 less the number of Yellow balls, all your uncertainties can be expressed in terms of a one-dimensional parameter, e.g., the number of Yellow balls or the overall proportion of Yellow.) This is in no sense a different problem from the one we have been considering all along. The diagram simply depicts the results of some calculations which many individuals (including both individuals who proceed to violate Postulate 2 and others who do not) claim to be relevant to their decision in that problem.

To choose reasonably among two actions whose known payoffs depend upon the uncertain value of a single parameter is a perfectly well-defined problem in terms of the "neo-Bernoullian" approach; and that approach supplies a general solution. You must choose "as if" you assigned a definite probability distribution over the possible values of the parameter and proceeded to maximize the mathematical expectation of utility. That proposition allows for considerable variation in individual beliefs and hence in preferences; but it still does *not* allow for the pattern of preferences: I $\cdot$> II, IV $\cdot$> III.

Consider first the special cases in which you might assign probability 1 to a particular proportion (or number) of Yellow balls and 0 to all others. Any proportion you might thus feel you "knew" would determine definite utility for each of the given actions, hence your order of preference. Any "known" proportion λ between 0 and $1/3$ (or, any given number of Yellow balls between 0 and 30) would imply III $\cdot \geq$ IV and I $\cdot \geq$ II; any "known" proportion λ between $1/3$ and $2/3$ would imply IV $\cdot \geq$ III and II $\cdot \geq$ I; if the proportion λ were "known" to be exactly $1/3$, IV $\doteq$ III and I $\doteq$ II. But *no* proportion λ, $0 \leq \lambda \leq 2/3$, would lead to an ordering in which IV $\cdot$> III and I $\cdot$> II; such preferences would contradict the assumption that you were certain of the proportion λ and maximized expected utility.

Moreover, the latter preferences would contradict the assumption that you act "as if" you were certain of the proportion and maximized expected utility; and the "neo-Bernoullian" proposition in this case can be shown to be equivalent to just that. Consider the cases in which you might assign positive probabilities to a finite set of λ's ($\xi_1, \ldots \xi_n$). Given the assignment of utilities 1, 0 to the two outcomes involved, the utility value of action II for any *given* proportion λ_j is equal to λ_j, and the expected utility for any given probability distribution ($\xi_1, \ldots \xi_n$) is thus ($\xi_1\lambda_1 + \ldots + \xi_n\lambda_n$), which is equal to the expected value of the proportion of Yellow balls (represented by a point on the horizontal axis between 0 and $2/3$). On the assumption that you assign a definite probability distribution over the possible proportions of Yellow balls, then I · > II implies $(\xi_1\lambda_1 + \ldots + \xi_1\lambda_n) < 1/3$, since the expected utility of action I equals the known proportion $(1/3)$ of Red balls. But given the same distribution, the expected utility of action III is equal to the expected value of the proportion of "Red and Black" balls, or $[\xi_1(1 - \lambda_1) + \ldots + \xi_n (1 - \lambda_n)]$. IV · > III would imply that the latter value is less than $2/3$, the value of action IV being equal to the known proportion $(2/3)$ of "not-Red" balls in the urn; hence, $[1 - (\xi_1\lambda_1 + \ldots + \xi_n\lambda_n)] < 2/3$. But these two conditions are incompatible, for any $(\xi_1, \ldots \xi_n)$, $\xi_j \geq 0$, $\Sigma_j \xi_j = 1$.

To say that a person who prefers IV to III and I to II is *not acting "as if" he assigned any definite probability distribution over the possible proportions of Yellow (Black) balls in the urn* is, in fact, to rule out as hypotheses explaining his behavior quite a variety of distinguishable states of mind and decision rules. To provide a familiar interpretation of the variables, a proposition that a given number λ_j represents the "true" proportion of Yellow balls in the urn would correspond to a "simple statistical hypothesis" (given our assumptions on your betting behavior, and interpreting the "likelihoods" of various outcomes given λ_j as definite subjective probabilities); a definite probability distribution over these propositions would correspond to "prior probabilities" for these hypotheses. We have considered (and ruled out for this person) cases where he assigns probability 1 to a given statistical hypothesis, and others where he assigns a different, definite probability distribution over a finite set of hypotheses. But more complex situations are possible.

From a different point of view ("objectivist," or "probability as statistical frequency"), Sir R. A. Fisher has categorized "levels of uncertainty" in a way that may easily be translated into terms of subjective probabilities.[1] He would refer to a proposition asserting a single statistical hypothesis as corresponding to "uncertainty of rank A" (as distinct from "certainty" as to relevant events, or consequences of actions), and to a "prior" distribution over such hypotheses as representing "uncertainty of rank B." Still higher ranks, C, D, E, etc., are also possible (Fisher prefers to speak of "levels of *deeper* uncertainty," hence his title, "The Underworld of Probability"). An individual confronted with our example might have in mind a *set* of possible probability distributions over the proportions, each of which corresponds to a "higher order hypothesis; we could imagine him assigning definite probabilities, or degrees of belief, to these higher hypotheses (each of which might determine the value of some parameter of the "lower" family of distributions). We could even imagine successively higher orders of hypotheses and corresponding super-distributions.

---

[1] Sir. R. A. Fisher, "The Underworld of Probability," *Sankhyā*, Vol. 18, Parts 3 and 4, September 1957, pp. 201–210.

Thus, you might assign definite probabilities (i.e., "definite" degrees of belief) to various processes by which a given experimenter (not, we assume, the friend who is offering you gambles) might have determined the proportion of Yellow balls in the urn, and "lower order" degrees of belief to various proportions ensuing from any given process; on a still higher level of uncertainty, you might have assigned probabilities to experimenters of different type, background, motivation or resources, for each of which you assign definite probabilities to various processes of determining the contents of the urn. Each of the "lower order" probability distributions, at any given level, is in effect a "conditional probability distribution"; if a hypothesis at any given level were "known," it would "eventually" determine definite degrees of belief for the possible proportions and hence definite utility values for the given actions. Assuming that at any level of uncertainty you did assign definite probabilities to the possible hypotheses, with some one "super-distribution" at a given, highest level, then if you proceeded to compound all these distributions appropriately and maximize expected utility, you would end up choosing "as if" you assigned definite probabilities to the possible proportions, or indeed (imagining all proportions between 0 and 2/3 possible), "as if" you were certain of a given proportion. Hence you would *never* prefer both I to II and IV to III. So if you do have these preferences, you aren't doing that. What else is there to do?

DECISION CRITERIA FOR "PARTIAL IGNORANCE"

There are, at least, the four criteria considered earlier in this chapter for "games against Nature"; we must reconsider them in this new context, interpreting the relevant events as proportions of Yellow (Black) balls. These criteria do not allow for any personal discrimination between the relative probabilities of events considered possible, and three of them (excluding the Laplace rule) conflict with the inference of any relative personal probabilities for these events. Therefore, if we admitted all proportions between 0 and 1 as "possible," all four of these criteria would be inappropriate for the same reason as before; virtually all subjects regard, and act "as if," proportions of Yellow (Black) balls greater than 2/3 were "less probable": indeed, "impossible" ("null"). But if we restrict attention to proportions between 0 and 2/3, on the basis of the information supplied in the experiment, the most obvious inadequacies of these rules vanish.

It will simplify discussion if we modify the example to allow only a small number of distinct, alternative "possible" proportions of Yellow balls in the urn: each proportion determining a distinct, "definite" probability distribution over the events Red, Yellow, Black in a single drawing from the urn. Let us imagine that the urn is known to contain not 90 balls but only *three*, of which one and only one is Red. You are informed that three possibilities for the composition of the remaining two balls are exhaustive: two Black; one Yellow and one Black; two Yellow. Other conditions are as before. You are not told by whom, or by what process, or for what purpose the composition was determined. As before, gambles are offered you by a friend who you are convinced (if you can imagine circumstances that would convince you) possesses no more, or no better, information on the contents of the urn than you.

If we assume that we know your von Neumann-Morgenstern utility function for outcomes (with utilities 1, 0 assigned arbitrarily to $100, $0), we can represent your utility evaluations of the familiar pairs of gambles as payoffs in a matrix, the columns representing alternative conditional probability distributions over Red, Yellow, Black corresponding respectively to 0, 1 or 2 Yellow balls. Given the utility payoffs, your choice between any pair of actions must reflect your definite opinions, if any, concerning the relative probabilities of these three possible "events". We are still trying to discover explicit decision criteria that *could* generate this choice pattern; or at least to reject those that could not.

Yellow balls:	0	1	2	
	(1/3, 0, 2/3)	(1/3, 1/3, 1/3)	(1/3, 2/3, 0)	
I	1/3	1/3	1/3	
II	0	1/3	2/3	Fig. 6.5
III	1	2/3	1/3	
IV	2/3	2/3	2/3	

Once again we must reject the Laplace criterion; since we have already concluded that you are not, with the pattern of choices premised, acting "as if" you assigned *any* given, definite probability distribution over the relevant events, you cannot be following the Laplace rule, which amounts to assigning the uniform distribution (1/3, 1/3, 1/3) over the three columns above.

Neither can the Savage minimax regret criterion lead to the given preferences. No criterion taking account only of "regrets"[1]—i.e., *differences* in corresponding payoffs between different strategies—could lead to that pattern, since the pair I, II and the pair III, IV have identical regret matrices:

---

[1]Besides *minimaxing* regret, we might postulate, for example, the criteria: (a) "lexicographic minimax regret"; instead of prescribing indifference between

Yellow balls

	0	1	2
I (III)	0	0	1/3
II (IV)	1/3	0	0

Fig. 6.6

That leaves the Hurwicz criterion, including the Wald criterion as a special case, to be considered. The Hurwicz criterion considers the smallest utility payoff a and the largest payoff A in each row and maximizes a convex linear combination, or weighted average, of these payoffs: $\alpha A + (1 - \alpha)a$, with α a given "personality/situation" constant, $0 \le \alpha \le 1$. For various values of α, this leads to the following *overall utility evaluation of the given actions:*

	a	A	(Minimax) $\alpha = 0$	$\alpha=1/4$	$\alpha=1/2$	$\alpha=3/4$	("Maximax") $\alpha = 1$
I	1/3	1/3	1/3	1/3	1/3	1/3	1/3
II	0	2/3	0	1/6	1/3	1/2	2/3
III	1/3	1	1/3	1/2	2/3	5/6	1
IV	2/3	2/3	2/3	2/3	2/3	2/3	2/3

Fig. 6.7

For different values of α, this criterion is capable of generating every pattern of preferences so far associated with this example.[1] For $\alpha < 1/2$, this application of the Hurwicz rule leads to the ordering: IV ·> III ·> I ·> II. For $\alpha > 1/2$, the pattern of preference is: III ·> IV ·> II ·> I. Only for $\alpha = 1/2$ does the rule *not* lead in this case to violations of the Sure-Thing Principle.

---

actions with identical maximum regrets, specify that the action whose "next highest regret" is lower be preferred; if these too are equal, consider "third highest regret," etc.; (b) maximize *expected* regret, assuming definite probabilities over events; this is equivalent to maximizing expected utility, within a given set of actions (see R. Schlaifer, *Probability and Statistics for Business Decisions*, Chapter 7, "Opportunity Loss and the Cost of Uncertainty").

Still other criteria are possible based on regrets; *none* would lead to patterns of choice violating the Sure-Thing Principle.

[1] Since the index value for a "constant action" will be the "von Neumann-Morgenstern utility" of the constant outcome, we can regard the payoffs in each column as the "worth" of the various actions to an individual for whom the "restricted

Having discovered rather exhaustively what you are *not* doing, if you assert these preferences, we shall examine some criteria in the next chapter that *can* serve to represent and generate your deliberated pattern of choices. We shall being with the "restricted Hurwicz criterion" above but proceed to developed others that seem more generally appropriate.

However, before considering more general criteria, let us take note of the fact that the "restricted Hurwicz criterion" can itself generate, formally and systematically, the precise patterns of behavior hypothesized by William Fellner, for the states of mind he describes.

> When our individual proves indifferent as between making a prize contingent upon E_x or $\sim E_x$, he usually knows that *he is ignorant of much potentially available information.* Consequently, his state of mind could be described by a statement such as this: 'the probability of E_x might be anywhere between 0.7 and 0.3, the probability of $\sim E_x$ anywhere between 0.3 and 0.7; I would need further objective guidelines of the right sort to narrow this range.' . . .

Hurwicz criterion" with the given value of α is appropriate. Equivalently, we can interpret the values in each column as the maximum *bids* (in utility) such an individual would offer for the various gambles. Recalling the underlying payoff matrix represented in Fig. 6.1 and the definitions in Chapter Three, the bids in a given column represent certain "lower betting probabilities": from top to bottom, respectively, $p_o(\text{Red})$, $p_o(\text{Yellow})$, $p_o(\text{not-Yellow})$, $p_o(\text{Not-Red})$.

Since by definition $p^o(E) = 1 - q_o(E) = 1 - p_o(\bar{E})$, we can derive "upper and lower betting probabilities" for the events Red and Yellow from the first three columns, for which the sets of bids are "coherent"; $\alpha > 1/2$ leads to "incoherent" sets of bids, for which "betting probabilities" are not defined. For all values of α, $p_o(\text{Red})$ = $p^o(\text{Red}) = 1/3$, a "definite" degree of belief. For $\alpha = 0$: $p_o(\text{Yellow}) = 0$, $p^o(\text{Yellow})$ = $2/3$. For $\alpha = 1/4$: $p_o(\text{Yellow}) = 1/6$, $p^o(\text{Yellow}) = 1/2$. For $\alpha = 1/2$, $p_o(\text{Yellow}) = p^o$ (Yellow) = $1/3$. The latter case illustrates a possible danger in interpreting $p_o(E) = p^o(E)$ as revealing a "definite degree of belief" in every case. And the difference between the bids in the first two cases indicates the danger of taking $p^o(E) - p_o(E)$ as an *impersonal* measure of "degree of ambiguity"; assuming Y^o is the same in both cases, the differences in bids do not reflect differences in underlying uncertainties but in the parameter α, i.e., individual differences in behavioral *response* to ambiguity, in the relative consideration given to "favorable" possibilities.

Note that $\alpha = 1/4$ leads to the same set of bids hypothesized in case (d), Fig. 3.6, Appendix to Chapter Three; see discussion there. The above application of the Hurwicz criterion with appropriate α thus represents one explicit normative principle that could generate a pattern of bids of the sort discussed by C. A. B. Smith, *op. cit.:* corresponding to "coherent" but "indefinite" degrees of belief, with positive intervals between "upper and lower betting probabilities."

It follows that our individual may prove indifferent as between staking a prize on E_x and staking the identical prize on *a standard-process event which has the probability 0.3;* and that his indifference point may be the same for $\sim E_x$ and an event in his standard process . . . That is to say, he knows for sure that either E_x or $\sim E_x$ will obtain, he is reluctant to judge whether the probability ratio is 0.7 ÷ 0.3 or 0.3 ÷ 0.7 or anything in between, and he is of such a disposition that in these circumstances *he assigns the weight 0.3 to that occurrence on which he stakes his fortunes (E or $\sim E$).*[1]

In terms of our example, Fellner's hypothetical subject might *know* that the urn contained *at least* 18 Yellow and 18 Black balls; these he might have seen placed in the urn, though he had no explicit information on the proportion of Yellow to Black in the *remaining* 24 non-Red balls in the urn. Or, in the "two-urn" example in Chapter Five, he might know that Urn I—whose proportion of Red to Black balls is not explicitly revealed—contains *at least* 30 Red and 30 Black balls, out of the 100. *If* he were to act "as if" he were "completely ignorant" with respect to all proportions not ruled out by this "knowledge," applying a "restricted Hurwicz criterion" with $\alpha = 0$ (a "restricted minimax criterion") to expected payoffs associated with these possible proportions, he would act in just the way Fellner suggests.

Moreover, there would be a very simple way to characterize this behavior. From the hypothesized statement describing his state of mind, we could infer that he assigns in Koopman's terms the "lower and upper intuitive probabilities" $p.(E_x) = 0.3$, $p^*(E_x) = 0.7$ respectively (likewise for $\sim E_x$). His use of a "restricted minimax criterion" leads to a pattern of choices that can be described as: *Maximizing the lower (intuitive) probability of the preferred outcome.*

This characterization may be compared to that corresponding to "Bernoullian" behavior in choices among gambles all offering the same two payoffs: "maximize 'the probability' of the preferred outcome." Before such concepts as "upper and lower" probabilities have been introduced, it is natural to wonder whether any other advice could possibly be reasonable; yet the latter advice is not, after all, so well defined in those "ambiguous" situations when "the probability" of a given event is simply not intuitively "definite" in the sense demanded. And as the criterion expressed above indicates, there *are* other ways to behave in such situations: no more difficult to express, perhaps much easier to follow, and, most important, possibly much truer to one's own deliberated preferences.

Fellner goes on to suggest other patterns of behavior corresponding to the state of mind described:

---

[1] Fellner, "Distortion of Subjective Probabilities as a Reaction to Uncertainty," p. 673.

Alternatively, he could be the kind of person who in such circumstances assigns the weight 0.7 to the event in which he acquires an interest. In general, this figure could be anywhere between 0.3 and 0.7. . . .all that matters here is that the number need not be 0.5.[1]

Obviously, these other patterns of betting behavior could be represented by a "restricted Hurwicz criterion" with $\alpha = 1$, or in general, with $0 \leq \alpha \leq 1$. The two extreme cases, corresponding to $\alpha = 0$, or $\alpha = 1$, have the interesting implication that it would be possible to infer the subject's "upper and lower intuitive probabilities" (in the Koopman/Good sense) from his observed "upper and lower *betting* probabilities" (in C. A. B. Smith's sense), knowing his decision rule. If $\alpha = 0$, then $p_\cdot(E) = p_o$ (E) and $p^*(E) = 1 - p_o(\bar{E}) = p^\circ(E)$; whereas if the subject "boldly" ("wishfully"?) maximized his *upper* intuitive probability of a "win," i.e., used a "restricted Hurwicz criterion" with $\alpha = 1$, then $p_\cdot(E) = p^\circ(E) = 1 - p_o(\bar{E})$, and $p^*(E) = p_o(E)$.

Fellner himself suggests quite a different characterization of the betting behavior he hypothesizes. Immediately following the passages quoted, he comments: "Let me repeat that we, as observers, will wish to infer that this individual's 'true' subjective probabilities for E_x and $\sim E_x$ are 0.5-0.5. This involves introducing the concept of *uncorrected* and of *corrected* subjective probabilities."[2] It is quite unclear to me why we should "wish" to infer that this individual's "true" probabilities are 0.5-0.5 or any other *definite* numbers; on the basis of Fellner's description of his state of uncertainty, it would seem much more appropriate to describe his partial belief in the event E_x in terms of the *interval* 0.3–0.7, and to describe the various patterns of behavior he might base upon this state of mind in terms of some decision criterion, such as the "restricted Hurwicz criterion," which takes as argument this whole *range* of values "reasonably acceptable" to him.[3]

---

[1] *Ibid.*

[2] *Ibid.*

[3] Fellner suggests that the "uncorrected probabilities" for E_x and $\sim E_x$ (corresponding to his observed "betting probabilities") be transformed in a way that preserves the *ratio* between them but ensures that they sum to unity. But it is not obvious to me that the resulting, definite, "corrected" numbers would have any special, behavioral significance in general.

If we consider the columns of "betting probabilities" corresponding to different values of α in Fig. 6.7 (interpreting this chart in terms of the problem as initially defined, with payoffs ultimately depending on the color of a ball drawn in a single drawing from the urn), we find that the *ratios* of the "betting probabilities" for Yellow and not-Yellow *vary* from 0 to 1. In any given column, this *ratio* depends not on

The notion of probabilities as "indefinite" within certain limits is, of course, explicit in the Koopman/Good approach. The question then arises as to how to *act* on such a state of mind. In 1954 I. J. Good described, independently of Hurwicz, as *one* among many reasonable ways to act what amounts to the "restricted minimax criterion" (i.e., the "restricted Hurwicz criterion" with $\alpha = 0$). Commenting on Wald's "apparently obvious negative recommendation that Bayes solutions cannot be applied when the initial distribution ξ is unknown," Good asserted:

> The word "unknown" is rather misleading here. In order to see this we consider the case of only two hypotheses H and H'. Then ξ can be replaced by the probability, p, of H. I assert that in most practical applications we regard p as bounded by inequalities something like $.1 < p < .8$. For if we did not think that $.1 < p$ we would not be prepared to accept H on a small amount of evidence. Is ξ unknown if $.1 < p < .8$? Is it unknown if $.4 < p < .5$; if $.499999 < p < .500001$? In each of these circumstances it would be reasonable to use the Bayes solution corresponding to a value of p selected arbitrarily within its allowable range.

> In what circumstances is a minimax solution reasonable? I suggest that it is reasonable if and only if the least favourable initial distribution is reasonable according to your body of beliefs. In particular a minimax solution is always reasonable provided that only reasonable ξ's are entertained. But then the minimax solution is only one of a number of reasonable solutions, namely, all the Bayes solutions corresponding to the various ξ's.[1]

---

the individual's state of uncertainty, which is presumed the same for each of the columns but, in a sense, upon his *response* to his uncertainty, in terms of his relative emphasis on favorable or unfavorable "reasonable possibilities." Thus, it does not seem to me that to determine a particular set of numbers on the basis of such observed "betting probabilities" as being the subject's "true" probabilities is a useful procedure, or that these "corrected" probabilities are behaviorally relevant. (In the next chapter, we shall consider the role that a particular set of "best guess" probabilities—determined on an intuitive basis—may have in decision-making even when behavior does not conform to the "Bernoulli proposition"; but in the "restricted Bayes/Hurwicz criterion" to be discussed, these "best guess" probabilities do not have such a simple relation to observed "betting probabilities" as do Fellner's "corrected probabilities").

[1] Good, "Rational Decisions," p. 114. See further references to Good's suggestions on this subject, next chapter.

Good defines here as "reasonable" not only the systematic use of the "least favorable distribution among reasonable ξ's"—in effect, use of the "restricted minimax criterion" which Good calls "Type II minimaxing"— but even more general patterns of behavior (including all those correspon- ding to the "restricted Bayes/Hurwicz criterion" discussed in the next chapter). But he nowhere draws attention to the fact that many of these "reasonable" patterns, e.g., "Type II minimaxing," will involve violations of Savage's Postulate 2, or of any corresponding "Bernoullian" axiom (see discussion in the next chapter of Rubin's axiom and Milnor's column lin- earity axiom). From a "neo-Bernoullian" point of view, such behavior would thereby be ruled *unreasonable.*

In response to my written query as to his attitude toward this implica- tion of such a pattern of behavior, and specifically as to the reasonableness, in his opinion, of preferring action I to II and action IV to III in the "three- color urn" example on the basis of some rule such as "Type II minimax- ing," Good was kind enough to express his views as follows:

> I naturally do not accept Savage's system of axioms in its entirety since, as you know, I regard subjective probabilities as only partially ordered. This is the essential point of disagreement, and the sure-thing principle only comes into question as a secondary matter, in distinguishing between Sav- age's and my systems. It seems to me to be consistent behavior to appear to be inconsistent, provided that the subject ("you") *states* that his subjec- tive probability judgment is vague enough to permit both choices. Thus *verbal* behaviour is an essential part of my system, but not of Savage's. Any violation of the sure-thing principle accepted as rational in my system can be rational only for this reason.[1]

As quoted earlier, it is Good's view that, where ξ is a "Type II hypoth- esis" asserting initial probabilities over a set of simple statistical hypothe- ses, there are typically "a number of different type II hypotheses, ξ, all of

---

[1] Good, private communication, 10 February 1962. Good notes that so far as his own preferences are concerned, choices I and II seem to him to be of equal value, and also choices III and IV. "But if I had the slightest suspicion that the experi- menter was dishonest, as most experimenters in psychology are these days, then I should prefer I to II and IV to III, the reason being that these choices do not give the experimenter a chance to cheat. (Unless of course he is a *flagrant* cheater.)" Some reflections follow on various "game" interactions with the experimenters. I have tried to abstract from these considerations in my presentation of the examples in Chapter Five.

which you regard as reasonable. Here 'you' is a technical term that may be singular or plural, but even if 'you' is singular the number of ξ's regarded as reasonable will usually be infinite."[1] In the next chapter, we shall consider various criteria that may be relevant and helpful when so many reasonable opinions clamor for "your" attention.

---

[1] Good, "Discussion on the Symposium on Linear Programming," *Journal of the Royal Statistical Society*, Series B, Vol. 17, No. 2, 1955, p. 195. In this note, Good elaborates on both the notions of a "type II hypothesis" (R. A. Fisher's "Uncertainty of Rank B") and the "type II minimax rule" which he had mentioned in "Rational Decisions" (1954). However, he redefines the "type II minimax rule" in terms of "regrets" ("expected defect"), describing his earlier formulation in terms of payoffs ("risks") as an "error." Apparently this "correction" reflected Savage's criticism of the "type I minimax rule" in terms of "risks," to which Good refers (Savage, Foundations of Statistics, p. 170).

As redefined, the rule might be described as a "restricted minimax regret criterion." It would no longer lead to violations of Postulate 2, though it would now entail the possibility of violations of Postulate 1. To my knowledge, only Good, in this 1955 note, has suggested that such a rule might be of normative or descriptive relevance; it would *not* correspond to any of the behavior patterns I have discussed.

Since the "type II minimax rule" using payoffs (1954 version; the "restricted minimax criterion") seems to me to correspond to empirically important and, I believe, reasonable behavior and the rule using "regrets," so far as I am aware, does not, I think Good was right the first time.

7

THE "RESTRICTED HURWICZ CRITERION"

WE HAVE AT last found one criterion for decision-making under uncertainty that can lead systematically to patterns of choice, conflicting with Savage's Postulate 2, frequently associated with the examples discussed in Chapter Five. These patterns of behavior may or may not be "irrational", as proponents of the "neo-Bernoullian" approach would suggest. What is indisputable is that they are *unpredicted* and *inexplicable* in terms of that approach. If the individuals who pursue them desire to systematize their decision-making along the lines of a formal logic of choice, they cannot look to the "neo-Bernoullian" theory for help; but the Hurwicz criterion, applied to a set of "possible" probability distributions, offers itself as one candidate (the first we have considered) for a normative principle corresponding to their deliberated preferences.[1]

---

[1] This application of the "Hurwicz α-criterion" to a subclass of "possible" probability distributions over certain events relevant to decision-making was first suggested by Leonid Hurwicz, "Some Specification Problems and Applications to Econometric Models," *Econometrics*, Vol. 19 (July, 1951), pp. 343–44 (abstract). I am indebted to Hurwicz for bringing this important note to my attention (on the occasion of my presenting an equivalent normative "solution" to the Econometric Society, St. Louis, 1960). This paper must be distinguished from another by Hurwicz, "Optimality Criteria for Decision Making Under Ignorance," *Cowles Commission Discussion Paper*, Statistics, No. 370, 1951 (mimeographed), which discusses the much more familiar application of the α-criterion in the case, considered earlier, of "complete ignorance of Nature's strategy": in which, in effect, *every* distribution over states of the world is considered "possible".

There is a useful discussion of the former paper by Hurwicz, and also of the related paper by Hodges and Lehmann considered below, in Luce and Raiffa,

The context in which Hurwicz first suggested this criterion was one in which it is natural, in fact inescapable, to think in terms of a family of distributions; this is the "specification" aspect of a standard statistical decision problem, the assumption that the observed sample has been drawn from a given class, say ^, of distribution functions F (usually regarded as "objective" distributions). It is frequently assumed that ^ is a parametric family of known functional form; Hurwicz points out that (1) in the maximum-likelihood and likelihood ratio approach and in Wald's minimax decision function theory, "no further knowledge concerning ^ is postulated," whereas (2) in the "Bayesian" formulation, "it is assumed that a probability measure ξ on ^ (an 'a priori distribution') is known to the statistician".

> In econometrics, as well as other applications, cases frequently arise where the statistician feels he is not quite as ignorant with regard to a given ^ as in (1) above, but cannot commit himself to a single ξ, as in (2) above. . .

> One type of answer is obtained by following a *generalized Bayes-minimax principle*. This corresponds to assuming that, while ξ is not known, some ξ's are excluded.[1]

Once again we must recall that within the strict "neo-Bernoullian" approach no meaning is defined for statements that one "knows" or "does not know" a probability distribution over the events affecting the consequences of his actions, or the notion that a reasonable man "cannot commit himself to a single" probability distribution. In that approach, the issue is not what you "know" but how you act. If you are "reasonable" and careful in your decision-making you are expected to act, willy-nilly, *"as if" you had* "committed yourself" to a single, definite probability distribution, whether or not non-behavioral tests would reveal that you "knew" one. Thus, when the Savage postulates or a similar set are regarded as universally compelling, the problem whether or not a decision-maker feels he "can" so commit himself appears a false dilemma; what other reasonable way is there to act?

If we believed that every decision-maker of interest obeyed the Savage postulates in unselfconscious, somnambulant fashion, we could avoid

---

Games and Decisions, pp. 304–305 (prior to the December, 1960, meeting, the applicability of this passage to the problems considered here had escaped my notice); the notation I shall use subsequently is borrowed in part from their treatment.

[1]Hurwicz, "Some Specification Problems and Applications to Econometric Models," pp. 343–44.

entirely the notions of "knowledge" or consciousness of a probability distribution, and hence all questions of "considering" or deciding among a *set* of probability distributions. But in practice, such notions enter even "neo-Bernoullian" (and more generally, "neo-Bayesian") discussion in connection with any *applications* of the theory or consultation to a decision-maker; and they are almost essential if we wish to deal formally with behavior that systematically *violates* the "neo-Bernoullian" principles.

As quoted earlier, Savage has commented upon "an important respect in which the personal theory of probability and utility does seem inadequate":

> If 'you' had a consistent and complete body of opinion, then every event would have a well-defined probability for you and every consequence a well-defined utility. Actually, *vagueness, or indecision, intervenes* at several stages to *prevent* this. . .
>
> I tell myself that if I had a consistent body of opinions and values I would have a P and a U [a definite probability function and a utility function]. *Actually there seem to be many different pairs P, U that are not conspicuously unacceptable to me.*[1]

Once we are allowed to talk about such circumstances formally (without cries of "meaningless" and "irrelevant" poisoning the air), we can begin systematically to compare the "neo-Bernoullian" theory and such criteria as the above Hurwicz principle as *alternative* modes of behavior in just this situation: when a *set* of "not conspicuously unacceptable" probability distributions are conscious candidates for use in our formal decision-making. The "neo-Bernoullian" approach, of course, requires the decision-maker "eventually" to settle upon *one* distribution[2] (or to act "as if"

---

[1] Savage, "The Subjective Basis of Statistical Practice," pp. 2.13–2.14; italics added.

[2] However, such comments as those cited above by Savage are tantalizing indications that even "neo-Bernoullians" may consider this degree of precision impractical in some circumstances. But these hints are almost always regrettably vague as to the specific *manner* in which "vagueness and indecision intervene" to "prevent" the inference of well-defined probabilities from your betting behavior. They imply that "vagueness" can affect even reasonable behavior in some way that involves violation of one or more of the Savage postulates, for otherwise there would be no "preventing" the measurement of precise probabilities. But which postulates are violated? What might this unspecified concomitant of "vagueness" be: *might it not be,* given certain alternative acts, the "definite" desire to make certain choices that conflict with Postulate 2?

he did) among all those "not unacceptable", for subsequent use in choosing among *any* given set of actions so long as his given state of mind, knowledge, information, opinion persists. The Hurwicz principle above and certain other criteria do not; they require, or permit, the decision-maker to "keep in mind"[1] a whole set of "reasonably acceptable" probability distributions, to be consulted in connection with different decision problems involving the same events: again, so long as his state of information, uncertainty, opinion does not change. But if the "neo-Bernoullian" approach, too, admits the possibility that the decision-maker may "have in mind" a number of closely-competing distributions, at least at an intermediate phase of the decision process in certain situations, then the two sorts of approaches can meaningfully be compared for the given situations.

Let us suppose henceforth that under most circumstances of decision-making you can *eliminate*, from the set Y of all possible probability distributions over the relevant states of the world, certain distributions as *unacceptable* for representing your opinions, your partial beliefs, your judgments of relative probability either "definite" or "vague." In effect, these rejected distributions embody all the probability comparisons that, in your given state of mind, you would *definitely not* affirm. But we shall further suppose that there may remain a sizeable subset Y^0 of distributions over the states of the world that still seem "reasonably acceptable," or as Savage puts it, "not conspicuously unacceptable." All of the distributions y in Y^0 must be consistent with your confident probability judgments, including your "definite" degrees of belief; but the number of distributions—comprising Y^0— that do not definitely contradict your ("vague") opinions may yet be large, particularly when relevant information is perceived as scanty, unreliable, contradictory, *ambiguous.*

Even when they admit the possible existence of a class of distributions Y^0 (with more than one member), "neo-Bernoullians" tend to be unhelpful when it comes to characterizing it precisely or identifying its members in a particular case. Indeed, it seems impossible to accomplish either of these tasks if one limits oneself (a) to non-verbal behavioral evidence, and specifically (b) to betting choices consistent with the Savage postulates: two working principles that distinguish the "neo-Bernoullians" from other "neo-Bayesians" such as Koopman, Good, and C. A. B. Smith. As discussed

---

[1] This phrase has an important technical implication. Quite literally, it means that a decision-maker utilizing one of these criteria must retain in his memory, or files, the whole set of distinct, "reasonably acceptable" distributions, since he may wish to base calculations upon one or another or different subsets of them in different decision problems, as available actions and payoffs change; he cannot simply store in his memory or retain access to *one* derivative or representative distribution for use in all problems.

in Chapter Four, Koopman and Good in particular depart from these constraints. On the basis of introspective judgments and verbal statements, generally in terms of inequalities, comparing probabilities (or asserting inability, lack of confidence, or absence of definite opinion with respect to certain comparisons), they have no conceptual difficulty in determining and describing Y^o in general. Once this characterization of Y^o has been supplied in terms of their operations and concepts, we can contrast meaningfully "neo-Bernoullian" to *alternative,* "non-Bernoullian" solutions of the problem: How to act reasonably when more than one personal probability distribution is "reasonably acceptable." The main points of contrast are apparent in connection with the example we have been discussing, in which it is relatively easy to arrive at a plausible characterization of Y^o.

For any given probability distribution y, a given action x will have a definite "von Neumann-Morgenstern utility" value, the relative values of various actions reflecting your actual preferences (assuming your "von Neumann-Morgenstern utilities" over outcomes are known). Let $\min_x$ be the minimum expected utility for an act x, and max x be the maximum expected utility as the probability distribution y ranges over the set Y^o.[1] What I shall call henceforth the "restricted Hurwicz criterion" would then require (for a fixed α between 0 and 1, depending upon the individual and perhaps the general nature of the situation): *Associate with each action x the index:*

$$\alpha \max_x + (1 - \alpha) \min_x$$

---

[1] This criterion differs from what might be called the "general Hurwicz criterion" in that it considers with respect to each act the "best" and "worst" distributions in the restricted yet Y^o, whereas the latter, better-known criterion considers, in effect, the "best" and "worst" distributions in the general set Y, which includes every distribution assigning probability 1 to any given state of the world. I.e., the "general Hurwicz criterion" considers with respect to each act the states of the world having the best and the worst consequences.

Hurwicz' own term for the "restricted" criterion—"generalized Bayes-minimax principle"—seems to exaggerate the role of Bayesian principles in this approach, while omitting any reference to the "maximax" aspects. His term is really better suited for the Hodges and Lehmann criterion discussed below. Names for this criteria do not yet seem well-established in the literature, and my main reason for relabelling them is to distinguish them clearly in the text.

With $\alpha = 0$ this rule might be termed the "restricted minimax criterion". As noted in Chapter Four, I. J. Good independently described what amounted to the letter criterion, terming it "type II minimaxing", as opposed to "type I minimaxing" or what we would call here the "general minimax criterion" ("Rational Decision," 1954).

Choose that act with the highest index.

Equivalently (assuming a finite number of relevant events), if y_x^{min} is the probability vector in Y° corresponding to min_x for action x, y_x^{max} is the probability vector in Y° corresponding to max_x and (X) is the vector of pay-offs for action x, the rule can be formulated: *Associated with each x the index:*

$$[\alpha\, y_x^{max} + (1 - \alpha)\, y_x^{min}]\, (X)$$

Choose that act with the highest index.

In the three-color urn example we have been discussing, assuming three balls only, we might imagine the set of "reasonably acceptable" distributions Y° over Red, Yellow, Black to be the three distributions: $(1/3, 0, 2/3)$; $(1/3, 1/3, 1/3)$; $(1/3, 2/3, 0)$. The possible expected utility values for each action have been shown in Fig. 6.5 above, and the corresponding index values in terms of the "restricted Hurwicz criterion," for different values of α, in Fig. 6.7 (where "a, A" stand for "min_x, max_x"). These index values would not be affected at all if we assumed that all convex linear combinations of the three distributions above were included in Y°: i.e., if we assumed that all probability distributions over Red, Yellow, Black resulting from applying what Good might call a "type II" personal probability distribution to the three given distributions were likewise "reasonably acceptable." This follows since the index values depend only on min_x and max_x for each action, and those would be the same for the larger (convex) set Y°.

As noted earlier, in the columns in Fig. 6.7 corresponding to $\alpha = 0$ (Good's "type II minimax rule") and $\alpha = 1/4$, the ordering of values implies I{> II and IV {>III. Moreover, the payoffs can be interpreted as "upper and lower betting probabilities," with those for the event Yellow enclosing those for the event Red, the latter corresponding to a "definite" degree of belief $1/3$.

However, although it thus merits closer attention from those individuals seeking a normative criterion not bound by the "Sure-thing Principle," there are aspects of the "restricted Hurwicz criterion" that raise questions about its general reasonableness. In particular, why the exclusive emphasis upon minimum and maximum expected utilities, "best" and "worst" distributions in Y°? Why should not other possibilities, in fact the whole spectrum of "reasonably acceptable distributions" be taken into account? Moreover, the gross distinction between y's that are "not conspicuously unacceptable" and those that *are*, represented by membership or not in Y°, seems inadequate to capture all the shades of opinion, doubt and confidence that might reasonably affect one's decision-making. As Luce and Raiffa put it: "Even if all 'reasonable' y are included in Y°, can't some y's be 'more reasonable' than others?"[1]

---

[1] Luce and Raiffa, *op. cit.*, p. 305.

This last point is clearly cogent, and it may be pertinent even to some of the behavior that appears consistent with the criterion in terms of the evidence so far considered. But it is possible to specify conditions under which this criticism would not apply; and it turns out that such conditions tend to justify the other peculiarity of the criterion, its preoccupation with extremes.

Just as the "general Hurwicz criterion" has been advanced as reasonable only for that (elusive) situation defined technically as "complete ignorance of the state of the world," so the "restricted Hurwicz criterion" would plausibly be associated with a state, similarly defined, of "complete ignorance" with respect to the distributions in $Y°$. At first glance, the behavioral conditions that serve operationally to define "complete ignorance'" might seem no more likely to be fulfilled in the latter sense than in the former. But you are at liberty to be ruthless in excluding any doubtful candidate distributions from the set $Y°$ to be taken into consideration in your decision-making; the subjective criteria for membership in $Y°$ might be made so rigorous as to include only those "conspicuously acceptable," and among those it might indeed be difficult or impossible for you to discriminate. Our artificial example, of course, has been deliberately constructed to achieve this effect.

To test whether the conditions defining "complete ignorance" are in fact satisfied for our example by a given individual, we must offer some new actions.

Yellow balls

	0	1	2
I	1	0	0
II	0	1	0
III	0	0	1

Fig. 7.1

Here we are offering a given prize staked alternatively upon the three possible proportions of Yellow (Black) in the urn, rather than upon the outcome of the next draw. You are given no explicit information on the process by which the proportion was determined, but, as ever, you cannot be prevented from making your own guesses. If you should, for example, for some reason be highly confident that the color of each ball other than the known Red ball was determined between Yellow and Black by independent flips of a fair coin, you might be willing to give even odds that the urn contains exactly one Yellow ball, whereas you would demand 3:1 odds in your favor to bet on zero or two. In other words, you would strongly prefer action II among the three actions above; you would act consistently "as if" you regarded the event labelled "1" as "more probable than" the others.

Hence your preferences among actions would *not* be independent of the labelling of the events, which is the first condition required for "complete ignorance" and which implies, in this case, indifference among the offers. Nor would the "restricted Hurwicz criterion" correspond to your preferences; it too dictates indifference, since all minimum and maximum expected payoffs here are equivalent.

However, with the given, "vague" information there should be no lack of individuals who *are* indifferent between these actions. Those among them who invariably obey the Savage postulates must, in subsequent gambles, continue to act "as if" they assigned the definite probabilities (1/3, 1/3, 1/3) to these three proportions. They will, then, fail the second condition that completes the definition of "complete ignorance," with respect to the offers below:

Yellow balls

	0	1	2
I	1	0	0
II	0	1	1
III	0	1	0
IV	1	0	1
V	0	0	1
VI	1	1	0

Fig. 7.2a

This second condition is that preference between actions be unaffected by the deletion of "repetitious" columns, or the "collapse" of two columns with identical payoffs into one.[1] In this case it implies, for example, that preference between actions I and II should not be affected if their payoffs are instead represented:

I	1	0
II	0	1

Fig. 7.2b

---

[1] See axiom 8, Milnor, *op. cit.*, p. 52; or axiom 11, Luce and Raiffa, *op. cit.*, p. 295 (see also p. 283). As noted earlier, the condition will not be met if (as would seem generally realistic) you act "as if" each event shown had "at least" some positive probability $\in$. On the other hand, you may "approximate" this condition by acting "as if" *each* of n disjoint, exhaustive events had "no more than" $\in$ probability, $\in < 1/n$.

The third, "repetitious" column may be regarded as having simply been dropped from consideration, or as having been "collapsed" into the second, which would not correspond to "1 or 2." This condition, or as it is usually termed, "axiom" of "complete ignorance," requires that whatever your preference between the actions was before this modification, it must remain the same. But the *initial* condition requires your preference to be independent of the labelling of events, i.e., to be unaffected by permutations of the columns of payoffs. Since each of these actions now offers a permutation of the payoffs of the other, you must now be indifferent between them; and likewise (by the second condition) in their original form. By a similar argument, the two conditions together require indifference also between III and IV, and between V and VI.

The "restricted Hurwicz criterion" has no difficulty passing this requirement; it implies indifference among all six actions, all of which have equivalent minimum and maximum expected payoffs (whether Y^0 consists of these three distributions only or the convex set of all "type II" probability distributions over them). The Savage postulates, on the other hand, obviously demand that anyone who is indifferent between I, III and V must *prefer* II to I, IV to III, and VI to V.[1]

The two modes of behavior are thus quite distinct. The one corresponding to the Savage postulates has an easy interpretation; consistently with your indifference between staking the prize on any one of three disjoint, exhaustive events or propositions ("the urn contains [zero, one, two] Yellow balls"), you are acting "as if" you assigned uniform probabilities, exactly 1/3 to each. Is there any sensible interpretation to the behavior implied by the "restricted Hurwicz criterion," or any behavior consistent with the second condition of "complete ignorance"? It is clear that with this pattern you would not be acting "as if" you assigned equal 1/3 probabilities to the three proportions of Yellow balls, since, for example, you are indifferent between staking the prize "on" or "against" the proposition that there are *no* Yellow balls in the urn. In fact, on that evidence alone we would infer by the Savage test that you assigned probability 1/2 to "zero" Yellow (1/2 to "non-zero"); however, your indifference among the other actions would imply probability 1/2 to "one" and you would still not be acting "as if" you assigned *unequal* probabilities; nor, indeed, "as if" you assigned any definite probabilities at all, in terms of which you maximized expected utility.

The issue is not so much whether you think you might follow this pattern of choices in terms of these particular events, as whether you can imagine yourself deliberately following a similar pattern under *any* circumstances.

---

[1] Given that I $\preceq$ III $\preceq$ V; by Postulate 3, admissibility, II {> {III, IV {> V, VI {> I; hence by Postulate 1, simple ordering of actions, II {> I, IV {> III, VI {> V.

One way to describe such a pattern, in its essential aspect, would be: *indifference between staking a given prize "on" or "against" any one of three or more mutually exclusive events, given that one will occur.* We could, now, make a meaningful guess as to "what" you might be doing if we observed this behavior, in the sense of what formal decision rule you might be following systematically: it could be a "restricted Hurwicz criterion." But "why"?

It is not hard to imagine the same verbal answers that are often used, in connection with the original example, to "explain" a *preference* for staking a prize on Red rather than on Yellow, now being used to explain *indifference* between staking the prize on or against zero Yellow balls, or one Yellow, or two. "Why should I act as if 'zero Yellow' were less probable than 'one or two Yellow'? I don't know what its probability is. For all I know, 'zero' is *more* probable than 'non-zero'." At this we must intervene to point out that such language does not seem to accord with the way we have agreed to use the word "probable": as an index of *opinion,* nothing more. But the statement can be reworded:

"Very well, I don't feel I know—or if you like, I don't know what I feel—which is more probable, zero or non-zero; or for that matter, one Yellow or more or less than one; or, two Yellow or less than two. I don't really know a whole lot about this urn, if you come down to it. (I've got some hunches about the way these things usually work; but when I try to add them up, they don't seem to tell me much about how many Yellow balls there ought to be in there).

"It's true that I don't care whether you stake the prize on zero, one or two Yellow balls: but not because I think they're 'equally probable.' If you won't let me say that I 'don't know' which is more probable, let me put it this way: If you ask me if I believe that a given one of these events is *more probable* than another given one, and I had to answer yes or no, I'd have to say 'No'; and if you asked me whether any two of them together seem to me to be *more probable* than the third, I would still say 'No'. Make of that what you can; it seems to me that it's just what I mean when I say I don't know the probabilities. *I know one thing, though: I don't feel like giving 2:1 odds "against" any one of those possibilities."*

We could not, perhaps, infer from the comments above that the subject would obey strictly the conditions of "complete ignorance," although the indications are strong that he would not obey the Savage postulates. However, before considering more general behavior (which might not conveniently be described by the "restricted Hurwicz criterion") we may take note of a powerful result that may be applicable if "you" *do* satisfy the conditions for "complete ignorance" with respect to some set of propositions or events.

For example, let us say that you *are* indifferent between actions I to VI in Fig. 7.2a, and that you would give the same maximum price α for any one of them, where α is a utility number between 0 and 1; i.e., where E represents any one of the "events" on which prizes are staked in actions I–VI, you are indifferent between I and II below:

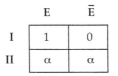

Fig. 7.2c

Then it can be proved that the *only* decision criterion which satisfies the conditions of "complete ignorance" and at the same time satisfies certain other axiomatic constraints of a sort that have generally, and without much controversy, been regarded as desiderata of a normative criterion is the Hurwicz criterion with index α. What makes this conclusion particularly interesting is that these additional requirements do seem, to me at least, to be relatively inoffensive, or plausible, or acceptable, to use the various words that are generally employed to described requirements that one suspects he does not ever want to violate. Moreover, it can be proved that any criterion satisfying a certain subset of these requirements takes into account *only the minimum and maximum utility associated with each act.*[1] These proofs, in effect, specify conditions under which the Hurwicz criterion is

---

[1]For a simple set of conditions and proofs, see Milnor, *op. cit.*, pp. 51–54. The basic proof is presented by Kenneth Arrow, "Hurwicz's Optimality Criterion for Decision-Making Under Ignorance," *Technical Report No. 6*, Department of Economics and Statistics, Stanford University, February 1, 1953, modifying a result due to Hurwicz, "Optimality Criteria for Decision Making Under Ignorance," *Cowles Commission Discussion Paper, Statistics*, No. 370, 1951.

See also the discussion in Luce and Raiffa, *op. cit.*, pp. 296–297.

The following statements of the requirements that, together, "characterize" the Hurwicz α-criterion are paraphrased from axioms stated by Luce and Raiffa.

Suppose that it is true of a decision criterion that satisfies the two conditions stated earlier for "complete ignorance" that for any specification of acts, utility payoffs and events defining a decision problem:

(1) the criterion determines an "optimal" act or sets of acts;

(2) the optimal set is invariant under the labeling of acts, i.e., the real acts singled out as optimal should not depend upon the arbitrary labeling of acts used to abstract the problem;

(3) every act which is equivalent to or which weakly dominates an act in the optimal set is also in the optimal set;

(4) the addition of new acts to the available alternatives never changes old, originally non-optimal acts into optimal ones and, in addition, either (a) all the old,

not merely compatible with the structure of one's preferences, but is uniquely so. The conditions imply the admittedly special requirement that you be indifferent between staking a prize *on* or *against* any one of several disjoint events ($n \geq 3$) given that one will obtain; but if this is true for *some*, suitably chosen set of events, then what seem very general and generally acceptable desiderata of your decision criterion lead inescapably to what otherwise seems the most "arbitrary" feature of the Hurwicz criterion, its emphasis upon extreme payoffs, maxima and minima. (Since, as noted earlier, the Hurwicz criterion can be regarded as a special case of Shackle's decision function, these conditions serve also to "characterize" Shackle's recommendations, in this special form; in particular, they provide a logical basis for his emphasis upon "focus outcomes").

THE "RESTRICTED BAYES/HURWICZ CRITERION"

Suppose, however, that while the hypothetical spokesman for the views above on "ignorance of probabilities" does not obey the Savage postulates, he does not strictly conform to the conditions for "complete ignorance" either. For example, his maximum (utility) bid for a unit utility stake on the event "0 Yellow balls" may be less than his maximum bid for a unit stakes *against* that event, although the sum of the two bids is less than unity. The same may be true for the events "1" and "2 Yellow balls"; moreover, the maximum bids for these three events, which again may not sum to unity, may not be equal.

It might be possible to account for such behavior by hypothesizing certain other propositions, each specifying a probability distribution over these three events, with respect to which he was, in effect, "completely ignorant." In effect, this would imply that he considered a smaller set of distributions over Red, Yellow, Black as being "reasonably acceptable," or included in Y^o, than we have been considering. It might not be as easy to

---

originally optimal acts remain optimal, or (b) none of the old, originally optimal acts remain optimal.

Then this criterion takes into account only the minimum and maximum utility associated with each act (this corresponds to the Arrow result); conditions above correspond to Luce and Raiffa Axioms, 1, 3, 4 and 7"; the two conditions of "complete ignorance" correspond to their Axioms 10 and 11 (*op. cit.*, pp. 286–297).

If in addition the criterion satisfies the condition (Luce and Raiffa Axiom 2):

(5) the optimal set of acts does not depend on the choice of origin and unit of the utility scale used to abstract the problem, i.e., it is invariant under an increasing linear transformation of the payoffs; then it must be the Hurwicz criterion with index α, where α is a number determined by indifference between actions I and II in Fig. 7.2c above.

characterize that smaller $Y°$ for him as it is to characterize $Y°$ for the man who fulfills the conditions of "complete ignorance" with respect to the events "0, 1, 2 Yellow balls." It may be much more convenient, and in certain respects more realistic, to suppose that his actions reflect certain "vague" discriminations in terms of probability among the various distributions in $Y°$, rather than an absolute narrowing of the distributions considered "reasonably acceptable."

I shall propose below a formal criterion that has the effect of expressing the notion that, as Luce and Raiffa put it, some y's in $Y°$ seem "more reasonable than others": without yet implying opinions so definite as to narrow $Y°$ down to a single distribution for purposes of decision-making. The decision criterion which follows has not, to my knowledge, been presented before, but it is based closely upon a criterion suggested by Hodges and Lehmann,[1] amounting, in fact, to a combination of their criterion with the "restricted Hurwicz criterion." To express it, we must introduce certain new concepts.

Let us suppose that after you have eliminated certain possible probability distributions over the states of the world as "unacceptable" representations of your opinions, leaving a set of $Y°$ of "reasonably acceptable" distributions, you force yourself to make further comparisons, probing your less "definite" opinions, consulting, as Fisher might put it, your judgments involving uncertainties of Rank C, D, E, etc., concerning the relative probability (ever more "vague" at successively higher levels) of propositions that determine conditionally the parameters of your lower-rank probability distributions. Let us suppose that you pursue this process until you can identify a single, "best guess" probability distribution $y°$ over the states of nature.

Actually, in general there might be many aspects of any one distribution that would have to be determined on a purely arbitrary basis, lacking any real guidance of personal opinion; even when your least definite opinions were taken into account, it might be more realistic to identify a *set* of "most acceptable" or "best guess" distributions than to specify a single one; or better yet, to describe *nested sets* of distributions reflecting decreasing degrees of "confidence" or definiteness of opinion. However, such complexity or refinement is scarcely suited to the present level of discussion. Let us confine ourselves, without pretending to talk in full generality, to cases when it may be possible to distinguish a particular distribution that, in some sense, "better" expresses your opinions as to relative probability than any other single distribution.

---

[1] J. L. Hodges, Jr. and E. L. Lehmann, "The Uses of Previous Experience in Reaching Statistical Decision," *Annals of Mathematical Statistics*, Vol. 23 (September 1952), pp. 396–407.

Even in these cases there may well remain a set Y^o of distributions expressing judgments you "might almost as well" have made, or that the degree of "vagueness" in your opinions (reflecting the degree to which your information is perceived as scanty, unreliable, ambiguous) does not permit you confidently to reject.

There is no reason to expect that Y^o must exhibit any sort of symmetry, in general, with respect to y^o; with respect to one dimension or another, your "best guess" might lie at the boundary of Y^o. Moreover, the degree to which y^o is distinguished from the other distributions in Y^o by virtue of greater "confidence" or "definiteness" may vary greatly with the situation.

The analogy suggested in the first chapter is highly *a propos* at this point: the decision-maker who relies upon a panel of experts to guide his "official opinions," and who finds in a particular case that each consultant produces a different, definite probability distribution. It may be convenient to think of some of the members of Y^o in the concrete form of probability distributions each written down on a separate piece of paper with the name of the forecaster attached. For simplicity, we may imagine a decision-maker who is compelled, in some sense, to base his own opinions, and hence his actions, upon this set of conflicting forecasts. He can ask himself: "Which one of these forecasters is most probably reliable on this sort of problem? (How to define 'this sort of problem' for this purpose?) To what extent do these predictions reflect individual biases; and which way do the biases go? When these fellows disagree, should I accept all the judgments on which they agree; i.e., should I limit the set of "reasonably acceptable" distributions to their distributions and to all probability distributions over their forecasts? Or do I suspect, when the experts differ this widely, that there are even more possibilities than they consider, so Y^o should be still larger?"

In the end, we can imagine this decision-maker evolving a particular distribution y^o over the relevant events, representing his own "best guess" opinions on all these questions that may influence, directly or remotely, his judgments of the relative probabilities of those events. He *could* now proceed, in every case, to maximize his expected utility on the basis of y^o. But the criterion presented below implies that he does not always do this; and that his occasion (or frequent) failure to *act upon y^o exclusively* reflects *another* sort of judgment, concerning the reliability, credibility or addquacy of his information, experience, advice, intuition taken as a whole: not about the relative support it may give to one hypothesis as opposed to another, but about its ability to lend support to any hypothesis—any set of definite opinions—at all.

Having exploited knowledge, guess, rumor, assumption, intuition, advice, to arrive at a "best" judgment that one event is more probable than another or that they are equally probable, one can still stand back and ask: "How much, in the end, is all this worth? How much do I really know about the problem? How firm a basis for choice, for appropriate decision and action, do I have?" It might be that the answers to these questions would fully justify confidence in a body of "definite" opinions that served to determine uniquely an overall probability distribution. But quite a different answer, "I don't know very much, and I can't rely on that," may also sound rather familiar, even in connection with markedly unequal estimates of relative probability. If "complete ignorance" over all states of the world is rare or non-existent, "considerable" ignorance is surely not.

Many writers, including Frank Knight and Lord Keynes, have insisted upon the feasibility and relevance of this sort of judgment, without indicating precisely how it might affect decision-making; we shall consider now a meaningful role. Let us here pursue the hypothesis that it influences choice by affecting the degree to which "you" evaluate alternative actions in terms of y° alone, as opposed to "considering" their utility expectations in terms of other distributions in Y°. There may, at one extreme, be situations in which you are quite prepared to act "as if" Y° consisted of the single distribution y°: i.e., in which you cannot conscientiously recognize more than one probability distribution as "reasonably acceptable" in the light of your definite opinions. At the other extreme, there may be a set of hypotheses, each corresponding to a different complete set of "definite" opinions, among which you are "completely ignorant" in our technical sense (as would be revealed by your choices among *side bets* concerning these hypotheses). Each of these hypotheses would correspond to a definite expectation of utility for each action; and if, in particular, your decision rule under these circumstances met the various desiderata alluded to above, you would act "as if" you took only the minimum and maximum expectations into account for each action and followed the "restricted Hurwicz criterion" with index α.

Various proposals might be imagined for decision-making in situations that seem to lie between these two extremes, but at this point let us examine what seems to be one of the simplest sorts of decision criteria that might reflect the various judgments and propensities discussed so far. Among its radical simplifications are the assumptions that one overall judgment (reflected in the parameter ρ) can be made of the "confidence" to be placed in the distribution y° as opposed to others in Y°, your relative willingness to rely upon it in your decision-making; and that various factors enter your decision criterion in linear combination.

The following notions have already been defined: $\min_x$, $\max_x$, y_x^{min} and y_x^{max} with respect to the action x and the set Y°; and α, a parameter dependent upon the personality (and perhaps, official "role" and overall situation) of the decision-maker, reflecting the relative influence of "favorable" versus "unfavorable" possibilities upon his decision-making under conditions of "complete ignorance." To these we must now add: y°, the "best guess" or "estimated" probability distribution; est_x, the expected utility payoff to the action x corresponding to $y°$; and ρ, a number between 0 and 1 reflecting the decision-maker's degree of confidence in or reliance upon the estimated distribution $y°$ in a particular decision problem.

I shall refer to the following decision criterion as the "restricted Bayes / Hurwicz criterion": *Associate with each x the index:*

$$\rho.est_x + (1 - \rho) + [\alpha.x_{max} + (1 - \alpha).x_{min}]$$

Choose that act with the highest index.

An equivalent formulation would be: *Associate with each x the index:*

$$\{\rho.y° + (1-\rho)\ [\alpha y_x^{max} + (1-\alpha)y_x^{min}]\}\ (X)$$

Choose that act with the highest index.

In strict "neo-Bernoullian" terms, of course, it is, in a sense, forbidden to speak of probability comparisons being made separately from or prior to a consideration of preferred *actions;* but even "neo-Bernoullians" permit themselves to use such notions on an intuitive basis in discussion, not to speak of the "neo-Bayesians" such as B. O. Koopman and I. J. Good who venture to construct the whole theory of probability explicitly upon the basis of such comparisons, providing a rigorous conceptual basis for doing so. From either point of view, it is not hard to give a plausible interpretation of the variables in the above criterion in terms of the example we have been discussing.

Let us return to the assumption that there are 90 balls in the urn, and let us suppose that with no sample from the urn and no explicit information except that exactly 1/3 of the balls are Red, your "best guess" distribution over Red, Black, Yellow is (1/3, 1/3, 1/3). An infinite number of distinguishable states of mind might all find expression in that same distribution; for example, you might assign equal probability to the cases (30 Red, 60 Black) and (30 Red, 60 Yellow) and exclude all others; or you might include the case (30 Red, 30 Yellow, 30 Black); or you might assign equal probability to every composition (30 Red, λ_iYellow, 60 – λ_iBlack), where λ_i = 0, 1, . . . 60. These different beliefs would "make a difference," for example, to the "value of information" to you, the maximum amount you would pay to observe a random sample of given size from the urn before choosing among gambles. But they would *not* make a difference to your behavior if (a) you had to choose without any additional information, and (b) you maximized expected utility on the basis of your "best guess" distribution.

Let us suppose that the set of "reasonably acceptable" distributions $Y°$ for you comprises the infinite set (1/3, λ,2/3 – λ), $0 \le \lambda \le 2/3$ (e.g., you might include all "Type II" distributions over the possibilities in the above paragraph as "reasonably acceptable"), and, for purposes of illustration, that the parameter α for you is $1/4$.

Then the formula for the "restricted Bayes / Hurwicz criterion" will be:

$$\rho \cdot \text{est}_x + (1 - \rho) \left[1/4 \cdot \text{max}_x + 3/4 \, \text{min}_x \right]$$

The relevant data (assigning utility values 1, 0 to \$100, \$0) would be, for various values of ρ:

	30		60				Bayes/Hurwicz Index			
	Red	Yellow	Black	Min_x	Est_x	Max_x	$\rho=0$	$\rho=1/3$	$\rho=1/2$	$\rho=1$
I	1	0	0	1/3	1/3	1/3	1/3	1/3	1/3	1/3
II	0	1	0	0	1/3	2/3	1/6	2/9	1/4	1/3
III	1	0	1	1/3	2/3	1	1/2	5/9	7/12	2/3
IV	0	1	1	2/3	2/3	2/3	2/3	2/3	2/3	2/3

Fig. 7.3

This simple model is obviously capable of encompassing a wide range of behavior patterns, even with given outcomes, given "von Neumann-Morgenstern utilities," and a given "best guess" probability distribution y^o. For particular values of ρ and or α, or special cases of y^o or Y^o, the formula reduces to one or another of the decision criteria we have already considered. In fact, *every* decision criterion we have discussed (except those based on "regrets") can be presented as a special case of this "restricted Bayes/Hurwicz criterion." The diagram below indicates some of these "reduced forms" of the criterion (assuming Y^o does not include every possible distribution over states of the world):

	$\alpha = 0$	$\alpha > 0$
$\rho = 0$	"Restricted minimax" (Hurwicz, Good)	"Restricted Hurwicz" (Shackle, Hurwicz)
$0 < \rho < 1$	"Restricted Bayes/minimax" (Hodges and Lehmann)	"Restricted Bayes/Hurwicz"
$\rho = 1$	"Bernoulli" (Savage, Raiffa and Schlaifer)	"Bernoulli"

Fig. 7.4

The case $\rho = 1$, which might be described as complete confidence in or total reliance upon a single, "best guess" probability distribution $y°$ with respect to which expected utility is maximized, corresponds to "neo-Bernoullian" decision-making. It leads to a pattern of choices obeying the Savage postulates; if appropriate choices are observed, the distribution $y°$ can be inferred by an observer. (Equivalent behavior follows from this rule when $\rho = 1$ or when $Y°$ consists of the single distribution $y°$; however, in general, the "size" of $Y°$ and the magnitude of the parameter ρ are to be regarded as independent variables, though often—inversely—correlated. *Each* seems useful as an operational index of "ambiguity," so long as $\rho < 1$; if decision situations are to be compared with respect to their "ambiguity" for a given decision-maker, it seems necessary to think of "ambiguity" as a vector with at least these two elements).

The "Laplace" criterion would be a special case of "neo-Bernoullian" decision-making, in which the "best guess" distribution $y°$ was a uniform distribution over the relevant states of nature; in what might be called the "restricted Laplace criterion," $y°$ would result from applying a uniform distribution over a set of "reasonably acceptable" distributions $Y°$.

If $o = 0$ (and $Y°$ contains more than one distribution), the rule reduces to the "restricted Hurwicz criterion." Thus, the column in Fig. 7.4 corresponding to $\rho = 0$ is equivalent to the column in Fig. 6.7 corresponding to $\alpha = 1/4$ (this value of α being assumed in Fig. 7.4); evaluations for this special case corresponding to other values of α appear in Fig. 6.7.

If $Y°$ includes all possible distributions over the states of the world, i.e., if the set of "reasonably acceptable" distributions includes every distribution assigning probability $= 1$ to a given state of the world, with $\rho = 0$, the rule may be interpreted as the ordinary "Hurwicz criterion," or the ordinary "Wald/minimax criterion" if $\alpha = 0$

Of course, it is only when $0 < \rho < 1$ that both the concepts $y°$ and $Y°$ are useful, and hence the concept ρ itself; when α, too, is strictly between 0 and 1, both the variables x_{min} and x_{max} (or, y_x^{min} and y_x^{max}) are relevant. I believe that it is possible for a decision-maker in given circumstances to assign meaningful values to these parameters appropriate to his state of mind and preferences in the particular situations, and that there are important circumstances in which values between 0 and 1 are appropriate both for α and ρ, so that *all* of the variables indicated in the formulation of the "restricted Bayes/Hurwicz criterion" are behaviorally relevant in a given decision problem. In other words, I do not propose that α and ρ be regarded as "dummy variables," useful for achieving pseudo-generality by combining in one portmanteau formula all earlier decision criteria.

It is true that for simplicity in exposition—and in some situations, with little loss in realism—it is possible to discuss most of the basic notions and behavior patterns under consideration in terms of a reduced form of this criterion, such as the "restricted Hurwicz criterion" or the "restricted Bayes-minimax criterion."[1] The latter criterion in particular, which introduces the notion of a "best guess" distribution y^o and a "confidence" parameter ρ, is useful to represent the observed shifts in behavior (or, from the point of view of a decision-maker, to generate systematically his desired shifts in behavior) as "ambiguity" *decreases*.

Suppose, in our example, that a subject were asked to express his maximum bids for the various options, I, II, III, IV represented in Fig. 6.1 initially before any explicit information had been offered on the proportion of Yellow to Black balls. Then suppose he were asked to bid again after a random sample of *two* balls had been drawn from the non-Red balls, resulting, let us say, in one Yellow and one Black. If his initial "best guess" distribution had been (1/3, 1/3, 1/3), this result would presumably not change it; on the contrary, his "confidence" in it, his desire to maximize expected utility with respect to that distribution, would presumably increase (if ρ were not already = 1). Likewise, if our interpretation of the behavioral (normative) significance of the parameter ρ is valid, we must assume ρ to increase as increasingly large samples are drawn from the non-Red balls, if we imagine each sample proportion to be close to 50:50.

To abstract from the effect on Y^o, which would presumably be contracting if these samples were replaced in the urn, and to simplify calculation of the effects of increase in ρ in the formula, let us assume that one Red ball is removed for every two non-Red, sample proportions of Yellow to Black are all exactly 1/2, and samples are not replaced. Then if all proportions

---

[1] Although in "Risk, Ambiguity, and the Savage Axioms" I alluded to the full "restricted Bayes/Hurwicz criterion" (not by that name), I relied for purposes of formal statement and full discussion upon the simpler "restricted Bayes/minimax criterion," since it reflected adequately the particular behavior patterns discussed, and also, as stated then: "because it most frequently corresponds to *advice* to be found on decision-making in ambiguous situations" (*op. cit.*,p. 664).

Since this criterion ignores $\max_x$ and α, the corresponding index can be stated simply: $\rho\text{-est}_x + (1-\rho)\min_x$

Hodges and Lehmann, who first proposed this criterion in "The Use of Previous Experience in Reaching Statistical Decisions," emphasized a different formulation with a special rationale (see below, Chapter Eight); their own term for an action optimal in terms of this criterion was "restricted Bayes solution" (*op. cit.*, p. 397).

of Yellow to Black from 0 to 2/3 remain in Y^o, the respective bids as ρ increases are shown below:

	30	60				Bayes/Hurwicz Index				
	Red	**Yellow**	**Black**	**Min_x**	**Est_x**	**ρ=0**	**ρ=1/4**	**ρ=1/2**	**ρ=2/3**	**ρ=1**
I	1	0	0	1/3	1/3	1/3	1/3	1/3	1/3	1/3
II	0	1	0	0	1/3	0	1/12	1/6	2/9	1/3
III	1	0	1	1/3	2/3	1/3	5/12	1/2	5/9	2/3
IV	0	1	1	2/3	2/3	2/3	2/3	2/3	2/3	2/3

Fig. 7.5

This over-all pattern of behavior corresponds closely to the pattern that many individuals assert they would (wish to) follow under the postulated conditions of information. It is not unique to this particular index; the same general pattern can be seen in Fig. 7.3 above, for the "Bayes/Hurwicz" index with $\alpha = 1/4$.[1] In both cases the set of bids approach closer and closer to those corresponding to the "best guess" distribution y^o as ρ increases. This is quite in line with the interpretation of ρ as indicating "confidence" in a single, given distribution as a basis for decision-making;[2] as ρ approaches 1, the relative influence upon the evaluation of various actions of probability distributions other than the "best guess" diminishes (hence, in this case, actions I and II approach closer and closer to indifference, as do actions III and IV). (Thus, the exact "size" and composition of Y^o grows less critical as ρ increases.)

---

[1] Note that the column ρ=1/2 above (α=0) presents the same set of bids corresponding to ρ=0, α=1/4 in Fig. 7.3. This is another indication of the ease of confounding what may be essentially different conditions of uncertainty or individual differences in normative criteria if we rely entirely upon non-verbal behavior for evidence of opinions (as implied not only in Savage's work but in the paper cited by C. A. B. Smith, which does recognize behavior patterns such as those in Figures 7.3 and 7.5

On the other hand, if we hypothesize, or infer on the basis of verbal or other evidence, the nature of an individual's normative criterion, we may be able to infer the values of various parameters from his choices. In particular, if (we assume) he is using a "restricted Hurwicz criterion" with o=0 (i.e., a "restricted minimax criterion" or what I. J. Good calls "type II minimaxing"), then p_o (E) and p^o(E) as revealed in his bids for a unit utility staked *on* and *against* the event E, "reveal" the lower and upper boundaries of the set of "reasonably acceptable" probabilities assigned to E in his set of distributions Y^o (i.e., p_*(E) and p^*(E), as defined below in Chapter Eight).

[2] Though it is natural to think of information being acquired in this artificial example—and, of course, in actual statistical problems—in the form of sample

However, the exclusive emphasis in the Hodges and Lehman "Bayes/minimax criterion" upon *unfavorable* possibilities among the set of "reasonably acceptable" distributions, relative to the "best guess" distribution, can make it—for many people, in frequent circumstances—*inappropriate as a normative criterion.* Preferences often asserted in connection with the following example indicate that favorable possibilities in Y^o may also be behaviorally relevant: i.e., that the full formulation of the "restricted Bayes/Hurwicz criterion" with positive values of α as well as ρ is frequently appropriate.

BOLDNESS AND PRUDENCE: THE "N-COLOR URN" EXAMPLE

Let us again imagine two urns, as in the first example in Chapter Five. In this case you are informed, and allowed to verify, that Urn I contains exactly 100 balls of ten different colors, ten of each: 10 Red, 10 Yellow, 10 Black, . . . 10 Green. You are informed (and, let us say, you believe) that Urn II also contains 100 balls, which may be in any proportion of the same ten colors; it contains no *other* colors, but you are given no other explicit information on what the proportions might be nor how they were determined. All other conditions are as before: including your assumption that the person measuring your opinions is as innocent as you of the proportions in Urn II, if you can imagine conditions that would support this conviction.

This investigator now offers you the opportunity to stake a large prize, say $1000, alternatively on one or another of the various colors that may occur in a single drawing from Urn I. Let us suppose that you are indifferent among these offers; i.e., let us limit discussion to those of "you" who are indifferent. Next, he offers you similar opportunities with respect to the drawing of a single ball, of given color, from Urn II. Again let us suppose that you are indifferent between staking the prize on one color or another.[1] Now, without indicating what subsequent offers may be made, he offers you a choice between the following two options: (I) $1000 if any color but

---

results, not all the relevant information about the events involved in a set of gambles can, in general, be represented in the form of sample-distributions. Hence, contrary to suggestions by John Chipman and N. Georgescu-Roegen (discussed in Chapter Eight), I do not think a "confidence" parameter can in general be identified with sample-size.

[1] I would have preferred to hypothesize 100 different possible colors, or possible numbers, in each urn, but it becomes somewhat harder to imagine strict indifference among all the various offers for Urn II, besides the problem of running out of color names; nevertheless, it may be useful for you to try to imagine a similar example with a number of alternative events greater than 10.

Green is drawn from Urn I (i.e., if "not-Green$_I$"occurs in a drawing from Urn I); (II) $1000 if "not-Green$_{II}$" occurs in a drawing from Urn II. Which do you prefer? Are you indifferent?

Many people of whom I have asked this question state that they would strongly prefer option I. They are, of course, violating the Sure-thing Principle, but warnings to this effect do not seem to deter them. So far, of course, their behavior pattern is similar to the one we have discussed at length: action I preferred to II, IV to III in the "three-color urn" example, Figs. 7.3, 7.5. If there is a difference, it is that the preference is more pronounced in this case, as shown, for example, by the maximum bids they would offer for option I or for option II. Once again, verbal comments tend to indicate that the preferred option is regarded as having a *less ambiguous probability distribution over payoffs,* and this judgment is described as critical to choice.

However, suppose you are offered a final pair of alternative options: (III) $1000 if a *Green* ball occurs, the drawing to be from Urn I; (IV) $1000 if a Green ball occurs, the drawing to be from Urn II. Which do you prefer? Or are you indifferent? How much would you pay for option III? For option IV?

Some of those who preferred option I to option II now prefer option IV to option III (again violating Postulate 2, the Sure-thing Principle), indicating that it is for the same reasons. Those who claimed indifference between I and II tend to be indifferent between III and IV. But a significant number of those who before preferred I to II now claim that they would prefer III to IV. These two pairs of preferences are not "inconsistent" with each other in terms of Postulate 2, (by themselves they would indicate that "Green$_I$" is believed "less probable" than "Green$_{II}$"), but *each* pair is inconsistent (in terms of Postulates 1 and 2) with the earlier indifference between staking a prize on any of the ten colors with respect to a given urn. In the latter pair, it is option III whose probability distribution of payoffs, and hence expected utility, is generally perceived as unambiguous. The expected utility for option IV is generally perceived as ambiguous; yet it is chosen over option III, and by the same people who appeared to shun ambiguity in earlier examples!

The latter pattern of behavior cannot be represented by the Hodges and Lehmann "restricted Bayes/minimax criterion" for any $y°$, $Y°$ or ρ (including $\rho = 1$, the "neo-Bernoullian" case; and $\rho = 0$, the "restricted minimax" case).

Yet the "restricted Bayes/Hurwicz criterion," with positive α, could generate this pattern of preferences under many different assumptions. For example, let us assume that $y°$ is the same for both urns, the uniform distribution over the ten colors $(1/10, 1/10, \ldots 1/10)$; that $Y°$ for Urn I consists of this one distribution $y°$, but that $Y°$ with respect to Urn II contains every possible distribution over the ten colors. For $\alpha = 1/4$, the calculations would be (for several values of ρ with respect to y° for Urn II):

Bayes/Hurwicz Index, α=1/4

	min$_x$	est$_x$	max$_x$	ρ=0	ρ1/4	ρ=1/2	ρ1
I	9/10	9/10	9/10	9/10	9/10	9/10	9/10
II	0	9/10	1	1/4	33/80	23/40	9/10
III	1/10	1/10	1/10	1/10	1/10	1/10	1/10
IV	0	1/10	1	1/4	1/5	7/40	1/10

Fig. 7.6

For $\rho = 0$, the criterion implies indifference between options II and IV, stakes on "not-Green" or "Green" in Urn II. This would not do for everyone; though there might be those who would profess a pattern of preferences corresponding to the conditions for "complete ignorance" of the proportion of Green balls in Urn II.

The column headed $\rho = 1/4$, corresponding to some slight degree of "confidence" in a "best guess" (uniform) distribution over the possible colors in Urn II, presents a set of bids that looks more typical. The bids for options II and IV are now *closer* to the values they would attain if you assigned "definite" uniform probabilities to the four colors that might be drawn from Urn II, i.e., if $\rho = 1$ or y° were the only "reasonably acceptable" distribution; the bid for option II is definitely higher than that for option IV. Yet the bid for option II is still *lower* than it would be if uniform probabilities were "definitely" assigned, the bid for option IV still *higher* than it would be: and *not*, so far as this decision criterion is concerned, because drawing a Green ball from Urn II is believed (definitely or even "vaguely") "more probable" than drawing any of the other nine, given colors from Urn II.[1]

---

[1] This corresponds exactly to the pattern of preferences reported by John Chipman in his controlled experiment investigating stochastic preferences among gambles, some of which correspond to actions I and III above (involving drawings from "urns" with exactly known proportions) and others of which corresponded to actions II and IV (involving drawings from "urns" from which only a small sample had previously been observed). To paraphrase the nature of these gambles, Chipman found a very strong tendency among his subjects to prefer: (a) to stake a prize on "Red" from an urn *known* to contain 60% Red than to stake it on an urn from which a 6:4 sample in favor of Red had been drawn; (b) to stake a prize on Red from an urn with known 50% Red than on Red from an urn from which a 5:5 sample had

The "restricted Bayes/Hurwicz criterion", unlike the others we have considered, thus seems capable of representing, formally, or of generating a certain pattern of choices: corresponding to the deliberated preferences asserted by some decision-makers. We may still ask whether it seems to reflect the actual considerations that influence their choices. To return to the question that opened Chapter Six: What do they think they are doing? What do they say they are trying to do?

It is noteworthy that a number of people who claim that they would make choices consistent with the Savage postulates in every earlier example decide that they would make conflicting choices, of the sort considered above, in this case. Others who are still not strongly tempted to violate the postulates begin to see the possibility of circumstances when they might wish to do so. In terms of the rather abstract setting of our example, such people claim that their decisions in this respect would be sensitive to the number of colors included in Urn I and the number *possible* in Urn II. As one individual put it, who had obeyed the Savage postulates in every hypothetical comparison until he was confronted with a choice between options I and II in an example similar to this one but with only four colors possible: "I might as well concede that I would prefer option I in this case; because I certainly would if there were *ten* colors possible in each urn, and the prize were staked on nine out of the ten." This same individual proceeded unhesitatingly to assert a preference, on the same grounds, for option IV over III.

However, many of those who in every earlier example violated the Savage postulates without hesitation (preferring actions whose distribution of payoffs seemed less ambiguous) are diffident, apologetic, and somewhat surprised when they now decide to state a preference for the "ambiguous" option IV, often prefacing their choice with phrases like:

---

been drawn; (c) to stake a prize on Red from an urn from which a sample of 10 balls, 4 of them Red, had been drawn, than to stake it on Red from an urn known to contain 40% Red balls. (To make the correspondence with our hypothetical results above complete, we might imagine that a sample of 10 balls had been drawn from Urn II, revealing 1 ball of each color). (John S. Chipman, "Stochastic Choice and Subjective Probability," *Decisions, Values and Groups,* ed. D. Willner, (New York, 1960); see Table III, p. 84, Table VIII, p. 88.)

Chipman does not, however, suggest a decision criterion that accounts adequately for this *triad* of preferences. He offers the plausible hypothesis that subjects "bias" an "unknown" (or, as we would say "ambiguous") probability (of winning) towards 1/2; but, as he points out, this cannot explain preference (b) above (*op. cit.,* p. 87). All three pairs of preferences, however, are quite consistent with the "restricted Bayes/Hurwicz criterion" with $0 < \alpha < 1/2$.

"Now, actually, this time I'm almost tempted to . . . ," "I really think, to tell the truth, I would prefer. . ."

This hesitancy undoubtedly reflects the fact that a tendency to give extra consideration to unfavorable possibilities in decision-making has a reassuring popular aura of "conservatism," "soundness," "prudence" even when it leads to violation of the Savage postulates, whereas a preference influenced significantly by extreme favorable possibilities is easily stigmatized as "wishful." To the extent that the decision-maker acts in a public role, his payoffs depending in part on his observed adherence to conventional standards of acceptable decision-making practice, this attitude might dissuade him from preferring option III to IV.

Nevertheless, the deliberated preferences in this example of some individuals—including myself—seem to reflect in a systematic way both favorable and unfavorable possibilities in an ambiguous situation. The way the relative influence of such considerations may vary in different situations is suggested by the diagram below. It shows the expected utilities for the four options described above as functions of the (unspecified) proportion of Green balls in Urn II (assuming your subjective probabilities for drawing a Green or not-Green ball from a given urn would correspond to a "known" proportion of Green, or to an "expected" proportion if "definite" probabilities were assigned to different proportions):

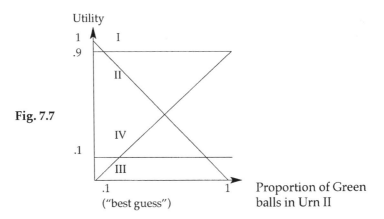

Fig. 7.7

The "flatness" of the payoff functions for options I and III does not imply that their outcome is certain. On the contrary, they are risky; but they involve "known" risks, with "definite" probabilities, and hence their evaluation in terms of "von Neumann-Morgenstern utilities" is equally definite. (They would not in this case, of course, be sensitive to the proportions of colors in Urn II, since they refer to drawings from Urn I.) If you assign "definite" probabilities to various proportions of Green balls in Urn II, your utility evaluation of options II and IV will be just as definite; in particular, if your "best guess" distribution y° (with $\rho = 1$) over the colors in Urn II is the same as for Urn I, you will regard the pair of options I, II as essentially indistinguishable, and likewise III, IV.

But if you are less confident of this particular y°—though it represents your single, "best guess" distribution—after you have pondered your scanty information on Urn II in the light of whatever additional evidence and experience you might bring to bear, you may feel uneasy with the results of a calculation indicating that options I and II are equivalent in value, and likewise options III and IV. "I feel *definitely* that option I is more favorable than option III," you might reflect; "in fact, the probability of winning seems definitely three times greater with option I than with option III (I would *give* 3:1 odds against a Green ball from Urn I). But can I judge as *definitely*, in any sense, that option II is as favorable as option I? Or more, or less favorable? Can I even say definitely that I believe option II to be more favorable than option III? Or more favorable than IV?"

"Definite" comparisons of the sort postulated would not require that you be certain of a particular proportion of Green balls in Urn II: merely that you assign "definite" probabilities to various proportions. But perhaps you can imagine, as I can, circumstances in which your information was such that a large number of probability distributions were "reasonably acceptable" representations of your "vague" opinions. In that case the questions posed above might have to be answered, "No." It is still not self-evident that such "vagueness" must color your preferences; on the other hand, neither does it seem self-evident that a "best guess" distribution based upon nothing more than a symmetry of ignorance about the relevant possibilities must be determinative of choice.

A person who felt that his "best guess" judgments of probability in a particular situation were an insubstantial basis for evaluating given actions might look for additional grounds of choice, new criteria, new questions to ask himself. In particular, he might ask: "What is the *worst* expectation of utility I might associate with this action, corresponding to probability judgments I don't definitely reject?" We might term this "worst" expectation ($\min_x$), corresponding to the *least favorable reasonable distribution* ($y^{\min}_x$ in Y°), the "security level" of the given action.

Rarely will the *only* fact worth noting about a prospective action be its "security level." But in situations of high ambiguity, such a consideration may appear worthy of *some* weight, relative to a given "best guess" expectation. In other words, in comparing two actions it might seem acceptable to "trade" some *decrease* in a ("vague") "best guess" expectation to achieve sufficiently great improvement in "security level."

One of the attractions of the "security level" as a consideration is that it *may* be possible to determine it for a given action much more "definitely" than the "best guess" expectation. Another question that may yield a relatively "definite" judgment, and which seems equally relevant, would be: "What is the *best* expectation that might be associated with this action, *consistent with all my 'definite' probability judgments?*" Again, this consideration might be considered as deserving *some* weight; i.e., some "trade-off" might be permissible between sufficient increases in "best reasonable expectation" (max_x) and sufficiently small decreases both in "worst reasonable" and "best guess" expectations. Appropriate weights for these various factors, determining acceptable "trades" between one or the other in comparing two actions, would depend on the individual and the situation.

The relative attention that a decision-maker will give to possible expected values other than the "best guess" expectation will depend upon his *confidence* in the probability judgments reflected in the latter expectation. The less confident he is, (the less "definite" his best judgments of probability), the more he may sacrifice in terms of "estimated" or "best guess" expected utility to achieve a given increase in "security level" or "best reasonable expectation"; the more confident, the greater increase he would demand in the latter aspects of a prospective action, compared to its alternative, to compensate for a given drop in "best guess" expectation. As between "best expectation" and "security level," personality and "role" characteristics may determine fairly constant relative weighting for a given individual in a given context of decision-making; thus, a given person may "use" one value of α in his role as a trustee, another in handling his own investments, a third as an elected official. In many roles, there would appear to be social pressures or conventions in favor of weighting the "worst" among *ambiguous* possibilities somewhat more than "best," even when the latter are not to be ignored. Thus, the value of α = 1/4 in Fig. 7.6 implies that it takes an increase of 3 utility units in "best reasonable expectation" to "compensate" for a drop of 1 unit in "security level," "other things (e.g., 'best guess' expectation) being equal."

Those decision-makers who conform to a "Bayes/minimax criterion," weighing only unfavorable factors in addition to "best guess" expectations, will choose a gamble whose distribution over payoffs is ambiguous over one with an unambiguous expectation *only when the "best guess" expectation for the ambiguous gamble is significantly better than the unambiguous expectation of the latter.* There seems a strong analogy here to the man whose "von Neumann-Morgenstern utilities" show diminishing marginal utility with respect to money; in comparing risky propositions to "sure things," he demands a positive premium in terms of the mathematical expectation of *money* before he will choose a risky proposition over a certain outcome. The same man, if he also uses a "Bayes/minimax criterion," will exhibit an

"ambiguity aversion" similar to his "risk aversion"; he will demand a positive premium in terms of the "best guess" mathematical expectation of
utility—the magnitude required varying inversely with his confidence in
the "best guess" distribution—before he will choose a gamble whose payoff probabilities are *ambiguous* over a risky proposition whose payoffs are
associated with "definite" probabilities. As between two ambiguous gambles with equivalent "best guess" expectations, he will always prefer the
one whose expectation is less sensitive to variation within the set Y°. In
Figures 7.6 and 7.7 above, he will prefer the "flat" payoff functions in both
pairs, I over II and III over IV.

To many people, however, such a degree of "ambiguity aversion" bor-
ders on the unreasonable;[1] in their own decision-making they wish to take
some account also of favorable possibilities in ambiguous situations. These
individuals will *not* exhibit a uniform tendency to "avoid ambiguity." In
general, the weight they give to favorable possibilities will reduce their relative aversion to a gamble with ambiguous payoffs, i.e., the premium they
may demand in terms of its "best guess" expectation before they will
choose it over a less ambiguous gamble. Moreover, even if they weight
favorable possibilities less heavily than unfavorable ($\alpha < 1/2$), they may
prefer an ambiguous gamble whose "best guess" expectation is no better
than the "definite" expectation of an unambiguous gamble, if both of these
expectations are sufficiently *low* relative to the "worst" and "*best*" reasonable expectations of the former. In terms of Fig. 7.7 their pattern of preferences in the examples above can be simply described: they prefer an unambiguous gamble (I) whose *probability of winning is definitely high* to an
ambiguous gamble (II) whose "best guess" expectation is equivalent but
which might "reasonably" be evaluated much lower; yet they prefer an
ambiguous gamble (IV), whose "best guess" expectation is low but which

---

[1] I sympathize with this view; but since my primary aim is to win tolerance
and understanding for a broad class of decision-makers who deviate from the
"Bernoulli proposition," I do not propose to join any witch-hunts at this point.

However, I would like to correct a false impression that I may inadvertently
have given in "Risk, Ambiguity, and the Savage Axioms." For expository reasons
only, I limited my discussion of "non-Bernoullian\#211> behavior there to patterns
formalized by the "Bayes/minimax criterion"; the rationale for that behavior
inevitably stressed preferences for "unambiguous" payoff probabilities. I did not
mean to suggest that such considerations constitute the sole acceptable motivation
for departure from the "Bernoulli proposition"; indeed, as my discussion above of
the "Bayes/Hurwicz criterion" should make clear, a normative criterion acceptable
for my own decision-making would certainly take account of favorable possibilities
in addition to "worst" possibilities. I suspect, in fact, that α for me is rather atypically—
some would say, pathologically—high.

might "almost as well" be evaluated much higher, to a gamble (III) whose *probability of winning is unambiguously low.*[1]

In slightly different terms, a person who preferred option I over II in Figures 7.6 and 7.7 might explain his calculations:

> On the basis of my definite opinions, I could assign a definite probability distribution over payoffs for option I; but I can't for option II. I don't really have strong opinions about the relative probabilities of the different outcomes in option II, though if I *had* to express a single set of opinions, II would end up with the same expectation as option I. But in terms of all the probability comparisons that are compatible with my definite opinions, I could judge option II to be a little more favorable than option I, or I could just as well judge it to be a great deal worse.

> Everything considered, I prefer option I. Its *definite* expectation is almost as good as the "best" expectation for option II, and its "security level" is *very* much better than the "worst" expectation I might reasonably assign to option II.

The same person might explain a preference for option IV over option III:

> I can evaluate option III "definitely"; its expectation is definitely a little better than the "worst" expectation I might assign to option IV, but its value is definitely not much better than that worst; whereas option IV has just as good a "best guess" expectation and without contradicting any of my definite opinions I could judge it to be very much more favorable. III does have a higher "security level," and in general I put a high weight on "insurance," but the price of insurance is just too high with option III.

Such language obviously lends itself to direct representation in terms of the "restricted Bayes/Hurwicz criterion." Yet as a rationale of deliberate decision-making, such an "explanation" would arouse only exasperation in a staunch "neo-Bernoullian," who might interject:

---

[1]For a given Y^o and α, there will be a "break-even" expectation = $\alpha \max_x + (1 - \alpha) \cdot \min_x$ for an action x with given payoffs (X), such that an alternative action with a *definite* expectation higher than this will be preferred to an ambiguous action x with the same, higher "best guess" expectation (but with $\rho < 1$); whereas the ambiguous action x will be preferred to any action whose *definite* expectation is *lower* than the break-even expectation, though it may be equivalent to the "best guess" expectation for x. For the actions considered in Fig. 7.6, the "break-even" expectation would be 1/4 (the payoffs and Y^o are such that this point will = α).

Why are you double-counting the "worst" and the "best" possibilities? They're already taken into account in your over-all estimates of probabilities, weighted in a reasoned, realistic way that represents—by your own claim—your best judgment. Once you've arrived at *one* probability distribution that reflects everything you know that's relevant, *use* it; stop worrying about the others you 'might almost as well' have assigned."

But the reply to this might be:

When it comes to choices concerning Urn II, as you very well know, my 'reasoned, realistic' calculations are based on a whole lot of nothing. And that's about what my 'best judgment' of the outcome is worth. Sure, when it comes to staking a prize on any one of the colors in Urn II, I'm indifferent; I don't know any reason not to be. And the only single probability distribution consistent with that is a uniform one; that's as much judgment as *that* "best guess" reflects. But what sort of basis does that give me for determining any *other* decisions?

You're asking me, in effect, to be willing to pay as much for option II as for option I. That amounts to my *giving* 9:1 odds *against* drawing a Green ball from Urn II.[1] Well, I don't mind giving 9:1 against Green from Urn *I*; but when I given 9:1 odds against some event, it has to be because I feel pretty definitely that it is *very much less likely than not* to occur. Why should I feel that about Green$_{II}$: or about *any other*, given color in Urn II? As a matter of fact, I don't. Given all the information I have about Urn II, what *reason* do I have to believe that drawing a Green ball from that urn is *any* less

---

[1] If you are indifferent between staking a prize on one or another of the ten colors in Urn II, then if you obey the "Bernoulli proposition" (or the Savage postulates) you must act "as if" you assigned probability $= 1/10$ to each color, given a drawing from Urn II. Then, with payoffs in your "von Neumann-Morgenstern utilities," you must be indifferent between I and II below:

	Green$_{II}$	not-Green$_{II}$
I	0	0
II	−9	1

I.e., you must find the bet II—which amounts to your giving 9:1 odds against Green—(barely) "acceptable." Likewise, you must be willing to give 9:1 odds against any other, given color in Urn II.

It is not always quite obvious just how very much you are committing yourself to when you pledge allegiance to the Savage postulates under all circumstances.

probable than drawing one that is not Green? Just why is it, again, you say that I 'ought' to be willing to put up 9 to 1 against Green$_{II}$?

I am not really sure just how a "neo-Bernoullian" would go about answering that last question. Of course, he can answer: "Because if you won't bet at 9:1 against Green$_{II}$, given your other choices, you are violating Savage's Postulate 2; and we won't be able to infer a definite probability for Green$_{II}$ for you. I know, you're going to say you don't *have* a definite probability for Green$_{II}$; but the fact remains, you aren't conforming to the 'Bernoulli proposition,' which makes you *unreasonable* in my book." These arguments might or might not, on reflection, pose to our hypothetical subject overwhelming imperatives to change his behavior, but they would sound rather weak to me. His own, extended rationale for his asserted preferences, on the other hand, has for me a seductive logic, a ring of plausibility to it that I would find hard to repudiate. In fact, I can hear myself saying it.

What is, after all, the alternative offered by the "neo-Bernoullian"? Let us conclude this chapter, and the main argument of this study, by further characterizing certain opposing positions.

IGNORANCE, PROBABILITY, AND THE VARIETIES OF GAMBLERS

"In some situations," Raiffa and Schlaifer assert, in their excellent manual for applying Bernoullian principles to practical decision problems, "the decision-maker will feel that the information available prior to obtaining actual sample evidence is virtually non-existent."[1] That is just the sort of situation our "urn" examples have been intended to represent; it is the situation upon which this study focuses. From the point of view of "intuitive probabilities" such a situation is probably characterized in the decision-maker's mind by a very large set Y° of probability distributions that are, as Savage puts it, "not conspicuously unacceptable." *What is he to do in this situation; how is he to choose; how might his "vague" opinions reasonably and usefully influence his decision?*

It *may be*, as all three authors above have pointed out, that his decision problem is such that:

> prior opinions and prior betting odds may have little or no effect on the decision actually chosen. Thus for example, we often find situations in which, *after a sample has once been taken*, the posterior expected utility of every act available is practically the same for every prior distribution that the decision maker is *willing to consider*.[2]

---

[1] Raiffa and Schlaifer, *Applied Statistical Decision Theory*, p. 62.
[2] *Ibid.*, p. 66.

In particular, Savage has emphasized the advantages and effectiveness of "subjective statistics" in the realm of problems involving *precise measurement* . . . the kind of measurement we have when the data is so incisive as to overwhelm the initial opinion, bringing a great variety of realistic initial opinions to practically the same conclusion."[1] There are, in short, a variety of situations in which the "neo-Bernoullian" advice, to pick a particular probability distribution from the family Y^o—if necessary, almost arbitrarily—and "act upon it"; will be readily and generally acceptable simply because it does not matter very much what prior distribution he chooses.

But we are concerned here with quite different situations, in which "terminal" decisions must be without further information and without benefit of prior observations of large samples of precise measurements, and in which the relevant acts, payoffs and Y^o are such that it *does make a difference* what weights are assigned to the relevant events in a decision criterion.[2] The decision-maker may announce emphatically in this situation that he finds virtually no basis in his information, his experience or his intuition for selecting any one distribution out of many in Y^o as a definite basis for decision-making. What normative counsel does the "neo-Bernoullian" approach provide him in this plight? The advice offered by Raiffa and Schlaifer is sympathetic but inexorable:

> . . . the decision maker may be *forced* to make a definite choice of the prior distribution with which he wishes his act to be consistent, no matter how vague or confused his initial psychological state may be. . . .

> In such situations it is therefore a vital and unavoidable responsibility of the decision maker to adopt a prior distribution which represents his best judgment as accurately as possible, however much he may wish that this judgment could be based on more evidence than is actually available.[3]

---

[1] Savage, "Subjective Probability and Statistical Practice," p. 15; italics added. See also his discussions of this topic in "Bayesian Statistics" and "The Subjective Basis of Statistical Practice."

[2] Similar problems arise, as Raiffa and Schlaifer point out, when the question "whether or not any sample should be taken at all and if so how large the sample should be" confronts a decision-maker whose prior opinions are "vague" (*op. cit.,* p. 67). "We cannot emphasize too strongly that, in situations where it is possible to take at most one sample or where each successive sample involves a substantial 'stage cost independent of sample size, answers to questions of this kind must *always* depend *critically* on the prior distribution.'"

[3] *Op. cit.,* pp. 67–68.

The news of this "responsibility" may fall harshly on the ears of a decision-maker who feels keenly his ignorance in given circumstances. He may realize, if he is alert, that Raiffa and Schlaifer are sentencing him to produce a set of "definite" betting odds which, whatever its exact structure, will commit him to *bet at long odds on some propositions* concerning which his opinions may, in fact, be exceedingly vague and unsure. There is no way he can escape this commitment if he is to conform to their advice, or to the Savage postulates, or in general, to the "Bernoulli proposition." No single distribution, of whatever shape (e.g., uniform or "diffuse") provides him an "out," if he should be "reluctant to gamble" in various senses we have earlier discussed.

Finding some one distribution that "represents his best judgment" (for what that is worth), that *expresses* his uncertainties as well as any other is not the problem. He can always calculate, one way or another, what Fisher calls his Uncertainties of Rank A, B, C, etc., assigning definite probabilities at each level, though one suspects that the assignment must become increasingly arbitrary as his opinions appear more and more fuzzy or "vague" at successively deeper levels. Harold Jeffreys has suggested one way you may always ensure that you will arrive at what we have earlier called a single, "best guess" distribution y^o:

> At any stage of knowledge it is legitimate to ask about a given hypothesis that is accepted, "How do you know?" The answer will usually rest on some observational data. If we ask further, "What did you think of the hypothesis before you had these data?" we may be told of some less convincing data; but if we go far enough back we shall always reach a stage where the answer must be: "I thought the matter worth considering, but had no opinion about whether it was true." What was the probability at this stage? We have the answer already. If there is no reason to believe one hypothesis rather than another, the probabilities are equal. . . . to say that the probabilities are equal is a precise way of saying that we have no ground for choosing between the alternatives. . . . it is merely the formal way of expressing ignorance.[1] . . . .

> Our first problem is to find a way of saying that the magnitude of a parameter is unknown, when none of the possible values need special attention. . . . If the parameter may have any value in a finite range, or from − ° to +°, its prior probability should be taken as uniformly distributed. . . .

> [But] how can we assign the prior probability when we know nothing about the value of the parameter, except the very vague knowledge just

---

[1] Harold Jeffreys, *Theory of Probability* (Oxford, 1948), pp. 33–34.

indicated? The answer is really clear enough when it is recognized that a probability is merely a number associated with a degree of reasonable confidence and has no purpose except to give it a formal expression. If we have no information relevant to the actual value of a parameter, the probability must be chosen so as to express the fact that we have none. It must *say nothing* about the value of the parameter, except the bare fact that it may possibly, by its very nature, be restricted to lie within certain definite limits.[1]

Now, it would appear that Jeffrey's rule here gives, in fact, fairly *unsatisfactory* expression to the notion that we "know nothing" about the value of the parameter. In the first place, a listener could not tell from your assertion of a uniform distribution over a finite range whether you felt you had "no information relevant to the actual value" or, on the contrary, "all possible relevant information" (and quite a lot at that). And far from "saying nothing," such an assertion says rather more than you may want to say about your "reasonable confidence." For example, it "says" that you judge it to be *nine times as likely as not, a fair 9:1 bet,* that the value lies within any given sub-interval 9/10 the length of the finite interval assigned positive probability (compare Urn II in the preceding example, or Figure 7.7). Are you really prepared to say that? *Are you prepared to bet that way?*

At this mention of betting, some "neo-Bernoullians" might enter the discussion, to disassociate themselves with Jeffrey's views. "*We* never proposed any Principle of Insufficient Reason," they might reassure you; "We don't lay down any rules at all for assigning uniform distributions or any other kind, that's up to you."[2] But this forbearance is a small favor. They must also inform you that from their point of view you may be *forced* to make a definite choice" of *some* prior distribution with which your acts are to be "consistent"; and one distribution will be as bad as another if you happen to be anxious to avoid making bets giving 9:1 odds, or worse, on *any* sub-interval of a given finite range. As a matter of fact, it is not so easy to escape this very same uniform distribution even from a Ramsey/de Finetti/Savage approach if your opinions are *uniformly* "vague." It is true that no one can tell you to assign uniform probabilities to any set of events, before watching you bet; but if your ignorance is so unflawed that you are

---

[1] *Ibid.*, p. 102.

[2] Criticizing the "Laplace rule" of assigning uniform distributions in circumstances of "ignorance," one of the founders of the subjectivist school comments: "This is not only inconsistent with the subjective point of view, but it seems to constitute in itself a very strange idea. On this point, I hope to be in accord with the supporters of the objective statistical theories.

"The belief that the *a priori* probabilities are distributed uniformly is a well defined opinion and is just as specific as the belief that these probabilities are

indifferent between staking a given price on any one of the events, your required betting behavior from that point on is hard to tell from that implied by Jeffreys.

The discussion by Raiffa and Schlaifer of the defects of any given distribution as an *expression* of "vague" opinions is detailed and frank. They demonstrate clearly that "vagueness" of opinion cannot, in general, reliably be *inferred* from any given, asserted probability distribution. It is tempting, they point out, to represent a lack of information about the "unknown parameter" of a given stochastic process, say μ by a distribution of μ with high variance, nearly uniform in the sense that the ratio of the probabilities of any two intervals of equal length approaches unity; this expression:

> . . . accords very well with two instinctive feelings: (1) that large variance is equivalent to great uncertainty and that great uncertainty is equivalent to little information, and (2) that when one knows very little about the value of some quantity, it is not unreasonable to assign roughly the same probability to every possible value of this quantity (strictly speaking, equal probabilities to equal intervals.)[1]

But the authors conclude, after analyzing several examples:

> Thus in general: if the distribution of one particular set of parameters θ has very great variance, the distributions of other, equally legitimate sets of parameters will have very little variance; so that if we choose one particular set of parameters and assign to it a very broad prior distribution, it must be because we have *reason* to assign such a distribution to these particular parameters and not to others. *The notion that a broad distribution is*

distributed in any other perfectly specified manner. Accordingly, there is no reason why the absence of opinion on the distribution of the *a priori* probabilities be taken as equivalent to the opinion that their distribution is of this or that specified form. To be misinformed of the prevailing temperature is not the same as to believe that it is zero degrees; moreover, "zero degrees" is not uniquely defined (Celsius or Fahrenheit?) and such arbitrariness in our case too." (Bruno de Finetti, "Recent Suggestions for the Reconciliation of Theories of Probability," *Proceedings of the Second Berkeley Symposium on Mathematical Statistics and Probability*, Berkeley, 1951, p. 222).

So much for the uniform distribution; clearly it is not to be *imposed* on someone of "vague" beliefs. But what *alternative* does de Finetti offer him? As de Finetti points out, *any* distribution is, from any point of view, the expression of "well defined opinion" and "specific belief" rather than of "absence of opinion."

[1] *Op. cit.*, p. 63.

an expression of vague opinions is simply untenable. There is no justification
for saying that a man who is willing to bet at odds of a million to one that
$1/$ $\mu= 0 \pm .0001$ hold an opinion which is either more or less vague or diffuse than that of a man who is willing to bet at the same odds that $\mu= 0 \pm$
$.0001.$[1]

This is well stated; but it does not seem to confront squarely the decision-maker's real problem, which is not after all to *express* opinions but to
act upon them. Suppose that his opinions really *are* "vague." Is it hard to
imagine that he is not really eager to bet at odds of a million to one *on either*
of those propositions, or on any other of the corresponding propositions
that would be implied by any given, definite probability distributions?
Offering nine to one is only the beginning, if "neo-Bernoullian" advice is
pursued conscientiously! (His discomfort will be extreme if he is, really, in
a mood to sympathize with Damon Runyon's adage: "*Nothing* is better
than five-to-three").

In their discussion of the problems of decision-makers afflicted with
"vagueness" and "lack of sureness," "neo-Bernoullians" sometimes hint at
one possible relief from the implications of their postulates that may be
allowed, as a concession to human imperfection: indecision, i.e., some violations of Postulate 1.

There is, however, an important respect in which the personal theory of
probability and utility does seem inadequate. It is not really true that any
of us knows his own mind, so-to-speak. If "you" had a consistent and
complete body of opinion, then every event would have a well-defined
probability for you and every consequence a well-defined utility. Actually, *vagueness, or indecision,* intervenes at several stages to prevent this.
Typically, you cannot tell even yourself exactly how much you would
give, to the penny, to acquire something that you want. Similarly, you cannot typically compare events. Suppose, for example, you have a coin that
you consider to be fair. Specifically you might consider all 220 possible
sequences of 20 throws with this coin to be equally probable. Most people
are able to provide themselves with such a coin or its equivalent without
perceptible doubt or vagueness. Twenty tosses of the coin will, in fact,
produce a binary fraction of twenty binary digits. Going back to the fundamental definition of "at least as possible as," you can ask yourself
whether a Republican victory in the next American presidential election
is at least as probable as the event that this binary fraction will not exceed
a specified value p. In this way, you could, in principle, determine what

[1] *Ibid.*, p. 66.

you hold the probability of a Republican victory to be with an inaccuracy of less than one part in a million. Of course, you cannot really do this, because there is a wide and vaguely defined *zone of indecision*.[1]

It does seem plausible that "vagueness" of opinion will be associated with "indecision" *in answering Koopman-type questions as to whether you "consider" one event to be at least as probable as another:* which is what Savage proposes here, implicitly accepting their meaningfulness. The question is, will such indecisiveness in committing yourself to any "definite" expression of opinion always be accompanied by "indecision" in choosing among gambles involving these events? In your *betting* behavior—say, in choosing whether to place a given stake on a certain fraction of Heads in 20 tosses of a fair coin or on a Republican victory, or in deciding at what odds you will bet *on* and at what odds you will bet *against* a Republican victory—are violations of Postulate 1 the only, or the only significant concomitant of "vagueness" in your political predictions?

Let us imagine, to the contrary, that in some circumstances you might decide quite firmly that you would *prefer* to stake the prize upon some given fraction of Heads rather than on the Republican victory: even when you would, if you put the offer to yourself, also prefer to stake the prize upon the complementary fraction of Heads than to stake it *against* the Republican victory. With respect to odds, even in terms of utilities, we might suppose you to demand at least seven-to-five in your favor to bet on the Republicans, when, if you asked yourself, you would also want seven-to-five in your favor to bet on the Democrats. Or, asymmetrically, you might *offer* five-to-three—the Runyon limit—against the Republicans, but demand at least two-to-one to bet on the Republicans: assuming, always, that you had the option not to bet.[2] This, of course, is a different

---

[1] Savage, "The Subjective Basis of Statistical Practice, p. 2.14.

[2] I.e., you might be roughly indifferent between I and II below, or between II and III, if either pair were offered to you in isolation; I and III represent the least favorable odds in utilities that would entice you to bet, respectively, on or against the Democrats in a particular election, if you had the option of "not gambling" (action II in either pair).

	Democrats	Republicans	
I	3	–5	
II	0	0	Fig. 7.9
III	–3	6	

category of violation from "indecision." Even to a "neo-Bernoullian" who can be tolerant of a certain randomness, arbitrariness, or inconstancy of decision in the presence of "ambiguity," systematic, decisive, deliberate violations of Postulate 2, the "Sure-Thing Principle," remain anathema. Yet confronted with certain choices among gambles of contrasting degrees of "ambiguity," some people—I am one—might wish to behave just this way. In other words, they might respond to such choices, and to their own "indefiniteness" of opinion, *purposefully:* though in terms of purposes the "Bernoullian" approach cannot measure, or express, or meaningfully comprehend.

To such a person, the "neo-Bernoullian" approach does not provide an adequate language to express certain considerations, certain differences among situations and states of mind, that are important to his decision-making. This is not surprising; every normative theory has the effect of telling one to ignore certain distinctions in circumstances that "should not make a difference" to behavior, and its adherents will feel no strong need for a language embodying such distinctions. Inadequacies of language, from the point of view of others, tend to be only symptomatic of more fundamental differences concerning the relevance of certain data—the importance of certain questions—to decision-making.

The Koopman/Good intuitive probability approach, for a "non-Bernoullian", "provides explicit notions of a *range* of what I have called "reasonably acceptable" opinions in given circumstances, of "upper and lower intuitive probabilities"; of "definite" comparisons of probability, with clear-cut rules of consistency relating them, contrasted with judgments distinctly less "definite," precise or sure. The related concepts of Y^0, of a distinguished distribution y^0, of a "confidence" factor ρ and a "boldness/prudence" parameter α: these are notions that a strict "neo-Bernoullian" simply does not need, yet which constitute *a language for expressing vagueness and desired responses* to it that may be highly useful to one for whom the "Bernoulli proposition" is not an adequate normative theory. And such a decision criterion as the "restricted Bayes/Hurwicz criterion" may express economically the way in which these factors influence the structure of their preferences, when they stop to think.

No normative theory has been suggested that would dictate the value of ρ, α, y^0 or Y^0 in given circumstances for a given person, any more than the "neo-Bernoullian" theory would dictate the shape of the probability distribution or the utility function. Different configurations of the variables represented in the "restricted Bayes/Hurwicz criterion" can account for many varieties of gamblers, as well as gambling situations. Yet for a given

---

(In terms of the Savage postulates, if these payoffs are utilities, then I ∄ II implies III ·> II; i.e., given I ∄ II, you should be willing to bet on the Republicans at 3:5 instead of demanding 3:6.)

individual in given circumstances, that criterion may imply no less structure to his deliberated preferences that would the "Bernoulli proposition," and inferences based upon it will be no less powerful and useful; the most prominent difference in applying it might be that he would ask himself, in his constructed, hypothetical model choices, not only how he would choose among prizes staked *on* certain propositions but also he would choose among prizes staked *against* them. It will still be true, for example, that a large range of choices "inconsistent" with his "definite" opinions will be ruled out, whatever values he assigns to ρ and α in a given situation.[1] (Assuming that Y^o is convex, choices implied by the "restricted Bayes/Hurwicz criterion" will always be compatible with all your "definite" opinions, which together define Y^o).

The "reluctant gambler" who strongly tends to "avoid ambiguity"— who demands a significant premium in terms of "best guess" expectation before he will choose an action whose expectation is "ambiguous" in preference to "not betting"—presents only one of the gambling personalities encompassed by the "restricted Bayes/Hurwicz criterion." (α is low or 0 for him, and ρ may tend to be low.) Others may be audacious, with a positive zest for ambiguity. Most may show traces of both tendencies, systematically avoiding vagueness of expectation when alternatives are available whose expectations are "definitely good," yet abandoning gambles whose expectations are "unambiguously bad" for others whose "best guess" values are no better but which offer some *basis for reasonable hope.*

What these decision-makers share is that differences in relative "vagueness" of opinion seem *relevant* to their choices. For their behavior in situations presenting such differences, the "neo-Bernoullian" theory gives wrong predictions and, by their lights, bad advice. Indeed, it sometimes seems to them, intolerantly, that the advice of the latter approach to *ignore* their own perceptions of ambiguity, their occasional unease with their best judgments of probability, could lead to *wildly irrational* decision-making; for they suspect that scarcely any faculty of discrimination is more closely related to survival than an ability to tell the difference between knowing a great deal about the consequences of their actions and knowing very little.

---

[1] Thus, the traditional (Good's "type I") minimax criterion may be criticized for "taking too many opinions into account," or acting "as if" one had no "definite" opinions whatever. In terms of a "restricted minimax criterion" this would mean acting "as if" the "lower intuitive probability" of any given proposition were indefinitely close to 0 and its "upper intuitive probability" indefinitely close to 1. This would be unacceptable to you when you "feel sure" that its probability (for you) can be confined within much narrower limits; and it would make you look foolish to those who felt strongly that you "should" feel that.

*

AMBIGUITY AND THE UTILITY AXIOMS

IN THE LAST two chapters the following testable propositions have been advanced: (1) certain information states can be meaningfully identified as ambiguous; (2) in these states, many otherwise reasonable people tend to violate the Savage axioms with respect to certain choices; (3) their behavior is deliberate and not *readily* reversed upon reflection; (4) certain patterns of "violating" behavior can be distinguished and described in terms of a specified decision rule; (5) this decision rule is one which has, in the past, been recommended or suggested as appropriate by reputable theorists; (6) many of the people concerned recognize the rule as reflecting the sort of considerations that influence their behavior and the rough character of actual mental processes by which they arrive at their decisions.

Yet is this behavior reasonable? The considerations above, if accepted, might seem to throw the burden of proof upon those who would claim it is *not*. But this is not likely to throw proponents of the Ramsey-Savage axioms into confusion; their whole approach, after all, is designed precisely to deal with this sort of challenge. They have been admirably explicit about the types of evidence and the tests of reasonableness they regard as valid, and "normality" is not one of them. They would not hesitate at all to conclude that many or all "generally reasonable" people, including themselves, behave on frequent occasion in quite unreasonable ways, unworthy of deliberate imitation.

---

*This chapter may be regarded as an appendix, the main argument of this study having concluded with Chapter Seven. A number of special topics are considered here, mainly dealing with relations between the "restricted Bayes/ *minimax*" criterion and various proposed "utility" axioms; the argument tends to be somewhat more speculative, controversial and introspective, even, than the preceding.

"A suitable theory" of reasonable behavior, as Good puts it, "must never force you into a position that *after mature consideration* you regard as untenable."[1] We have used just this test to question the suitability of the Savage theory; in fairness, we must apply it just as stringently to the decision rule under consideration. The most direct way to do this is to seek out, systematically, situations in which the rule would imply behavior violating the various propositions that have been advanced as defining criteria of rationality.

Thus, in this chapter we shall ask: Are *all* of the choices and their consequences comprising or implied by the given pattern of decision likely to prove acceptable to the decision-maker, on mature reflection in the light of all the proposed postulates and *all logical consequences* of those postulates? To the extent that such probing fails to discredit this rule, it will have demonstrated not only its acceptability but its *superiority*, for certain people, at least, in certain situations, as normative theory over those axioms and theorems with which it conflicts.

I have already asserted that many people will persist in certain choices, consistent with this rule, despite the knowledge that they are directly violating one of the Savage postulates. This would seem to constitute in itself quite a powerful test, since those postulates (and the Sure-Thing Principle above all) have been chosen as foundation-stones precisely because their intuitive appeal is considered maximally compelling, and because they put meaningful restrictions on acceptable behavior with minimum requirements of prior observation. If you violate one of the postulates, then consistent behavior must lead you to violate indefinitely many of the propositions deducible from the postulates; and it might seem that anyone who shamelessly violates the Sure-Thing Principle will have no qualms about violating any of the more complex propositions based upon it.

However, this cannot be taken for granted. It might be argued that choices directly testing one of the postulates require such special circumstances as to be somewhat unnatural, leading to unrepresentative behavior. This is a dubious point, since these "artificial" situations have been designed expressly to permit *decisive* inferences from a small body of observed choices; but it is true that if we do have access to the larger body of observations that is required to make more complex postulates meaningful, it becomes possible to apply consistency tests in a much wider variety of situations, some of which may be more natural to the subjects and provide firmer basis for their intuition.

When we have observed only a few of his choices among bets, a subject's subsequent choices are constrained by the Savage axioms only within

---

[1] I. J. Good, *Probability and the Weighing of Evidence*, p. 5, italics added.

very wide limits. We can as yet make only very general predictions of his behavior with the aid of the theory; it is "hardest," at this stage, to detect him in a definite inconsistency (though all the more significant when we do!). But by the time we have gathered enough information to enable us to assign definite probabilities to a number of events and definite utilities to various consequences, he is thoroughly pinned down; the theory *determines* all his choices among bets involving these events and consequences, and every new choice among such bets is fraught with potential inconsistency. If we imagine, then, that we have already observed a significant number of your choices, it becomes "easy" to test you for subtle and complex "inconsistencies," conflicts with theorems that were simply untestable at the earlier stage of investigation.

In particular, if we suppose that you have obeyed the axioms in a sufficient number of cases to enable us to assign definite probabilities to many events, we can proceed to test propositions—deducible from the postulates—concerning your consistent choices among bets with "known" probabilities. Certain of these propositions antedate the Savage postulates themselves, having appeared as axioms in their own right in the von Neumann-Morgenstern or subsequent axiomatizations of utility. Although these "utility axioms," which are meaningful only to the extent that certain probabilities are "known," are necessarily of more limited applicability than the Savage postulates (which do not require such prior measurements), they are quite generally regarded as intuitively compelling within their sphere of application: perhaps even more so than the Savage postulates, to some theorists for whom they are more familiar. We must proceed, then, to confront our presumptive violator with the several varieties of violation to which his decision rule may expose him. As we shall see, Howard Raiffa and John Pratt have conjectured that people who lightheartedly violate the Sure-Thing Principle may yet be dismayed to find their behavior conflicting with certain utility axioms (or theorems, as they are in the Savage approach).

To begin, we shall apply the decision rule mechanically in certain hypothetical situations, without direct appeal to intuition, to expose the fact that it does, in special circumstances, lead to violation of the utility axioms. Since we are ultimately interested in the reasonableness of this behavior in the light of such consequences, we must then focus upon similar situations which are simple enough to afford valid play to intuition. (However, whatever the results of mature reflection upon this behavior pattern, the fact that it does follow from the given decision rule is of considerable independent interest. For to the extent that the rule is *descriptively* valid, we shall have isolated a significant class of situations in which systematic violation of the utility axioms is *to be expected*, among many otherwise reasonable and at least moderately reflective subjects. To put it in other terms, there may be an important class of "consequences" to which it is impossible to assign von Neumann-Morgenstern utilities, for the subjects in question.)

The utility axioms[1] impose restrictions on "rational"[2] preferences among risky *prospects*, i.e., actions whose uncertain outcomes are associated with "known" probabilities of occurrence. In the von Neumann-Morgenstern discussion, these probabilities are interpreted as known, "objective frequencies"; however, it is a natural extension of their approach to regard them as subjective probabilities we have derived from observation of a subject's prior betting behavior. These earlier bets enabling us to measure his probabilities, may have involved only *two* distinct outcomes. If he follows the von Neumann-Morgenstern axioms in his choices among prospects (or, if he *continues* to obey the Savage axioms with respect to these new choices), we can proceed to assign "von Neumann-Morgenstern utilities" to all outcomes and prospects, so that mathematical expectations of utility computed on the basis of these numbers will correspond to his actual preferences among prospect and outcomes. Hence the name, "utility axioms."

Prospects are known metaphorically as "lottery tickets" in which the alternative outcomes are "prizes." If A and B are prizes, the lottery tickets offering either A with probability p or B with probability $(1-p)$ may be symbolized: $(A,B; p)$. In formal treatments of the theory, the "prizes," "outcomes" or "consequences" are primitive notions, not defined explicitly; they are abstract entities, among which certain relationships are postulated. They have been variously interpreted, as "events,"[3] as amounts of money, as "market-baskets" of goods or more general vectors, and as other

---

[1] John von Neumann and Oskar Morgenstern, *The Theory of Games and Economic Behavior*, Princeton, 1944, pp. 24–29, 617–632. Jacob Marschak presents an alternate set in "Rational Behavior, Uncertain Prospects, and Measurable Utility," *Econometrica*, May 1949, pp. 139–140.

[2] This interpretation of the von Neumann-Morgenstern axioms and the later sets has been almost universal. It is particularly insisted upon by Marschak; like rules of logic and arithmetic, Marschak says, the utility axioms serve to describe the behavior of men "who, it is believed, cannot be 'all fools all the time.'" See also, "Why 'Should' Statisticians and Businessmen Maximize Moral Expectation?", *Proceedings of the Second Berkeley Symposium on Mathematical Statistics and Probability*, University of California Press, 1951, pp. 493–506. However, it is interesting to note that von Neumann and Morgenstern themselves deliberately refrained from associating the notion of "rationality" with their axioms on risk-behavior, to which *they* assigned no normative significance.

[3] von Neumann and Morgenstern, *op. cit.*, p. 19; they use the term as equivalent to what Savage calls "consequences."

lottery tickets; no discussion has ruled out more general interpretations. Marschak, for example, asserts: "If the space X of 'outcomes' and the space S of strategies are defined, this permits us to take care of all human decisions, transcending conventional economics and including the private man's choice of profession or wife, the legislator's choice of election tactics or national policies or military and administrative decision."[1][2] The axioms imply that an individual has a complete preference ordering over all prizes and over all lottery tickets, and they specify certain additional restrictions on his preferences among lottery tickets.

For example, the von Neumann-Morgenstern axiom 3:B:b[2] requires that if outcome A is preferred to B, then A must be preferred to any prospect (A,B;p) where p is less than 1. This property of the preference-system including prospects is known as "monotonicity."

In later formulations of the axioms, a key position has been ascribed to what Samuelson calls the Special (or Strong) Independence Assumption. In one form, this states: if you are indifferent between A and B, you must be indifferent between (A,C;p) and (B,C;p) for any C and p (the same in both prospects). The same relationship applies if "indifference" is replaced by "preference" throughout. Samuelson has also stated this in the form: If lottery ticket A is better than B, and lottery ticket C is better than D, then an even chance of getting A or C is better than an even chance of getting B or D.[3] Samuelson comments that, "This is simply a version of what Dr. Savage calls the 'sure-thing principle.' . . . It is this independence axiom that is crucial for the Bernoulli-Savage theory of maximization of expected cardinal utility."[4] The relationship of this postulate to Savage's Postulate 2 becomes obvious if we assume that the outcome C not only has the same probability p in both prospects but is contingent in both upon the occurrence of the same event:

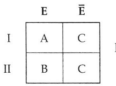

Fig. 8.1

---

[1] Marschak, "Why 'Should' Statistics and Businessmen Maximize Moral Expectation?", p. 499.

[2] *Op. cit.*, p. 26.

[3] This is paraphrased from: Samuelson, "Probability, Utility, and the Independence Axiom," *Econometrica*, Vol. 20, No. 4, October 1952, p. 672.

[4] *Ibid.*, p. 672. "Around 1950, Marschak, Dalkey, Nash and others independently recognized the crucial importance of the independence axiom"; *ibid.*, p. 673.

The Strong Independence Assumption then becomes the familiar proposition that action I is preferred to II, or II is preferred to I, or I and II are indifferent, as A is preferred to B, B preferred to A, or A and B are indifferent. The only difference, in this instance, from the Sure-Thing Principle is that the probability of E is assumed "known," and A, B, C are lottery tickets with known probabilities (including such "lotteries" as [A;1], [B;1], etc., otherwise known as "sure prospects").[1]

In early critiques of the axioms, the counter-examples that turned up were rather an odd lot. They included the player of Russian Roulette, or the mountaineer who sought out (without publicity) the most dangerous peaks;[2] another is a man who would not bet a dime to a dollar that the sun will rise tomorrow.[3] It is possible to explain such behavior in other terms, but even if such persons *are* interpreted as violating the axioms, they do not contradict strongly the view expressed by Robert Strotz: "In my opinion, it would be a strange man indeed who would persist in violating them."[4] These people *are* pretty strange. Russian roulette players may not be crazy, but it might well be argued that a working theory of rational choice could afford to ignore them.

More recently, Maurice Allais and others have produced some examples, one of which we shall consider later, which tempt less eccentric subjects to violate the axioms. Of course, even the most pronounced adherents of the axioms expect that people will "frequently and flagrantly behave in disaccord with the utility theory,"[5] just as they will violate any normative theory, or principles of logic or arithmetic. What is claimed is that it is *unreasonable* for them to do so, and that it should be possible through analysis and demonstration to persuade an intelligent person to see this and to "correct" his decisions, at least if he were given "a couple of years to brood over his answers."[6]

---

[1] The close relation, in spirt, to the notion of "admissability" or "non-domination" is evident here; but note that A, B and C are not, in general, "consequences," but are sets of possible consequences corresponding to the separate "states of the world" that *comprise* the *events* E and $\bar{E}$. Neither I nor II will, in general, *dominate* the other; i.e., have a preferred or indifferent consequence for *every* "state of the world."

[2] Both of these could be held to violate Axiom 3:B:b; of two prospects offering the same two outcomes, they prefer one with a higher probability of the less desirable outcome.

[3] He violates 3:B:c, the Continuity axiom: if A is preferred to B and B is preferred to C, there must be *some* prospect (A,C:p) that is preferred to B, with p less than 1.

[4] Robert H. Strotz, "Cardinal Utility," *American Economic Review*, May 1953, pp.

[5] Savage, *op. cit.,* p. 100.

[6] Samuelson, *op. cit.,*

Let us now consider *prospects that offer as "outcomes" actions whose consequences are ambiguous;* in other terms, lottery tickets which offer (with "known" probabilities) other *bets* as prizes. We could say, "with other lottery tickets as prizes," except that I wish to reserve the terms prospect and lottery ticket for bets the probabilities of whose outcomes are stipulated to be known *definitely* to the subject: i.e., the outcomes of which are contingent upon events *with respect to which he obeys the the Savage axioms.* We shall assume that such events exist. Specifically, let us assume that we have discovered a coin you are convinced is fair; you act "as if" you assigned definite probabilities to every finite sequence of heads and tails, and the same probability to every sequence of the same length.[1] We shall further suppose that we have used this coin to calibrate your utility scale, by constructing lottery tickets with amounts of cash contingent upon the occurrence of given sequences and observing your choices among these prospects. Thus, assuming we have started by assigning arbitrarily to the money outcomes A and C the utility numbers 10 and 0, if we represent the outcome B by the utility number 5 this means that you have actually been *observed* to be indifferent between B and the prospect (A,C;1/2) (where A is contingent upon, say, the occurrence of Heads on a single flip of the fair coin); or else it means that you can reliably be expected to be indifferent, on the basis of other observed choices and your general consistency with the utility axioms in choosing among prospects. To specify a particular set of von Neumann-Morgenstern utilities, as we shall do below, is to postulate that you are a person with particular, well-defined preferences among given *prospects.*

Let us suppose that the outcomes A and C above are $100 and $0, respectively, and that you happen to be indifferent between the sure possession of $40 and a prospect offering $100 if a fair coin comes up Heads and $0 if it comes up Tails. We assign $40 the utility number 5. Suppose, further, that we have found you indifferent between the following two actions, where R_{II} signifies drawing a red ball, B_{II} a black ball, from our original Urn II (in the two-urn example, Chapter Five) known to contain exactly 50 red and 50 black balls.

	50 R_{II}	50 B_{II}
I	$100	$ 0
II	$ 40	$ 40

Fig. 8.2

---

[1]This disproving my earlier, pessimistic conjectures about the ease of finding such a coin, or, I should say, such a subject; again we see the advantages of hypothetical experiments as a basis for discussion.

In other words, you are willing to pay up to "$40 for $100 on Red." Similarly, we suppose that you are willing to pay the same amount if you are offered, alternatively, "$100 on Black." Substituting the known utility numbers for money outcomes, we assert: $p.10 + (1-p).0 = 5$, when p is your subjective probability of drawing a red ball from Urn II, so that we can calculate directly:

$$p = \tfrac{1}{2}.$$

But even without this calculation, we could have derived the result immediately from the observations that lie behind it if we assume that you obey Savage's Postulate 1, the complete ordering of actions. The fact that you are willing to pay the same amount for "$100 on Red$_{II}$" as for $100 on Heads" with your fair coin, and the same amount for "$100 on Black$_{II}$" (or "$100 against Red$_{II}$") as for "$100 on Tails" means that you assign the same probability to Red$_{II}$ as to Heads; and we have already found the latter probability to be $1/2$. The utility calculations merely reflect these observed correspondences.

Now we consider bets with respect to Urn I, for which you have not been told the proportion of red to black balls. Let us assume that you are one of those who would pay something *less* for "$100 on Red$_I$" or for "$100 on Black$_I$", if *one* of these contingencies were offered you, than you would for "$100 on Red$_{II}$". For a specific example, suppose that you follow the "Bayes/minimax" rule $[\rho \cdot y^\circ + (1 - \rho)y^{min}{}_x](X)$, that having observed a certain sample of balls from Urn I your "best guess" distribution y° over (Red$_I$, Black$_I$) is $(1/2, 1/2)$ with $\rho = 1/2$, and the set of "reasonably acceptable" distributions Y° ranges from $(1/4, 3/4)$ to $(3/4, 1/4)$. The bet on Red$_I$ would then have a utility value to you of $[1/2(1/2 \cdot 10) + 1/2(1/4 \cdot 10)] = 3.75$, or something less than $40 (since $40 has utility 5).

Finally, we offer you the following option: if a fair coin comes up Heads, you will be offered action III below; if it comes up Tails, you will be offered action IV.

| | 100 | |
	Red$_I$	Black$_I$
III	$100	$ 0
IV	$ 0	$100

Fig. 8.3

This is a *lottery ticket with actions III and IV as prizes:* the prospect (III, IV;1/2). Since you are indifferent between III and IV and would pay the same amount X for either of them (X < $40, U(X) = 3.75) then *if you were to obey the utility axioms when actions of this nature were offered as prizes in lot-*

teries you would be indifferent between this lottery ticket and either III or IV considered separately; you should be willing to pay for this prospect the same amount X you would give, say, for III.

But consistent application of your decision rule would decree otherwise. Your payoffs now depend on the joint results of flipping a coin and drawing a ball; there are four possibilities shown below with the corresponding outcomes:

	Red (p)		Black (1–p)	
	Heads ($\frac{1}{2}$)	Tails ($\frac{1}{2}$)	Heads ($\frac{1}{2}$)	Tails ($\frac{1}{2}$)
(III,IV; $\frac{1}{2}$)	$100	$0	$0	$100

Fig. 8.4

The probability of any *one* of these *joint events* will depend on the probability *p* assigned to a drawing of Red from Urn I, and we have assumed that this might vary between 1/4 and 3/4. But the probability distribution *over payoffs* "given" that a Red ball is drawn is unambiguously (1/2, 1/2); and the probability distribution over payoffs given that a Black ball is drawn is the *same*, (1/2, 1/2). Thus there is no "least favorable distribution" distinct from the "most favorable distribution" *over payoffs*. Whether Red or Black is drawn, and hence for every component distribution over (Red, Black) there is the same distribution over payoffs, probability 1/2 of $100 and probability 1/2 of $0.[1]

---

[1] A somewhat less "logical" grouping of the same joint outcomes of the coin toss and the drawing may make this result more obvious:

	$\frac{1}{2}$·p Heads/Red	$\frac{1}{2}$(1–p) Tails/Black	$\frac{1}{2}$(1–p) Heads/Black	$\frac{1}{2}$·p Tails/Red	
(III,IV; $\frac{1}{2}$)	$100	$100	$0	$0	Fig. 8.5

$$\underbrace{\qquad\qquad}_{\frac{1}{2}}\qquad\underbrace{\qquad\qquad}_{\frac{1}{2}}$$

The probability of any *one* of these joint *events* will depend on the probability *p* assigned to a drawing of Red from Urn I, which we have assumed might vary between 1/4 and 3/4. But for every probability *p* within these limits (and in fact, for every *p* between 0 and 1), the *combined* probability of the first two columns or joint events is 1/2, and similarly for the last two columns. Hence, there is a single, unambiguous distribution over the payoffs, $100, $0.

In terms of expected utilities, $\min_x = \text{est}_x = 5$, so the decision rule gives: $\rho \cdot 5 + (1-\rho)5 = 5$. This implies that you should be willing to pay $40 for this lottery ticket, or more than you would for either of its "prizes," actions III or IV, if offered separately. The rule clearly forces you to violate Samuelson's Independence Axiom, since you *prefer* (III,IV;1/2) to (III,III;1/2) although you were indifferent between III and IV. Likewise, it implies that you should be indifferent between the prospect (III,IV;1/2) and the prospect (I,II;1/2), despite the fact that both I and II are preferred either to III or to IV considered separately.

So much for the implications of the decision rule; are these results likely to be accepted as corresponding to the decision-maker's actual preferences? As we have analyzed the prospect (III,IV;1/2) above, it offers *exactly the same distribution of payoffs* as action I or action II; we should be disturbed if the decision rule did *not* assign them the same value, and surprised if a decision-maker were not, after such an analysis, indifferent between them.

The utility axioms would then compel us to reconsider our earlier evaluation of the two component "prizes", actions III and IV. In comparing each of them, separately, with the lottery ticket (III,IV;1/2), we note that all three alternatives offer the same "best guess" distributions over the payoffs $100, $0, but that the former two alternatives are ambiguous and the latter, subjectively, is not. It is entirely consistent with a pattern of "penalizing" ambiguity of payoff probabilities to prefer the lottery ticket, or "mixed strategy," to either of these two ambiguous components.

It is something of a coincidence that the payoff distribution to this particular prospect is unambiguous where the component strategies are not, and this fact may not be immediately obvious to many subjects. However, the following argument, suggested by Howard Raiffa,[1] may clarify the situation for them.

Imagine that the ball has already been drawn from Urn I, but you have not yet seen its color. If, on the one hand, it is actually red, then the prospect (III,IV;$\frac{1}{2}$) offers you an unambiguous 50-50 chance of $100 or $0; for if the coin turns up Heads, you choose action III and collect $100 when the ball is revealed, and if it is Tails, you choose action IV and collect nothing. Likewise if the ball is black; the prospect offers you exactly a 50-50 chance of III (paying $0 in this case) or IV (paying $100). So you are "guaranteed" exactly a 50-50 chance of $100 or $0 "whether the ball is red or black" (assuming the probabilities of Heads or Tails to be unambiguous, or "definite," for you).

---

[1] Howard Raiffa, "Risk, Ambiguity, and the Savage Axioms: Comment,: *Quarterly Journal of Economics*, Vol. LXXV, No. 4, November 1961, p. 693.

Raiffa points out that you should be willing to pay at least as much as you would pay for this prospect—or for actions I or II with respect to Urn II—for the opportunity to *choose freely* between actions III and IV with respect to Urn I. For given this opportunity, nothing can prevent you from flipping a coin between the two actions, choosing III if heads, IV if tails. In other words, if you are allowed to choose either III or IV, you are also free to choose (III, IV; 1/2), so the opportunity should be worth at least as much as the latter option. Raiffa has conducted such hypothetical experiments with many classes of students at the Harvard Business School and graduate classes in statistics. He reports that a majority of students will offer considerably more initially for the opportunity to choose between actions I and II than for the opportunity to choose between actions III and IV: e.g., $35 in the first instance and $5 in the second. However, when the availability of a "mixed strategy" based on coin-flipping is brought to their attention, he asserts that eventually they change their opinions and offer as much for the second opportunity as for the first. As we have seen, this conclusion does not contradict the hypothesis that they follow our decision rule concerning ambiguity. If they do obey the Savage axioms with respect to *some* hypothetical coins and urns with known, 50-50 composition, then they should indeed conclude, after analysis, that these various options are equivalent.

By the same token, it is important to notice that such experiments are crucially different from those suggested in Chapter Five in which you were never invited to choose both a color and an urn freely; in those, randomized strategies with the effect of banishing ambiguity were infeasible. It would be interesting to know how much students who had finally been persuaded by Raiffa to offer as much for a free choice between III and IV as for a free choice between I and II would *subsequently* be willing to pay for, say, action III alone, offered in isolation as the sole option. (Raiffa conducted no experiments in which the students were not offered free choice of color.) My conjecture is that they might well go back to their original, low bids, e.g., $5. It is clear that the rationale used effectively to influence their choices in the earlier situation would no longer be available. If they tend to act "as if" the outcomes of "a bet on Red$_1$" were ambiguous, no amount of coin-flipping should serve to lessen this tendency, for it cannot remove the ambiguity.

Anyone who uses this rule, then, will violate the von Neumann-Morgenstern utility axioms in his choices between certain prospects that offer ambiguous bets as prizes. Is this a powerful argument for rejecting the reasonableness of his behavior?

At least two proponents of the Savage approach have argued that it is. Although we have already covered the substance of their comments above, it is worthwhile at the cost of some duplication to examine their arguments in detail, since their language appears to throw the actions of our hypothetical violator into a more questionable light than might appear from my discussion.

THE PRATT/RAIFFA CRITICISMS AND THE VALUE OF RANDOMIZATION

John Pratt has focused his comments upon the following examples from Chapter Five:

	R_I	B_I	R_{II}	B_{II}
1	a	b	b	b
2	b	a	b	b
3	b	b	a	b
4	b	b	b	a

With column group labels: 100 spanning R_I and B_I; 50 over R_{II}; 50 over B_{II}.

If there are 50 each of R_{II} and B_{II} and 100 I's divided in an unknown way, you would prefer 3 to 1 and 4 to 2, and you claim this is not unreasonable. Suppose you are now offered the following opportunity: you may flip an "unambiguously" fair coin (or better, do the equivalent with another urn); if you get heads, you may choose 1 or 3; if tails, you may choose 2 or 4. *If you make your choice after flipping, you will surely choose 3 or 4.* If you are required to choose before flipping, *it certainly does not seem reasonable to me to make a decision you will soon regret (after flipping), so you seem to me to be forced to choose 3 and 4.* Now this choice gives you an "unambiguous" probability 1/4 of obtaining the preferred prize a, and the opposite choice (1 and 2) does also. It certainly seems unreasonable to me to prefer (3,4) to (1,2) when they give identical, "unambiguous" probability distributions over the consequences. (My italics.)[1]

The example here is, of course, precisely the one that we have been discussing above. Again we consider the choice between the "compound lottery tickets" (1,2;1/2) and (3,4;1/2) where 3 and 4 are actions with unambiguous distributions of payoff, and where, considered as pure alternatives, 3 is preferred to 1 and 4 is preferred to 2. It will be clear from our earlier discussion that I agree thoroughly with Pratt's assertion that the two

---

[1] Private communication. In this case, "you" is me. Pratt refers to "Risk, Ambiguity, and the Savage Axioms."

"mixed strategies" give "identical, 'unambiguous' probability distributions over the consequences," and hence that, like Pratt, I see no reasonable basis for preferring one to the other. But I do not agree that indifference between these two mixed strategies is necessarily inconsistent with the earlier pattern of preferences between the alternative pure actions. Let us examine closely Pratt's reasons for thinking otherwise.

Pratt's key assumption is in the first sentence italicized above: that *after flipping a coin* to determine the pair of actions available to me, I would, if the coin came up heads, prefer 3 to 1, and if the coin came up tails, prefer 4 to 2. He concludes from this that if I had to commit myself to a choice from each pair *before* knowing which pair would become available as a result of the coin toss, I would be "forced to choose 3 and 4," because to choose instead 1 and 2 would be to make a decision I would surely "soon *regret* (after flipping)." (By Pratt's logic, a choice of 1 and 4 or of 2 and 3 would expose me to a 50% chance of "regret after flipping" with no compensating chance of gain over the choice of 3 and 4.) If, on the contrary, I committed myself to 1 and 2 before flipping, Pratt argues, then if the coin came up heads I would be willing to pay a dollar (say) to be released from my commitment to 1 so that I could choose the action I really prefer, 3; and likewise, if the coin came up tails I would be willing to pay a dollar to be able to choose 4 instead of 2. Why not save the dollar by picking 3 and 4 in the first place: even if I had to pay a small premium for this option?

The flaw in this argument is that, on the basis of my own introspection and analysis of the problem, I would *not* be willing to pay a dollar, or anything, to be released from a commitment to 1 and 2 *after flipping*. The reasoning that leads me to this conclusion is not self-evident, which is just why the somewhat duplicative discussion of this example seems worthwhile.

It remains true that if confronted with a choice between actions 1 and 3, I would consider it reasonable to prefer 3 to 1 and might pay a premium of a dollar to get it: if these were the only alternatives available and I did not know enough—or knew too much that was contradictory—about the process that had made this particular pair of alternatives available instead of some other to assign definite probabilities to all possible offers. Yet I maintain that I might be indifferent between committing myself to 1 or to 3 in advance of the particular compound lottery that Pratt describes, and indifferent between these two actions *after* flipping, in the event that the *given* lottery presented me with this particular pair of actions and I were permitted to choose freely after all.

My rationale for indifference between the two compound lottery tickers (1,2;1/2) and (3,4;1/2) is perhaps sufficiently clear; it is essentially the same one that Pratt gives. What may be less clear is why I would not be anxious to be released from a commitment to 1 or 2 *after* the "super-lottery" had been conducted. This attitude is closely related to another aspect of my preferences to which Pratt does not refer but which he would, no doubt, find equally paradoxical. In saying that I would pay the same amount for one compound lottery as for the other, I am saying, in particular, that I might pay *more* for the lottery ticket (1,2;1/2) than I might pay for *either* of its "prizes," the pure strategies 1 or 2, if either of these had become available to me through circumstances other than the operation of a "stochastic process" of precisely these assumed characteristics (i.e., involving this set of "prizes" and these "known" probabilities). And if action 1 (or action 2) *had* become available to me as a result of this particular process, I might pay more for it than if it had become available through some other, undefined process.

This pattern of preferences has nothing essentially to do with "suspicion" of the unknown circumstances that might have led to the offer of action 1. It could hold even though I were convinced that the person offering me these bets had no pecuniary interest in the outcome of a given bet; that he had, for example, only an unprejudiced interest in determining my actual expectations and degrees of uncertainty, and that he had no more and perhaps much less information than I on the actual outcomes to be expected from the bets. The point is not that I *distrust* the nature of the process that might have led to an offer of action 1 in isolation, but that I simply do not know what it was; whereas if 1 became available to me as the result of a compound lottery (1,2;1/2) I know that the same process provided an "equal probability" of giving me the opportunity to choose action 2. It does not follow necessarily, nor in every case, that this will be "a difference that makes a difference;" yet it may be, with these particular payoffs. For if my decision is to choose whichever action results from the lottery (1,2;1/2), I feel that *my probabilities for the payoffs "win" and "lose"* (1, 0) associated with this decision are "definite," in a way that they are *not* "definite" for, say, action 1 when offered by itself; but in the *same* way that they are "definite" for actions 3 or 4, or for the lottery (3,4;1/2). (It so happens in the latter three cases that I *also* assign definite probabilities to the occurrence of the various possible *events*, R_{II}, B_{II}, but this is irrelevant to my choices. *It is my probabilities over payoffs, not probabilities over events, that determine my decisions.*)

In principle, my choices among a given set of gambles reflect my opinions, which may take the form of "definite" probabilities, concerning the possible outcomes of those particular gambles. These opinions need not be derived from any opinions concerning average outcomes or frequencies in some large set of known or hypothetical trials under "similar" conditions involving "similar" events (i.e., I need not consider explicitly or even admit the possibility of other trials under conditions essentially "similar" to the ones that affect these particular gambles, in order to have "definite" opinions about the outcomes). On the other hand, when it *is* plausible to imagine large sets of "independent" experiments under "similar" conditions, then "definite" probabilities assigned to the outcomes of a particular trial should lead to the assignment of "definite" probabilities to average outcomes or frequencies in the overall set of trials. If, under conditions when "independence" and "similarity" could plausibly be assumed, I do *not* act "as if" I assigned "definite" probabilities to average outcomes, it could be inferred that I would not act "as if" I assigned "definite" probabilities to the outcomes possible in a single trial.

D. R. Cox has made this point concerning consistency between one's subjective probabilities for the outcomes of a single trial and one's opinions concerning average outcomes or frequencies, in commenting upon the "neo-Bayesian" (*not* "neo-Bernoullian") paper by C. A. B. Smith discussed above in Chapter Three:

> Suppose that the product law in its usual form is introduced into the theory of subjective probability. Let A_1, A_2, ... be independent events all with the same [subjective] probability p; for instance the A_1 may refer to different fields of application. By the weak law of large numbers, for large n Dr. Smith's consistent man will bet very heavily that nearly a proportion p of the events A_1, ..., A_n are true, i.e., he will bet heavily that his probabilities can be given a frequency interpretation. (Of course, this can be extended to events not all of the same probability, events that are not independent, etc.)[1]

---

[1] D. R. Cox, "Discussion on Dr. Smith's Paper," *Journal of the Royal Statistical Society*, Series B, Vol. 23, No. 1, 1961, pp. 27–28; commenting on C. A. B. Smith, "Consistency in Statistical Inference and Decision," (*op. cit.*).

Cox goes on to ask, "Would it not be better to start from this point? This would be akin to the attitude of Reichenbach." The answer of a "neo-Bayesian" to this would be: (a) In order to measure your current probabilities for the outcomes of a particular experiment (which may be what concerns us directly) it is not *necessary* for us to investigate your opinions concerning average, "long run" outcomes in independent trials; (b) in order for you to "have" definite probabilities for the outcomes of a single experiment (i.e., for us to be able to infer definite probabilities from your choices among various gambles offered), it is not necessary that it be *possible* for us to find definite probabilities for you over any given large set of experiments including this one (i.e., you need not admit that *any* given experiments we might propose were either "independent of" or "similar to" the present one).

Smith's reply to this comment is also pertinent:

> Dr. Cox's suggestion of a relationship between pignic probabilities and anticipated frequencies seems correct . . . If we are willing to offer odds w: 1 on each of a series of events A_1, A_2. . . ., this means that we anticipate this betting to be profitable, i.e., that, in the long run, a fraction at least as great as $w/(1+w)$ of the events will occur."[1]

In seeking to understand the distinction that I recognize in my betting behavior between events whose probabilities are "unambiguous" or "definite" and those whose probabilities are not, it is useful to ask what sort of evidence would enable me to *predict* it. What evidence would lead me to *infer* that, if I were offered gambles involving a particular event, I would *not* act "as if" I assigned a "definite" probability to that event? The comments above suggest that, if a large class of "independent" trials involving essentially "similar" events could be defined in a way acceptable to me, my choices among gambles concerning average outcomes in that class of events should provide such evidence; the possibility of inferring "definite" probabilities for me concerning a single trial should be predictable from the "definiteness" or lack of "definiteness" of my opinions concerning "long run" frequencies in a large sequence of similar, independent trials, *when* the latter can be appropriately defined.

It seems to me that my own preferences and opinions, so far as I can determine them by conscientious reflection, would be consistent with this hypothesis. In terms of the gambles we have been discussing, I would be willing to bet heavily, *giving long odds*, that in a large set of bets involving "independent" events which I identified beforehand as being, in terms of my subjective uncertainties of the outcomes, "similar to" gambles 3 or 4 or the prospect (3,4; 1/2), I would *win* "almost exactly" a definite, specified percentage of the gambles. Specifically, I would offer long odds that I would *win* "very nearly" 25 per cent of the time, neither more nor less. With payoffs of 1, 0, I would expect (and would back my opinion with bets at long odds) my average payoff in a long series of independent but closely similar bets to be "very close" to .25.

I would make similar predictions, and lay similar long-odds bets, on the long-run average consequences of accepting lotteries "like" (1, 2; 1/2). This is one more difference, so far as my opinions and my betting behavior are concerned,

---

[1] C. A. B. Smith, *ibid.*, p. 35. Smith also, of course, assumes "independence" of the events in question here. On propositions concerning "odds," see Appendix to Chapter Three, above. Smith's "pignic probabilities" are what I have renamed "betting probabilities."

between that mixed strategy and its ambiguous component strategies. *I would not at all be willing to give long odds on a proposition that the average rewards of accepting a large sequence of bets "like" action I would be "very close" to any particular, specified number.*

My *reluctance to gamble at high odds* on the latter proposition does not reflect a definite opinion that the average rewards of such "ambiguous" gambles will be *lower* than the average for gambles "like" action 3 (i.e., a definite belief that "Nature is against me," in situations when my opinions are "vague"). What it does reflect in my state of mind is precisely the "vagueness" of my beliefs; I do not feel I *have* definite opinions as to the relative probabilities of various average rewards to "bets like this." (My opinions would be much more "definite" if I *had* a distinct belief that Nature was for me, or against me, or rigorously neutral, in situations when my confused or ambiguous information and opinions left "Nature's choice of strategy" so unconstrained).

I do not offer these comments on my preferences among gambles concerning long-run average outcomes of sequences of events as "explaining" or revealing the "cause" of my postulated betting behavior with respect to the single-trial situations we have discussed throughout this thesis. I merely conjecture that my overall betting behavior, covering choices among both sorts of gambles, reveals a certain, rough "logical consistency not with the Savage postulates, but with some such decision criterion as the "restricted Bayes/Hurwicz criterion."[1]

To assign "definite" probabilities over all possible utility *payoffs* to a given action—implying a "definite" expected utility for that action—it may not be necessary to assign "definite" probabilities to all relevant *events*. By the same token, it may be possible for me to assign "definite" probabilities to long-run average payoffs for a certain class of gambles without acting "as if" I assigned "definite" probabilities to the relative frequencies of relevant events.

We have already discussed the argument for assigning "definite" probabilities to the payoffs associated with the prospect (1, 2; 1/2), or the decision to let a choice between 1 and 2 (both having been offered) depend on the toss of a coin. There are still other, quite different experimental conditions in which bets on R_I or B_I might have, for me, an unambiguous prob-

---

[1] Not, probably, with $\alpha = 0$; I have focussed here upon the "Bayes/minimax criterion" because Pratt and Raiffa (see below) addressed their comments to my use of that criterion in "Risk, Ambiguity, and the Savage Axioms." The difference between the two criteria is not important in this context (though $\alpha > 0$ would reduce, and α sufficiently high would eliminate, the "value" of a mixed strategy, or randomisation, relative to the value of its "ambiguous" component strategies).

ability distribution over payoffs: (a) I might *know* that the person offering me the choice had flipped a coin to decide whether to offer me action 1 or action 2, as an alternative to action 3; or (b) I might *know* that the 100 R_I and B_I balls had been chosen by random drawing from a large population of red and black balls in 50-50 proportions; or (c) I might *know* that a number p had been chosen at random from the integers between 0 and 100, and that this had determined the number p of R_I balls and the number $(100-p)$ of B_I balls.

I do not pretend that the implications of such "knowledge" for my choices among gambles, or my bids for gambles, involving R_I or B_I would be so obvious as to determine my initial, hasty choices. But upon analysis and reflection, I conclude that this "knowledge" would influence my deliberated preferences just as would the opportunity to flip a coin between the two offers, 1 and 2. I would bid as much for 1, or 2, if I believed with certainty that any of the above circumstances obtained, as I would for 3 or 4, or for $(1, 2; \frac{1}{2})$.

Likewise, I would be willing to give long odds on propositions concerning the average payoff in a large sequence of "bets like these" (i.e., in which such "knowledge" was available). This is true despite the fact that in none of these cases would I give high odds that I could predict closely the average number of red balls that would be drawn in a large series of drawings from a particular urn. In cases (b) and (c) I would predict the average outcomes of drawings from a large number of urns whose contents had been similarly, but independently, determined; but I would not even do this for case (a), in which I "do not know" how the contents of the urn were determined.

Under condition (a), for example, my policy might be: "Accept the bet that is offered: when the offer results from a random drawing from a set of offers like 1 and 2." I would expect this policy, in a large series of trials, to be on the average very nearly *as* profitable, neither appreciably more nor less, as the average results of the policy: "Accept bets like action 3, when offered." But I have no such definite expectation about the long-run consequences of accepting bets like 1 or 2 when none of the above conditions of information and certainty are satisfied: when I am "ignorant" of the process by which one of these bets became available or by which the relative proportion of R_I to B_I balls was determined. Again, I offer this as a (purported) fact about my preferences among gambles on long-run frequencies. It is consistent with my preferences among gambles on single events, but not necessarily prior or necessary to the latter preferences in any sense; I am undecided to what extent it might be useful to "explain" the latter preferences in terms of the former.

However, there is an important class of decision-makers who may be strongly influenced in their professional capacities by a *preference for gambles such that definite predictions can be made (i.e., bets at long odds are acceptable) on the long-run average payoffs for the whole class of gambles accepted.* One setting in which choices among "prospects offering ambiguous strategies as prizes" are ubiquitous is precisely that of the standard statistical decision problem, when the question arises of selecting a *randomized or non-randomized sample.* A "taste" among many statisticians for randomization in this context is well known. From a strict, "neo-Bernoullian" point of view, positive preferences of this sort are, at first sight, somewhat paradoxical. As Savage says, "Bayesian statistics has no formal reason to recommend randomization at all."[1]

> The problem of analyzing the idea of randomization is more acute, and at present more baffling, for subjectivists than for objectivists, more baffling because an ideal subjectivist would not need randomization at all. He would simply choose the specific layout that promised to tell him the most. The need for randomization presumably lies in the imperfection of actual people and, perhaps, in the fact that more than one person is ordinarily concerned with an investigation.[2]

---

[1]Savage, English summary of "On the Manner of Choosing Initial Probabilities," by Bruno de Finetti and L. J. Savage (to be published under the auspices of *Metron* as "Sul Modo di scegliere le probabilita iniziali"), mimeographed.

The "neo-Bernoullian" approach assumes that you act "as if" you attached a definite "von Neumann-Morgenstern utility" to each of your actions (its mathematical expectation of utility); a mixed strategy, or probability mixture of actions, would then have a utility equal to a weighted mean of the utilities of the component actions. But a weighted mean cannot be strictly greater than every one of its terms; hence the mixed strategy cannot be strictly preferable to all of its components. If the Savage postulates are obeyed, there must be a "pure" strategy available which is at least as good as any mixed strategy available; hence one need never choose, or even *consider*, randomized acts. (See discussion in Chernoff, *op. cit.*, pp. 437–439. A certain intellectual tension then results from the fact that, as Savage remarks, "the usual preference of statisticians for random samples represents a preference for certain mixed acts" (*Foundations of Statistics*, p. 163).

[2] L. J. Savage, "Subjective Probability and Statistical Practice," University of Chicago, SRC-91028S14, mimeographed (to be published in *The Foundations of Statistical Inference* (Methuen, London, 1962).

In discussion of this paper at the London symposium to be published by Methuen, Savage added the comment that the objectives of randomization were "to make the experiment useful to others and to guard against one's own subconscious. What remains delicate and tentative for me is to understand when, and to what extent, randomization really can accomplish these objectives. . . . It seems to me that, whether one is a Bayesian or not, there is still a good deal to clarify about randomization."

Without disagreeing with any of these comments, and without entering at all into a controversy concerning the definitive, exhaustive set of possible motives for randomization, I suggest that *among* those motives may be certain considerations of the very sort that lead, in general, to use of normative principles such as the "Bayes/minimax" or "Bayes/Hurwicz" criteria for decision-making under "ambiguous" circumstances. This is not to say that to find a statistician deliberately randomizing is to prove that he uses such a criterion or that he departs in principle from the Savage postulates; as Savage indicates, incentives to convince others, to reach agreement on experimental design among people of differing opinions, or to play a "game" against one's own unconscious biases can "explain" deliberate randomization even within a strict, "neo-Bernoullian" framework. Yet are these *all* the reasonable incentives? May not some preferences for randomized strategies remain, even when all incentives that are "legitimate" in the eyes of a strict "neo-Bernoullian" are eliminated?

I suspect that there may be occasions in which many statisticians would definitely prefer to choose randomly from a set of samples rather than to select any one of them without explicit randomization, even though *none* of the reasons acceptable to a "neo-Bernoullian" could be said truly to apply. That is, their reasons, related to "ambiguity" in their opinions concerning the appropriateness of any one sample they might deliberately select, might be quite similar to the reasons advanced above for preferring the prospect (1, 2; 1/2) either to 1 or to 2 considered separately. Such reasons must be adjudged quite unreasonable, the resulting behavior quite unworthy, by a "neo-Bernoullian." But the "Bayes/Hurwicz criterion" may, in fact, be an appropriate normative theory for these statisticians in these circumstances.

The motivation in question is one particularly identified with the statistical profession, though not peculiar to it. As Savage had observed, a decade ago: "Traditionally, the central problem of statistics is to draw statistical inferences, that is, to make *reasonably secure statements* on the basis of incomplete information."[1] The newer theory, which he was then expounding,

> centers about the problem of statistical action rather than inference, that is, deciding on a reasonable course of action on the basis of incomplete information. . . . it can be argued that all problems of statistics, including those of inference, are problems of action, for to utter or publish any statement is, after all, to take a certain action."[2]

---

[1] Savage, "The Theory of Statistical Decision," *Journal of the American Statistical Association*, Vol. 46, No. 253, March, 1951, p. 55; italics added.

[2] *Ibid.*

But the translation from "statements" to "actions" as the product pursued by statisticians tends to lose some overtones associated with the key phrase, "reasonably secure." *There* is a requirement that is readily understandable within a frame of reference that includes notions of relative "ambiguity," of "confidence," of "vague" versus "definite" opinions (less so in the framework of statistical "decision," in which such a phrase is in danger of being held "meaningless"). Its possible import for the advantages of randomization follows directly from our example.

With a random sample a statistician may be able to *state definitely* his expectations as to the *long-run average payoff* to a certain decision procedure in a large number of similar trials (where payoff might be measured, for example, in distance from an estimate of a parameter to its "true value"— as ascertained subsequently, by specified methods—or in some function of this distance). To say that he can state "definitely" is to say that he will be willing to do so with some precision, feeling "reasonably secure:" an assurance he would be willing to evidence by offering bets on his predictions at high odds. This would be true, for example, when with a random sample his probability distribution over *payoffs* for this rule would be the *same* for every one of the probability distributions over events that were "reasonably acceptable" to him as expressions of his opinions. (This is precisely the effect of the randomizations we have been discussing in this chapter). Under the same conditions, he might not feel willing to make such a definite statement— or to offer comparable bets at high odds—on the average payoff to any decision rule involving a non-random sample. That might well be, in his mind, a difference that made a difference: in favor of randomization.

In terms of the above example, we might imagine that tickets entitling one to actions 1 and 2, respectively, were enclosed in envelopes, each marked only "1 or 2." If *one* of these were offered to such a statistician, he might offer, say, $30 for it, where he might offer $40 for a ticket to action 3. But if the envelope to be offered, out of the two, were to be determined by flipping a fair coin, he might (after analysis) be willing to pay $40 to have whichever envelope should result from the toss. Likewise, if the envelope had already been selected when the offer was made to him, but he was convinced that it had been chosen as an offer by just this process among these candidates, he might make the same offer. And after he had paid his $40 and had opened the envelope to find, say, a ticket to action 1, he need *not* be willing to pay another dollar, or 10 cents, to exchange this for a ticket to action 3 before being told the results of the drawing from the urn. For after analyzing the implications of his knowledge or assumption concerning the "prospect" he had purchased, he might decide that he could not expect to *improve* either his immediate expectations or his expectations of long-run rewards by such an exchange.

In other words, the analogy is deceptive between this situation and one in which he held an envelope marked "1 or 2" *without* the assurance that it had been chosen randomly from the set of two. In the latter case, he might indeed be willing to pay $10 to exchange the envelope for a ticket to action 3, or to action 4, or for a random selection between 3 and 4; or for a random selection between 1 and 2 (i.e., for the opportunity to flip a coin between the *two* envelopes marked "1 or 2," knowing each strategy to be contained in one):

Such behavior might indeed seem counterintuitive in most ordinary contexts; but then, problems of experimental design and analysis are not "ordinary" in this sense. Moreover, *whatever* its motivation, randomization in statistical procedures must be regarded as a "sophisticated" practice, based upon insight, fairly subtle reasoning, and analysis in the light of the peculiar objectives of the statistician (if it should turn out to be based in some instances upon self-deception from a "neo-Bernoullian" point of view, it is very sophisticated self-deception, available only to subtle minds: really, a credit to the victim). That is, its advantages in statistics should not necessarily be expected to be immediately apparent, particularly to someone who does not share the same objectives. Among these objectives may be a particular desire to make "objective" statements on the "long run" payoffs to be anticipated from repeated use of a particular statistical strategy: i.e., *statements that not only the statistician, but the members of his audience, will be willing to bet on with heavy stakes giving high odds,* given the evidence he presents. To the extent that his listeners disagree, in their initial, "definite" opinions, with each other and with the statistician, this goal may lead him to use mixed strategies even though each of these persons conforms to the "Bernoulli proposition" in all of his choices. But I conjecture that, in many cases where initial opinions all agree but all are "vague," this goal may also lead to the choice of mixed strategies through the operation of some normative principle similar to the "restricted Bayes/Hurwicz criterion,"[1] in recognition precisely of differences in relative "ambiguity" between statements concerning the long-run consequences of those mixed acts of available, non-randomized acts.

---

[1] It also seems plausible to conjecture that: (a) in the application of this rule, the demands of their profession and, perhaps, also their personal predilections, may lead many statisticians to assign a value to α close or equal to 0 (i.e., in effect, to use the "Bayes/minimax criterion"), which tends to enhance the calculated value of randomization; (b) the sets of actions normally available in statistical decision problems may be such that randomized acts which have the special property of eliminating ambiguity (offering the *same* distribution of payoffs for every y in Y^o) tend to be more often available to the statistician than in other decision-making contexts.

Howard Raiffa's published counterexample to my argument is virtually equivalent to the one discussed above, raising exactly the same issues. However, without pursuing that particular discussion any further, it is worth quoting certain of his remarks, because they lead naturally into consideration of some proposed postulates not yet considered. Raiffa addresses his comments to the second example presented in Chapter Five, the "three-color" urn experiment examined at length in Chapters Six and Seven (see Fig. 6.1). After concurring, on the basis of interrogating his graduate students in mathematical statistics and his classes at the Harvard Business School, that "most subjects choose act I over II and IV over III, thus violating the Savage Axioms," and that "many of these subjects are reluctant to change their choices when it is pointed out to them that their behavior is inconsistent with the Sure-thing Principle," he states that he would like to "undermine further their confidence in their initial choices! I find the following argument is quite persuasive":

Suppose you register I ·> II and IV ·> III. I now offer you the paired comparison between the following two options: In option A a fair (unbiased) coin is tossed and act I is taken if heads appears, whereas act IV is taken if tails appears; with option B, heads leads to act II and tails to act III. In table form we get:

	Heads	**Tails**
Option A:	Act I	Act IV
Option B:	Act II	Act III

Fig. 8.7

Now *by strict dominance*[1] option A is better than B *for you* since you prefer I to II and IV to III. So far there is no trouble but let's take a closer look at options A and B. The final outcomes of either option depend on the toss of the coin and the selection of a ball. Now let's do the accounting by analyzing the implications of the options conditional on the color of the withdrawn ball. Our analysis takes the form:

	Red		**Yellow**	**Black**
Option A	(An "objective" 50-50 chance of $100 and $0)	→	same →	same
Option B	same		→ same →	same

Fig. 8.8

---

[1] Italics added.

But this reasoning should lead everyone to assert that options A and B are *objectively identical!* Something must give! I cannot see how anyone could refute the logic leading to the conclusion that given your initial choices, you should prefer option A to option B. This bit of logic is certainly not the weak link in the argument. But then again these options look awfully alike to me! Therefore, on thinking it over, wouldn't you like to change your mind about your initial preferences?[1]

It is, no doubt, clear by now that my own answer to Raiffa's appeal is: No. Yet I agree that options A and B do offer the same, "unambiguous" probability distribution over possible payoffs: which is why, contrary to Raiffa's conjecture, I would be indifferent between them despite my preference for I over II, or for IV over III, if either of these pair were offered to me in isolation (and in the absence of the various sorts of knowledge mentioned earlier that might "make a difference" to me). As Raiffa says, something must give; for me, the weak link in the "neo-Bernoullian" argument is precisely where Raiffa least expects it, the inference that I must prefer option A to option B given my initial preferences.

No doubt it is the magic phrase, "by strict dominance" that makes the latter "bit of logic" so irrefutable in Raiffa's eyes. I have already commented (Chapter Four) on what appears to me to be Raiffa's misuse of that phrase in this context. The notion of *domination,* and the related notion of *admissibility,* are used, elsewhere, virtually universally as defined in Luce and Raiffa's *Games and Decisions;* where A′ and A″ are two arbitrary but specific acts in a decision problem:

   i. A′ ~ A″ : means that the acts are equivalent in the sense that they yield the same utilities for *each state of nature.*

  ii. A′ > A″ : means that A′ *strongly dominates* A″ in the sense that A′ is preferred to A″ for *each state of nature.*

 iii. A′) A″: means that A′ *weakly dominates* A″ in the sense that A′ is preferred to A″ for at least one state and is preferred or indifferent to A″ for *all other states.*

An act A′ is said to be *admissible* if there is no act A in α such that A) A′, i.e., A′ is admissible if A′ is not weakly dominated by any other act.[2]

---

[1] Raiffa, "Risks, Ambiguity, and the Savage Axioms: Comment," p. 694. I have reversed the yellow and black columns to conform to my discussion in Chapters Five-Seven.

[2] Luce and Raiffa, *op. cit.,* pp. 286–287; italics supplied for references to states of nature.

It is easy to see that by these definitions, neither option A nor option B "dominates" the other; both are "admissible." The relevant states of nature on which the outcomes depend are, as Raiffa points out, the joint results of "the toss of the coin and the selection of a ball." The corresponding outcomes for the two options can be shown:

	$\frac{1}{3}$ $\quad$ $\frac{1}{2}$ Red/Heads	$\frac{1}{3}$ $\quad$ $\frac{1}{2}$ Red/Tails	P_y $\quad$ $\frac{1}{2}$ Yellow/Heads	P_y $\quad$ $\frac{1}{2}$ Yellow/Tails	$(\frac{2}{3}-P_y)\frac{1}{2}$ Black/Heads	$(\frac{2}{3}-P_y)\frac{1}{2}$ Black/Tails
Option A	$100	$ 0	$ 0	$100	$0	$100
Option B	$ 0	$100	$100	$ 0	$0	$100

Fig. 8.9

The absence of domination is fairly evident in this diagram (which merely "expands" Fig. 8.8). The notions of dominance and admissibility, applied rigorously, are simply not relevant to a comparison of these two options (nor can they be applied directly, without further analysis, to any pair of options whose possible "consequences" are shown explicitly only as "acts," as in Figure 8.8). The reason for emphasizing what may seem merely a point of terminology is that among the "reasonable desiderata for decision criteria to fulfill" listed, for example, by Luce and Raiffa, the two that are *accepted most generally* as significant normative criteria are the two that rely upon the notions defined formally above:

Axiom 4. If A' belongs to [the optimal set] and A'') A' or A'' ~ A', then A'' belongs to [the optimal set].

Axiom 5. If A' belongs to [the optimal set], then A' is admissible.[1]

Since neither of these potent axioms, nor any other commonly associated with the strict notions of "dominance" and "admissibility" (e.g., Sav-

---

[1] Luce and Raiffa, *op. cit.*, p. 287. The authors include Axiom 4 in a set that they describe as "quite innocuous in the sense that, if a person takes serious issue with them, then we would contend that he is not really attuned to the problem we have in mind" (*ibid.*). Axiom 5 is generally regarded as equally "innocuous," though powerful. As Savage says, "The one clear guide to analysis to which [frequentists] have come is the principle of admissibility" ("The Foundations of Statistics Reconsidered," p. 579).

age's Postulate 3) does in fact constrain a choice between Options A and B, just what *is* the bit of logic that Raiffa has in mind?

It is easy to see from Figure 8.9 that if you regard the probabilities of (Heads, Tails) as "unambiguously" (1/2, 1/2), then for *either* option you will assign "definite" probabilities of 1/2 each to $100 and to $0; there is no reason (of any sort we have considered, or will) to be other than indifferent between them.[1] On the other hand, there is no denying the *plausibility*, when the options are displayed as they are in Figure 8.8, of the proposition that a person who prefers act I to II, when that pair is considered in isolation, and IV to III likewise, should prefer option A to B. It is plausible, in other words, that postulates which *extrapolated* the notions of domination and admissibility to cover "prospects which offer other strategies as prizes" should be just as compelling, as normative criteria, as are Axioms 4 and 5 above, or Savage's Postulate 3. As we have already noted, it is Savage's Postulate 2 (in combination with Postulate 1) or, among the "utility" axioms, Samuelson's Independence Axioms, that lend themselves to this precise interpretation. And indeed, before I had pondered my own preferences among gambles subject to gross "ambiguity," such as the examples we have discussed, I would have guessed that postulates having this effect would be quite acceptable to me as normative criteria, reflecting the underlying logic of my own, deliberated choices.[2]

---

[1] The probabilities shown in the diagram correspond to a set of "reasonably acceptable" distributions Y^o: $(1/3, p_y, 2/3 - p_y)$, $0 \le p_y \le 2/3$. The sum of the probabilities of states leading to the outcome $100 for, Option A is: $1/6 + 1/2 \cdot p_y + 1/2$ $(2/3 - p_y) = 1/2$; likewise for $0 under Option A: and likewise for the outcomes $100 and $0 under Option B. Thus, for any p_y, $0 \le 2/3$ (i.e., for any y in Y^o), the probability distribution over ($100, $0) is identical for Options A and B: $(1/2, 1/2)$.

[2] After listening to me expound the unacceptability of Postulate 2 and the Independence Axiom for decision-making under "ambiguity" at Northwestern University (March, 1962), Jacques Drèze dryly recalled to me that I had once urged him to abandon his own, quixotic attacks upon the Sure-Thing Principle, to look for less invulnerable targets. It was true; I remember, now, that until the fall of 1957 I probed for the source of my doubts (related, even then, to circumstances of ambiguity) among quite other axioms and postulates (my suspicions centered upon Savage's Postulate 4). When I had finally constructed counterexamples that evoked in me unequivocal preferences contrary to the "Bernoulli proposition," I was, in fact, considerably surprised to discover that it was Postulate 2 I wanted systematically to violate.

Drèze having exposed as apostasy what I had been regarding, in myself, as insouciant, more or less instinctive irreverence, an even more disturbing recollection led me to look up some conjectures I had expressed on the utility axioms exactly a

Nevertheless it is, after all, Postulate 2 (in combination with Postulate 1, complete ordering of actions among the Savage postulates) that is violated by the pattern of preferences: Option A indifferent to Option B, but action I preferred to II and IV preferred to III. That particular transgression has lost by now, presumably, its power to surprise, or perhaps to shock. We have already seen that this pattern likewise violates, among the utility axioms, Samuelson's Independence Axiom; this may pose certain problems for the measurement of utility, to which we shall return below (see, "Winning at Russian Roulette").

Neither of these axioms has an exact counterpart among the axioms listed by Luce and Raiffa as possible desiderata of decision-making criteria. However, a preference for a mixed strategy over any of its pure strategy components—which is one aspect of the pattern of preferences criticized by Raiffa—violates the "anticonvexity property of the optimal set,"[1] which is a consequence of their Axiom 3 (optimal set invariant under labeling of

---

decade ago, and published in 1954. To reveal my youthful views honestly is to present my current position in disconcerting but, I suppose, useful perspective:

"It is the 'Strong Independence Axiom' [as a special case of the "Sure-Thing Principle"] ruling out this sort of preference which Samuelson has emphasized, presenting it as the 'crucial' axiom. It seems rather hard to justify this emphasis, since the axiom seems indubitably the most plausible of the lot. After all, all of the axioms are necessary to the final result, and this particular one is almost impregnable (even people who did not follow it in practice would probably admit, on reflection, that they should) whereas others (such as 3:C:b) are contradicted by much everyday experience. One might also suspect Samuelson, who counts himself a 'fellow traveller' of the von Neumann-Morgenstern theory, of using the axiom (his invention) as a man-trap, luring critics past the really vulnerable points to waste their strength on the 'Independence Assumption,'" ("Classic and Current Notions of 'Measurable Utility,'" *Economic Journal*, Vol. LXIV, 1954, p. 544).

I cannot, now, congratulate myself on my choice of (English-speaking) audience for these remarks; but as a wise man once said: "It is anything but a casual thing to have and know one's complete ordering or set of indifference curves; and if you ask a casual question, you must expect to get a casual answer."

[1] This consequence of Axioms 3, 7 and 8 may be stated: "If an optimal act of a given decision problem under uncertainty is equivalent to a probability mixture of two other acts, then each of these acts is also optimal" (Luce and Raiffa, *op. cit.*, p. 291n). In other words, the mixed act cannot be strictly preferred to all its components. Various "utility" axioms also embody this notion; see, for example, the von Neumann-Morgenstern axioms 3:B:a, 3:B:b (*Theory of Games and Economic Behavior*, p. 26), or Marschak's Postulate IV ("Rational Behavior, Uncertain Prospects, and Measurable Utility," *Econometrica*, Vol. 18, 1950, pp. 120–122).

acts(, Axiom 7 (addition of acts cannot make a non-optimal act optimal; which rules out "minimaxing regret"), and Axiom 8 ("Rubin's axiom"; see below). Axioms 3 and 7 are described by the authors, with reason, as "extremely reasonable," Axiom 8 being the "weakest link in the argument" leading to the anticonvexity property.

RUBIN'S AXIOM

Axiom 8, which is due to Herman Rubin, does deserve our attention. In the axiom systems presented by Chernoff and by Luce and Raiffa, this axiom plays the logical role of Postulate 2 in Savage's system; in each case it is the *only* desideratum violated by the minimax criterion, which it thereby rules out (along with the Hurwicz α-criteria and our modification, the "restricted Bayes/Hurwicz criterion"). Moreover, it is the axiom in these lists that would rule out the initial pattern of preferences—I preferred to II and IV preferred to III in our example—and it is the key element in the "bit of logic" that rules those preferences incompatible with indifference between Options A and B. Although recognizing Rubin's axiom as controversial and presenting some possible counterexamples to it, Luce and Raiffa defend it as "perfectly reasonable," adding: "This is a matter of taste!"[1]

The following informal characterization, by Luce and Raiffa, of Rubin's axiom will do for our purposes:

> Suppose a decision maker is given two decision problems having the same sets of available acts and states but differing in payoffs. Suppose the second problem is trivial in the sense that the payoff depends only upon

---

[1] Luce and Raiffa, *op. cit.*, p. 291. Despite the authors' own "taste" for Axiom 8, their treatment of it suggests strongly that its violation is far from the felony indicated by loose mention of "strict dominance" (which would invoke Axioms 4 or 5, or Savage's Postulate 3). They devote two pages (more space than any of their other 11 axioms receive) to stating, illustrating and responding to three common objections to it (I would subscribe to all three). Later, when they conclude that their Axioms 1 through 11 are mutually incompatible, they comment: "Something will have to be deleted, and one possible candidate is Rubin's Axiom 8." All this, with the estimate that Axiom 8 is the "weakest link in the argument" leading to the anticonvexity property, is in interesting contrast to Raiffa's assertion above: "I cannot see how anyone could refute the logic leading to the conclusion that given your initial choices, you should prefer option A to option B. This bit of logic is certainly not the weak link in the argument" (*op. cit.*, p. 694).

As a matter of fact, surely few readers of *Games and Decisions* would hesitate for a moment to respond to Raiffa's expostulation, "Something must give!" by nominating Rubin's axiom.

the state and not upon the act adopted. In other words, in the array representing problem 2, all entries in the same column are the same. If the decision maker knows only that he is playing problem 1 with probability p and problem 2 with probability $1 - p$ when he has to adopt an act, then he should adopt an act which is optimal for problem 1, since problem 2, which enters with probability $1 - p$, is irrelevant as far as his choice is concerned.[1]

It is clear that meaningful application of this requirement to your behavior must rely upon "knowledge" (i.e., prior measurement) of your "von Neumann-Morgenstern utilities" for the outcomes in question and of "definite" probabilities relating the two decision problems. It is for this reason that no such constraint is accorded status as a fundamental postulate in The Foundations of Statistics. However, we have accepted throughout most of our discussion the assumption that there are *some* events and consequences with respect to which you do strictly obey the Savage postulates, which is all that is required to permit a test of the acceptability of this postulate, or of others defined in terms of "known, definite" utilities and probabilities.

Another interpretation of the role of "problem 2" in each case is that an "umpire" will make a decision by a random device with "definite" probabilities known to you whether to give you the utility payoff indicated for problem 1 (which depends, in general, both on your choice of act and on the state that obtains) or to give you a utility payoff that is determined only by the state that obtains, not by your choice. Suppose that the random process is the toss of a coin, Heads leading to payoffs from problem 1, Tails, leading to payoffs (constant with respect to your choice of act) from problem 2. Reasoning along the lines of the "Sure-Thing Principles": If you "know" that the coin would fall Heads, you would, in effect, confront payoffs corresponding to problem 1; you would have a definite preference, or indifference, between two given actions, I, II. Let us say you do *not* prefer I to II. On the other hand, if you "know" that Heads would *not* obtain—that the coin would certainly fall Tails—you "wouldn't care" what you chose, since your payoff would be independent of your choice; you would be indifferent between I and II. So, since you would not prefer I to II "in either event"—i.e., either *knowing* that Heads will obtain or *knowing* that Heads will not obtain[2]—you should not (according to the "Sure-Thing Principle") prefer I to II when you *do not know* which event will obtain.

---

[1] Luce and Raiffa, *op. cit.*, p. 290.

[2] Statements of the "Sure-Thing Principle" do not always spell out—as I have done here—the fact that the "events" alluded to in the phrase "in either event" must be interpreted as including, as part of their definition, your subjective state of

If nothing were specified about your subjective uncertainty concerning the outcome of the coin-toss, we would be back to the "Sure-thing Principle" itself, in its more general forms such as Savage's Postulate 2. But if we specify that the outcome of tossing *this* coin is an event with respect to which you obey the Savage axioms and for which your "definite" subjective probability has been measured, we can represent the "consequence" corresponding to a given act i and a given state j as a "lottery ticket" offering the corresponding payoffs u_{ij}^1 and u_{ij}^2 from problems 1 and 2, with "definite" probabilities p, $1 - p$, respectively. Thus: $u_{ij}^3 = U(u_{ij}^1, u_{ij}^2; p) = p \cdot u_{ij}^1 + (1 - p) \cdot u_{ij}^2$.

The simple examples below illustrate the effects of this probability mixture of problems 1 and 2 on the utility payoffs implied for the "combined" problem 3; in each case, problem 3 is a mixture of problems 1 and 2 in which each is assigned probability *1/2*.

	1/2 Problem 1		+	1/2 Problem 2		→	Problem 1	
	E	Ē		E	Ē		E	Ē
I	100	0		100	0		100	0
II	0	100		100	0		50	50

Fig. 8.10a

---

uncertainty: specifically, your postulated "knowledge" or subjective certainty that some specific event *otherwise* defined will obtain. When this is explicit, use of the phrase "in either event" begins to appear distinctly misleading: for the states of mind corresponding to your "knowing" one thing or another are quite obviously not an exhaustive set of possible states of mind (hence, they are not a *partition* of states of the world, when the latter are defined, in part, with respect to your state of mind). In addition to "knowing," *there is also "not knowing,"* in its variety of forms: various degrees of partial belief between 0 and 1, or other "ambiguous" states such as we have discussed. To say that you would prefer action I to II in all those states of mind corresponding to "certainty" concerning certain relevant facts does *not logically imply* that you prefer I to II in those states of mind corresponding to *lack* of certainty with respect to those facts. It *may be a fact* that your preferences in the former subset of subjective states in those cases when they "agree" for every member of that subset, your preferences in all remaining states of mind; but that is precisely the proposition at issue, when we consider the acceptability of postulates like Savage's Postulate 2, Samuelson's Independence Axiom, Rubin's axiom, or Milnor's "column linearity" axiom (below).

	1/2 Problem 1		+		1/2 Problem 2		→		Problem 1	
	E	Ē			E	Ē			E	Ē
I	100	-100		I	100	-100		I	100	-100
II	-100	100		II	100	-100		II	0	0

Fig. 8.10b

	1/2 Problem 1		+		1/2 Problem 2		→		Problem 1	
	E	Ē			E	Ē			E	Ē
I	100	-100		I	100	-100		I	100	-100
II	-100	100		II	100	-100		II	0	0

Fig. 8.10b

With respect to each of these examples, Rubin's axiom requires that: *whatever the event E and whatever your preference between actions I and II in Problem 1, your preference should be the same in Problem 3.*

It is, perhaps, necessary to emphasize that this required pattern of preferences is not already implied by the prior assertion that the payoff

---

[1] In fact, it is impossible to tell from the numbers alone whether different outcomes are involved in these two sets of problems, or whether the outcomes are the same but the scale and origin of the utility scale have been changed. "Positiveness/negativeness" and "size" of von Neumann-Morgenstern utility numbers have no operational meaning *with respect to choices among prospects.* This does not rule out, however, the possibility of a meaningful "zero" point—e.g., your current "status quo" position, a "no gain-no loss" outcome—in terms of which meaningful and useful notions of "positive" and "negative" payoffs could be defined for purposes of analyzing your choices among *ambiguous* gambles (with respect to which you did *not* obey the Savage postulates, or the von Neumann-Morgenstern axioms). Egon Neuberger, among others, has emphasized to me the possible importance of such notions in explaining certain differential patterns of behavior. I believe he is right. The possibility of utilizing utility functions limited to a narrower class of admissible transformations than are the von Neumann-Morgenstern utility functions to explain certain types of behavior deserves much more investigation than it has so far received.

numbers represent your "von Neumann-Morgenstern utilities" for the respective outcomes. The von Neumann-Morgenstern utility axioms apply only to choices among gambles ("prospects") whose outcomes are contingent upon events with "known, definite" probabilities. In order to measure any "von Neumann-Morgenstern utilities" for you, it must be true that you obey the Savage postulates, or some equivalent set, with respect to *some* events, so that it is possible to measure definite probabilities for them and hence definite utilities for outcomes in gambles involving those events. For example, to say that the payoff numbers 100, –100 and 0 in Figure 8.10b represent your "von Neumann-Morgenstern utilities" for the corresponding outcomes, it must be true that *if* you acted in all your choices involving the event E "as if" you assigned the "definite" probability 1/2 to E (1/2 to E̅), then you would be indifferent between actions I and II both in Problems 1 and 3. The same applies to the payoff numbers 100, 0 and 50 in Fig. 8.10a. Moreover, *if* the event E in these various examples is such that you act "as if" you assigned *any* "definite" probability to it, then the assertion that the payoff numbers are "von Neumann-Morgenstern utilities" does *imply* that your preference, or indifference, between I and II in Problem 1 must also hold in Problem 3. But that premise concerning the particular event E has nothing to do with the issue of whether or not the payoffs are valid "von Neumann-Morgenstern utilities" for you.

To translate from these payoff numbers to "real" outcomes that give your intuition something to work on,[1] imagine, first, that the event E in Figure 8.10b is itself the outcome Heads on a toss of a fair coin, the utility numbers –100 and 0 correspond to the outcomes –$1000 and $0, respectively, and the utility number 100 corresponds to that positive reward that would make you indifferent between actions I and II in Problem 3: $1000, $1500, $2000, whatever outcome would just compensate you for a "definite" *even* chance of losing $1000 (assuming that Heads has "definite" probability 1/2 for you).

Now, with those, fixed money outcomes, ask yourself if it is true that for *every* event E that you can imagine, such that you would be indifferent between actions I and II in Problem 1 in Figure 8.10b, you would still be indifferent between I and II with the outcomes corresponding to Problem 3. For example, suppose that E were the drawing of a Red ball in Urn I in the "two-urn example" in Chapter Five, where the proportion of Red to Black balls in Urn I was unspecified; or suppose that E were the proposition, "there are at least as many Yellow as Black balls" in the "three-

---

[1] The necessity of doing this is a major disadvantage of propositions like Rubin's axiom when proposed as fundamental normative criteria, compared to Savage's postulates.

color urn" example. Would you still be indifferent in Problem 3? Or, might you now *prefer*, say, action II: so that it would take a greater possible reward, or smaller posssible loss, to action I to restore your indifference? The latter pattern might result if you applied, say, a "restricted Bayes/Hurwicz criterion" with $\alpha < 1/2$ to these payoffs: on the basis of precisely the same sort of rationale as that considered toward the end of Chapter Seven.[1]

Likewise, if E were similarly "ambiguous" in the example in Figure 8.10c, this criterion might lead you to prefer action I in Problem 1, but to prefer action II (with its now-unambiguous utility expectation) in Problem 3. In particular, if the "O" point in this utility scale represents a "status quo, no gain/no loss outcome," a preference for II in Problem 3 but not in Problem 1 would mean that you "prefer not to gamble" either *on* E or *against* E—at the odds represented by I and II in Problem 1 or I in Problem 3—when you are offered the chance to avoid it.

As mentioned earlier, Rubin's axiom rules out the use of such a criterion in any of these examples. Might it be ruling out, at the same time, choices "you" would actually prefer, upon reflection?

Luce and Raiffa discuss an example similar in structure to that in Figure 8.10c; they come close to agreeing with the argument, which they consider, that insistence upon strict conformity to Rubin's axiom in such a case, *for every E,* is counterintuitive. In fact, the form of the argument they present for the reader's consideration is remarkably similar to the rationale suggested in Chapters Six and Seven above for patterns of choice violating Savage's Postulate 2. They state (in language that applies fairly to our example in Figure 8.10c):

> Intuitively, a plausible method for analyzing these [decision problems] is to be somewhat pessimistic and to behave as if the less desirable state is somewhat more likely to arise. The extreme example of this rule is the maximiner who focuses entirely on the undesirable state, but our point holds equally well for one who *emphasizes the undesirable state only* slightly. In problem 1, [E] is less desirable, and so one is led to choose [I]. In problem 3, [E] is less desirable, and so one might be led to choose [II]. But if one subscribes to axiom 8, the same alternative must be chosen in both cases, and so we are led to doubt the axiom.[2] [Italics added.]

---

[1] Given that the payoffs are your "von Neumann-Morgenstern utilities," and given a coin that you consider "fair," another way for you to arrive at the payoffs of action II in Problem 3, in Figures 8.10a and 8.10b, is to flip the coin between actions I and II in problem 1.

[2] Luce and Raiffa, *op. cit.*, p. 291.

The phrase italicized above comes closest of any I have found in *Games and Decisions*—close indeed!—to suggesting a decision criterion of the form of the "restricted Bayes/Hurwicz criterion,"[1] though I have generally avoided using terms like "pessimism" to characterize such a criterion. A person using that criterion does not, in general, "definitely expect" the worst (as a true "pessimist" might); but it is, of course, correct to say that *he chooses to act "as if" the worst (among "reasonable" expectations of utility) were somewhat more likely than his "best guess" judgments of probability would indicate.*

If that mode of behavior is close to what Luce and Raiffa had in mind in their comments above, then I quite agree that—under circumstances of "ambiguity" I can readily imagine—it is intuitively plausible, and it does lead me to doubt Rubin's axiom.

The counterblow in Luce and Raiffa's dialectic seems rather week: "The very compelling *a priori* quality of Rubin's axiom argues against the analysis which led us to choose I in problem I and II in problem 3."[2]

---

[1] (It so happens that Luce and Raiffa describe the closely-related Hodges and Lehmann criterion in quite a different form from that discussed in Chapter Seven above, using terms that do not lend themselves to this interpretation; *ibid.*, p. 305).

I suspect that any writer who has tried to produce original work in any of the fields covered by *Games and Decisions*, subsequent to its publication, will know why I find this assertion—hinting at a certain lack of overlap—worthy of comment. It is simply dishearteningly difficult to evolve an idea in those areas so novel, so unheralded, so previously unthinkable, that one does not find on re-examining that book at least a paragraph in small print devoted to it (if not a page, judiciously summarizing, formalizing, illustrating and criticizing one's "invention"). I feel I have gotten off lightly on this one.

[2] *Op. cit.*, p. 292. The authors attempt further to undermine the thesis suggested earlier by asserting: "Certainly, the intuitive analysis cannot be used without restriction, for it would also lead us to choose [II] again in:

	E	Ē
I	500	-0.01
II	100	0

Fig. 8.11

and that seem counterintuitive" (*ibid.*).

This is the sort of payoff array that is familiar as a counterexample against the strict minimax (Wald) criterion. It is important to note that the counterintuitive

Chernoff has shown that Rubin's axiom implies that a constant payoff may be subtracted from (added to) a given column of payoffs (or, a different constant subtracted from each column) without affecting one's choice.[1] The latter proposition is used as an axiom by Milnor,[2] and an equivalent requirement is proposed by Blackwell and Girshick, who describe it as asserting that "in deciding between [actions] f_1 and f_2, the decision maker is guided only by the change in utility, as a function of the unknown state ω, resulting from a change from f_1 to f_2."[3] The latter formulation has some intuitive appeal, but there are problems in giving the notion of "adding" or "subtracting" "von Neumann-Morgenstern utilities" operational meaning in terms of relevant behavior.

These latter axioms, like Rubin's axiom or Savage's Postulate 2, would have the effect of ruling out any form of the minimax or Hurwicz criteria, including the "restricted Bayes/Hurwicz criterion." Savage's Postulate 2 can, in fact, be considered a special application of such a requirement, to the case of decision problems with one or more "constant columns" of payoffs; it implies that a constant payoff can be added to, or subtracted from, a constant column of payoffs without affecting your ordering of actions (where a finite number of states of the world is considered).[4]

The application of any one of these requirements to our "three-urn" example is straightforward; we have already covered it, at great length, for all of them except Rubin's axiom, which may be illustrated briefly. You are informed, as before, that the urn contains 30 Red balls and 60 Yellow and Black balls in unspecified proportions. An "umpire" flips a fair coin between the payoff matrices represented in Problem 1 and Problem 2.

---

inference does not follow at all from the (general or "restricted") Hurwicz criterion with $\alpha > 0$, nor from the "restricted Bayes/ minimax criterion" with $\rho > 0$, all of which are much more nearly suggested by the "intuitive analysis" above than is the former criterion. In none of the latter criteria would action II be preferred here unless E were believed "definitely almost impossible" (or ρ and α were infinitesimal).

[1] Herman Chernoff, "Rational Selection of Decision Functions," p. 433; Theorem 2 ("Relevance of Regret").

[2] Milnor, "Games Against Nature," p. 51; axiom 7, "column linearity."

[3] Blackwell and Girshick, *Theory of Games and Statistical Decisions*, p. 117.

[4] Milnor's "column linearity" axiom (*op. cit.*, p. 51) simply extends Savage's Postulate 2, so stated, to columns of payoffs in general, not merely "constant columns" (in which all payoffs are identical). Luce and Raiffa remark that they might have taken a similar proposition—that a adding a constant to each entry of a column of the payoff matrix does not alter the optimal set—instead of Rubin's axiom; "however, we feel, as do Rubin and Chernoff, that this property is not as intuitively compelling as the axiom given" (*op. cit.*, p. 290).

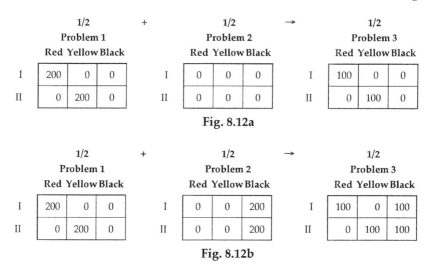

Fig. 8.12a

Fig. 8.12b

Rubin's axiom implies that it should make no difference to your choice of action whether the payoff matrix of Problem 2—to be "combined," by the umpire's random action, with that of Problem 1—is that shown in Figure 8.12a or that in Figure 8.12b. In either case, whatever your preference between actions I and II in Problem 1, it should be preserved in Problem 3; from the point of view of this axiom, the two (familiar) payoff matrices for Problem 3 in Figures 8.12a and 8.12b are to be considered identical for purposes of decision-making.

And just what *is* the difference between them, from any point of view? That challenge is implicit in any one of the related set of axioms considered above. What significant difference should it make to your preferences between I and II in Problem 3, "merely" to raise the constant payoff to the event "Black" by a constant amount for the two actions: why should that *make* a difference, in your choices?

For purposes of testing the acceptability of proposed normative criteria for you, it may be enough to know the fact that it *does* make a difference to you, upon reflection: if that *is* a fact. But if further analysis is acknowledged as desirable, we can point to a significant effect of this shift in payoffs in terms of concepts introduced in preceding chapters. If we accept the notion that there may be a *set* of personal probability distributions Y^0 that are not excluded by a decision-maker's "definite" probability judgments, then to a given action there will correspond, in general, a *set* of expected utility values, among which he cannot discriminate in terms of "definite" probabilities.

It may be that a decision-maker chooses between two actions in a way that reflects the *whole set* of "reasonably acceptable" values for each action.

He may take this range of values for each action into account formally and systematically, using some such decision rule as a "restricted Bayes/Hurwicz criterion;" or he may compare various possible values within each range less formally, though perhaps arriving at behavior patterns that still may be approximated by such a criterion. The set of expectations associated with an action reflect both the nature of the set $Y°$ and the nature of the payoff function (over events) for the action. By changing the "shape" of the payoff functions for given actions, changes in payoffs of the sort considered *irrelevant* by the Chernoff/Milnor/Blackwell-Girshick "column linearity" axioms, by Rubin's axiom or by Savage's Postulate 2 (changes in the payoffs for which two actions "agree") can change the nature of the *set* of expected utility values associated with a given action.

For example, such a change can reduce that set from an infinite class of "reasonably acceptable" expectations, all those within certain wide boundaries, to a single, "definite" expectation, perhaps at one former boundary or the other. In fact, most of our examples have been constructed so that such changes in payoff will produce, for at least some individuals, just this effect.

Given that we are dealing with "von Neumann-Morgenstern utilities," it is true that none of these changes would be relevant to decision-making *if* the decision-maker had in mind a single, "definite" probability distribution over events: or acted "as if" he did. But if he does *not* act always "as if" he assigned definite probabilities to events—and hence, to payoffs—then such shifts in the payoff function can make a diference to his decisions (without contradicting any assumptions properly relating to his "von Neumann-Morgenstern utility function" over outcome).

ALLAIS AND THE SURE-THING PRINCIPLE

A position somewhat related to that above has frequently been expressed by Maurice Allais, both in connection with the von Neumann-Morgenstern and with the Savage postulates.[1] Since the examples discussed by Allais presume "definite" subjective probabilities on the part of the decision-maker (in fact, Allais generally assumes these probabilities to be identical

---

[1] Maurice Allais, "Le Comportement de l'Homme Rationel devant le Risque. Critique des Postulats et Axiomes de l'École Américaine," *Econometrica*, "Fondements d'Une Théorie Positive des Choix Comportant Un Risque et Critique des Postulats et Axiomes de l'École Américaine," *Annales des Mines*, numéro spécial 1955 (I am indebted to M. Allais for sending me a copy of this paper). The latter paper contains a wealth of illustrations, conjectures and hypotheses deserving close attention by anyone interested in the general subject-matter of the present study; there is not space to do full justice to it here.

with "objective" probabilities, without much discussion of the problem of determining the latter in every case), they would not appear at first glance to involve problems of "ambiguity," which has been our concern in this study. It was not until recently that I noticed certain relations between the considerations raised by Allais in criticism of the *utility* axioms and those I have emphasized as limitations of the *probability* axioms. Before studying carefully certain hypothetical examples proposed by Allais, I would have conjectured that the Savage postulates would prove acceptable to me as normative criteria in any situation providing a clear basis for "definite" probabilities: e.g., urns with known proportions of balls (we have, in effect, been assuming this for "you" throughout this study). Now I am not so sure.

The examples I have proposed, with respect to which I conjecture that many reasonable people will wish to violate the Sure-Thing Principle, involve comparisons between gambles in which the subjective probability distribution of payoffs is (for many persons) "definite" and others in which the distribution of payoffs is (for many persons) "ambiguous." The comparisons posed by Allais involve, on the one hand, risky gambles in which the subjective probability distribution of payoffs is "definite" though the outcomes are uncertain, and on the other, propositions that offer a definite outcome with certainty. The pattern of violations of the Sure-Thing Principle that he expects in these examples is quite similar to that I have hypothesized for mine.

The best-known of the examples by Allais is described by Savage as follows:

> Consider an example based on two decision situations each involving two gambles.
>
> Situation 1. Choose between
>
> Gamble 1. $500,000 with probability 1; and
> Gamble 2. $2,500,000 with probability 0.1, $500,000 with probability 0.89, status quo with probability 0.01.
>
> Situation 2. Choose between
>
> Gamble 3. $500,000 with probability 0.11, status quo with probability 0.89; and
> Gamble 4. $2,500,000 with probability 0.1, status quo with probability 0.9.
>
> Many people prefer Gamble 1 to Gamble 2, because, speaking qualitatively, they do not find the chance of winning a *very* large fortune in place

of receiving a large fortune outright adequate compensation for even a small risk of being left in the status quo. Many of the same people prefer Gamble 4 to Gamble 3; because, speaking qualitatively, the chance of winning is nearly the same in both gambles, so the one with the much larger prize seems preferable. But the intuitively acceptable pair of preferences, Gamble 1 preferred to Gamble 2 and Gamble 4 to Gamble 3, is not compatible with the utility concept or, equivalently, the sure-thing principle. Indeed that pair of preferences implies the following inequalities for any hypothetical utility function.

$$U\ (\$500,000) > 0.1U\ (\$2,500,000) + 0.89U\ (\$500,000) + 0.1U(\$0),$$

$$0.1U\ (\$2,500,000) + 0.9U\ (\$0) > 0.11U\ (\$500,000) + 0.89U\ (\$0);$$

and these are obviously incompatible.

Examples like the one cited do have a strong intuitive appeal; even if you do not personally feel a tendency to prefer Gamble 1 to Gamble 2 and simultaneously Gamble 4 to Gamble 3, I think that a few trials with other prizes and probabilities will provide you with an example appropriate to yourself.[1]

The principle on which Allais constructed this example was to contrast a prospect of risky rewards with an offer of a "sure" gain, where the rewards have great value compared to the capital of the gambler: in order to demonstrate "the considerable psychological importance that the advantage of certainty, as such, can have."[2] Allais implies that when *both* gambles offer rewards that are "far from certain" (as in Situation 2), a given person may obey the von Neumann-Morgenstern postulates or the Sure-Thing Principle. That same person may violate the Sure-Thing Principle, he believes, in choosing among "risky prospects in the neighborhood of certainty," i.e., when *one* of the alternatives offers a *certain* consequence (as in Situation 1); because "experience shows that some people, judged as perfectly rational, but prudent . . . attach great value to certainty."[3]

---

[1] Savage, *Foundations of Statistics*, pp. 101–102. See Allais, "Fondements d'une Théorie Positive des Choix," p. 39.

[2] Allais, *op. cit.*, p. 39; my translation.

[3] *Ibid.*, pp. 40–41. Similarly, one could describe someone who used a "restricted Bayes/minimax" criterion or a "restricted Hurwicz criterion" with $\alpha = 0$ as *attaching great value to lack of ambiguity*, in choosing among gambles none offering "certainty" but some offering more "definite" probability distributions of payoffs than others. Experience suggests that such people do exist and, often, are popularly regarded—like those described by Allais—as "prudent" rather than "irrational."

In an example like this, Allais asserts, he himself would accept a great diminution in potential reward in order to lower the probability of *losing*, or of winning *nothing*, from a small, positive value to *zero*; whereas he would not accept the same diminution to achieve a like reduction in the probability of losing when that probability remained that high (i.e., when it would be impossible, merely by lowering one's sights on potential profit, to achieve "the neighborhood of certainty" with respect to *some* level of improvement over the status quo).

> This is, so far as we are concerned at least, an attitude *quite calculated, quite deliberate,* and no one could persuade us to change our attitude if we were put *actually* face to face with such risky choices. *Our psychology is such that we have a stronger preference for security in the neighborhood of certainty than in the neighborhood of great risks,* and we do not think that it could be regarded, in anything whatever, as irrational.[1]

Given this psychology, the flaw in the "Sure-Thing Principle" (e.g., Savage's Postulate 2 or Samuelson's Independence Axiom) is that changes in those payoffs for which two actions "agree", or the formation of "compound lottery tickets" with other "lottery tickets" as "prizes," may be *relevant* to choice precisely because they may change *the availability of certainty of reward within a given set of actions.* Allais describes all the tests which he proposes for probing the adequacy of the Sure-Thing Principle as inspired by the fundamental idea that the psychological value of a payoff associated with an event of given probability is not independent, as the Bernoulli hypothesis would have it, of the payoffs associated with other events.[2] For as these other payoffs vary, so the possibility of achieving *certainty* of reward varies. (Similarly: as these other payoffs vary, the possibility of achieving an *unambiguous probability distribution*—hence, expectation— of payoffs may vary, as in the "three-color urn" example). The value to us

---

[1] Allais, *op. cit.,* p. 48; my translation (italics in original). There is an interesting relationship between the "psychology" described here and the pattern of bids associated with the example discussed at the end of Chapter Seven; see Figures 7.6 and 7.7. In that example a "restricted Bayes/Hurwicz criterion" with $0 < \alpha < 1/2$ would imply a pattern of choice—which seems to correspond to preferences actually asserted—such that, between two actions with the same "best guess" probability of winning a given prize, one would prefer the less ambiguous action when that probability was high, but not prefer it (or even prefer the more ambiguous action: a sort of possibility Allais does not discuss) when that probability was low.

[2] *Ibid.,* footnote (94), p. 39.

of a given ticket in a lottery among ten tickets, Allais points out, is not independent of whether or not we already possess the other nine tickets.[1]

It is clear from his account of his own preferences—"*très calculée, très réfléchie*"—that the "Sure-Thing Principle" is not an appropriate normative criterion for *Allais*, by the tests we have been applying in this study.

It is in the course of discussing this same Allais example that Savage makes the unequivocal statement of principle quoted earlier which has guided the course of my own argument:

> *If, after thorough deliberation, anyone maintains a pair of distinct preferences that are in conflict with the sure-thing principle, he must abandon, or modify, the principle;* for that kind of discrepancy seems intolerable in a normative theory. Analogous circumstances forced D. Bernoulli to abandon the theory of mathematical expectation for that of utility. In general, a person who has tentatively accepted a normative theory must conscientiously study situations in which the theory seems to lead him astray; he must decide for each *by reflection*—deduction will typically be of little relevance—whether to retain his initial impression of the situation or to accept the implications of the theory for it.[2]

Savage's subsequent comments upon his own reaction to this example, quoted below, provide the clearest possible model of the process of applying this principle; nothing could illustrate better what is meant by our familiar phrase, "honest, conscientious deliberation." At the same time, his reflections seem to lead him to a remarkably counterintuitive conclusion.

> When the two situations were first presented, I immediately expressed preference for Gamble 1 as opposed to Gamble 2 and for Gamble 4 as opposed to Gamble 3, and I *still feel an intuitive attraction to those preferences.* But I since accepted the following way of looking at the two situations, which amounts to repeated use of the sure-thing principle.

> One way in which Gambles 1–4 could be realized is by a lottery with a hundred numbered tickets and with prizes according to the schedule shown in Table 1.

---

[1] Frank Ramsey hints at this phenomenon at one point in "Truth and Probability"; he mentions that the method of measuring a person's belief by seeing the lowest odds he will accept in a given bet "suffers from being necessarily inexact . . . partly because the person may have a special eagerness or reluctance to bet, because he either enjoys or dislikes excitement or for any other reason, e.g., *to make a book*" (*op. cit.*, p. 172; italics added).

[2] Savage, *op. cit.*, p. 102.

Table 1 Prizes in Units of $100,000 in a Lottery Realizing Gambles 1–4

| | | Ticket Number | | |
		1	2–11	12–100
Situation 1	{Gamble 1	5	5	5
	{Gamble 2	0	25	5
Situation 2	{Gamble 3	5	5	0
	{Gamble 4	0	25	0

Now, if one of the tickets numbered from 12 through 100 is drawn, it will not matter, in either situation, which gamble I choose. *I therefore focus on the possibility* that one of the tickets numbered from 1 through 11 will be drawn, in which case Situations 1 and 2 are exactly parallel. The subsidiary decision depends in both situations on whether I would sell an *outright gift* of $500,000 for a 10-to-1 chance to win $2,500,000—a conclusion that I think has a claim to universality, or objectivity. Finally, consulting my purely personal taste, I find that I would prefer the gift of $500,000 and, accordingly, that I prefer Gamble 1 to Gamble 2 and (contrary to my initial reaction) Gamble 3 to Gamble 4.

It seems to me that in reversing my preference between Gambles 3 and 4 I have corrected an error.[1]

Let us look closely at the reasoning process by which Savage uncovers the "error" in his intuitive preferences. It involves, first, throwing away the information on payoffs represented by the third column, having ascertained that the payoffs in each situation are the same for both gambles in this column. He simplifies the problem in this way automatically, because the Sure-Thing Principle assures him that this column would, in the end, prove irrelevant to his decision even if he "stopped to think."

Of course, it is one of the main functions of a normative criterion to suggest how one may profitably and "safely" simplify a complicated problem; a useful criterion guides one's self-interrogation directly to *relevant* abstractions, models, analogies. The question is, always, whether this process of abstraction is suppressing *significant* distinctions or information in the original data.

In this case, the Sure-Thing Principle tells Savage to choose in both situations *as if he "knew" that a ticket from 1 to 11 would be drawn.* Why? Because if he "knew" that a ticket from 1 to 11 would *not* be drawn, he would be

---

[1] Savage, *op. cit.*, p. 103; italics added.

indifferent between the gambles, in either situation. Focusing, then, upon the first two columns only, Savage asks himself whether he would prefer $500,000 *for certain* or a 10-to-1 chance to win $2,500,000, at the risk of winning nothing. That is, he consults his personal taste only with regard to this "reduced" problem, for the Sure-Thing Principle tells him that his answer to *this* question should determine his choice in *both* the given situations.

But notice that in turning his attention away from the problem as presented to this "reduced" problem, Savage has *suppressed from his direct consideration* the very difference between the two situations that Allais considers essential. After formalizing the problem, the only question that Savage puts directly to his intuition involves a choice "in the neighborhood of certainty": a comparison between "an outright gift" and a risky prospect (with a high probability of winning). The essence of Situation 2, as Allais designed it, is that, quite unlike Situation 1, *neither* gamble offers a high probability of winning. But as Savage describes his calculations, he never proceeds to ask himself directly which gamble he would prefer in a situation "like" 2 (in this specific sense); because, according to the Sure-Thing Principle, he does not need to. In other words, he no longer really puts to a direct test the main Allais hypothesis about his preferences: i.e., the hypothesis that his behavior may be affected by this sort of *difference* (in the availability of certainty) between two situations.

It is obviously impossible for Savage to discover discrepancies between his actual preferences and those implied by Postulate 2, so long as he consults his intuition directly only with respect to certain comparisons and then "uses" Postulate 2 to *infer* his preferences in other situations, on the *assumption* that the Sure-Thing Principle constitutes an adequate theory of his own deliberated preferences.

There are, in fact, rather strong indications in Savage's comments that he might have the sort of taste for certainty that could lead, in examples like those suggested by Allais, to violations of the Sure-Thing Principle: if he were to examine his whole set of relevant preferences directly, so as to *test* the acceptability of that principle as his own normative criterion.

Thus, his "personal taste," in his hypothetical comparison, for the "outright gift" of $500,000 rather than a 10-to-1 chance of $2,500,000 seems quite in harmony with his initial, immediate preference for Gamble 1 over Gamble 2, where Gamble 1 offered the certainty of $500,000 and Gamble 2 offered no certain outcome (with a 1% chance of winning nothing). In other words, from Allais' point of view, one would not hesitate to predict from Savage's preference in his hypothetical comparison what his deliberated preference would be in Situation 1, which is "essentially" similar. But one would be less confident of predicting his deliberated choice in Situation 2, where *neither* option offers an outcome "in the neighborhood of certainty."

Savage's conclusion that he decides in favor of certainty in the hypothetical comparison and *"accordingly,* that I prefer . . . (contrary to my initial reaction) Gamble 3 to Gamble 4" raises some doubts as to whether we are learning his "true," deliberated preference, after reflection, or whether he is simply reporting the results of applying the Sure-Thing Principle. One is tempted to challenge him: "Yes, indeed, that is what Postulate 2 says you *should* prefer, given your other preferences. Now: which gamble do you *really* prefer, 3 or 4, when you stop to think about it?" Savage's earlier comment that "I *still* feel an intuitive attraction" for Gamble 4 as opposed to Gamble 3, looks remarkably like an answer to that very question! And after consulting my own preferences, it would be hard for me to empathize with anyone who would give a different answer.[1]

Since it is postulated in this example that subjective probabilities are "definite," the pattern of choices to which Savage reports an "intuitive attraction" would violate not only Savage's Postulate 2 but Samuelson's special version of the Sure-Thing Principle, his "Strong Independence

---

[1] Referring to Savage's inference, based on the Sure-Thing Principle, that his initial choice of 4 over 3 was an "error," Andrew Marshall has made to me the comment, with which I agree, that an actual preference for Gamble 3 over Gamble 4 would represent a rather extraordinary degree of "risk-aversion." The expected *money* value of Gamble 3 is $55,000; of Gamble 4, $250,000 (with the probability of "loss," or $0 outcome, "almost the same" for both, .11 vs. .1). A "von Neumann-Morgenstern utility function" representing a preference for 3 would show what would seem unusually marked curvature over the range $0 to $2,500,000, looking almost totally flat for amounts over $500,000; if we assign the arbitrary values 0 to $0 and 100 to $2,500,000, then a preference for Gamble 3 over Gamble 4 would imply: .11 ·U($500,000) > .1(100), or U($500,000) > 90.

Like Marshall, I would find the choice between Gambles 1 and 2 *difficult* (in most moods, I would be inclined to choose 2; which would not bring me into conflict with the Sure-Thing Principle) but the choice of 4 over 3 "obvious." We could easily imagine someone choosing 1 over 2 — for example, Bernoulli's "very poor man"— and in "moods of extreme caution," as Chipman puts it, we might do it ourselves.

Yet we would generally expect (i.e., give odds on) even Bernoulli's pauper to pick 4 over 3 without much hesitation.

We may simply be projecting our strong tastes on this matter; but Savage's account of his own instinctive preferences, and his persistent "intuitive attraction" to them, does not seem contradictory. Yet, if his tastes were, really, *at all* like ours, then an application of the Sure-Thing Principle that required a choice of 3 over 4 would mean forcing himself to violate a particularly strong personal preference. Faced with such a demand, one could almost agree with some vivid writing by Allais:

Axiom" relating to choices among *prospects*, or gambles with "known" probabilities. To prefer an "outright gift" of $500,000 to a 10-to-1 chance to win $2,500,000 is to prefer the "sure" prospect ($500,000; 1) to the risky prospect ($2,500,000, $0; 10/11); let us denote the first prospect A and the second prospect B, and define prospect C as the "sure" prospect ($0; 1). Now let us consider the "compound lottery tickets": (A, C; 11/100) and (B, C; 11/100). As can be seen in Table 1, Situation 2, these are equivalent to Gambles 3 and 4, respectively. To prefer prospect A to prospect B and Gamble 4 to Gamble 3 is to violate the Strong Independence Axiom, which asserts (in one form):

A ≥ B <=> (A, B; p) ≥ (B, C; p), for any prospects A, B, C, and any positive probability p.[1]

The "recognizability" of behavior-patterns such as those Allais describes, which involve violations of the Sure-Thing Principle even when personal probabilities are "definite," suggests that the following notion may have considerable heuristic value: *Certainty is to Risk, as Risk is to Ambiguity.* This expression suggests a relationship between the sorts of violations of Savage's Postulate 2 discussed by Allais and those I have described. In the Allais examples, a change in the payoffs for which two actions "agree" (e.g., the payoffs in a "constant column") converts *one* of two alternative actions from a risky proposition to a "sure thing." Correspondingly, in the "three-color urn" example, a shift in the rewards on which two actions "agree" (the payoff under Black) can produce a "definite" probability distribution over payoffs for *one* of the actions, where both actions before had been associated with an "ambiguous" set of mathematical expectations of utility, corresponding to different, "reasonably acceptable" probability dis-

---

Cet example montre bien *le caractère pseudo-évident* de [Postulate 2] de Savage. *Si tant de personnes admettent si facilement cet axiome, c'est en fait parce qu'elles n'en aperçoivent pas toutes les implications dont certaines, loin d'être rationnelles, peuvent être au contraire dans certaines situations psychologiques . . . parfaitement irrationnelles. (Op. cit.,* p. 40.)

In Dickensian English (my translation): "If the Sure-Thing Principle supposes that, . . . the Sure-Thing Principle is a ass."

[1] Paul Samuelson, "Utilité, Préference et Probabilité," *Colloque International d'É-conometrie,* 12–17 May 1952, on "Fondements et Applications de la Théorie du Risque en Économetrie," Paris, Centre National de la Recherche Scientifique, 1953, p. 147. See also, "Probability, Utility, and the Independence Axiom," p. 672; and Samuelson's closing comment: "I sometimes feel that Savage and I are the only ones in the world who will give a consistent Bernoulli answer to questionnaires of the type that Professor Allais has been circulating—but I am often not too sure about my own consistency."

tributions over payoffs. In either case, there may be many people for whom this change makes a significant difference (not, necessarily, always in a direction favoring the action no-longer risky or no-longer-ambiguous).

WINNING AT RUSSIAN ROULETTE

In 1957, in a paper with the above title, I drew attention to the fact that a person who accepted as a normative criterion for decision-making under conditions of what I would now call "ambiguity," either the minimax criterion, the Hurwicz criterion or the minimax regret criterion would violate the von Neumann-Morgenstern utility axioms in choosing among prospects that offered as prizes "strategies in a game against Nature" or, under some conditions, "strategies in a game against a rational opponent."[1] The same is true, as we have seen in this chapter, for an individual who applies a "restricted Hurwicz criterion," a "restricted Bayes/minimax criterion" or a "restricted Bayes/Hurwicz criterion," and for the same reasons. The phenomenon is essentially that (as Raiffa and Pratt point out) such criteria lead, under certain conditions of payoffs and uncertainty, to preference for such a prospect over any of its "prizes" (i.e., preference for a mixed strategy over any of its "pure" strategy components).

For someone who follows such criteria under given circumstances, it will be impossible to assign for him definite "von Neumann-Morgenstern utility" values to the "ambiguous" strategies (actions) offered as "prizes." As I pointed out in the earlier paper, such a conclusion cuts two ways. To those who do not question the normatively compelling quality of the von Neumann-Morgenstern-Samuelson utility axioms, this implication is a telling argument against the reasonableness of the criteria in question; this is the position taken by Raiffa and Pratt (and, in 1957, by Robert Strotz, among others). On the other hand, to the extent that the latter criteria seem normatively (or even descriptively) valid, one must accept certain limitations on the applicability, both normatively and predictively, of the utility axioms; they could be applied only very circumspectly, if at all, to "compound lottery tickets" in which not all probabilities could be assumed to be "definite."[2]

With respect to this tension between the von Neumann-Morgenstern-Samuelson utility axioms and the criteria then current for use in "games

---

[1] Paper read at the September meetings of the Econometric Society, Atlantic City, 1957; abstract, *Econometrica*, Vol. 26, 1958, p. 325.

[2] To the extent that one accepts the Allais hypotheses on reasonable but "non-Bernoullian" preferences among certain prospects whose probabilities all *are* "definite," this same conclusion would apply to the latter sorts of prospects.

against Nature," I was, in 1957, relatively neutral. I did point out the ubiquity of situations (involving both "risk" and "ambiguity") in which this
tension might arise. For example, various formal interpretations could be
designed to fit the notion of offering a player in a game against a rational
opponent (or in 100 simultaneous plays against 100, independent opponents;
like a checker champion in simultaneous play) a forced choice between two
"pure" strategies and a single, specified "mixture" of the two. Or, with certain modifications, the same conclusions would extent to prospects offering
games as prizes; e.g., in poker, players might flip a coin to decide whether to
play stud or draw, or whether to allow "sand-bagging," and in business or
war, similar lotteries might be introduced in the course of "bargaining over
the rules of the game." Of course, an extremely broad interpretation can be
put upon the notion of "strategies in a game against Nature" (where conditions of "complete ignorance" are not assumed).

A proponent of the von Neumann-Morgenstern axioms who was willing to exclude all such "consequences" from their jurisdiction would be
accepting fairly radical limitations on their applicability. Just how radical,
might not appear at first glance: Is it not enough to measure the utility of
all the "sure things" in the world, starting with fixed amounts of money?
But in a highly original and stimulating passage in *The Foundations of Statistics*, L. J. Savage has pointed out just how rare "sure things," in a strict
and useful sense, may be:

> Consider a simple example. Jones is faced with the decision whether to
> buy a certain sedan for a thousand dollars, or to buy neither and continue
> carless. The simplest analysis, and the one generally assumed, is that Jones
> is deciding between three definite and sure enjoyments, that of the sedan,
> the convertible, or the thousand dollars. Chance and uncertainty are
> considered to have nothing to do with the situation. This simple analysis
> may well be appropriate in some contexts; however, it is not difficult to
> recognize that Jones must in fact take account of many uncertain future
> possibilities in actually making his choice. The relative fragility of the con-
> vertible will be compensated only if Jones's hope to arrange a long vacation
> in a warm and scenic part of the country actually materializes; Jones would
> not buy a car at all if he thought it likely that he would immediately be faced
> by a financial emergency arising out of the sickness of himself or of some
> member of his family; he would be glad to put the money into a car, or
> almost any durable goods, if he feared extensive inflation. This brings out
> the fact that what are often thought of as consequences (that is, sure expe-
> riences of the deciding person) in isolated decision situations typically are
> in reality highly uncertain. Indeed, in the final analysis, a consequence is
> an idealization that can perhaps never be well approximated. I therefore

suggest that we must expect acts with actually uncertain consequences to play the role of sure consequences in typical isolated decision situations.[1]

If one believes—*as I do now*—that it can be reasonable to exhibit a pattern of preferences among "acts with actually uncertain consequences" such as that implied, for example, by the "restricted Bayes/Hurwicz criterion," then the strict applicability of the utility axioms comes into question for an extraordinarily large number of erstwhile "sure consequences," under the blinding illumination of Savage's comment.

No such paradox confronts the "neo-Bernoullian" who limits his attention to those decision-makers who conform to the "Bernoulli proposition" under *all* circumstances. But as quoted earlier (Chapter Seven), Savage, on one occasion, suggested circumstances when he himself might accept, in particular, the "minimax regret" criterion: situations in which an "aura of vagueness" attached to his judgments of personal probability. Since "minimaxing regret" can lead to a preference for mixed acts, like other instances of minimax principles, this behavior (which Savage might no longer espouse as reasonable) would raise obstacles to measuring the utility of any "consequences" whose actual uncertainties, suggested by Savage above, were subject to an "aura of vagueness." How many consequences would this *not* affect?

Undoubtedly, for many minor, short-run decisions it is possible to abstract from uncertainties associated with the individual "consequences," or to represent those uncertainties in terms of "definite" probability distributions over payoffs. But let us recall Marschak's characterization of the intended scope of the utility axioms:

> If the space X of "outcomes" and the space S of strategies are defined, this permits us to take care of all human decisions, transcending conventional economics and including the private man's choice of profession or wife, the legislator's choice of election tactics or national policies or military and administrative decisions.[2]

These "consequences" scarcely escape the paradox. The choice of a wife, indeed!—the oldest game against Nature. Who will deny that his prenuptial anticipations possessed, to put it mildly, an "aura of vagueness"?

---

[1] Savage, *op. cit.*, pp. 83–84. "It may fairly be said that a lottery prize is not an act, but rather the opportunity to choose from a number of acts. Thus a cash prize puts its possessor in a position to choose among many purchases he could not otherwise afford." (p. 86)

[2] Jacob Marschak, "Why 'Should' Statisticians and Businessmen Maximize Moral Expectation?", p. 499.

Election tactics, military decisions: these are strategies in a game! Allow sufficient "vagueness" of opinion to make criteria for decision-making under partial ignorance appropriate, and in choosing among lotteries with campaigns or brides for prizes, the legislator or prospective husband slip out from Marschak's theory.

In fact, who will remain? It is hard to tell; if the axioms are to apply to lotteries with only "sure consequences" (not "strategies") for prizes, it no longer seems an easy problem to decide when in reality these conditions are approximated. Once more, only conscientious deliberation with respect to a variety of specific circumstances can determine this for a given individual.

This does not guarantee that the considerations introduced in this study serve to rationalize the behavior of the "classical violators" of the utility axioms described at the beginning of this chapter: the reckless mountaineer and the player of Russian Roulette, for example. Still, it may be worthwhile to take a second look at them. My 1957 suggestions for optimal play in Russian Roulette have not previously been published (except in abstract). To quote them, below, will end this chapter, which has been somewhat introspective and speculative, on a note of practical application.

> As in the case of Marschak's "mountaineer" (who likewise violates Axiom 3:B:b), the possible consequences of alternative actions open to the Russian Roulette player have always been described as "Life" or "Death." Yet even the crudest simplification must allow the possibilities that Death may be associated either with Heaven or Hell, and it is plausible to suppose that the probabilities of these eventualities are subject to an "aura of vagueness" for typical players.

> To simplify the game, let us also assume that the subject has strong time-preference, ignoring consequences beyond the next few years (it seems plausible that Russian Roulette players do not tend to live in the future). If we arbitrarily choose the origin of his utility function so that the value of living a few more years is zero, the payoff function for a player might appear as in Fig. 8.13a (where the strategy Death represents six bullets in the cylinder, and Life, none).

	Heaven	Hell
Life	0	0
Death	1000	-5000

Fig. 8.13a

An appropriate criterion here would be to minimax *regret*.[1] After all, the possibility of foregoing Heaven in the immediate future is a mark against Life; and the prospect of experiencing Hell sooner than necessary is a deterrent to Death. The player may, then, turn his attention to the "regret" matrix in Fig. 8.13b.

	Heaven	Hell	
Life	1000	0	
Death	0	5000	**Fig. 8.13b**
(Life, Death, 5/6)	833	833	

He will prefer Life to Death, if he is restricted to those "pure" alternatives. But his *optimum* strategy, in terms of his criterion, is (Life, Death; 5/6). The "best" way for him to play is to put one bullet in the chamber and spin it.

This is, in fact, the traditional strategy. That testifies to the realism of our assumptions. But our results are not cut-and-dried; it does not follow that the traditional choice is really best-suited to the tastes of every player. To play optimally, each person must determine for himself his own payoff function and the criterion that seems most acceptable to him. One player, for example, may minimax regret but place a higher value than assumed

---

[1] Since 1957, when this analysis was written, the "minimax regret" has come to seem less appropriate to me; of the standard criteria for "games against Nature," it is the *one* that does *not* appear to correspond to patterns of deliberated choices among "ambiguous" gambles that I have observed or have heard defended, even in a "restricted" form applied to "reasonably acceptable" probability distributions.

With somewhat different payoffs, it might be possible to generate behavior typically chosen in Russian Roulette with some other criterion, e.g., the "restricted Hurwicz criterion." However, I preserve the criterion originally presented here, out of respect to Savage's own account of his taste for it under conditions of "vagueness" (*Foundations of Statistics*, p. 169). The "non-neo-Bernoullian" is always tolerant of the other fellow's normative criterion. Besides it is, after all, possible that the decision problem considered here is precisely the practical context in which minimaxing regret is appropriate.

above on Heaven: say, 2500. The reasonable course for him is to put *two* bullets in the chamber.

On the other hand, if the player follows, say [the "restricted Bayes/mini-max"] criterion, at these payoffs he might as well live.

Bibliography

Publisher's note: the bibliography appears as in original form.

Allais, Maurice, "Fondements d'Une Théorie Positive des Choix Comportant Un Risque et Critique des Postulates et Axiomes de l'École Américaine," *Annales des Mines*, numéro spécial 1955.

Anderson, N. H., and R. E. Whalen, "Likelihood Judgments and Sequential Effects in a Two-Choice Probability Learning Situation," *Journal of Experimental Psychology*, Vol. 60, 1960, pp. 111–120.

Angell, James W., "Uncertainty, Likelihoods and Investment Decisions," *The Quarterly Journal of Economics*, Vol. LXXIV, 1960, pp. 1–28.

Arrow, Kenneth J., "Alternative Approaches to the Theory of Choice in Risk-Taking Situations," *Econometrica*, Vol. 19, 1951, pp. 404–437.

――――, "Mathematical Models in the Social Sciences," *The Policy Sciences*, Daniel Lerner and H. D. Lasswell, ed. (Stanford, 1951), pp. 129–154.

――――, "Hurwicz's Optimality Criterion for Decision-Making Under Ignorance," *Technical Report 6*, Department of Economics and Statistics, Stanford University, 1953.

Atthowe, J. M., Jr., "Types of Conflict and Their Resolution: A Reinterpretation," *Journal of Experimental Psychology*, Vol. 59, 1960, pp. 1–9.

Baumol, William J., "The Neumann-Morgenstern Utility Index—An Ordinalist View," *Journal of Political Economy*, Vol. 59, 1951, pp. 61–66.

Bayes, Thomas, "Essay Towards Solving a Problem in the Doctrine of Chances," *The Philosophical Transactions*, Vol. 53, 1763, pp. 370–418; reprinted in *Biometrika*, Vol. 45, 1958, pp. 293–315.

Bernoulli, Daniel, "Specimen Theories Novae de Mensura Sortis," *Commentarii Academiae Scientiarum Imperialis Petropolitanae*, Tomus V (Papers of the Imperial Academy of Sciences in Petersburg, Vol. 1) 1738, pp. 175–1952; translated by Dr. Louise Sommer, as "Exposition of a New Theory of the Measurement of Risk," *Econometrica*, Vol. 22, 1954, pp. 23–36.

Bitterman, M. E., and Calvin W. Kniffin, "Manifest Anxiety and 'Perceptual Defense,'" *Journal of Abnormal and Social Psychology*, Vol. 48, 1953, pp. 248–252.

Blackwell, David, and Girshick, M. A., *Theory of Games and Statistical Decisions* (New York, 1954).

Borel, Emile, "A propos d'un Traité de Probabilités," pp. 134–146, Note II of *Valeur Pratique et Philosophie des Probabilités*, Gauthier-Villars, (Paris, 1939). [Originally in *Revue Philosophique*, Vol. 98, 1924, pp. 321–336.]

Boulding, Kenneth E., *The Image* (Ann Arbor, 1959).

Bowman, Mary Jean (Ed.), *Expectations, Uncertainty, and Business Behavior*, (New York, 1958).

Braithwaite, Richard B., *Theory of Games as a Tool for the Moral Philosopher* (Cambridge, 1955).

———, *Scientific Explanation, A Study of the Function of Theory, Probability and Law in Science* (New York, 1960).

Brim, Orville G., Jr., "Attitude Content - Intensity and Probability Expectations," *American Sociological Review*, Vol. 20, 1955, pp. 68–76.

Bross, Irwin D. J., *Design for Decision* (New York, 1953).

Brown, C. B., "Concepts of Structural Safety," *Journal of the Structural Division*, Vol. 86, 1960, pp. 39–57.

Bruner, Jerome S., and Cecile C. Goodman, "Value and Need as Organizing Factors in Perception," *Journal of Abnormal and Social Psychology*, Vol. 42, 1947, pp. 33–34.

———, and Leo Postman, "Symbolic Value as an Organizing Factor in Perception," *Journal of Social Psychology*, Vol. 27, Second Half, 1948, pp. 203–208.

———, Jacqueline J. Goodnow, and George A. Austin, *A Study of Thinking* (New York, 1958).

———, and Henri Tajfel, "Cognitive Risk and Environmental Change," *Journal of Abnormal and Social Psychology*, Vol. 62, 1961, pp. 231–241.

Cantril, Hadley, "The Prediction of Social Events," *Journal of Abnormal and Social Psychology*, Vol. 33, 1938, pp. 364–389.

Chernoff, Herman, "Rational Selection of Decision Functions," *Econometrica*, Vol. 22, 1954, pp. 422–443.

———, and Lincoln E. Moses, *Elementary Decision Theory* (New York, 1959).

Chipman, John S., "Stochastic Choice and Subjective Probability," *Decision, Values and Groups*, ed. D. Willmer (New York, 1960), pp. 70–95.

Christie, Richard, and Marie Jahoda (Ed.), *Studies in the Scope and Method of "The Authoritarian Personality"* (Illinois, 1954).

Churchman, C. West, "Problems of Value Measurement for a Theory of Induction and Decisions," *Third Berkeley Symposium on Mathematical Statistics and Probability* (Berkeley, 1956), Vol. V, pp. 53–59.

———, *Prediction and Optimal Decision* (New Jersey, 1961).

Coombs, C. H., and D. G. Pruitt, "Components of Risk in Decision Making: Probability and Variance Preferences," *Journal of Experimental Psychology*, Vol. 60, 1960, pp. 265–277.

Cooper, W. W., C. J. Hitch, W. J. Baumol, M. K. Shubik, T. C. Schelling, S. Valavanis, and D. Ellsberg, "Economics and Operations Research: A Symposium," *Review of Economics and Statistics*, Vol. XL, 1958, pp. 195–229.

Cowen, Emory L., "The Influence of Varying Degrees of Psychological Stress on Problem-Solving Rigidity," *Journal of Abnormal and Social Psychology,* Vol. 47, 1952, pp. 512–519.

Cox, D. R., "Discussion on Dr. Smith's Paper," *Journal of the Royal Statistical Society,* Series B, Vol. 23, 1961, pp. 27–28.

Davidson, Donald, J. C. C. McKinsey, and Patrick Suppes, "Outlines of a Formal Theory of Value, I," *Philosophy of Science,* Vol. 22, 1955, pp. 140–160.

———, Sidney Siegel, and Patrick Suppes, *Some Experiments and Related Theory on the Measurement of Utility and Subjective Probability,* Applied Mathematics and Statistics Laboratory, Stanford University, *Technical Report No. 1,* August, 1955.

———, and Patrick Suppes, "A Finitistic Axiomatization of Subjective Probability and Utility," *Econometrica,* Vol. 24, 1956, pp. 264–275.

———, and Jacob Marschak, *Experimental Tests of a Stochastic Decision Theory,* Applied Mathematics and Statistics Laboratory, Stanford University, *Technical Report No. 17,* July, 1958.

de Finetti, Bruno, "La Prevision: Ses Lois Logiques, Ses Sources Subjectives," *Annales de l'Institut Henri Poincare,* Vol. 7, 1937, pp. 1–68.

———, "Recent Suggestions for the Reconciliations of Theories of Probability," *Proceedings of the Second Berkeley Symposium on Mathematical Statistics and Probability* (Berkeley, 1951), pp. 217–226.

———, "The Bayesian Approach to the Rejection of Outliers," *Proceedings of the Fourth Berkeley Symposium on Mathematical Statistics and Probability* (Berkeley, 1961), Vol. 1, pp. 199–210.

de Jouvenel, Bertrand, "Les Recherches sur la Decision," *Bulletin SEDEIS, Futuribles,* No. 809 Supplément, 20 January 1962, pp. 2–32.

Duesenberry, James S., *Income, Saving, and the Theory of Consumer Behavior* (Cambridge, 1949).

Edwards, Ward, "Probability-Preferences in Gambling," *American Journal of Psychology,* 1953, Vol. 66, pp. 349–364.

———, "Probability Preferences Among Bets with Differing Expected Values," *American Journal of Psychology,* Vol. 67, 1954, pp. 56–67.

———, "The Reliability of Probability Preferences," *American Journal of Psychology,* Vol. 67, 1954, pp. 68–95.

———, "The Theory of Decision Making," *Psychological Bulletin,* Vol. 5, 1954, pp. 380–417.

———, "Variance Preferences in Gambling," *American Journal of Psychology,* Vol. 67, 1954, pp. 441–452.

———, "Utility, Subjective Probability, Their Interaction, and Variance Preferences," *Journal of Conflict Resolution,* Vol. VI, 1962, pp. 42–51.

Erlich, Danuta, Isaiah Guttman, Peter Schonbach, and Judson Mills, "Postdecision Exposure to Relevant Information," *Journal of Abnormal and Social Psychology,* Vol. 54, 1957, pp. 98–102.

Ellsberg, Daniel, *Theories of Rational Choice Under Uncertainty: The Contributions of von Neumann and Morgenstern* (undergraduate honors thesis), Harvard University, June, 1952.

——, "Classic and Current Notions of 'Measurable Utility,'" *Economic Journal*, Vol. LXIV, 1954, pp. 528–556.

——, "Theory of the Reluctant Duelist," *American Economic Review*, Vol. XLVI, 1956, pp. 909–923.

——, "Winning at Russian Roulette" (abstract), *Econometrica*, Vol. 26, 1958, p. 325.

——, "A Final Comment: Symposium on Economics and Operations Research," *Review of Economics and Statistics*, Vol. XL, 1958, pp. 227–229.

——, "Risk, Ambiguity and the Savage Axioms" (abstract), *Econometrica*, Vol. 29, 1961, pp. 454–455.

——, "review, *Decision Making* (Donald Davidson and Patrick Suppes), *American Economic Review*, Vol. LI, 1961, pp. 420–421.

——, "The Crude Analysis of Strategic Choices," *American Economic Review*, Vol. LI, 1961, pp. 472–478.

——, "Risk, Ambiguity, and the Savage Axioms," *Quarterly Journal of Economics*, Vol. LXXV, 1961, pp. 644–661.

Erikson, Charles W., "Defense Against Ego-Threat in Memory and Perception," *Journal of Abnormal and Social Psychology*, Vol. 47, 1952, pp. 230–235.

Feather, N. T., "Subjective Probability and Decision Under Uncertainty," *Psychological Review*, Vol. 66, 1959, pp. 150–164.

Festinger, Leon, *A Theory of Cognitive Dissonance* (Illinois, 1957).

Filer, Robert J., "Frustration, Satisfaction, and Other Factors Affecting the Attractiveness of Goal Objects," *Journal of Abnormal and Social Psychology*, Vol. 47, 1952, pp. 203–212.

Fisher, Charles, "Dreams and Perception," *American Psychoanalytic Association Journal*, Vol. 2, 1954, pp. 389–445.

Fisher, Ronald A., *The Design of Experiments* (London, 1947).

——, *Statistical Methods and Scientific Inference* (New York, 1956).

——, "The Underworld of Probability," *Sankhyā*, Vol. 18, Parts 3 and 4, 1957, pp. 201–210.

Frenkel-Brunswik, E., "Intolerance of Ambiguity as an Emotional and Perceptual Personality Variable," *Journal of Personality*, Vol. 18, 1949, pp. 108–143.

Friedman, Milton, and L. J. Savage, "The Utility Analysis of Choices Involving Risk," *Journal of Political Economy*, Vol. 56, 1948, pp. 279–304.

——, "The Expected-Utility Hypothesis and the Measurability of Utility," *Journal of Political Economy*, Vol. 60, 1952, pp. 463–474.

Georgescu-Roegen, Nicholas, "Choice, Expectations, and Measurability," *Quarterly Journal of Economics*, Vol. LXVIII, 1954, pp. 503–534.

——, "The Nature of Expectation and Uncertainty," in *Expectations, Uncertainty, and Business Behavior*, ed. M. J. Bowman (New York, 1958), pp. 11–29.

Good, I. J., *Probability and the Weighing of Evidence* (London and New York, 1950).

————, "Rational Decisions," *Journal of the Royal Statistical Society*, Ser. B., Vol. 14, 1952, pp. 107–114.

————, "The Population Frequencies of Species and the Estimation of Population Parameters," *Biometrika*, Vol. 40, Parts 3 and 4, 1953, pp. 237–264.

————, "Saddle-Point Methods for the Multinomial Distribution," *Annals of Mathematical Statistics*, Vol. 28, 1957, pp. 861–881.

————, "Significance Tests in Parallel and in Series," *Journal of the American Statistical Association*, Vol. 53, 1958, pp. 799–813.

————, "Could a Machine Make Probability Judgments?, Part 1," *Computers and Automation*, Vol. 8, 1959, pp. 14–16. Concluding part in Vol. 8, 1959, pp. 24–26.

————, "Kinds of Probability," *Science*, Vol. 129, 1959, pp. 443–447.

————, "The Paradox of Confirmation," *The British Journal for the Philosophy of Science*, Vol. XI, 1960, pp. 145–149.

————, "A Causal Calculus (I)," *The British Journal for the Philosophy of Science*, Vol. XI, 1961, pp. 305–318; "A Causal Calculus (II)," Vol. XII, 1961, pp. 43–51.

————, "Subjective Probability as the Measure of a None-Measurable Set," *Proceedings of the International Congress for Logic, Methodology and Philosophy of Science* (1960) (forthcoming).

————, "Weight of Evidence, Causality, and False-Alarm Probabilities," *Proceedings of the Fourth London Symposium on Information Theory*, ed. Colin Cherry (London, forthcoming).

Goodnow, J. J., "Determinants of Choice-Distribution in Two-Choice Probability Situations," *American Journal of Psychology*, Vol. 68, 1955, pp. 106–116.

Hake, Harold W., and Ray Hyman, "Perception of the Statistical Structure of a Random Series of Binary Symbols," *Journal of Experimental Psychology*, Vol. 45, 1953, pp. 64–74.

Hamilton, Vernon, "Perceptual and Personality Dynamics in Reactions to Ambiguity," *British Journal of Psychology*, Vol. 48, 1957, pp. 200–215.

Helmer, Olaf, and Nicholas Rescher, *On the Epistemology of the Inexact Sciences*, The RAND Corporation, Report R-353, February 1960.

Hitch, Charles J., and Roland N. McKean, *The Economics of Defense in the Nuclear Age* (Cambridge, 1960).

Hitch, Charles J., *The Uses of Economics*, The RAND Corporation, Paper P-2179, November 1960.

Hodges, J. L., Jr., and E. L. Lehmann, "Some Problems in Minimax Point Estimation," *Annals of Mathematical Statistics*, Vol. 21, 1950, pp. 182–197.

————, "The Use of Previous Experience in Reaching Statistical Decisions," *Annals of Mathematical Statistics*, Vol. 23, 1952, pp. 396–407.

Hurst, Paul M., and Sidney Siegel, "Prediction of Decisions from a Higher Ordered Metric Scale of Utility," *Journal of Experimental Psychology*, Vol. 52, 1952, pp. 138–144.

Hurwicz, Leonid, "Optimality Criteria for Decision Making Under Ignorance," *Cowles Commission Discussion Paper*, Statistics, No. 370 (Chicago, 1951), (mimeographed).

———, "Some Specification Problems and Applications to Econometric Models," *Econometrica*, Vol. 19, 1951, pp. 343–344.

Hyman, Ray, "Stimulus Information as a Determinant of Reaction Time," *Journal of Experimental Psychology*, Vol. 45, 1953, pp. 188–196.

Irwin, F. W., "Stated Expectations as Functions of Probability and Desirability of Outcomes," *Journal of Personality*, Vol. 21, 1953, pp. 329–335.

Jeffreys, Harold, *Theory of Probability* (Oxford, 1948).

Kaysen, Carl, "The Minimax Rule of the Theory of Games, and the Choices of Strategies Under Conditions of Uncertainty," *Metroeconomica*, Vol. 4, 1952, pp. 5–14.

Kemeny, John G., "Fair Bets and Inductive Probabilities," *Journal of Symbolic Logic*, Vol. 20, 1955, pp. 263–273.

Keynes, John Maynard, *A Treatise on Probability* (London and New York, 1921, 2d ed. 1929).

———, *The General Theory of Employment Interest and Money* (New York, 1935.

———, *Essays and Sketches in Biography* (New York, 1956).

Klein, George S., Herbert J. Schlesinger, and David E. Meister, "The Effort of Personal Values on Perception: An Experimental Critique," *Psychological Review*, Vol. 58, 1951, pp. 96–112.

Klein, George S., "Perception, Motives and Personality," in *Psychology of Personality*, ed., J. L. McCary (New York, 1956).

Knight, Frank H., *Risk, Uncertainty and Profit* (Boston, 1921).

Kogan, Nathan, and Michael A. Wallach, "Certainty of Judgment and the Evaluation of Risk," *Psychological Reports*, Vol. 6, 1960, pp. 207–213.

Komorita, S. S., "Factors Which Influence Subjective Probability," *Journal of Experimental Psychology*, Vol. 58, 1959, pp. 386–389.

Koopman, B. O., "The Axioms and Algebra of Intuitive Probability," *Annals of Mathematics*, Ser. 2, Vol. 41, 1940, pp. 269–292.

———, "Intuitive Probabilities and Sequences," *Annals of Mathematics*, Ser. 2, Vol. 42, 1941, pp. 169–187.

———, "The Bases of Probability," *Bulletin of the American Mathematical Society*, Vol. 46, 1940, pp. 763–774.

Latané, Henry Allen, "Criteria for Choice Among Risky Ventures," *Journal of Political Economy*, Vol. LXVII, 1959, pp. 144–155.

Lehmann, R. Sherman, "On Confirmation and Rational Betting," *Journal of Symbolic Logic*, Vol. 20, 1955, pp. 251–262.

Lerner, Daniel, ed., *Evidence and Inference* (Illinois, 1958).

Lindley, Dennis V., "Statistical Inference," *Journal of the Royal Statistical Society*, Ser. B, Vol. 15, 1953, pp. 30–76.

———, "A Statistical Paradox," *Biometrika*, Vol. 44, 1957, pp. 187–192.

———, "The Use of Prior Probability Distributions in Statistical Inference and Decisions," *Proceedings of the Fourth Berkeley Symposium on Mathematical Statistics and Probability* (Berkeley, 1961), Vol. 1, pp. 453–468.

Lindzey, Gardner, ed., *Assessment of Human Motives* (New York, 1960).

Little, I. M. D., *A Critique of Welfare Economics* (Oxford, 1950).

Luce, Duncan, and Howard Raiffa, *Games and Decisions* (New York, 1957).

Manne, Alan S., "The Strong Independence Assumption - Gasoline Blends and Probability Mixtures," *Econometrica*, Vol. 20, 1952, pp. 665–669.

Markowitz, Harry, "The Utility of Wealth," *Journal of Political Economy*, Vol. 60, 1952, pp. 151–158.

Marks, Rose W., "The Effect of Probability, Desirability, and 'Privilege' on the Stated Expectations of Children," *Journal of Personality*, Vol. 19, 1951, pp. 332–351.

Marschak, Jacob, "Neumann's and Morgenstern's New Approach to Static Economics," *Journal of Political Economy*, Vol. 54, 1946, pp. 97–115.

———, "Role of Liquidity Under Complete and Incompete Information," *Cowles Commission Papers*, New Series, No. 37 (Chicago, 1949).

———, "Rational Behavior, Uncertain Prospects, and Measurable Utility," *Econometrica*, Vol. 18, 1950, pp. 111–141.

———, "Why 'Should' Statisticians and Businessmen Maximise 'Moral Expectation'?," *Proceedings of the Second Berkeley Symposium on Mathematical Statistics and Probability* (Berkeley, 1951).

———, "Three Lectures on Probability in the Social Sciences," *Cowles Commission Papers*, New Series, No. 82 (Chicago, 1954).

———, "Towards an Economic Theory of Organization and Information," *Cowles Commission Papers*, New Series, No. 95 (Chicago, 1954).

———, "Norms and Habits of Decision Making Under Certainty," *Mathematical Models of Human Behavior* (Connecticut, 1955), pp. 45–54.

———, "Suggested Experiments on Tastes and Beliefs," *Cowles Foundation Discussion Paper No. 7* (Chicago, 1955).

———, "Remarks on the Economics of Information," *Contributions to Scientific Research in Management*, (Berkeley, 1961).

Marshall, Alfred, *Principles of Economics* (London, 1925).

Martin, Barclay, "Intolerance of Ambiguity in Interpersonal and Perceptual Behavior," *Journal of Personality*, Vol. 22, 1953–1954, pp. 494–503.

McGinnies, Elliott, and Howard Sherman, "Generalization of Perceptual Defense," *Journal of Abnormal and Social Psychology*, Vol. 47, 1952, pp. 81–85.

McGregor, Douglas, "The Major Determinants of the Prediction of Social Events," *Journal of Abnormal and Social Psychology*, Vol. 33, 1938, pp. 179–204.

Milnor, John, "Games against Nature," in *Decision Processes*, ed. Thrall, Coombs, and Davis, (New York, 1954) pp. 45–59.

Minsky, Marvin, "Steps Toward Artificial Intelligence," *Proceedings of the IRE*, Vol. 49, 1961.

Mosteller, Frederick and Philip Nogee, "An Experimental Measurement of Utility," *Journal of Political Economy*, Vol. LIX, 1951, pp. 371–404.

Myers, J. L. and E. Sadler, "Effects of Range of Payoffs as a Variable in Risk Taking," *Journal of Experimental Psychology*, Vol. 60, 1960, pp. 306–309.

Nelson, Richard R., *The Economics of Parallel R and D Efforts*, The RAND Corporation, Paper P-1774, August, 1959.

————, *Uncertainty, Prediction, and Competitive Equilibrium*, The RAND Corporation, Paper P-1687, May, 1960.

————, "Uncertainty, Learning, and the Economics of Parallel Research and Development Efforts," *Review of Economics and Statistics*, Vol. XLIII, 1961, pp. 351–364.

Nelson, Richard R. and Sidney G. Winter, Jr., *Weather Information and Economic Decisions, A Preliminary Report*." The RAND Corporation, Research Memorandum RM-2620-NASA, August, 1960.

Neyman, Jerzy, *Lectures and Conferences on Mathematical Statistics and Probability*, (Washington, 1952).

O'Connor, Patricia, "Ethnocentrism, 'Intolerance of Ambiguity,' and Abstract Reasoning Ability," *The Journal of Abnormal and Social Psychology*, Vol. 47, 1952, pp. 526–530.

Polya, G., *Mathematics and Plausible Reasoning: Volume I, Induction and Analogy in Mathematics; Volume II, Patterns of Plausible Inference*, (New Jersey, 1954).

Postman, Leo and Jerome S. Bruner, "Personal Values as Selective Factors in Perception," *Journal of Abnormal and Social Psychology*, Vol. 43, 1948, pp. 142–154.

Postman, Leo and Donald R. Brown, "The Perceptual Consequences of Success and Failure," *Journal of Abnormal and Social Psychology*, Vol. 47, 1952, pp. 213–221.

Postman, Leo, Wanda C. Bronson, and George L. Gropper, "Is There a Mechanism of Perceptual Defense?," *The Journal of Abnormal and Social Psychology*, Vol. 48, 1953, pp. 215–224.

Pratt, John W., review of *Testing Statistical Hypotheses*, by E. L. Lehmann, *Journal of the American Statistical Association*, Vol. 56, 1961, pp. 163–167.

Quastler, Henry (Ed), *Information Theory in Psychology*, (Illinois, 1955).

Radner, Roy and Jacob Marschak, "Note on Some Proposed Decision Criteria," *Cowles Commission Papers*, New Series, No. 96 (Chicago, 1954).

Raiffa, Howard, and Robert Schlaifer, *Applied Statistical Decision Theory* (Boston, 1961).

Raiffa, Howard, "Risk, Ambiguity, and the Savage Axioms: Comment", *Quarterly Journal of Economics*, Vol. LXXV, pp. 690–694.

Ramsey, Frank P., *The Foundations of Mathematics and Other Logical Essays*, (London and New York, 1931).

Reichenbach, Hans, "Philosophical Foundations of Probability," *Proceedings of the Berkeley Symposium on Mathematical Statistics and Probability* (Berkeley, 1949), pp. 1–20.

————, "Probability Methods in Social Science," *The Policy Sciences*, (Stanford, 1951).

Robbins, Herbert, "Asymptotically Subminimax Solutions of Compound Statistical Decision Problems," *Proceedings of the Second Berkeley Symposium on Mathematical Statistics and Probability*, (Berkeley, 1951)

Rokeach, Milton, "Generalized Mental Rigidity as a Factor in Ethnocentrism," *Journal of Abnormal and Social Psychology*, Vol. 43, 1948, pp. 259–278.

————, "The Nature and Meaning of Dogmatism," *Psychological Review*, Vol. 61, 1954, pp. 194–204.

Samuelson, Paul, "Probability and the Attempts to Measure Utility", *Economic Review, Tokyo University of Commerce*, Hitotsubashi University, Vol. 1, 1950, pp. 167–173.

————, "Utilité, Préférence et Probabilité," *Colloque International d'Économétrie* May 12–17, 1952, on "Fondements et Applications de la Théorie du Risque en Économétrie," Paris, Centre National de la Recherche Scientifique, 1953, pp. 141–150.

Samuelson, Paul, "Probability, Utility, and the Independence Axiom," *Econometrica*, Vol. 20, 1952, pp. 670–678.

Savage, Leonard J., "The Theory of Statistical Decision," *Journal of the American Statistical Association*, Vol. 46, 1951, pp. 55–67.

————, review of I. J. Good's, *Probability and the Weighing of Evidence, Journal of the American Statistical Association*, Vol. 46, 1951, pp. 383–384.

————, review of Rudolf Carnap's *Logical Foundations of Probability Econometrica*, Vol. 20, 1952, pp. 688–690.

————, "Une Axiomatisation de Comportement Raisonnable Face a L'Incértitude," *Colloque International d'Econometrie*, May 12–17, 1952, on "Fondements et Applications de la Théorie du Risque en Économétrie" Paris, Centre National de la Recherche Scientifique, 1953, pp. 29–33.

————, *The Foundations of Statistics*, (New York, 1954).

————, *The Casino That Takes a Percentage and What You Can Do About It*, The RAND Corporation, Paper P-1132, July, 1957.

————, "The Foundations of Statistics Reconsidered," *Proceedings of the Fourth Berkeley Symposium on Mathematical Statistics and Probability*, (Berkeley, 1961) Vol. 1, pp. 575–587.

————, "Bayesian Statistics," lecture at the *Third Symposium on Decision and Information Processes*, Purdue University, April, 1961, to be published in *Decision and Information Processes*, (New York, Macmillan)

————, "The Subjective Basis of Statistical Practice," University of Michigan, July, 1961 (hectographed).

————, "Subjective Probability and Statistical Practice," SRC-91023S14, University of Chicago mimeographed; to be published in 1962 in *The Foundations of Statistical Inference*, Methuen, London.

Schlaifer, Robert, *Probability and Statistics for Business Decisions*, (New York, 1959).

Scodel, Alvin, Philburn Ratoosh and J. Sayer Minas, "Some Personality Correlates of Decision Making Under Conditions of Risk," *Behavioral Science*, Vol. 4, 1959, pp. 19–28.

Scott, Dans, and Patrick Suppes, *Foundational Aspects of Theories of Measurement*, Applied Mathematics and Statistics Laboratory, Stanford University, Technical Report No. 6, April, 1957.

Seeman, William, and Roger Buck, "On a Behavioristic Approach to the Concept of Wish-Fulfillment," *Journal of Abnormal and Social Psychology*, Vol. 47, 1952, pp. 17–24.

Shackle, G. L. S., *Expectation in Economics* (Cambridge, 1952).

———, *Uncertainty in Economics* (Cambridge, 1955).

Shimony, Abner, "Coherence and the Axioms of Confirmation," *Journal of Symbolic Logic*, Vol. 20, 1955, pp. 1–28.

Shubik, Martin, "Information, Theories of Competition, and the Theory of Games," *Journal of Political Economy*, Vol. 60, 1952, pp. 145–150.

———, "Information, Risk, Ignorance and Indeterminacy," *Quarterly Journal of Economics*, Vol. LXVIII, 1954, pp. 629–640.

Siegel, Sidney, "A Method for Obtaining an Ordered Metric Scale," *Psychometrika*, Vol. 21, 1956, pp. 207–216.

Simon, Herbert A., "A Behavioral Model of Rational Choice," *Quarterly Journal of Economics*, Vol. CXIX, 1955, pp. 99–118.

Smith, Cedric A. B., "Consistency in Statistical Inference and Decision," *Journal of the Royal Statistical Society*, Series B., Vol. 23, 1961, pp. 1–25.

Solley, Charles M., Douglas N. Jackson, and Samuel J. Messick, "Guessing Behavior and Autism," *Journal of Abnormal and Social Psychology*, Vol. 54, 1957, pp. 32–36.

Suppes, Patrick, and Donald Davidson, "A Finitistic Axiomatization of Subjective Probability and Utility," *Econometrica*, Vol. XXIV, 1956, pp. 264–275.

———, *Decision-Making* (Stanford, 1957).

Suppes, Patrick, and Muriel Winet, "An Axiomatization of Utility Based on the Notion of Utility Differences," *Management Science*, Vol. 1, 1955, pp. 259–270.

Thistlethwaite, Donald, "Attitude and Structure as Factors in the Distortion of Reasoning," *Journal of Abnormal and Social Psychology*, Vol. 45, 1950, pp. 442–458.

Thrall, R. M., C. H. Coombs, R. L. Davis, ed., *Decision Processes* (New York, 1954).

Townsend, Elias Carter, *Risks: The Key to Combat Intelligence*, (Pennsylvania, 1955).

von Neumann, John, and Oskar Morgenstern, *The Theory of Games and Economic Behavior* (Princeton, 1943, 2d edition, 1947).

Wald, Abraham, "Contributions to the Theory of Statistical Estimation and Testing Hypotheses," *Annals of Mathematical Statistics*, Vol. 10, 1939, pp. 299–326.

———, "Generalization of a Theorem by von Neumann Concerning Zero-Sum Two-Person Games," *Annals of Mathematics*, Vol. 46, 1945, pp. 281–286.

———, "Statistical Decision Functions which Minimize the Maximum Risk," *Annals of Mathematics*, Vol. 46, 1945, pp. 265–280.

———, *Statistical Decision Functions* (New York, 1950).

———, "Basic Ideas of a General Theory of Statistical Decision Rules," *Proceedings of the International Congress of Mathematicians*, Vol. I, pp. 231–243 (Providence, 1952).

——, *Selected Papers in Statistics and Probability* (New York, 1955).

Wallach, Michael A., and Nathan Kogan, "Aspects of Judgment and Decision Making: Interrelationships and Changes with Age," *Behavioral Science,* Vol. 6, 1961, pp. 23–26.

Wohlstetter, Albert J., *Systems Analysis Versus Systems Design*, The RAND Corporation, Paper P-1530, October, 1958.

Wold, H., "Ordinal Preferences or Cardinal Utility?", *Econometrica,* Vol. 20, 1952, pp. 661–664.

Wolfowitz, J., "On ??379??-Complete Classes of Decision Functions," *The Annals of Mathematical Statistics,* Vol. 22, 1951, pp. 461–465.

Made in the USA
San Bernardino, CA
07 January 2018